GUIDE TO AMERICA'S
FEDERAL JOBS

A Complete Directory of U.S. Government Career Opportunities

THIRD EDITION

Bruce Maxwell and the Editors at JIST

JIST Works

America's Career Publisher

Guide to America's Federal Jobs, Third Edition
A Complete Directory of U.S. Government Career Opportunities

© 2005 by JIST Publishing, Inc.

Published by JIST Works, an imprint of JIST Publishing, Inc.
8902 Otis Avenue
Indianapolis, IN 46216-1033

Phone: 1-800-648-JIST   Fax: 1-800-JIST-FAX
E-mail: info@jist.com   Web site: www.jist.com

About career materials published by JIST. Our materials encourage people to be self-directed and to take control of their destinies. We work hard to provide excellent content, solid advice, and techniques that get results. If you have questions about this book or other JIST products, call 1-800-648-JIST or visit www.jist.com.

Quantity discounts are available for JIST products. Please call 1-800-648-JIST or visit www.jist.com for a free catalog and more information.

Visit www.jist.com for information on JIST, free job search information, book excerpts, and ordering information on our many products. For free information on 14,000 job titles, visit www.careeroink.com.

Acquisitions Editor: Susan Pines
Contributing Editor: Holli Cosgrove
Assistant Editor: Stephanie Koutek
Cover Designer: Trudy Coler
Interior Designer: Aleata Howard
Interior Layout: Carolyn J. Newland
Proofreaders: Jeanne Clark, David Faust
Indexer: Tina Trettin

Printed in the United States of America

09 08 07 06 05   9 8 7 6 5 4 3 2

Library of Congress Cataloging-in-Publication Data
Guide to America's federal jobs : a complete directory of U.S. government
career opportunities / Bruce Maxwell and the editors at JIST. -- 3rd ed.
      p. cm.
   Includes index.
   ISBN 1-59357-116-X (alk. paper)
   1. Civil service positions--United States--Directories. I. Title : America's
federal jobs. II. Maxwell, Bruce, 1959- III. JIST Works, Inc.
   JK692.G85 2005
   351.73'023--dc22

                                        2004030566

We have been careful to provide accurate information throughout this book, but it is possible that errors and omissions have been introduced. Please consider this in making any career plans or other important decisions. Trust your own judgment above all else and in all things.

Trademarks: All brand names and product names used in this book are trade names, service marks, trademarks, or registered trademarks of their respective owners.

ISBN 1-59357-116-X

This Book Can Save You Many Hours of Frustration

With more than 1.8 million employees, the federal government is the country's largest employer. Yet untangling the terminology and procedures used in federal job hunting may leave you frustrated and discouraged.

Where do you start? Which departments and agencies have jobs that interest you? Are federal jobs available in your area? What's the best and easiest way to find out about federal openings? How do you make sense of vacancy announcements that ask for information like "KSAs" and even dictate what kind of envelope *not* to use when mailing your application?

Take heart! The federal government offers between 16,000 and 18,000 job openings on an average *day,* and you learn how to find and apply for them with this book's help. *Guide to America's Federal Jobs* is your best overall resource on federal employment and gives you the most current information, step-by-step guidance, and helpful tips throughout.

We conducted extensive research for the most useful details on federal employment and present them clearly in this book. We hope it saves you many hours of frustration, answers your questions, and leads you to a federal job.

Table of Contents

Summary of Major Sections

Introduction. The introduction explains how this book can help you and how to best use the information. *The introduction begins on page 1.*

Part I: Understanding, Finding, and Applying for Federal Jobs. The three chapters in this part unravel the complexities of federal job hunting. **Chapter 1** explains why now is a great time to work for the federal government and overviews opportunities, pay, and benefits. **Chapter 2** covers—in clear language—how the government fills jobs, how to find openings, how take advantage of the Internet in the process, and how to avoid scams. **Chapter 3** takes you step-by-step through applying for federal jobs. *Part I begins on page 5.*

Part II: Descriptions, URLs, and Sample Job Vacancies for Federal Agencies and Departments. The book's longest section provides details on nearly 90 agencies and departments that hire the most employees. In addition, this part summarizes agencies' actual job announcements to give you an excellent grasp of the types of jobs available and their application requirements. Uniform Resource Locators, or URLs, lead you to helpful Web sites. **Chapter 4** covers the legislative branch. **Chapter 5** highlights the judicial branch. **Chapter 6** profiles the executive branch and its many departments, agencies, and boards. The Department of Homeland Security is covered in Chapter 6. *Part II begins on page 41.*

Part III: Special Federal Job Opportunities. **Chapter 7** explains federal job opportunities that veterans can receive. **Chapter 8** covers federal opportunities for people with disabilities. **Chapter 9** reviews federal job programs for students. *Part III begins on page 367.*

Part IV: Appendixes. The appendixes offer numerous helpful resources, including federal jobs listed by college major, a complete sample vacancy announcement, sample federal-style resumes, and more. *Part IV begins on page 383.*

Detailed Table of Contents

Introduction

Over the years, many myths have arisen about job opportunities with the federal government. Some of the most common are that the government hires only faceless bureaucrats to shuffle papers; federal jobs pay poorly; the jobs are unrewarding; and they're all located in Washington, D.C.

This book should shatter those myths forever.

Most important, this book should help you navigate the federal employment maze by clearly explaining everything you need to know—from how to find a federal job to how to make your application stand out. Although the federal government has made serious efforts in recent years to improve its hiring process, in too many cases applying for a job remains a bewildering, complex, and frustrating experience. Don't be discouraged.

In most cases, you'll find that the extra effort required to apply for a federal job is well worthwhile.

How This Book Is Organized

Part I of this book disentangles the process from beginning to end, using plain language (something the government generally isn't known for) to lead you step by step along the way.

But what types of jobs does the federal government offer? The second part of this book tells you. It profiles dozens of federal agencies and departments and then summarizes information from actual job announcements to describe a sampling of jobs that are offered. For each job, you'll learn the title, the salary, the location, the duties, what qualifications are required, what application materials are necessary, and any special requirements for applicants. All of the jobs are full-time, permanent positions unless otherwise noted. Note that some agencies and departments had no openings as of this writing.

Application periods for all the jobs listed in Part II have closed, but the descriptions should give you an excellent understanding of some of the types of jobs the federal government offers. Many of the jobs may surprise you. For example, did you know that the U.S. Forest Service (part of the Department of Agriculture) employs archeologists?

In Part III, you'll find helpful information on special opportunities in the federal government for veterans, for people with disabilities, and for students.

Hundreds of Uniform Resource Locators—URLs—lead to additional information on the Web and are sprinkled throughout this book. URLs for the main Web site of each agency or department are listed, and for most departments you'll also commonly find URLs for sites that provide basic employment information, lists of job openings, descriptions of internship opportunities, employee directories, and information about smaller components within the overall department. Other URLs lead to everything from detailed information about employee benefits to the most important Web sites for federal job applicants. All URLs were current at press time.

A Few Helpful Notes About This Book

Before you start reading, it might be helpful for you to know the following:

★ To save you time, this book is not designed to be read from front to back (unless you really want to). You might want to start with the second part that describes actual federal jobs and then return to the first part to learn how to find and apply for similar jobs. Or you may want to browse through the book initially, looking for things that catch your eye. If you're looking for something specific, you may want to use the Table of Contents and the Index to quickly find the relevant information.

★ Making generalizations about federal hiring and personnel management practices, as we do in this book, is a dangerous business. This is especially true today because selected agencies are obtaining permission to throw out the regular rules to improve the hiring process. Even in agencies that abide by the normal rules, many variations and exceptions exist that only the agency's personnel specialists fully understand. Once you find a federal job for which you'd like to apply, protect yourself by carefully reading every word in the vacancy announcement (more about this in Part I) and by checking the agency's Web site for information about its current hiring and personnel management practices.

★ The second part of this book is organized in the same order as the *United States Government Manual*. The manual provides information on a large number of U.S. government agencies. Along with entries on the agencies of the executive, judicial, and legislative branches of government, it includes details on quasi-official agencies; international organizations in which the U.S. participates; and other boards, commissions, and committees. If you're familiar with the *United States Government Manual,* you will find this book very easy to navigate.

★ To help you focus on the entities with the most career opportunity, the second part of the book provides details about federal agencies and departments that employ only 100 or more people. Smaller agencies listed in the *United States Government Manual* are not included in this book.

★ This book touches briefly on opportunities at the U.S. Postal Service and the active-duty portion of the Department of Defense. Both have their own hiring and personnel systems. For detailed information on active-duty positions with the Department of Defense, consult *America's Top Military Careers* (available from JIST Publishing).

★ We obtained virtually all the information in this book from federal government publications, Web sites, and databases. We examined an enormous amount of material, and we've included only the information we think will be directly useful in your federal job search. We also condensed and clarified the materials from federal sources to save you time and to make the information easier to understand.

★ We obtained all statistics in this book from databases and publications produced by the federal Office of Personnel Management (OPM) unless otherwise noted.

★ No source exists for data covering *every* federal employee. The main source we relied on is the OPM's Central Personnel Data File, which provides data regarding selected civilian employees. It primarily covers the Executive Branch, which is the largest part of the federal government. When we cite statistics about "federal employees," they're from the OPM's Central Personnel Data File. But it has some limitations:

- It covers civilians in all Executive Branch agencies except the Board of Governors of the Federal Reserve, the Central Intelligence Agency, the Defense Intelligence Agency, the National Imagery and Mapping Agency, the National Security Agency, the Office of the Vice President, the Postal Rate Commission, the Tennessee Valley Authority, the U.S. Postal Service, and the White House Office.

- Coverage of the Federal Bureau of Investigation is limited.

- It does not cover the Legislative Branch except for the Government Printing Office, U.S. Tax Courts, and selected committees.

- The Judicial Branch is excluded.

We Hope You Find This Book Helpful

We've tried to include in this book everything you need to know to apply for federal jobs. We hope it answers your questions about the types of jobs that are available and about federal employment and personnel issues. It's impossible to answer every conceivable question in one book, but we've designed this one to point you toward additional information about a wide variety of subjects.

Good luck in your federal job hunt!

Understanding, Finding, and Applying for Federal Jobs

Working for the Federal Government—The Best Opportunities and Benefits in Decades

Can you name the employer that

★ Employs more people than any other organization in the United States?

★ Seeks workers at all levels of education and experience?

★ Employs people in virtually every county in the United States and in most foreign countries?

★ Offers between 16,000 and 18,000 job openings on an average day?

★ Loses an average of 4,155 employees *each week*, which opens up vast numbers of jobs?

★ Faces a retirement boom over the next few years that will open up even more jobs?

★ Gives all employees annual pay raises that averaged 2.76 percent over the last 10 years?

★ Provides special employment opportunities for veterans, people with disabilities, and students?

★ Repays the college loans of recent graduates that qualify?

Since this book is about federal jobs, the answer is probably no great surprise: The employer is the United States government. If you look back over the list, though, you may be surprised by some of the facts and statistics.

Ever since the horrific terrorist attacks of Sept. 11, 2001, an increasing number of Americans have sought civilian (or military) federal jobs because they want to serve their country. "A new organizational chart or wiring diagram will not defeat terrorists–people will," said Tim Roemer on Sept. 9, 2004. Roemer was a member of the 9/11 Commission that investigated the attacks.

Max Stier, president and CEO of the private Partnership for Public Service, echoed Roemer's sentiment five days later at a congressional hearing. "If you look at the missed opportunities [to stop the 9/11 attacks]," Stier said, "you will see one dominant continuing theme–people."

He added: "Getting the right people with the right skills into the right positions in government must be a primary focus of our response to the [recommendations] of the 9/11 Commission."

Although some of those drawn to government service since 9/11 have applied for jobs directly related to homeland security, many others have not. They just want to do their part to help the government as it fights back against terrorists and tries to protect the nation from further attack.

"In a sense, every federal employee, political or career, is now responsible for the nation's security," said Dr. Paul C. Light, a senior fellow at the Brookings Institution, at a congressional hearing on Sept. 14, 2004. The Brookings Institution is a think tank in Washington, D.C.

The new generation of information technology workers is increasingly drawn to federal employment, according to an article published by *Federal Computer Week*. "Many are motivated by patriotism and a desire to give something back after witnessing the terrorist attacks on Sept. 11, 2001," the magazine said. But it added that for many IT applicants, patriotism was not the sole motivator: New graduates are "looking for job security, a healthy benefits package and a chance to move up before they turn gray, all of which the federal government offers," it said. "The stereotype of government workers being paper pushers punching time clocks no longer exists, according to the new generation."

Why Now Is the Time to Apply for Federal Employment

In many ways, this is the best time in decades to apply for federal employment. Here are just four reasons:

1. The government is rapidly hiring for jobs related to homeland security, and this trend shows no sign of ending anytime soon. The "war on terrorism" declared by President George W. Bush isn't going to end next month or next year–and it may never end. In the latest edition of its *Career Guide to Industries,* the U.S. Department of Labor said, "Demand will continue to grow for specialized workers in areas related to border and transportation security, emergency preparedness, public health, and information analysis."

2. Even if you're not interested in homeland security positions, the government is continuing to hire massive numbers of people to replace employees who leave government service because of retirement, a move to the private sector, or other reasons. In 2003 alone, the government lost 216,336 employees. That's just a few hundred more than the annual average for the period from 1999 to 2003.

3. The federal workforce has been graying, and the government faces a retirement explosion. In 2003, 50,032 federal employees retired–well above the government's projection of 44,305. Hundreds of thousands more are either eligible for retirement now or will be soon. The evidence comes from government data that counted the number of federal employees by age group:

   ★ 50–54: 339,791   ★ 60–64: 101,429

   ★ 55–59: 254,012   ★ 65 and above: 42,444

4. The federal government is seriously working to improve its hiring and employment practices in an effort to attract the "best and the brightest" to federal jobs. "More progress in addressing human capital challenges has been made in the last 3 years than in the last 20 years," said J. Christopher Mihm, managing director of strategic issues for the Government Accountability Office—the investigative arm of Congress—at a congressional hearing on Sept. 14, 2004. He added, however, that "much more needs to be done." Some of the improvements have included attempting to

★ Make vacancy announcements easier to understand.

★ Shorten the period of time between the deadline for applications and making a job offer.

★ Provide selected agencies with Direct Hire Authority to fill critical positions (some applicants for information technology positions have started work within two weeks).

★ Provide incentives for people who accept selected federal jobs, such as lump-sum hiring bonuses of up to 25 percent of the employee's basic pay.

★ Recruit top college students by creating internship programs that lead directly into federal jobs or offering to repay all of a student's loans.

★ Attract and retain outstanding employees in some positions by paying them more than less-talented employees who hold similar jobs.

★ Keep the best employees by providing them with a retention allowance of up to 25 percent of their basic pay (a bill before Congress as we went to press would authorize retention allowances of up to 50 percent of basic pay).

★ Reward employees for special accomplishments by giving them one-time bonuses of up to $10,000.

The federal government has not yet fully implemented some of these improvements. For example, you'll still find many vacancy announcements have the same readability level as hieroglyphics. In addition, in some cases only certain agencies—or parts of agencies—have received special authority to offer a particular incentive such as signing bonuses. And one more caveat: Some of these incentives are in the experimental stage and could be changed at any time.

Despite the caveats, the government is really trying to make federal jobs more attractive and desirable. The efforts are essential as the government competes with the private sector for the top candidates.

J. Christopher Mihm, the Government Accountability Office official quoted earlier in this chapter, put it best in testimony at a congressional hearing on July 13, 2004. "The federal government is now facing one of its most transformational changes to the civil service in probably over half a century," he said. "Federal agencies need effective hiring processes to compete for talented people in a highly competitive job market. Given that the executive branch…may continue significant hiring over the coming years, improving the federal government's hiring process is absolutely critical."

What Types of Jobs Are Available?

The federal government has jobs for you no matter what your interests may be, the level of education you've attained, or the number of years you have (or haven't) worked. For just a sampling of federal job titles, take a look at Chart 1. You'll see some titles that you'd expect but also some you might not, such as botanist, deckhand, geologist, historian, landscape architect, locksmith, photographer, sheet metal mechanic, and veterinarian.

CHART 1
A Sampling of Federal Career Opportunities

Accountant	Economist	Land surveyor
Agricultural market reporter	Electrician	Landscape architect
Air conditioning equipment mechanic	Electronics mechanic	Laundry worker
Aircraft engine mechanic	Engineer	Law enforcement officer
Aircraft pilot	Entomologist	Linguist
Air traffic controller	Environmental protection specialist	Loan specialist
Animal caretaker	Financial institution examiner	Lock and dam operator
Archeologist	Food inspector	Locksmith
Astronomer	Foreign affairs specialist	Machinist
Attorney	Forester	Mail deliverer
Boilermaker	Gardener	Maintenance mechanic
Botanist	Geographer	Materials handler
Budget analyst	Geologist	Meatcutter
Carpenter	Health insurance administrator	Medical records technician
Cemetery administrator	Highway safety specialist	Microbiologist
Community planner	Historian	Model maker
Computer specialist	Hydrologist	Museum curator
Consumer safety specialist	Illustrator	Nuclear medicine technician
Cook	Immigration inspector	Nurse
Correctional officer	Industrial property manager	Occupational therapist
Crane operator	Intelligence specialist	Oceanographer
Custodian	Interior designer	Painter
Deckhand	Investigator	Paralegal specialist
Document analyst		Park ranger
		Patent examiner

Personnel management specialist	Psychologist	Teacher
Pharmacist	Public affairs specialist	Telecommunications specialist
Photographer	Sandblaster	Toolmaker
Physiologist	Secretary	Veterinarian
Pipefitter	Sheet metal mechanic	Wastewater treatment plant operator
Plumber	Small arms repairer	
Podiatrist	Shipwright	Welder
Printer	Social worker	Wildlife biologist
	Supply program manager	

Two other sections of this book provide additional information about the types of jobs the federal government offers. The book's second part describes selected federal jobs in detail. And if you're in college or a recent graduate, the appendix titled "Federal Jobs by College Major" will help you match your major with federal job opportunities.

The range of job types and the number of vacancies is far larger if you qualify for a white-collar rather than a blue-collar job. Like the entire U.S. economy, the federal government has been steadily shedding blue-collar workers. As of this printing, the federal government had 203,527 blue-collar employees, compared to 1,646,000 white-collar workers.

How Much Do Federal Jobs Pay?

As a general rule, government salaries are roughly comparable to those in the private sector. However, numerous exceptions exist where government pay is lower. If you're offered a federal job, you'll need to know the salary for a similar position in the private sector to help you determine whether it's a good opportunity. Following is a look at the system—make that *systems*—that most government agencies use today to pay their employees.

The General Schedule

The vast majority of federal employees—77 percent—are on the General Schedule pay system. The General Schedule covers white-collar and service employees. It has 15 "grades" of pay, and 10 "steps" within each pay grade. In addition to a base salary, every federal employee on the General Schedule also receives locality pay. This ranges from 10.9 percent to 24.21 percent of the base salary, depending on location.

Chart 2 shows the range of base pay for every grade in the General Schedule and the range with the minimum 10.9 percent locality pay added. Salaries are provided in ranges because each grade has 10 steps, and the chart shows the minimum and maximum salaries within each grade. The average employee on the General Schedule makes $60,109. However, to put that number in perspective, it's important to know that the same average employee had worked for the federal government for 15.9 years.

CHART 2
General Schedule Pay

Grade	Base Pay Range	Range with Locality Pay*
GS-1	$15,625–19,543	$17,328–21,673
GS-2	$17,568–22,109	$19,482–24,518
GS-3	$19,168–24,919	$21,257–27,635
GS-4	$21,518–27,971	$23,863–31,019
GS-5	$24,075–31,302	$26,699–34,713
GS-6	$26,836–34,891	$29,761–38,694
GS-7	$29,821–38,767	$33,071–42,992
GS-8	$33,026–42,935	$36,625–47,614
GS-9	$36,478–47,422	$40,454–52,590
GS-10	$40,171–52,222	$44,549–57,914
GS-11	$44,136–57,375	$48,946–63,628
GS-12	$52,899–68,766	$58,664–76,261
GS-13	$62,905–81,778	$69,761–90,691
GS-14	$74,335–96,637	$82,437–107,170
GS-15	$87,439–113,674	$96,969–126,064

Note: Each grade has 10 steps, which leads to a range of salaries within each grade. Employees' actual salaries depend on their step within the grade.

* All federal employees on the General Schedule receive locality pay in addition to their base salaries. Locality pay ranges from 10.9 percent to 24.21 percent of the employee's salary, depending on location. The calculations in this section use the lowest locality rate possible of 10.9 percent.

As the chart shows, locality pay can significantly increase an employee's overall salary. This is especially true in areas where locality pay is above 10.9 percent and at the higher grades in the General Schedule. For example, the base pay for a GS-9 worker at the first step is $36,478. With the minimum 10.9 percent locality pay added, the salary jumps to $40,454–a nice increase of $3,976. For a GS-11 worker at the tenth step, the base pay is $57,375. Adding the minimum locality pay raises the salary to $63,628–an increase of $6,253.

Note: Salaries in Vacancy Announcements

Every federal vacancy announcement lists the job's salary. The salary number combines the job's base pay and its locality pay. Keep this in mind so that when you look at a vacancy announcement, you don't think that locality pay will be added to the listed salary.

Where in the General Schedule will you likely fall based on your qualifications? Here are some general guidelines:

★ If you don't have a high school diploma and are hired as a clerk, you'll start at GS-1.

★ If you have a high school diploma, even as a clerk you'll start at GS-2 or GS-3.

★ If you have some technical training or experience, you'll likely start at GS-4.

★ If you have a bachelor's degree, you'll start at GS-5 or GS-7 depending on your grades.

★ If you have a master's degree or a Ph.D., you'll likely start at GS-9 or GS-11.

These examples are baselines. If you have relevant paid or unpaid work experience, you may start at a higher grade than those listed. The same is true if you have education beyond a Ph.D. And it can be true if the government needs to fill a critical position but has trouble finding qualified candidates. Typically, new employees start at the first step of a grade (keep in mind that each grade has 10 steps). But this also isn't written in stone. If the job is difficult to fill or you have particularly strong qualifications, you may start at a higher step—and thus at a higher salary.

Some federal jobs are specially designed so that workers can rapidly move up the General Schedule grade ladder. For example, you might start as a GS-7. In your first year you could be promoted to a GS-9, in the second year to a GS-11, and in the third year to a GS-12. At current General Schedule rates with the lowest locality pay included, this means that in three years you'd jump from a minimum salary of $33,071 to a minimum salary of $58,664. As long as your performance is satisfactory, each year at a minimum you should expect to be promoted to the next step within your grade and receive a related pay increase.

Every federal job announcement lists the starting grade for a position and the maximum grade that can be achieved with promotions. The larger the range between these grades, the greater potential there is for significant promotions. Some job announcements list a variety of grades at which a new employee could start. Exactly what grade you'll be hired at depends on your education and professional experience. The announcement should clearly list the minimum requirements for each grade.

The Federal Wage System

Slightly more than 202,000 workers—or 11 percent of the government workforce—are paid under the Federal Wage System. This system covers blue-collar employees who work in craft, repair, operator, and laborer occupations. These federal workers receive wages that are designed to be comparable with prevailing regional wages for similar types of jobs. Because wages are based on prevailing local rates, the salary for the same position can vary widely across the country. The average worker covered under the Federal Wage System makes $41,657. However, to reach that salary, the same average worker had to put in 16 years with the federal government.

The Senior Executive Service

Slightly less than 6,000 employees who are top government managers belong to the Senior Executive Service. This is the highest level that federal workers can reach without being specifically nominated by the President and confirmed by the U.S. Senate. Competition for these jobs is intense. Members of the Senior Executive Service have salaries ranging between $104,927 and $158,100.

Other Pay Plans

If you've been adding employment numbers as we've gone along, you've realized that the two major federal pay systems—the General Schedule and the Federal Wage System—cover 88 percent of federal workers. But what about the remaining 12 percent, or 226,400 people? Government statistics lump them under "Other Pay Plans." That's fine with us, since explaining the details of every pay plan the government uses would add innumerable pages to this book—and, more than likely, put you in a deep sleep. But if you really want more information about federal pay systems, it's available at http://www.opm.gov/oca.

More About Pay Raises

In addition to promotions (and accompanying pay increases) that individual federal employees may receive, each year Congress approves a raise in base salary for all federal workers. Federal employees have received this increase each of the last 10 years, unlike many of their counterparts in other levels of government or the private sector who have faced pay freezes or even pay cuts in some years.

Over the last 10 years, Congress has increased the base pay for all federal workers by an average of 2.7 percent annually. In 2005, it's projected that federal workers will get a 3.5 percent pay hike. Every federal worker gets the same percentage increase through these Congressional actions. To make things even sweeter, some years Congress also boosts locality pay rates. For example, in 2004 Congress approved a 2.7 percent base pay raise for all federal workers. But because Congress also boosted locality rates, the average federal worker ended up with a total pay raise of 4.1 percent—and that's before individual raises from promotions are added.

All this means that if you work for the federal government for even a relatively brief time, your salary can really jump. As Chart 3 shows, the average federal worker who had been employed for less than one year earned $39,188. But the average federal worker who had been employed for just three to four years earned $49,197. And the average worker who remained with the government for 10 to 14 years earned $59,986.

CHART 3
Average Salaries Based on Length of Service

Length of Service	Average Salary	Number of Employees
Less than 1 year	$39,188	109,898
1–2 years	$43,111	202,768
3–4 years	$49,197	128,257
5–9 years	$53,143	222,527
10–14 years	$59,986	243,325
15–19 years	$62,973	305,625
20–24 years	$68,951	253,081
25–29 years	$70,455	203,112
30–34 years	$74,663	129,640
35 years or more	$78,004	51,136

Many employees who leave government service find that the contacts they've made and expertise they've developed are extremely valuable to private-sector employers. In some cases, moving to the private sector results in a hefty paycheck that's far above what the person made as a government employee. For example, if you've worked for a while as a procurement officer in the General Services Administration, any company that sells products to the federal government—and there are a lot of them—would likely jump at the chance to gain your expertise about how to win more government contracts. Likewise, if you've worked as a top aide for one of the congressional banking committees, banking trade associations and large banking firms likely would be thrilled to hire you for the inside knowledge you've gained about how to move banking legislation through Congress.

What Benefits Do Federal Workers Receive?

The benefits package provided by the federal government is one of its strongest selling points in attracting employees. Following are brief descriptions of the major benefits:

★ Health insurance coverage that continues into retirement. Employees can choose among at least a dozen different health plans, and the government pays the bulk of the premium. The portion of the employee's salary that pays the remainder of the premium is not taxed. More information: http://www.opm.gov/insure/health/index.asp.

★ An optional long-term care insurance program that offers a choice of benefits. Employees can obtain coverage for themselves, their spouse, their adult children, their parents, their parents-in-law, and their stepparents. More information: http://www.itcfeds.com.

★ An optional group life insurance program where employees can choose to continue coverage for their entire lives. The government pays a portion of the premium. More information: http://www.opm.gov/insure/life/index.htm.

★ A pension that's based on the employee's years of service and salary history. Employees make a small, mandatory contribution toward the pension. More information: http://www.opm.gov/retire/index.htm.

★ An optional Thrift Savings Plan that's very similar to a 401(k) plan. It's one of the best benefits the government offers. All employees automatically receive a Thrift Savings Plan account and an annual contribution by the government that's equal to one percent of their base pay. If the employee contributes to the plan, the government provides a 100 percent match for the first three percent of the employee's base salary and a 50 percent match for the next 2 percent. The government match is free money flowing into your retirement account. Employee contributions are tax deferred, and employees can contribute up to 14 percent of their base salary. Federal workers have a choice of five investment funds. More information: http://www.tsp.gov.

★ Voluntary Flexible Spending Accounts that allow employees to pay for certain health and dependent-care expenses with pre-tax dollars. More information: http://www.fsafeds.com/fsafeds/index.asp.

★ Annual leave that includes 10 paid federal holidays and vacation time. Workers receive 13 days of vacation annually for the first 3 years of employment; 20 days annually for the next 12 years; and 26 days a year after year 15 of employment.

★ Sick leave of 13 days annually. Any unused time is rolled over into the next year. Sick leave can be used for personal medical needs, the care of a family member, or adoption-related purposes. More information: http://www.opm.gov/oca/index.htm.

★ Flexible work schedules and teleworking. A flexible work schedule allows employees to adjust their work hours so their normal 10-day time commitment is covered in 9 days, providing a 3-day weekend. More information: http://www.opm.gov/oca/leave/index.htm.

Many agencies also offer the following benefits:

★ Public transit subsidies in areas where public transportation is available.

★ Recruitment bonuses for new employees who possess exceptional skills or who accept jobs that are difficult to fill. The bonus can be up to 25 percent of the employee's base pay and is paid in a lump sum prior to the employee starting work. Employees who receive recruitment bonuses must agree to remain with the government for a specified length of time and must pay back some or all of the bonus if they leave early. More information: http://www.opm.gov/oca/pay/html/recbonfs.htm.

★ Relocation bonuses for new employees who move to a different area to accept a job that's difficult to fill. Like the recruitment bonus, the relocation bonus can be up to 25 percent of the employee's base pay. Employees who receive retention bonuses must agree to remain in government employment for a specified amount of time and must pay back some or all of the bonus if they leave early. More information: http://www.opm.gov/oca/pay/html/relbonfs.htm.

★ Tuition assistance for employees who take classes that directly relate to their official duties. More information: http://www.opm.gov/wrkfam/html/FAS.asp.

★ Repayment of student loans for selected federal employees. More information: http://www.opm.gov/oca/pay/studentloan.

Where Are Federal Jobs Located?

Contrary to a common misperception, the vast majority of federal jobs are not located in Washington, D.C. Currently 286,989 people—just over 15 percent of the federal civilian workforce—work in the Washington Metropolitan Statistical Area, which includes all of the city and parts of Maryland, Virginia, and West Virginia. This leaves an awful lot of federal employees—1,562,133, to be exact—working outside the Washington area.

The federal government employs people in every state, every U.S. territory, and most foreign countries. Among federal employees who do not work in the Washington area, 1,498,935 work in other parts of the United States, 14,091 work in U.S. territories, and 49,115 work in foreign countries. Chart 4 shows how many people the federal government employs in each state—including yours. The number of federal workers in each state ranges from a low of 2,774 in Delaware to a high of 152,507 in California. These numbers mean good federal jobs that you may not even know existed are likely available in your community or nearby.

CHART 4
Number of Federal Employees by State

State	Number of Employees
Alabama	34,940
Alaska	12,872
Arizona	34,617
Arkansas	13,098
California	152,507
Colorado	35,263
Connecticut	7,665
Delaware	2,774
District of Columbia	151,871
Florida	74,344
Georgia	68,019
Hawaii	22,341

(continued)

(continued)

CHART 4
Number of Federal Employees by State

State	Number of Employees
Idaho	8,762
Illinois	45,527
Indiana	19,781
Iowa	8,120
Kansas	16,265
Kentucky	21,184
Louisiana	20,994
Maine	9,534
Maryland	111,490
Massachusetts	27,878
Michigan	25,394
Minnesota	15,986
Mississippi	17,575
Missouri	34,465
Montana	9,950
Nebraska	9,477
Nevada	9,730
New Hampshire	3,545
New Jersey	28,261
New Mexico	23,082
New York	63,645
North Carolina	34,504
North Dakota	6,042
Ohio	43,927
Oklahoma	34,766
Oregon	20,087
Pennsylvania	65,898
Rhode Island	6,744

State	Number of Employees
South Carolina	17,583
South Dakota	7,712
Tennessee	26,169
Texas	113,092
Utah	28,731
Vermont	3,961
Virginia	121,296
Washington	48,510
West Virginia	13,138
Wisconsin	13,205
Wyoming	5,257

What Are the Demographics of the Federal Workforce?

For years, federal jobs have been a stepping-stone for women, members of minority groups, and people with disabilities into the middle class. Consider these numbers:

★ The federal government employs 830,459 women, who comprise 45 percent of the total federal workforce.

★ According to the latest data available, minorities comprise 30.8 percent of the federal workforce. Seventeen percent of federal workers are black, 6.9 percent are Hispanic, 4.7 percent are Asian/Pacific Islanders, and 2.2 percent are American Indians or Alaskan Natives.

★ Consistently for the last decade, people with disabilities have made up 7 percent of the federal workforce.

The federal government also employs people of all ages. It even employs 6,806 people who were less than 20 years old. Chart 5 shows the number of federal employees by age group and their average salaries.

CHART 5
Federal Employment by Age Group

Age Group	Number of Employees	Average Salary
Less than 20	6,806	$21,119
20–24	53,186	$31,036
25–29	98,896	$41,103
30–34	148,260	$49,643
35–39	205,355	$56,606
40–44	278,400	$60,660
45–49	321,103	$62,264
50–54	339,791	$64,470
55–59	254,012	$65,732
60–64	101,429	$65,790
65 or more	42,444	$65,321

Isn't the Federal Workforce Shrinking?

No, at least not in recent years. Here are the total numbers of federal civilian employees by year:

★ 1999: 1,772,333

★ 2000: 1,762,559

★ 2001: 1,772,533

★ 2002: 1,819,107

★ 2003: 1,839,600

★ 2004: 1,849,690

You may have read about federal employees receiving RIF notices. Reduction in Force is the government's fancy term for layoffs. While the federal government does lay off some workers each year (mostly because their jobs have become obsolete), layoffs affect only a tiny fraction of the workforce. Between 1999 and 2003, the number of federal workers who were laid off ranged from a high of 3,295 in 1999 to a low of 1,360 in 2002.

Now that you know the merits of federal employment, in the next chapter we'll explain how to find the perfect federal job.

CHAPTER 2

How to Find a Federal Job

Finding a job in the federal government is much like finding one in the private sector, but some crucial differences exist. We'll explore them in this chapter. We'll also briefly explain how the federal government fills jobs, provide insider advice about how to take maximum advantage of the Internet to find a federal job, tell you how to receive e-mail alerts when federal jobs that match your precise criteria become available, and discuss why the Internet shouldn't be the only tool you use in a job search.

The Federal Job Hunt

Looking for a federal job is very similar to looking for one with any other type of employer. But some differences exist, both major and minor. Here are some of the biggest differences:

★ The classified ads in your local newspaper list selected private-sector job openings, but you'll rarely see a federal job in the classifieds. Instead, the federal government lists most of its job openings through USAJOBS, a system that provides job information at a Web site and by telephone. We discuss USAJOBS in detail later in this chapter. An important caution: Some scam artists run classified ads that appear to offer federal jobs or special "study guides." Read "How to Avoid Federal Job Scams" for more information.

★ You'll probably need to slightly adjust your resume to apply for a federal job. The government requires that your resume contain specific information, some of which you wouldn't normally include in a standard resume. For example, the government requires that you include your Social Security number. We provide instructions for creating a federal-style resume in Chapter 3.

★ If you have excellent qualifications and interview well, a private-sector employer may offer you a job on the spot. This rarely happens with federal jobs because government regulations usually require that agencies follow a series of procedures to hire employees. However, the situation is changing a little as selected agencies receive permission to be more flexible in hiring. The flexibility may exist for all job openings at an agency or be limited to specific types of positions, such as information technology jobs.

★ You'll probably wait longer–sometimes a *lot* longer–to receive a job offer from a federal agency than from a private-sector employer. We discuss this issue further in Chapter 3.

You should note one very important similarity between federal and private-sector jobs: The best way to get your foot in the door is through an internship. We discuss internships and special employment opportunities for students in Chapter 9.

How to Avoid Federal Job Scams

The federal government—including the U.S. Postal Service—provides complete information about job openings to the public at no cost. However, scam artists use Web sites or classified ads in newspapers to victimize an untold number of Americans each year. Some brazenly use names that imply an affiliation with the federal government, such as "U.S. Agency for Career Advancement" or "Postal Employment Service."

Here are some of the most common promises made by scam artists in their ads—and the accompanying reality:

The promise: To "guarantee" that you'll be hired.

The reality: No one can guarantee you'll be hired. Federal laws and rules govern all hiring decisions.

The promise: To give you the low-down about "hidden" or unadvertised federal jobs.

The reality: The federal government doesn't have hidden or unadvertised jobs. Some jobs are not publicly advertised because they're only open to current federal employees.

The promise: To sell you booklets containing lists of federal job openings.

The reality: Most federal job openings are listed at USAJOBS, and the rest appear on agency Web sites. In both cases, the sites provide powerful, easy-to-use search engines to help you quickly identify jobs that match your interests and qualifications. These custom, up-to-the-minute searches are far more valuable than any printed booklet.

The promise: To sell you practice questions for the "Civil Service Exam."

The reality: There is no such thing as a "Civil Service Exam." In fact, you don't have to take tests of any kind to apply for most federal jobs. In the few cases where tests are required, the hiring agency typically provides sample questions at no charge.

Some legitimate companies offer to perform customized searches of USAJOBS or agency Web sites to find jobs that meet your criteria. They typically e-mail you the information—for a fee, of course. If you don't want to do the searching yourself, a service like this may be worthwhile. Just make sure you actually receive something of value for your money.

How the Federal Government Fills Jobs

The federal government has two classes of jobs. How it fills a particular position depends on the job's class:

1. Most jobs are in the competitive civil service. When vacancies occur in these jobs, all applicants are judged in open competition. Federal law also requires that agencies use merit system principles to fill these jobs. The principles are designed to ensure that all job applicants receive fair and equal treatment in the hiring process. The section of the law that covers job applicants is available in the shaded box titled "Merit System Principles for Federal Job Applicants."

Merit System Principles for Federal Job Applicants

1. Recruitment should be from qualified individuals from appropriate sources in an endeavor to achieve a work force from all segments of society, and selection and advancement should be determined solely on the basis of relative ability, knowledge, and skills, after fair and open competition, which assures that all receive equal opportunity.

2. All employees and applicants for employment should receive fair and equitable treatment in all aspects of personnel management without regard to political affiliation, race, color, religion, national origin, sex, marital status, age, or handicapping condition, and with proper regard for their privacy and constitutional rights.

Source: U.S. Code, Title 5

2. Jobs in the excepted service are filled using qualification requirements established by a particular agency and are not subject to the same laws as civil service positions. All jobs in some agencies, such as the Federal Bureau of Investigation, the Central Intelligence Agency, and the Library of Congress are in the excepted service. Some agencies have both types of positions. For a list of major excepted service agencies, see the shaded box below titled "Major Excepted Service Departments and Agencies."

Major Excepted Service Departments and Agencies

Administrative Office of the U.S. Courts	Library of Congress
Agency for International Development	National Security Agency
Central Intelligence Agency	Nuclear Regulatory Commission
Defense Intelligence Agency	Postal Rate Commission
Department of State (Foreign Service only)	Tennessee Valley Authority
	U.S. Claims Court
Department of Veterans Affairs (Health Services and Research Administration only)	U.S. House of Representatives
	U.S. Mission to the United Nations
Federal Bureau of Investigation	U.S. Postal Service
Federal Reserve System (Board of Governors only)	U.S. Senate
	U.S. Supreme Court
Government Accountability Office	

Federal agencies must post all of their competitive civil service openings on USAJOBS, which includes a Web site and an interactive voice response telephone system. Many agencies also post their excepted service openings on USAJOBS, although they're not required to do so.

Tip: Excepted Service Jobs

If you'd like to work at a particular excepted service agency, first check USAJOBS for any job openings the agency lists. Whether or not you find anything at USAJOBS, then check the agency's own Web site for job openings. Web addresses for all federal agencies are listed in Part II of this book.

USAJOBS: The Basics

Back in the old days (that's any time before the Internet became ubiquitous), trying to find information about job openings in the federal government was usually an arduous, bewildering, wearying quest. But you're in luck: Since you're part of the Internet generation, everything you need to know about federal job openings around the world is at your fingertips. Just have them type http://usajobs.opm.gov into your Web browser and behold the wonders of USAJOBS.

Tip: Using Computers at Libraries

If you don't have a computer or you have one but lack an Internet connection, check your local public library. Nearly all public libraries offer free use of computers that are hooked to the Internet, and many offer free classes about the basics of using computers, using the Internet, and related topics.

The Office of Personnel Management operates USAJOBS, which is the official job site for the federal government. On an average day, USAJOBS provides complete information regarding 16,000 to 18,000 federal job openings. It also features dozens of articles about working for the federal government.

If you create a personal account at USAJOBS (it's easy, fast, and free), you can access three great features:

1. The first lets you store multiple versions of your resume and cover letter online so you can zap them right out when you see an interesting federal job opening.

2. The second gives you the option of making your resume available to federal personnel managers who search USAJOBS when they have job openings.

3. The third lets you create up to five Job Search Agents that automatically send you e-mail alerts when new jobs are posted that meet your criteria.

Tip: USAJOBS by Phone

If you're uncomfortable using computers, you can access almost all of the information available at the USAJOBS Web site through the USAJOBS interactive voice response telephone system. In some cases you can even apply for a job by phone. The phone number for the USAJOBS telephone system is 703-724-1850 (TDD 978-461-8404). But a warning: The telephone numbers are not toll free. If the numbers are outside your local calling area, you'll pay long-distance charges.

USAJOBS: Getting Started

If you have more than a passing interest in federal employment, it's best to create a personal account at USAJOBS so you can access all of the site's features. However, if you just want to see what kinds of federal jobs are available, you can search the database of job vacancies without registering. You can always go back and register later.

To register, on the home page click the bar labeled "Create your account now!" This takes you to a page where you plug your personal information into a short fill-in-the-blanks form and create a username and password so you can access your account in the future.

You next have to answer two simple questions. The first asks whether you're a U.S. citizen. If you are, click the button labeled "Yes." If you're not a U.S. citizen, click the button labeled "No" and enter your country of citizenship. Most federal jobs are only open to U.S. citizens.

The second question asks whether you claim a veterans' preference. By law, veterans who are disabled or who served on active duty in the Armed Forces during certain time periods are entitled to a hiring preference over non-veterans. If you qualify for veterans' preference, click on the most appropriate button (there are five choices). If you don't qualify for veterans' preference, click the button labeled "No."

> ### Note: Job Opportunities for Veterans
>
> Information about veterans' preference and special job opportunities for veterans is provided in Chapter 7.

To finish, click the "Submit" button. When you do, the site automatically logs you into your new USAJOBS account.

USAJOBS: Searching the Jobs Database

The heart of USAJOBS is its database of federal job openings around the world. The database provides powerful tools to narrow your search, yet it's also remarkably easy to use. If you're already in the USAJOBS site, you can reach the jobs database by clicking the "Search Jobs" button that's located at the top of nearly every page. If you're not already in USAJOBS, the URL http://jobsearch.usajobs.opm.gov takes you directly to the database.

USAJOBS offers five slightly different methods for searching the database:

★ Basic Search

★ Agency Search

★ Series Search

★ Advanced Search

★ Senior Executive Search

We'll start with the Basic Search, since it meets the needs of most users. Like the other search methods, it provides multiple fields where you can type in information or select items from drop-down menus. And like the other search methods, you can use any or all of the fields to narrow your search. You're only required to complete one field of your choice. The four fields offered in the Basic search include

1. Keyword: In this box you can type a job title (such as archeologist), words that may appear in a job description (such as investigate), the name of the agency where you'd like to work (such as Department of Education), the job location (such as Omaha), the number for a particular vacancy (if you know it), or any other words that you think might appear in a relevant vacancy announcement. Don't enter a lot of keywords—the more you use, the narrower your search will be. You want to narrow your search, but you don't want to narrow it too far. We provide some tips for using keywords with USAJOBS in the shaded box below titled "Keyword Search Tips."

Keyword Search Tips

You can just type any words that seem relevant into the keyword field at USAJOBS and you'll probably do fine. However, you'll likely get better results if you fine-tune your query using Boolean operators. We'll skip the history about Boolean operators and go straight to explaining how you can use them at USAJOBS:

AND. If you place AND between two words, you'll only receive results where both words appear in the job title or description. Example: marine AND biology.

OR. Using OR is helpful if you aren't sure what words the government might use in a job title or description. Example: environment OR ecology. This search would return job announcements that contain at least one of the words. You also can string words together using OR. Example: environment OR ecology OR refuge.

AND NOT. The AND NOT operator ensures that the word you specify does not appear in the titles or descriptions of job openings returned in your search. Example: clerk AND NOT mailroom.

Parentheses. Using parentheses to separate keyword subsets helps refine your search. Example: (writer OR editor) AND NOT technical. This is a good search to run if you're looking for a writing or editing job but you don't have technical writing skills.

Quotation marks. To use an exact phrase in a search, place quotation marks around the words. Example: "social work." This ensures that the words appear next to each other in the job title or description.

An asterisk. An asterisk is a wildcard. If you put it at the end of a root, you'll retrieve job listings that contain any variations on that root. Example: investigat* returns job listings that contain the words investigator, investigation, investigations, or investigative in the job title or description.

2. Location: The location field lets you select a city, region, state, or foreign country where you'd like to work. It offers a drop-down list that you scroll through. The location field is especially helpful if you live in a city and don't intend to move or you're moving to a specific place. In either case, you can obtain announcements for all federal job openings in the area by clicking on the appropriate city or region. If you'd like to work in a foreign

country, the list includes many individual countries where the federal government has employees. You also can select from the following: Atlantic overseas area, Central and Southern Europe, Pacific overseas area, South America, Southeast Asia, Southwest Asia, the Middle East, Throughout Europe, and Throughout the World.

Tip: Making Multiple Selections

Many USAJOBS fields provide drop-down lists that you scroll through. If you just want to select one item in the list, click on it. But if you want to select multiple items, hold down the Control key on a PC or the Command key on a Mac while clicking your selections.

3. Job Category: This field provides a drop-down list you can scroll through to select a particular occupational area or areas. The available choices are listed in the shaded box below titled "Job Categories at USAJOBS."

Job Categories at USAJOBS

The Job Category field at USAJOBS allows you to select from the following professional areas:

Accounting, Budget, and Finance	Management, Administration, Clerical, and Office Services
Biological Sciences	Mathematics and Statistics
Business, Industry, and Procurement	Medical, Dental, and Public Health
Copyright, Patent, and Trademark	Physical Sciences
Education	Postal Service
Engineering and Architecture	Quality Assurance and Grading
Equipment, Facilities, and Services	Safety, Health, Physical and Resource Protection
Human Resources	Social Science, Psychology, and Welfare
Information, Arts, and Public Affairs	Supply
Information Technology	Trades and Labor
Investigation and Inspection	Transportation
Legal and Claims Inspecting	Veterinary Medical Science
Library and Archives	

4. Salary Range: You can type in your desired salary to search for job announcements based on compensation. We recommend that you ignore the Salary Range field unless you absolutely have to make a certain amount of money to survive. If you type in a salary range, you may miss out on good jobs that pay either more or less than you've listed.

You next have to answer one question and make two easy selections before you can search the jobs database. The Applicant Eligibility field asks whether you're one of the following:

★ A current permanent federal employee in a competitive position or a former employee with reinstatement eligibility

★ A current federal employee in an excepted service position covered by an interchange agreement

★ A person eligible for veterans' preference or a person separated from the armed forces under honorable conditions after three years or more of continuous military service

★ A person with non-competitive appointment eligibility

If all of this is gibberish to you, simply click the "No" button. But if you fit one of the categories listed, be sure to click the "Yes" button. Your choice helps USAJOBS show you relevant job openings.

Next, you must decide whether to sort the job openings you'll receive by date or keyword relevance. If you expect to search the site frequently, you'll probably want to sort by date so you always see the newest jobs first.

Next, you must choose whether to have the job openings listed in brief view or detailed view. The brief view is really brief: it just lists the date, job title, agency, and location for each job. The detailed view includes all of that information and the first couple lines of the job description, the job type, the job status (full-time, part-time, and so on), and the salary. We recommend choosing the detailed view because it provides more information, thus making it easier for you to decide whether to read the full vacancy announcement.

Finally, click the "Search for Jobs" button to run your search.

USAJOBS: Search Results

Your search will result in a list of jobs, and each job will link to its full vacancy announcement. "Vacancy announcement" is the federal government's fancy term for a document that describes a job opening. This document lists things like the job title, the location, the salary, the duties, the qualifications required, how to apply, and the all-important date by which you must submit your application materials.

Vacancy announcements are not designed for reading by the faint-of-heart. They often appear to be written in Klingon instead of anything approaching English. The federal government is trying hard to make vacancy announcements more concise and readable. But don't despair: We walk you through an announcement's typical components and decipher the jargon next. An appendix reproduces an actual announcement so you can prepare yourself for its language and structure.

Vacancy announcements are long. The shortest are usually 5 or 6 pages, but it's not uncommon for them to run 15 to 24 pages. Because of this, it's best to start by scanning the results from your search to determine which announcements are most likely to be useful.

When you find a job in your search results that looks good, click on the job title to get the full vacancy announcement. It's best to first scan the announcement for highlights. Then if the job still looks good, you can go back and read the announcement more carefully. If you'd like to apply for a job, it's best to print the announcement so you can consult it carefully, highlight the most important parts, and keep it for your records.

Vacancy announcements differ regarding the exact types of information they provide and the order in which they present it. Typically, an announcement begins with a summary that highlights the document's most important details. After the summary, you'll likely find the following types of information:

★ **Position Title.** The federal government uses a standardized list of job titles. This is helpful because when you find a job you like, you can go back to the search screen and plug the title into the keywords field to find similar positions.

★ **Series and Grade.** The four-digit series number identifies the federal occupational series assigned to the position. The government groups similar positions together in an occupational series. For example, all secretarial jobs are in the 0318 occupational series. The series number is most helpful if you want to run another search at USAJOBS to find similar jobs. Descriptions of the occupations included in each series are available at http://www.opm.gov/fedclass/text/HdBkToC.htm. The grade (GS-9, GS-12, and so on) indicates where the job falls among the 15 grades in the General Schedule pay system, which we discussed in Chapter 1.

★ **Salary Range.** If the vacancy announcement lists just one grade for the job, your education and experience will determine where you fall in the range. Many jobs are listed at multiple grades. In these cases, the salary range runs from the lowest grade to the highest. Your education and experience will determine the grade for which you qualify.

★ **Promotion Potential.** The top grade level you can achieve in the job with promotions.

★ **Type of Appointment.** This may indicate whether the job is full-time or part-time, or whether it's permanent or temporary.

★ **Location.** The city and state where the job is located.

★ **Area of Consideration:** Check this carefully, because it indicates what types of people are eligible to apply. Here are some of the most common areas of consideration:

• All U.S. Citizens: Anyone who is a U.S. citizen can apply. The announcement might instead list "non-status candidates," which is another term for all U.S. citizens.

• All U.S. Citizens in the Local Commuting Area: Only U.S. citizens who live within a reasonable driving distance of the job are eligible.

• Status Applicants Only: Only current federal employees may apply.

• [Agency] Employees Only: Only current employees of the named agency may apply.

★ **Announcement Number.** Each job opening has a unique announcement number. You should always include the announcement number on your resume and any other materials you submit so everything ends up in the correct file.

★ Opening and Closing Dates. The date range during which applications are accepted. It's usually a period of two to four weeks. Pay special attention to the closing date because if your application is late, you won't be considered. If you're mailing your application materials, you also should check very carefully to see whether your application must *arrive* at the agency by the closing date or be *postmarked* by the closing date.

★ Duties. Describes the primary job responsibilities.

★ Qualifications. Describes the main qualifications you must possess to be considered for the job.

★ Application Information. This lists the materials you must submit to apply. Read this list carefully because if you leave out anything, your application will be automatically rejected. This area also may describe how to apply (fill out an online application, send documents by postal mail, and so on) and provide the relevant Web or postal addresses.

★ Significant Working Conditions. Describes any unusual working conditions for the job, such as a requirement that you travel.

★ Contact Information. The phone number and usually the e-mail address for a person you can contact if you have any questions.

Many job announcements include links that you can click to apply online through USAJOBS or a Web site operated by the agency.

USAJOBS: Other Search Methods

Earlier in this chapter, we described the Basic Search method for USAJOBS. Four other methods are available by clicking the appropriate tab at the top of the search page:

1. The Agency Search lets you search for jobs within a selected federal agency. You can type the agency or department's name in the appropriate field or select the name from a drop-down list. For many large departments, the list also includes individual components. For example, you can select the entire Interior Department or individual components such as the Bureau of Indian Affairs, the Bureau of Land Management, the National Park Service, the U.S. Fish and Wildlife Service, or the U.S. Geological Survey, among others. The Agency Search page also has fields for location, series number, occupational series, and salary range or pay grade range.

2. The Series Search lets you look for jobs by occupational series number. You can type the series number in the appropriate field or select the series from a drop-line list. The Series Search page also has fields for location and salary range or pay grade range. Brief descriptions of the occupations included in each series are available at http://www.opm.gov/fedclass/text/HdBkToC.htm.

3. The Advanced Search lets you to search for jobs by combining some or all of the fields available at USAJOBS, many of which offer drop-down lists. The fields include keyword, occupational series number, location, agency, and salary range or pay grade range.

4. The Senior Executive Search lets you search for high-level executive jobs. The Senior Executive Search page has fields for keywords and location.

USAJOBS: How to Create Job Search Agents

A job hunt, whether in the federal government or the private sector, can take a while. Visiting USAJOBS every day to search for new job openings may become a chore. And who can remember which combination of keywords and search fields produced great results the other day? Wouldn't it be great if someone could search USAJOBS for you and send you e-mail alerts when new jobs were posted that met your precise criteria? You probably could hire someone to perform this task for you, but some *thing* will do it for free. This "thing" is the job search agents at USAJOBS. You can create up to five agents to find jobs that perfectly match your selected criteria.

You must be registered with USAJOBS to use the agents. To create a job search agent, log into your account and then click on the "My USAJOBS" button at the top of the page. This takes you to your personal page. In the section titled "My Job Search Agents," click on the link labeled "Manage Agents." On the next page, click on the button labeled "Create New Agent." This takes you to the page where you actually create agents.

This page will look familiar if you've previously searched the jobs database. Once again, you choose search criteria from fields. You're only required to complete two fields: the locations field and the "Agent Title" field where you type in a name for the agent.

The first four fields–location, job categories, occupational series, and agency–provide drop-down menus. You can select up to ten items in any drop-down menu. To make multiple selections, hold down the Control key on a PC or the Command key on a Mac while clicking on your choices. For the remaining seven fields, you must click on a selection or type in information:

★ Salary range. If you wish, you can type numbers into this field. However, as before we recommend that you leave this field blank to avoid missing out on great opportunities that may pay more or less than you expect.

★ Senior Executive. If you click this field's button, your agent will only search for jobs in the Senior Executive Service. These jobs are high-level executive positions, but there are only about 6,000 of them in the federal government.

★ Applicant eligibility. This is the same field we discussed under Basic Search earlier in this chapter. Click the "Yes" button if you meet the listed eligibility criteria or the "No" button if you don't.

★ How Often Do You Want to Receive Email Notification? Five choices are available in this field: daily, weekly, bi-weekly, monthly, or none. We recommend choosing daily or weekly because some jobs would already be closed by the time you'd receive bi-weekly or monthly alerts. If you choose none, the agent will store searches in your personal account but not send you e-mail alerts when it finds new jobs.

★ Position Type. You can select part-time, full-time, or both.

★ Keywords. You can type words or phrases into this field that you think are likely to appear in relevant vacancy announcements. For example, you might use words that describe your educational and professional experiences and skills.

★ Agent Title. Type a name for your agent in this field.

Finally, click the "Save Agent" button at the bottom of the page. You can always edit or delete agents by returning to your personal account page.

USAJOBS: Two Last Points

Before we leave USAJOBS, you should know two final points:

★ The site offers dozens of publications about federal employment at http://www.usajobs.opm.gov/faqs.asp. The publications discuss topics such as employment of non-citizens, employment opportunities for attorneys, federal employment overseas, qualification requirements, transfers, pay and benefits, and special opportunities available for veterans and students.

★ USAJOBS provides just about any form you might need to apply for a federal job at http://www.usajobs.opm.gov/forms.asp. There are forms that apply government-wide, such as the Optional Application for Federal Employment (OF-612), and forms required by individual agencies.

A Final Word

USAJOBS is a terrific tool for finding and applying for federal jobs. However, it should not be the only tool you use in your hunt for federal employment. Look at every tool you'd normally use to find a job in the private sector to see whether you can use it–perhaps in modified form–in your federal job search.

For example, an old standby–the informational interview–can be just as useful in getting a federal job as it is in landing a job in the private sector. For an informational interview, you make an appointment with an employer to learn more about it. While you're asking smart, carefully prepared questions, the employer gets a chance to look you over for possible future job openings.

Informational interviews are particularly helpful if you live outside Washington, D.C., and want a federal job in the area where you live. The federal government employs people in just about every county in the country. To find out which federal agencies have offices in your area, look in the blue pages of your telephone directory. In most places, the blue pages list phone numbers for governmental offices at the local, state, and federal levels that are located in the area. The federal numbers are usually listed at the end of the blue pages. If you look in the blue pages, you'll probably be surprised at the number of federal agencies that have offices near you.

Once you find an interesting federal job opening, you need to apply. As you've probably already guessed, government rules and regulations can make it more complicated to apply for a federal job than for one in the private sector. The process really isn't too painful–you just have to follow each step precisely. We'll lead you through the application process in the next chapter.

CHAPTER 3

How to Apply for a Federal Job

Using the information we provided in the previous chapter, you've found a great federal job opportunity through USAJOBS and you want to apply. What's required?

Unfortunately, there isn't a single answer to this question because the application process is not standardized across the federal government. Each agency has its own procedures regarding what information you must submit and how you must submit it. Some agencies give you options; others do not unless you specifically request them.

Your guide to the application requirements for a specific job is its vacancy announcement. The announcement will list the exact materials you must submit. Read this list carefully and follow it precisely. The announcement also will say how you must submit your materials (by e-mail, a Web form, fax, courier service, and so on) and provide the necessary address(es).

As we said in the previous chapter, when you find a job opportunity you should print the vacancy announcement so you can refer to it frequently as you put together your application. The vacancy announcement also will provide keywords that you'll want to use in your resume or other application materials.

Your Federal-Style Resume—Step by Step

Whether you're applying for a job in the federal government or elsewhere, the employer wants to know who you are and what you can do. For federal jobs you most commonly supply this information through a resume and brief essays that respond to KSAs, which are questions about your knowledge, skills, and ability to perform the specific job.

You can't just submit your standard resume when applying for a federal job. Your standard resume can serve as the base for your federal-style resume, but the government requires additional information.

Many federal agencies have developed their own automated, online resume builders that you must use. Some let you use the online resume builder at USAJOBS. Some let you submit a paper or e-mailed resume as long as it contains certain required information. And some let you fill out a form called OF-612, the Optional Application for Federal Employment, instead of a resume. You can download OF-612 from the USAJOBS forms page at http://www.usajobs.opm.gov/forms.asp.

If you expect to apply for multiple federal jobs, you'll save lots of time by creating a federal-style resume in a word-processing program so you have all the necessary information at hand. You then can submit the document when doing so is an option or you can copy and paste information from it into online resume builders.

Federal-style resumes frequently run two to four pages because of all the information that's required or that you have the option to include. You can format your federal-style resume any way you like.

However, it must contain the information detailed in the following sections.

1. Job Information

Your federal-style resume must include information on the job for which you are applying:

★ The announcement number and position title, which you can copy from the vacancy announcement.

★ The job's grade (GS-5, GS-7, and so on), which you also can copy from the vacancy announcement. If the announcement lists more than one grade, list the lowest grade you would accept. For example, if the announcement describes the job as "GS-5/7," decide whether you would take the GS-5 or if you would only accept a GS-7.

★ For information about applying at more than one grade, see the box titled "Applying for a Job at Multiple Grades." Also refer to Chapter 1 for an explanation of the GS or General Schedule system.

Applying for a Job at Multiple Grades

Some federal vacancy announcements list multiple grades (GS-7, GS-9, and so on) at which you can apply. Higher grades require higher skills but also provide higher pay.

Be sure you qualify for the grade you choose. If you pick a level that is too high based on your skills, your application will not be considered. However, in most cases if the level you pick is too low, the agency will upgrade you automatically.

There are exceptions where you should consider applying at different grade levels because the agency probably won't upgrade you automatically. These are cases where answers to different KSAs (questions about how your knowledge, skills, and abilities apply to the job) are required at different grades. Generally, the complexity of the KSAs increases as the grade increases.

To find the lowest grade at which you should apply, look in the announcement for the grade where you absolutely meet all requirements. To find the highest grade at which you should apply, look for the grade where you meet most but not all of the requirements. You can apply at these grades and any in between.

This strategy increases the chances you'll be hired at the highest possible grade. Unfortunately, it also increases the number of separate applications you must submit.

2. Personal Information

Your resume needs to include the following personal details:

★ Your full name, mailing address with ZIP Code, and day and evening telephone numbers (with the area code).

★ Social Security number.

★ Country of citizenship.

★ Veterans' preference (if applicable).

★ Reinstatement eligibility (if applicable; for former federal employees only).

★ Highest federal civilian grade held (if you've previously worked for the federal government). Also provide the job series number and the dates you were employed.

3. Work Experience

Include the following information about your work experience on your resume:

★ For each job you've held, provide the job title; the starting and ending dates (including month and year); the employer's name and address; the average number of hours worked per week (or just say "full-time"); the salary; and your supervisor's name, address, and telephone number. Also indicate whether your most recent supervisor can be contacted.

★ For each job you've held, also describe your duties and accomplishments. Give examples that shed additional light on the scope of your experience. Be specific. If you won an award, say what it was for. If you helped your employer save money or streamline a process, describe how you did it and the results. Use numbers to quantify your accomplishments whenever possible. Study the vacancy announcement and emphasize the parts of your work history that match the qualifications listed there. Also check the vacancy announcement for any keywords you can repeat in your descriptions.

Tip: Using Keywords in Your Resume

Using as many keywords as possible from the announcement in your resume helps if a computer initially screens your application. Just be sure the keywords accurately match your skills.

★ If you've previously worked for the federal government, include the occupational series numbers and the starting and ending grades of those positions.

★ If you have volunteer experience that's relevant to the job for which you're applying, describe it. Once again, use concrete examples to tell about your duties and accomplishments.

4. Education

On your resume, provide these details about your education:

★ High school (include name, city, state, and date of diploma or GED).

★ College or university (include name, city, and state; majors; and type and year of any degrees).

★ If you are working toward a degree, list the number of credits you've earned. Include the month and year you expect to graduate.

★ List specific courses you've taken that relate to the job and the number of credits you've earned.

★ Include your grade point average if it's high enough to help (some automated forms require your GPA). College graduates with GPAs of at least 2.5 or 3.0 sometimes qualify for higher starting pay and expedited hiring programs.

5. Other Qualifications

Explain your other qualifications on your resume, including

★ Any other skills relevant to the job that are not immediately obvious from other parts of your resume. These skills might include experience with specific computer software or knowledge of a foreign language.

★ Job-related training courses (include title and year).

★ Job-related honors or special accomplishments such as publications, memberships in professional or honor societies, speaking appearances, and performance awards (include dates).

You might want to consider including a separate section in your resume that summarizes your qualifications. Summaries can be especially helpful in explaining long or varied work histories. Whenever possible, use the summaries to focus on the qualifications listed in the vacancy announcement.

Making Sure Your Resume Is Complete

Tip: A Complete Resume Is Important

All of the information listed in the preceding sections must be included on any resume submitted as part of an application for a federal job.

Some vacancy announcements are sloppy about listing what's required on your resume. They list some required elements, but leave out others. It's your responsibility to make sure your resume is complete.

If you submit a paper resume, make sure that each page includes the vacancy announcement number and your name and Social Security number. This helps reviewers keep your paperwork together.

To help you prepare your federal-style resume, we've provided some sample resumes in an appendix.

Tackling the KSAs

Many people are unnecessarily intimidated when it comes time to respond to KSAs, which are questions about your knowledge, skills, and ability to perform the job for which you're applying. Most federal vacancy announcements have KSAs, although you sometimes have to dig through a lot of gobbledygook to find them.

Tip: Do Not Dread Responding to KSAs

You should view KSAs for what they are: Opportunities to help ensure your application lands on top of the pile instead of getting buried at the bottom.

A lot of confusion exists about KSAs, much of it caused by people who write federal vacancy announcements. For example, KSAs are not phrased as questions, although that's what they really are. "Knowledge of human resources rules and regulations" might be a KSA for a human resources specialist job. What it really means is "What experience do you have using human resources rules and regulations?"

Some vacancy announcements also confuse matters by calling KSAs other names, such as "specialized experience requirements" or "selective factors." To confuse matters further, some announcements don't make it clear that you must respond to each KSA with an essay of one page or less, each on a separate sheet of paper. Instead of being clear, the announcement may say something like "Candidates will be evaluated in terms of the following quality ranking factors, which must be addressed separately to ensure full consideration."

In a final effort to throw you off track, some announcements say that responding to KSAs is optional. Don't believe it for a minute. Your KSA responses are a critical part of your application. Applications that lack KSA responses go to the bottom of the pile–if they're considered at all.

Most importantly, though, failing to respond to KSAs would deprive you of a glorious opportunity to showcase your talents that are directly related to the job for which you're applying. Who would want to do that?

In short, KSAs give you the chance to explain why you're the best candidate for the job. You should handle your responses with care because they're your best chance to show who you are, what you can do, and what kinds of experiences you've had that directly relate to the job for which you're applying. Although you should take care with your answers, there's no reason to be intimidated.

Tips for Writing Your KSAs

Here are a few tips to help get you started:

★ Carefully read the vacancy announcement, highlighting along the way any keywords or phrases that describe the job responsibilities. Use these keywords or phrases in your KSA responses where appropriate.

★ For each KSA, review your resume and outline a list of experiences you've had that might address it. Look for examples that demonstrate initiative, innovation, leadership, teamwork, or the ability to solve a complex problem. Winnow down each list until you have the best example or examples that illustrate a link between your experience and the KSA.

★ When you write about your experiences, link each example explicitly to the KSA. The experiences don't necessarily have to be from paid jobs. Perhaps you coached a youth athletic team, volunteered at a nursing home, or wrote for your college newspaper. Examples from these activities are relevant for your KSAs if they demonstrate your special talents to perform the work described in the announcement.

★ Write your KSAs in the first person using short, direct sentences. Include as many concrete examples as possible to illustrate your skills. Examples carry much more weight than simple assertions that you have a certain knowledge, skill, or ability.

★ Clearly indicate who you interacted with and how. Did you provide critical information to a key manager? Did you work with a group of your peers to successfully complete a project? Did you direct other people in an activity?

★ Try to make each of your responses between half a page and a page in length. Don't load them with fluff to make them long. Shorter, targeted responses are much more effective.

★ After you write your KSA responses, let them sit for anywhere from a few hours to a few days (you are writing them well before the application deadline, aren't you?). Then go back and reread them to check for clarity. Chop off sentences that run forever. Replace acronyms with plain language. Take out any extraneous words, phrases, or sentences. Carefully proofread everything.

What Not to Do on Your KSAs

Here are some things you should never do when preparing or submitting your application:

★ Do not forget to put your name and announcement number on everything you submit as part of your application.

★ Do not "embellish" your experiences, your education, or anything else included in your application package. If you make a false statement of any kind, you may not be hired; you may be fired after you begin work; or you may be subject to fine, imprisonment, or other disciplinary action.

★ Do not rely on the spell checker or grammar checker on your computer to find spelling mistakes or other errors. Proofread everything you're submitting.

★ Do not include in your package articles you've written, reference letters, or any other unsolicited material. You can refer to these items in your cover letter, resume, or KSA responses.

★ Do not include college transcripts in your application unless the vacancy announcement specifically requests them.

★ Do not put your application materials in a notebook, binder, or other cumbersome cover.

★ Do not use postage-paid government envelopes, federal stamps, or federal postage meters to send your application. If you disregard this, your application will not be considered.

Submitting Your Application

Make sure that you complete and submit your application well before the closing date. Check the vacancy announcement to see whether your application must be *received* or just *postmarked* by the closing date.

If you're submitting your materials online, be aware that federal computer servers can become congested or even crash in the minutes or hours immediately preceding an application deadline, especially if a number of vacancy announcements have the same closing date. Deadline extensions are not granted because of computer malfunctions, no matter where they occur.

Tip: Avoiding Postal Problems

If you're sending paper application materials to a federal office in the Washington, D.C., area, avoid using the U.S. Postal Service. Mail deliveries to federal offices in Washington have been delayed ever since anthrax was sent in letters to top government officials. If you must send paper materials, use a fax machine or a courier service such as Federal Express.

If you do submit your application at the last minute, get some sort of proof that you sent it before the deadline. Federal agencies aren't always careful in handling applications, and they can erroneously decide you missed the deadline. This dooms your application unless you can prove they're wrong.

The agency should send you confirmation that it has received your application. If you don't hear anything within a month, call or e-mail the contact person listed on the vacancy announcement to check on the status of your application.

Don't be surprised if it takes the agency a long time to consider your application and let you know the results. As of this writing, it took federal agencies an average of 102 days from the application deadline to make a job offer. The agencies were trying to cut that average to 45 days, which is still longer than you'll wait to hear from most private-sector employers.

Preparing for an Interview

Like most managers, federal managers usually interview applicants before deciding whom to hire. There are no special rules for federal interviews.

You can prepare for them as you would any others. Learn more about the job by visiting the agency Web site, skimming its publications and mission statements, and reviewing its organizational chart. You also should review the job announcement and your application.

On the day of the interview, take a notepad and pen and copies of the materials you submitted. Give yourself enough time to find the correct office and navigate security procedures. You probably need to bring photo identification as well as any materials that the hiring manager requests.

You might meet with the hiring manager alone or with a panel of managers and coworkers. The standard advice about interviews applies, including listening well, being ready with specific examples of your skills, and sending thank-you notes. Ask those who interview you for their business cards so you have accurate names and job titles.

Negotiating Salary and Accepting the Job

When you are selected for a job in the federal government, a human resources specialist will telephone you with an offer. This is a good time to ask questions about pay and benefits. Negotiating for pay is not as common in federal work as it is in the private sector because pay ranges are set by law.

Note: Agencies Have Some Flexibility in Pay

Agencies can start experienced workers at the high end of the pay range, based on qualifications, market conditions, the applicant's past salary, and agency regulations. Some agencies can also offer signing bonuses, student loan repayment, and relocation assistance.

In addition to answering questions about pay and benefits, the human resources specialist will explain the process of getting a security clearance or other background check, if such checks are required for the job.

If you need time to decide whether to accept the job, ask for it. If you do accept, the specialist will give you a start date and tell the hiring manager—who will probably be your new boss.

On your first day, you will sign or say an oath of office and become a public servant. Then, you can stop the job hunt and start your federal career.

Part II

Descriptions, URLs, and Sample Job Vacancies for Federal Agencies and Departments

CHAPTER 4

Legislative Branch

Congress

The Capitol
Washington, D.C. 20510
202-224-3121 (Senate)
202-225-3121 (House of Representatives)

* Web site, Senate: http://www.senate.gov/index.htm

* Web site, House: http://www.house.gov/Welcome.html

* Job vacancies, House: http://www.house.gov/htbin/caohr_vacancies

* USAJOBS By Phone: 912-757-3000

* House of Representatives Job Line: 202-226-4504

* Senate Job Line: 202-228-JOBS

* Senate Employment Bulletin: http://www.senate.gov/visiting/resources/pdf/seb.pdf

* Senate Pages: http://www.senate.gov/reference/reference_index_subjects/Pages_vrd.htm

* Committee directory, House: http://clerk.house.gov/committee/index.html

* Committee directory, Senate: http://www.senate.gov/pagelayout/committees/
  b_three_sections_with_teasers/membership.htm

The Congress comprises the Senate and the House of Representatives, in which are vested "all legislative powers." The Senate is composed of 100 members, 2 from each state, who are elected to serve for a term of six years. The House of Representatives comprises 435 Representatives, who are elected for a term of two years. The number representing each state is determined by population, but every state is entitled to at least one representative. Both the senators and the representatives must be residents of the state from which they are chosen. A resident commissioner from Puerto Rico (elected for a four-year term) and delegates from American Samoa, the District of Columbia, Guam, and the Virgin Islands complete the composition of the Congress. Delegates are elected for a term two years. The resident commissioner and delegates may take part in the floor discussions but have no vote in the full House or in the Committee of the Whole House on the state of the Union. They do, however, vote in the committees to which they are assigned.

Due to the high volume and complexity of their work, the Senate and House divide their tasks among committees and subcommittees. The Senate has 20 committees and 68 subcommittees. The House has 21 committees and 97 subcommittees. There are 4 joint committees. Committees generally have legislative jurisdiction. Subcommittees handle specific areas of the committee's work. Committees receive varying levels of operating funds and employ varying numbers of aides. Each hires its own staff. The majority party controls most committee staff and resources, but a portion is shared with the minority.

Selected Committees Within the Senate

The **Committee on Banking, Housing, and Urban Affairs** handles legislation related to the following: banks, banking, and financial institutions; control of prices of commodities, rents and services; deposit insurance; economic stabilization and defense production; export and foreign trade promotion; export controls; federal monetary policy, including the federal reserve system; financial aid to commerce and industry; issuance and redemption of notes; money and credit, including currency and coinage; nursing home construction; public and private housing (including veterans housing); renegotiation of government contracts; urban development and urban mass transit. It has five subcommittees: Securities and Investment; Financial Institutions; Housing and Transportation; Economic Policy; and International Trade and Finance.

★ Web site: http://banking.senate.gov/

★ Committee members: http://banking.senate.gov/
index.cfm?FuseAction=Information.Membership

★ Subcommittee members: http://banking.senate.gov/
index.cfm?FuseAction=Information.Subcommittees

The **Finance** committee handles legislation related to the following: bonded debt of the United States; customs, collection districts, and ports of entry and delivery; deposit of public moneys; general revenue sharing; health programs under the Social Security Act and health programs financed by a specific tax or trust fund; Social Security; reciprocal trade agreements; revenue measures; tariffs and import quotas; and transportation of dutiable goods.

★ Web site: http://finance.senate.gov/

★ Contact information: http://finance.senate.gov/sitepages/contact.htm

★ Committee members: http://finance.senate.gov/sitepages/committee.htm

★ Subcommittee members: http://finance.senate.gov/sitepages/2001HearingF.htm/
subcommittees.htm

The **Foreign Relations** committee is responsible for the foreign policy activities of the U.S. Senate. It evaluates all treaties with foreign governments; approves all diplomatic nominations; and writes legislation pertaining to U.S. foreign policy, the State Department, Foreign Assistance programs, and many associated topics.

★ Web site: http://foreign.senate.gov/

★ Contact information: http://foreign.senate.gov/contact.html

★ Committee members: http://foreign.senate.gov/about.html

The duty of the **Indian Affairs** committee is to conduct a study of any and all matters pertaining to problems and opportunities of Indians, including Indian land management and trust responsibilities; Indian education, health, special services, and loan programs; and Indian claims against the United States.

★ Web site: http://indian.senate.gov/index.html

★ Internships: http://indian.senate.gov/intern.htm

★ Contact information and staff: http://indian.senate.gov/staff.htm

★ Committee members: http://indian.senate.gov/members.htm

The **Special Committee on Aging** was first established in 1961 as a temporary committee. It was granted permanent status on February 1, 1977. While special committees have no legislative authority, they can study issues, conduct oversight of programs, and investigate reports of fraud and waste. Throughout its existence, the Special Committee on Aging has served as a focal point in the Senate for discussion and debate on matters relating to older Americans. Often, the Committee will submit its findings and recommendations for legislation to the Senate. In addition, the Committee publishes materials of assistance to those interested in public policies which relate to the elderly.

★ Web site: http://aging.senate.gov/

★ Internships: http://aging.senate.gov/index.cfm?Fuseaction=Intern.Home

★ Contact information: http://aging.senate.gov/index.cfm?Fuseaction=Contact.Home

★ Committee members: http://aging.senate.gov/index.cfm?Fuseaction=Members.Home

Other Senate Committees

Agriculture, Nutrition, and Forestry
http://agriculture.senate.gov/

Appropriations
http://appropriations.senate.gov/

Armed Services
http://armed-services.senate.gov/

Budget
http://budget.senate.gov/

Commerce, Science, and Transportation
http://commerce.senate.gov/

Energy and Natural Resources
http://energy.senate.gov/

Environment and Public Works
http://epw.senate.gov/

Governmental Affairs
http://govt-aff.senate.gov/

Health, Education, Labor, and Pensions
http://health.senate.gov/

Judiciary
http://judiciary.senate.gov/

Rules and Administration
http://rules.senate.gov/

Small Business and Entrepreneurship
http://sbc.senate.gov/

Veterans Affairs
http://veterans.senate.gov/

Select Committee on Ethics
http://ethics.senate.gov/

Select Committee on Intelligence
http://intelligence.senate.gov/

Selected Committees Within the House of Representatives

The **Committee on Education and the Workforce** handles legislation related to the following: child labor, Gallaudet University and Howard University and Hospital, convict labor and the entry of goods made by convicts into interstate commerce, food programs for children in schools, labor standards and statistics, education or labor generally, mediation and arbitration of labor disputes, regulation or prevention of importation of foreign laborers under contract, workers' compensation, vocational rehabilitation, wages and hours of labor, welfare of minors, and work incentive programs.

★ Web site: http://edworkforce.house.gov/

★ Internships: http://edworkforce.house.gov/interns/internindex.htm

★ Contact information: http://edworkforce.house.gov/committee/contact.htm

★ Committee members: http://edworkforce.house.gov/members/108th/mem-fc.htm

The **Committee on Transportation and Infrastructure** handles legislation related to highways, transit, and pipelines; aviation; coast guard and shipping; water resources and environment; and public buildings.

★ Web site: http://www.house.gov/transportation/

★ Committee members: http://www.house.gov/transportation_democrats/members.htm

★ Subcommittees: http://www.house.gov/transportation/

The **Committee on Ways and Means** handles legislation related to the following: customs, collection districts, and ports of entry and delivery; reciprocal trade agreements; revenue measures; bonded debt of the United States; deposit of public monies; transportation of dutiable goods; tax exempt foundations and charitable trusts; and Social Security.

★ Web site: http://waysandmeans.house.gov/

★ Internships: http://waysandmeans.house.gov/Special.asp?section=1139

★ Contact information: http://waysandmeans.house.gov/contact.asp

★ Committee members: http://waysandmeans.house.gov/members.asp

★ Subcommittee members: http://waysandmeans.house.gov/About.asp?section=3

The **Select Committee on Homeland Security** holds hearings and studies issues related to protecting the country from future terrorist attacks.

★ Web site: http://hsc.house.gov/

★ Internships: http://hsc.house.gov/internships.cfm

★ Committee members: http://hsc.house.gov/members.cfm

★ Subcommittees: http://hsc.house.gov/subcommittees.cfm

Other House Committees

Committee on Agriculture
http://agriculture.house.gov/

Committee on Appropriations
http://appropriations.house.gov/

Committee on Armed Services
http://armedservices.house.gov/

Committee on the Budget
http://www.house.gov/budget/

Committee on Energy and Commerce
http://energycommerce.house.gov/

Committee on Financial Services
http://financialservices.house.gov/

Committee on House Administration
http://www.house.gov/cha/

Committee on International Relations
http://wwwc.house.gov/international_relations/

Committee on the Judiciary
http://www.house.gov/judiciary/

Committee on Resources
http://resourcescommittee.house.gov/

Committee on Rules
http://www.house.gov/rules/

Committee on Science
http://www.house.gov/science/

Committee on Small Business
http://wwwc.house.gov/smbiz/

Committee on Standards of Official Conduct
http://www.house.gov/ethics/

Committee on Veterans Affairs
http://veterans.house.gov/

Joint Committee on Printing
http://www.house.gov/jcp/

Joint Committee on Taxation
http://www.house.gov/jct/

House Permanent Select Committee on Intelligence
http://intelligence.house.gov/

Sample Job Vacancies

Lead Inventory Control Specialist

Agency: Office of the Secretary of the U.S. Senate, Stationery Room
Salary: $34,496 to $51,744
Location: Washington, D.C.

Job description summary: Assists in organizing and participating in all physical inventories; receives, counts, stocks and distributes merchandise; maintains adequate and accurate inventory; resolves discrepancies with vendors and accounting personnel; enters merchandise into inventory tracking system; advises sales associates of inventory availability; notifies front office of reordering requirements; ensures timely completion and delivery of orders to Senate offices; prepares special order deliveries for warehouse clerks to deliver; ensures warehouse associates adhere to departmental procedure and policy; schedules and approves leave requests for warehouse clerks to ensure adequate staffing; and assists in various areas of the Senate Stationery Room as needed.

Minimum qualifications required: High school diploma or GED with three to five years of warehouse/retail experience; OR an equivalent combination of education and experience. Must have knowledge of applicable inventory and accounting systems and methods; ability

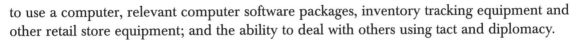

to use a computer, relevant computer software packages, inventory tracking equipment and other retail store equipment; and the ability to deal with others using tact and diplomacy.

Minimum application materials required: Fax a resume with salary history and applicable cover letter.

Director, Contractor Management

Agency: Office of Contractor Management, Office of House Support Services, U.S. House of Representatives
Salary: $6,858 to $8,664/month
Location: Washington, D.C.

Job description summary: Performs administrative oversight of departmental staff, which consists primarily of contracting officer representatives, in the oversight of specific projects. Maintains high level of knowledge relative to developments and practices in order to set strategic direction and provide consultative services. Ensures team policy and procedure compliance along with a consistent approach to policies and procedures.

Minimum qualifications required: Must have a strong customer service orientation and leadership skills; be results oriented with the ability to motivate people to achieve; be able to identify priorities and achieve results with a sense of urgency and give honest and straightforward opinions on related issues; possess excellent departmental planning, project management, and systems/process development skills as well as excellent strategic thinking skills; be able to manage multiple complex programs and to resolve cross-group issues; be able to develop metrics and measurement techniques to track performance; have excellent oral and written presentation and communication skills for reporting to senior management; have excellent interpersonal skills and the ability to develop and maintain strong working relationships with other Congressional departments.

Minimum application materials required: Submit a resume online, by fax, or by mail.

Special requirements: Must pass a criminal background check.

Web Content Specialist

Agency: Office of Publications Services, Office of the Clerk, U.S. House of Representatives
Salary: $56,837
Location: Washington, D.C.

Job description summary: Supports the creation of electronic information. Responsible for content development in support of the Office of the Clerk's Web sites. Acts as a liaison for all Web content issues and inquiries. Assists in the creation and support of new methodologies for electronic dissemination of House information through Web projects.

Minimum qualifications required: Three or more years' experience in electronic publishing and Web site development is required. Must be proficient in HTML, Photoshop, Acrobat/Distiller, and browser compatibility issues. Working knowledge of Section 508 guidelines, Dreamweaver, Photoshop, Fireworks or ImageReady, JavaScript, PHP, and Flash is helpful. Should have the ability to exercise discretion and independent judgment in fulfillment of responsibilities. Strong communication and written abilities are desired. Should be competent in the operation of PCs, have a working knowledge of the congressional legislative process, have an analytical mind, and be detail-oriented. College degree preferred.

Minimum application materials required: Submit a resume and cover letter by fax or mail.

Systems Administrator

Agency: Senate Judiciary Committee Majority
Salary: Commensurate with experience
Location: Washington, D.C.

Job description summary: Supports all aspects of the computer operations for the Majority Staff, Senator Orrin Hatch (R-UT), including all Republican subcommittees. This is a full-time, exempt position, requiring 45 or more hours per week. Some weekend and evening hours may be required. A one-year commitment is desirable. Primary responsibilities include maintaining and troubleshooting the local area network, training staff in computer use, as well as building and maintaining a Web site that properly addresses the Committee's activities, including hearings, markups, press releases, etc.

Minimum qualifications required: The position requires discretion, independent judgment, prioritizing staff needs in the development, deadlines, and utilization of technology. Additionally the position requires the ability to work well under pressure and deadlines, and the ability to work cooperatively and courteously with others. Must possess the ability to anticipate and systematically solve problems to enhance the office's functioning. Knowledge of Windows Operating System and standard Microsoft Office software, as well as strong oral and written communication skills are required. Hill experience is a plus.

Minimum application materials required: Submit a resume and cover letter by fax or in person.

Deputy Press Secretary

Agency: U.S. Senate
Salary: Commensurate with experience
Location: Washington, D.C.

Job description summary: Progressive Midwestern Democratic Senator seeks Deputy Press Secretary with Capitol Hill experience and strong writing skills. Primary responsibilities will include writing speeches, columns, and advisories. Assists Communications Director and Press Secretary in message development and day-to-day operation of three-person press shop. Duties will include a variety of writing assignments including speeches, columns, floor statements, advisories, and other short writing assignments. Responsible for updating and maintaining press files and lists, pitching press events and new stores, and other related duties.

Minimum qualifications required: Must exhibit extremely strong writing skills and demonstrate ability to handle multiple tasks and deadlines in a fast-paced office.

Minimum application materials required: Fax a cover letter and resume.

Legislative Assistant

Agency: U.S. Senate
Salary: Commensurate with experience
Location: Washington, D.C.

Job description summary: Senior Midwestern Republican Senator seeks Legislative Assistant to handle military and veterans' issues. LA will be expected to write floor statements, talking points, briefs on legislative issues, and responses to constituent mail. LA will also handle meetings with constituents and assist with related constituent matters.

Minimum qualifications required: Hill experience preferred and a background in military or veterans' issues a must. Must have strong analytical, research, and writing skills, and the ability to handle multiple tasks in a fast-paced environment.

Minimum application materials required: Fax a cover letter and resume, along with a short writing sample.

Director, House Child Care Center

Agency: U.S. House of Representatives
Salary: $64,395 to $72,440
Location: Washington, D.C.

Job description summary: Administers the House Child Care Center, providing a nurturing and caring learning environment for children, while motivating staff to peak performance.

Minimum qualifications required: Bachelor's degree in early childhood education. Master's preferred. Must have five to seven years of directly applicable experience in leading and administering an Early Childhood Program. Leadership experience will include effectively communicating with staff, parents, children, and various stakeholders of the Child Care Center. Must be able to demonstrate ability and experience in developing world class curriculum planning, implementation, principles of collaborative instruction, and supervising and training staff.

Minimum application materials required: Submit a cover letter and resume online or by fax.

Architect of the Capitol

U.S. Capitol Building
Washington, D.C. 20515
202-228-1793

★ Web site: http://www.aoc.gov

★ Job vacancies: http://jobsearch.usajobs.opm.gov/

★ USAJOBS By Phone: 912-757-3000

The Architect of the Capitol is responsible to the United States Congress for the maintenance, operation, development, and preservation of the United States Capitol Complex, which includes the Capitol, the congressional office buildings, the Library of Congress buildings, the Supreme Court building, the U.S. Botanic Garden, the Capitol Power Plant, and other facilities. Duties include the mechanical and structural maintenance of the buildings, the upkeep and improvement of the Capitol grounds, the arrangement of inaugural ceremonies and other events and ceremonies held in the building or on the grounds, the care and repair of all works of art in the Capitol, and the maintenance and restoration of murals and other architectural elements throughout the Capitol Complex.

Sample Job Vacancies

Electromotive Equipment Mechanic Helper
Agency: Subway Branch of the Elevator and Subway Division, Architect of the Capitol
Salary: $14.43 to $23.93/hour
Location: Washington, D.C.

Job description summary: Performs electrical and mechanical repairs in connection with inspection, maintenance, and repair of the subway car systems. Overhauls, maintains, modifies, and repairs electronic parts, assemblies, and components. Independently controls an electromotive system and monitors it for irregularities, such as identifying improper operating indications for a subway system and taking action in case of malfunctions. Works in conjunction with the supervisor to determine the operational mode of the subway cars and guide way. Monitors the system for alarms via remote control and takes immediate action to ensure the continued safe operation of the subway system and the safety of its passengers.

Minimum qualifications required: Applicants will be evaluated on their ability to perform the duties of the position rather than length of experience. Eligibility will be determined by the relevance, scope, and quality of all experience and training, regardless of where or how acquired. Applicants will be ranked and rated based on their knowledge of the job elements identified in this announcement.

Minimum application materials required: Submit an online application and resume. Application must include narrative responses to the following KSAs: 1) ability to interpret instructions and specifications, including reading blueprints; 2) ability to troubleshoot; 3) ability to use and maintain tools and equipment; 4) knowledge of equipment assembly, installation, repair, etc.

Gardener
Agency: U.S. Botanic Garden, Conservatory Division, Gardens and Grounds Team, Architect of the Capitol
Salary: $13.09 to $15.27/hour
Location: Washington, D.C.

Job description summary: Performs seasonal gardening tasks such as fertilizing, preparing seedbeds, transplanting, laying sod, aerating, pruning, trimming, and applying chemicals according to specific directions. Assists with various tasks related to planning and implementing USBG exhibits and special events throughout the year, such as planting in terrace boxes and moving, carrying, and arranging potted flowers, equipment, and materials. Receives instruction on installing aesthetic or educational displays related to the plants or plant families maintained within the division. This may include layout and design of the display, selecting and properly labeling the plants, maintaining and rotating plants in the exhibit. Ensures that plants are healthy and well grown and that display areas are clean, orderly, and operated in accordance with professional horticultural standards on a daily basis.

Minimum qualifications required: Applicants will be evaluated on their ability to perform the duties of the position rather than length of experience. Eligibility will be determined by the relevance, scope, and quality of all experience and training, regardless of where or how acquired. Applicants will be ranked and rated based on their knowledge of the job elements identified in this announcement.

Minimum application materials required: Submit an online application, resume, and copy of driver's license. Application must include narrative responses to the following KSAs: 1) ability to do the precise and/or artistic work of the occupation; 2) ability to interpret instructions and specifications; 3) ability to use and maintain gardening tools and equipment.

Special requirements: Applicants must possess a valid driver's license.

Occupational Health Nurse
Agency: Office of the Attending Physician of the United States Capitol, Architect of the Capitol
Salary: $59,951 to $75,818
Location: Washington, D.C.

Job description summary: Provides nursing services to members of Congress, staff, and visitors to the buildings under the jurisdiction of the AOC. This includes providing emergency assessment, diagnosis, and initial treatment of injuries or illnesses. Notifies the attending physician when necessary for advice and assistance. Administers life-saving procedures to stabilize a patient. Administers electrocardiograms to diagnose abnormalities of heart actions. Refers patients to their personal physicians as necessary. Dispenses or performs first aid or palliative treatment for conditions which the employee would not reasonably be expected to seek the attention of their personal physician. Administers certain treatments such as allergens, vaccines, vitamins, and similar treatments requested by the employee's physician. Administers required immunizations as requested. Serves as an informational resource. Maintains accurate, complete, and confidential medical records. Maintains a supply of emergency drugs, a record of drugs and supplies issued, and other inventory records required to ensure orderly resupply of the pharmacy. Maintains an automated database of patients treated, and operates a personal computer for required reports and data input and retrieval. Assists employees in identifying and locating private physicians and dentists as required.

Minimum qualifications required: Degree or diploma from a professional, state-accredited nursing program. Must have an active, current registration as a professional nurse in a state, the District of Columbia, the Commonwealth of Puerto Rico, or a territory of the United States. One year of specialized experience that is in or related to the position of occupational health nurse and that has equipped the applicant with the specific knowledge, skills, and abilities to successfully perform the duties of the position.

Minimum application materials required: Submit an online application and resume. Application must include narrative responses to the following KSAs: 1) skill in assessing and treating minor illnesses to include preventive care for the common illnesses through interviews; 2) skill in providing cardiopulmonary resuscitation and other life-saving emergency procedures; 3) ability to communicate effectively both verbally and in writing; 4) skill in the application of established nursing concepts, principles, practices, and procedures; 5) skill in assessing the condition of patients, nursing care, and advising of health care needs.

Special requirements: Must be a U.S. citizen.

General Accounting Office

441 G Street NW
Washington, D.C. 20548
202-512-3000

* ★ Web site: http://www.gao.gov/
* ★ Job vacancies: http://jobs.quickhire.com/scripts/gao.exe
* ★ USAJOBS By Phone: 912-757-3000
* ★ Internship information: http://www.gao.gov/jobs/intern.htm
* ★ GAO telephone directory: http://www.gao.gov/about.gao/phonebook/orgphonebook.pdf
* ★ Basic employment information: http://www.gao.gov/jobopp.htm

The General Accounting Office (GAO) is the investigative arm of the Congress and is charged with examining all matters relating to the receipt and disbursement of public funds. It has offices in Atlanta, Georgia; Boston, Massachusetts; Chicago, Illinois; Dallas, Texas; Dayton, Ohio; Denver, Colorado; Huntsville, Alabama; Los Angeles, California; Norfolk, Virginia; San Francisco, California; and Seattle, Washington. GAO is organized into 13 teams that work on specific subject areas.

The ability to review practically any governmental function requires a multidisciplined staff. More than half of GAO's employees have doctoral or master's degrees from leading universities in such areas as public administration, public policy, law, business, computer science, accounting, economics, and the social sciences. GAO has more than three thousand employees from coast-to-coast, two-thirds of whom work at GAO headquarters in Washington, D.C., minutes from Capitol Hill. Major career tracks include analyst, financial auditor, and specialist (including information technology specialist, economist, actuary, and communications analyst).

Selected Teams Within GAO

More than 200 billion tax dollars are spent each year buying sophisticated weaponry, complex space and satellite systems, advanced technologies, and a broad range of goods and services needed to make the federal government run. This sum comprises the largest element of discretionary spending in the federal budget. The **Acquisition and Sourcing Management Team** examines whether this money is being spent efficiently and effectively and whether acquisitions maximize agencies' ability to meet their mission objectives. The Team also analyzes commercial practices and how they can be applied to government.

★ Web site: http://www.gao.gov/jobs/asm.pdf

The **Defense Capabilities and Management Team** leads GAO's efforts to support congressional oversight of the Department of Defense. It studies a wide range of current and future defense issues, including assessing defense plans and force capabilities to deal with adversaries who are more likely to strike in nontraditional ways.

★ Web site: http://www.gao.gov/jobs/dcm.pdf

The **Natural Resources and Environment Team** provides Congress with fact-based analyses on a variety of issues, including the safety of the food supply, farm income, management of national lands, quality of water and air, and hazardous waste cleanup and storage.

★ Web site: http://www.gao.gov/jobs/nre.pdf

The **Physical Infrastructure Team** helps Congress address the challenge of maintaining a safe, secure, and effective national physical infrastructure (transportation, postal and communications networks, and federal buildings and facilities) by identifying best practices and assessing improvement efforts and alternative options.

★ Web site: http://www.gao.gov/jobs/pi.pdf

Other GAO Teams and Offices

Applied Research and Methods Team
http://www.gao.gov/jobs/arm.pdf

Education, Workforce, and Income Security Team
http://www.gao.gov/jobs/ewi.pdf

Financial Management and Assurance Team
http://www.gao.gov/jobs/fma.pdf

Financial Markets and Community Investments Team
http://www.gao.gov/jobs/fmci.pdf

Health Care Team
http://www.gao.gov/jobs/hc.pdf

Homeland Security and Justice Team
http://www.gao.gov/jobs/hsj.pdf

Information Technology Team
http://www.gao.gov/jobs/it.pdf

International Affairs and Trade Team
http://www.gao.gov/jobs/iat.pdf

Office of the General Counsel
http://www.gao.gov/jobs/ogc.pdf

Office of Special Investigations
http://www.gao.gov/jobs/osi.pdf

Strategic Issues Team
http://www.gao.gov/jobs/si.pdf

Sample Job Vacancies

Human Capital Specialist

Agency: Office of Policy, Compensation, and Best Practices
Salary: $85,210 to $110,775
Location: Washington, D.C.

Job description summary: Develops and provides policy guidance on a wide range of compensation programs. Provides expert technical advice and assistance to program managers and Human Capital (HC) personnel. Analyzes proposed pay and leave legislation and regulations for impact on agency HC policies and programs. Advises management officials on pay flexibilities for alleviating recruitment and retention problems. Provides advice on employee grievance and claims involving pay and leave entitlements. Analyzes regulations to develop operating procedures for recruitment, relocation, and retention incentive programs. Advises on setting and adjusting pay for GAO employees, special salary rates pay limitations, allowances, differentials, hours of duty, Fair Labor Standards Act, overtime pay, grade and pay retention, severance pay, back pay and settlement of claims, and applications of single-agency compensations authorities.

Minimum qualifications required: Must have one year of specialized experience that equipped you to deliver a wide range of integrated services and products that support complex compensation programs and initiatives. Experience must demonstrate a high level of independence and work products must have been relied on as technically authoritative. Must be experienced in applying the full range of advanced HC principles, concepts, and practices with a concentration on pay administration policies, principles, and practices. In addition, advanced consultative skills are required to provide advice to major agency components in the development of solutions to complex problems in the area of compensation. Experience must have included a broad application of a wide range of qualitative and quantitative analytical techniques and methods in order to analyze trends and marketing surveys to determine and evaluate compensation strategies.

Minimum application materials required: Submit an online application, resume, and Notification of Personnel Action (SF-50) Application includes 20 questions relating to specific knowledge, skills, and abilities outlined above, including eight essay questions.

Senior Analyst

Agency: Acquisition and Source Management Team
Salary: $72,282 to $110,876
Location: Washington, D.C.

Job description summary: Works collaboratively, either as a team leader or member, to conduct research and produce reports or other products for Congress and for internal customers related to sourcing management.

Minimum qualifications required: Must have at least one year of professional experience showing analytical, data gathering, and research skills. Must have been responsible for independently planning, designing, and carrying out projects and studies where results of the work are considered technically authoritative and normally accepted without significant change. Must have demonstrated experience in an organization where the predominant work involves leading and working on a wide range of professional services engagements requiring complex analysis of management and organizational deficiencies, development of audit findings, and implementation of corrective actions. Applicant must have independently and interdependently developed and presented recommendations to support audit findings orally and in writing that specifically deal with sourcing strategies to address staffing and workforce issues of organizations with intensive knowledge-based systems. Requires strong analytical, writing, and oral communications skills, with a customer-service orientation and the ability to build and sustain productive working relationships.

Minimum application materials required: Submit online application and resume.

Special requirements: Must possess or be able to obtain a TOP SECRET security clearance.

Government Printing Office

732 North Capitol Street NW
Washington, D.C. 20401
202-512-0000

★ Web site: http://www.gpo.gov/

★ Job vacancies: http://www.gpo.gov/employment/job1.html

★ USAJOBS By Phone: 912-757-3000

★ Application information: http://www.gpo.gov/employment/of512.html

★ General employment information: http://www.gpo.gov/employment/index.html

The Government Printing Office (GPO) keeps America informed by producing, procuring, and disseminating printed and electronic publications of the Congress as well as the executive departments and establishments of the federal government. Created initially to satisfy the printing needs of Congress, the GPO today is the focal point for printing and information dissemination for the entire federal community. In addition to Congress and the White House, approximately 130 federal departments and agencies rely on the GPO's services. Congressional publications, federal regulations and reports, census and tax forms, and U.S. passports are among the documents produced by or through the GPO. The GPO provides government information in a wide range of formats, including print, microfiche, CD-ROM, and online through GPO Access. GPO sells approximately nine thousand different printed and electronic publications that originate in various government agencies. It administers the federal depository library program through which a comprehensive range of government publications are made available for the free use of the public in approximately 1,300 libraries throughout the country. GPO also provides online access to more than 200,000 federal government titles, including the Congressional Record and the Federal Register.

GPO employs about 3,500 people nationwide, about half of them in the graphics arts and related blue-collar occupations. Most are based at the GPO's central office facility in Washington, D.C., making the GPO the largest industrial employer in the District of Columbia. Also located in the National Capital area are a bookstore and a publications warehouse. GPO operates a printing plant in Denver, Colorado; a technical documentation facility in Atlantic City, New Jersey; a publication distribution facility in Pueblo, Colorado; and regional and satellite procurement offices throughout the country.

Sample Job Vacancies

Supervisory Content and Development Specialist
Agency: Office of Education & Development
Salary: $72,108 to $110,775
Location: Washington, D.C.

Job description summary: Coordinates the planning and delivery of Web content management for the GPO Access Service and provides consultation and advice to federal agency customers and partners interested in working with GPO on informational Web sites. Leads a team of information technology professionals in the development of asynchronous education and training products to support the Federal Depository Librarians and other partners, customers, and GPO clients. Collaborates with key leaders and managers in GPO program offices to identify strategic objectives, goals, and long-range plans. Writes, edits, and manages content that comprises GPO Access. Coordinates design, prototypes, and specifications of Web site presentation, and develops new, and updates existing, Web pages and applications on GPO Access. Conducts routine reviews of training and education development products with the objective of discovering better, faster, and less expensive ways of getting products to our partners as promptly as possible. Advises on how the products and services of the unit can enhance various organizations functional capabilities.

Minimum qualifications required: Must have one year of specialized experience which is directly related to this position and has equipped you with the particular knowledge, skills, and abilities in order to successfully perform the duties described above.

Minimum application materials required: Submit an Optional Application for Federal Employment (OF-612), an Application for Federal Employment (SF-171), or a resume. Respond in narrative form to the following KSAs: 1) knowledge of state-of-the-art information systems design, development, and documentation concepts, methods, tools, and techniques associated with Internet and Web-based computing, and enterprise information architectures; 2) ability to supervise a staff responsible for Web-based training application development, including design, planning, testing, security, implementation, monitoring, and maintenance;

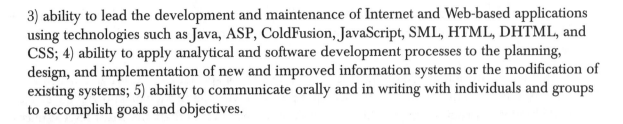

3) ability to lead the development and maintenance of Internet and Web-based applications using technologies such as Java, ASP, ColdFusion, JavaScript, SML, HTML, DHTML, and CSS; 4) ability to apply analytical and software development processes to the planning, design, and implementation of new and improved information systems or the modification of existing systems; 5) ability to communicate orally and in writing with individuals and groups to accomplish goals and objectives.

Supervisory Librarian

Agency: Office of Bibliographic Services
Salary: $60,638 to $93,742
Location: Washington, D.C.

Job description summary: Plans, coordinates, and directs the creation of bibliographic and authority records for all products in scope of the National Bibliography Program. Reviews workflow and practices to identify opportunities for improving efficiency or controlling expenses. Works with staff in Bibliographic Services Support Section responsible for ILS operations to facilitate and implement changes. Manages cataloging and service contracts. Works with appropriate personnel in the development and procurement of services from commercial vendors. Oversees the execution and evaluation of contract deliverables. Prepares and presents budget requests to Office Director. Prepares and delivers presentations to GPO upper management, library professional associations, and library constituent groups. Prepares proposal, position, and project documents.

Minimum qualifications required: Must have one year of specialized experience that demonstrates knowledge of automated cataloging and indexing applications, systems, and related operations, and practices that are consistent with national cataloging standards and current library practices.

Minimum application materials required: Submit an Optional Application for Federal Employment (OF-612), an Application for Federal Employment (SF-171), or a resume. Respond in narrative form to the following KSAs: 1) ability to direct, motivate, and supervise a large and diverse workforce; 2) knowledge of library science and management, particularly automated bibliographic authority, and metadata record creation and systems; 3) knowledge of controlled vocabularies and taxonomies; 4) knowledge of national and international data tagging schemes; 5) ability to analyze and assess data in order to make recommendations significantly affecting operational polices and processes relating to cataloging, indexing, classification priorities, and activities; 6) ability to communicate orally in order to deliver presentations to GPO upper management, library professional associations and library constituent groups; 7) ability to communicate in writing in order to draft and prepare executive quality proposals, position and project documents, and related papers.

Visual Information Specialist (Graphic Designer)

Agency: Government Printing Office
Salary: $41,815 to $78,826
Location: Washington, D.C.

Job description summary: Consults with agency representatives for planning, scheduling, and budgeting; develops visual concepts that satisfy customer needs; prepares designs for print,

Web, or multimedia products; and helps specify production techniques and materials. In the absence of a supervisor, may assume duties in the planning, assigning, and reviewing of the section's work.

Minimum qualifications required: Must have one year of specialized experience which is directly related to this position and has equipped you with the particular knowledge, skills, and abilities in order to successfully perform the duties described above. Must have a master's or equivalent degree in commercial art, fine arts, art history, industrial design, architecture, drafting, interior design, photography, or visual communication OR at least two full years of progressively higher-level graduate education leading up to such a degree.

Minimum application materials required: Submit an Optional Application for Federal Employment (OF-612), an Application for Federal Employment (SF-171), or a resume. In addition, submit a portfolio including at least six examples of your original work. Respond in narrative form to the following KSAs: 1) ability to design various types of products including: logos, identity materials, annual reports, newsletters, magazines, posters, displays, books, and digital materials such as Web sites and interactive CDs; 2) skill in developing design for the Web or skill using the following software programs: Dreamweaver, Director, and Flash; 3) expertise in the following software: Adobe InDesign or QuarkXPress, Adobe Photoshop, Adobe Illustrator, and Adobe Acrobat; 4) ability to specify ink, paper, and binding for printed jobs and the ability to prepare electronic files according to industry standards.

Special requirements: Must be a U.S. citizen.

Library of Congress

101 Independence Avenue SE
Washington, D.C. 20540
202-707-5000

★ Web site: http://www.loc.gov/

★ Job vacancies: http://www.loc.gov/hr/employment/jobposts.html

★ USAJOBS By Phone: 912-757-3000

★ Internship information: http://www.loc.gov/hr/employment/umbrella/
jobs-umbrella.html#internships

★ Volunteer opportunities: http://www.loc.gov/loc/visit/volunteer.html

★ Fellowships: http://www.loc.gov/hr/employment/umbrella/
jobs-umbrella.html#fellowships

★ Employee benefits: http://www.loc.gov/hr/employment/jobs-benefits.html

★ Contact information: http://www.loc.gov/help/contact-general.html

The Library of Congress is the nation's oldest federal cultural institution and serves as the research arm of Congress. It is also the largest library in the world, with nearly 128 million items on approximately 530 miles of bookshelves. The collections include more than 29 million books and other printed materials, 2.7 million recordings, 12 million photographs, 4.8 million maps, and 57 million manuscripts. The Library's mission is to make its resources available and useful to the Congress and the American people and to sustain and preserve a universal collection of knowledge and creativity for future generations.

Selected Agencies Within LOC

The **Congressional Research Service** is where members of Congress turn for the nonpartisan research, analysis, and information they need to make informed decisions. The CRS staff comprises nationally recognized experts in a range of issues and disciplines, including law; economics; foreign affairs; public administration; and the information, social, political, and natural sciences. The breadth and depth of this expertise enables CRS staff to come together quickly to provide integrated analyses of complex issues that span multiple legislative and program areas.

★ Web site: http://www.loc.gov/crsinfo/

★ Job vacancies: http://www.loc.gov/hr/employment/

★ Salary and benefits: http://www.loc.gov/crsinfo/crsbenefits.html

The **Copyright Office** is an office of record, the place where claims to copyright are registered and where documents relating to copyright may be recorded when the requirements of the copyright law are met. The Copyright Office furnishes information about the provisions of the copyright law and the procedures for making registration, explains the operations and practices of the Copyright Office, and reports on facts found in the public records of the Office. The Office also administers various compulsory licensing provisions of the law, which include collecting royalties. Additionally, the Copyright Office and the Library of Congress administer the Copyright Arbitration Royalty Panels, which meet for limited times for the purpose of adjusting rates and distributing royalties. The Copyright Office also provides expert analysis, advice, and assistance to Congress on national and international intellectual property matters.

★ Web site: http://www.copyright.gov/

★ Job vacancies: http://www.usajobs.opm.gov/

★ Headquarters contacts: http://www.copyright.gov/help/contact.html

Other LOC Agencies

American Folklife Center
http://www.loc.gov/folklife/

Center for the Book
http://www.loc.gov/loc/cfbook/

Children's Literature Center
http://www.loc.gov/rr/child/

John W. Kluge Center
http://www.loc.gov/loc/kluge/

Law Library
http://www.loc.gov/law/public/law.html

Motion Picture Conservation Center
http://www.loc.gov/rr/mopic/mpcc.html

National Film Preservation Board
http://www.loc.gov/film/

National Recording Preservation Board
http://www.loc.gov/rr/record/nrpb/

Poetry and Literature Center
http://www.loc.gov/poetry/

Recorded Sound Reference Center
http://www.loc.gov/rr/record/

Sample Job Vacancies

Historian
Agency: American Folklife Center
Salary: $50,593 to $65,769
Location: Washington, D.C.

Job description summary: Makes records available in response to individual requests. Supports professional researchers and provides advice and consultation to government officials or to scholars. Uses knowledge of the holdings as well as subject matter expertise to identify and locate germane source materials, explain the background, suggest secondary sources or documents that might be useful to the inquirer, and provide the information requested. Plans and accomplishes historical studies and projects. Defines the preliminary approaches and techniques, scope, depth, and major areas of focus for historical projects. Obtains and evaluates historical evidence in several forms and gathered through a variety of means, such as the search of records that are in written, physical, or oral formats. Carries out documentary publication, historical editing, and exhibition of archival materials. Holdings may be published either comprehensively or selectively in printed volumes, as facsimiles, or on microfilm, or may be exhibited in the interest of greater popular understanding of events and persons in American history. Selects items that are suitable for publication or display and determines the form and scope of publication or exhibit. Conducts extensive research in secondary works and in a number of record groups or collections of private papers to bring together all the relevant and related information. Writes introductory or descriptive material and creates a proper arrangement of materials.

Minimum qualifications required: Must have had progressively responsible experience and training sufficient in scope and quality to furnish you with an acceptable level of the knowledge, skills, and abilities to perform the duties of the position without more than normal supervision.

Minimum application materials required: Apply online or submit a completed applicant job kit. Include written responses to the following KSAs: 1) ability to communicate orally and in writing; 2) ability to provide research and reference services; 3) ability to organize, analyze, and interpret historical research and materials into various formats or media; 4) ability to work effectively with a variety of publishing and broadcasting media.

Specialist in Terrorism and International Crime

Agency: Congressional Research Service
Salary: $100,231 to $130,305
Location: Washington, D.C.

Job description summary: Prepares a variety of descriptive, background, and analytical reports, memoranda, and written materials on subjects or public policy issues within your area of professional knowledge. Participates in planning, organizing, and coordinating group research efforts. Through personal consultation, assists committees, members, and staff with consideration of legislative issues by providing information and analysis and applying professional subject-area knowledge. Participates in CRS seminars, workshops, or outreach programs for committees, Members, and staff. Locates and provides information requested by members of Congress or their staff.

Minimum qualifications required: Must have had progressively responsible experience and training sufficient in scope and quality to furnish you with an acceptable level of knowledge, skills, and abilities to perform the duties of the position without more than normal supervision.

Minimum application materials required: Apply online or submit a completed applicant job kit. Include written responses to the following KSAs: 1) knowledge of terrorism and international crime; 2) ability to analyze public policy issues; 3) ability to design and utilize research and analytical methods and techniques; 4) knowledge of Congressional decision-making; 5) ability to write in a public policy context; 6) ability to convey analysis and information orally through briefings, consultations, and other presentations; 7) ability to work collaboratively with others and build and maintain a professional network; 8) ability to exercise objectivity in all phases of analysis and consultation; 9) ability to work effectively in a high-pressure environment; 10) ability to exercise judgment and discretion; 11) ability to lead tasks and people effectively.

Supervisory Librarian (Domestic and Social Policy Research)

Agency: Congressional Research Service
Salary: $100,231 to $130,305
Location: Washington, D.C.

Job description summary: Supervises a group of employees performing work at a variety of levels. Analyzes major issues in information access and dissemination and develops new approaches to resolve critical reference information problems. Directs users to research sources and helps them evaluate the sources. Organizes and develops projects utilizing critical judgment to determine scope, emphasis, approach, appropriate techniques, and manner of presentation. Develops technical standards or protocols applicable to a library function.

Participates in planning the work of a unit, defining goals and objectives and identifying opportunities for improvements. Develops professional relationships with librarians and other specialists in order to share resources and information as well as to coordinate workflow within CRS. Participates in professional organizations, which may include presenting papers at conferences, seminars, or meetings in librarianship and other relevant fields. Serves as a principal liaison for the organization at professional conferences, seminars, and exhibits. Collaborates on projects both inside and outside CRS and the LOC.

Minimum qualifications required: Must have had progressively responsible experience and training sufficient in scope and quality to furnish you with an acceptable level of the knowledge, skills, and abilities to perform the duties of the position without more than normal supervision.

Minimum application materials required: Apply online or submit a completed applicant job kit. Include written responses to the following KSAs: 1) ability to manage projects; 2) ability to lead and inspire change; 3) ability to convey information in writing and orally through briefings, consultations, and other presentations; 4) ability to apply knowledge of information research within public and domestic social policy research frameworks; 5) ability to innovate; 6) ability to interact collaboratively with others; 7) ability to supervise; 8) ability to exercise judgment and discretion.

Congressional Budget Office

Second and D Streets SW
Washington, D.C. 20515
202-226-2600

- ★ Web site: http://www.cbo.gov/

- ★ Job vacancies: http://www.cbo.gov/jobs.cfm

- ★ USAJOBS By Phone: 912-757-3000

- ★ Internship information: http://www.cbo.gov/Intern.cfm

- ★ Fellowship information: http://www.cbo.gov/Fellowships.cfm

- ★ Benefits: http://www.cbo.gov/Benefits.cfm

The Congressional Budget Office (CBO) is a small, nonpartisan agency that produces policy analyses, cost estimates, and budget and economic projections that serve as a basis for the Congress's decisions about spending and taxes. Every piece of legislation affecting the use of the nation's resources undergoes CBO's scrutiny. The Congress depends on CBO to help it find its way each year through the intricate maze of programs competing for funds and to serve as a "reality check" for partisan advocacy.

CBO is a public-sector "think tank" that employs more than 230 people at levels ranging from undergraduate and graduate interns to seasoned researchers with doctorates and substantial experience. Well over half of its staff has advanced degrees in economics, public administration, or a wide variety of other disciplines.

Selected Agencies Within CBO

The **Macroeconomic Analysis Division** is responsible for preparing CBO's economic projections, analyzing the effects of fiscal policy on the economy, and advising the Congress on general macroeconomic issues. Macroeconomics, the study of the economy as a whole, focuses on key economic indicators, such as employment, production, income, saving, investment, trade, interest rates, and inflation.

The Macroeconomic Analysis Division employs approximately 20 Ph.D.-level economists. It also offers opportunities to a few assistant analysts. The Division gives economists who are interested in public policy a unique opportunity to apply their training in economics. Its staff write CBO studies, draft testimony to be delivered at Congressional hearings, and carry out original research for publication in academic journals.

★ Web site: http://www.cbo.gov/divlist.cfm?Pass=MAD

★ Job vacancies: http://www.cbo.gov/jobs.cfm

The **National Security Division** analyzes budgetary issues related to national defense, international security, and veterans' affairs. Its research focuses on defense budgets, military forces and weapon systems, the demand for and supply of military personnel, the military's industrial and support facilities, and U.S. foreign assistance programs. The division's analyses examine the budgetary effects of proposed legislation, the cost-effectiveness of current and potential defense programs, and the impact on the private sector of legislative initiatives concerning defense.

Analysts in the National Security Division bring the tools of applied microeconomic analysis, cost-benefit analysis, and related academic disciplines to their work. Many of the Division's 20 staff members hold Ph.D.s, and others have master's degrees. Economics and public policy are the most common fields of study, but the Division also includes people with degrees in political science, international affairs, and physics. Some analysts have served in the military, but most gained their knowledge of defense issues as civilians while working at CBO, nonprofit research organizations, or the Department of Defense.

★ Web site: http://www.cbo.gov/divlist.cfm?Pass=NSD

★ Job vacancies: http://www.cbo.gov/jobs.cfm

Other CBO Agencies

Budget Analysis
http://www.cbo.gov/divlist.cfm?Pass=BAD

Health and Human Resources
http://www.cbo.gov/divlist.cfm?Pass=HHRD

Management, Business, and Information Services
http://www.cbo.gov/divlist.cfm?Pass=MBISD

Microeconomic and Financial Studies
http://www.cbo.gov/divlist.cfm?Pass=MFSD

Tax Analysis
http://www.cbo.gov/divlist.cfm?Pass=TAD

Sample Job Vacancy

Economist
Agency: Tax Analysis Division
Salary: Commensurate with experience and education
Location: Washington, D.C.

Job description summary: Prepares in-depth CBO studies and conducts short-term analyses of current legislative proposals. The position offers the opportunity to conduct empirical research on a wide variety of federal tax policy issues, including tax incidence, behavioral responses to changes in tax law, and the consequences of tax reform proposals for economic efficiency. Staff members are encouraged to present papers at conferences and publish articles in conference volumes and academic journals.

Minimum qualifications required: A Ph.D. or equivalent experience. Post-graduate research experience in the field of taxation or public finance in an academic, research, or government setting is desirable. Must have strong quantitative skills, including econometrics, and the ability to initiate and complete independent research projects. Experience using large microdata files, especially panel data, is a plus. Must write well and be able to communicate technical matters effectively to nonspecialists.

Minimum application materials required: Submit cover letter, resume, salary history, academic transcripts, three references, and a writing sample via e-mail.

CHAPTER 5

Judicial Branch

The Supreme Court of the United States

One First Street NE
Washington, D.C. 20543
202-479-3000

★ Web site: http://www.supremecourtus.gov/

★ Job vacancies: http://www.usajobs.opm.gov

★ USAJOBS By Phone: 912-757-3000

★ Internship information: http://www.supremecourtus.gov/jobs/jip/jip.html

★ Fellows program: http://www.fellows.supremecourtus.gov/index.html

★ Volunteer docent program: http://www.supremecourtus.gov/jobs/docentprogram.pdf

The Supreme Court has original jurisdiction in cases involving public ministers and those in which a state is a party. In all other cases, it is the court of last resort. The court consists of the chief justice and eight associate judges. Power to nominate the justices is vested in the president of the United States, and appointments are made with the advice and consent of the Senate. Court officers assist the Court in the performance of its functions. They include the administrative assistant to the chief justice, the clerk, the reporter of decisions, the librarian, the marshal, the director of budget and personnel, the court counsel, the curator, the director of data systems, and the public information officer. The administrative assistant is appointed by the chief justice. The clerk, reporter of decisions, librarian, and marshal are appointed by the Court.

Sample Job Vacancies

Assistant Clerk—Case Analyst
Salary: $40,712 to $58,285
Location: Washington, D.C.

Job description summary: Screens new case submissions for jurisdictional and procedural compliance with the statutes and Rules of the Court, enters new cases into the automated docket, and corresponds with counsel and pro se litigants concerning jurisdictional and procedural defects.

Minimum qualifications required: Bachelor's degree and at least three years' general experience in progressively responsible positions in an appellate court or other legal environment. A working knowledge of the Rules of the Court and applicable sections of the U.S. Code is desirable. Ability to analyze complex situations; to communicate clearly, effectively, promptly, and courteously; and to use a word processor and a computer terminal required.

Minimum application materials required: Fax a Declaration for Federal Employment (OF-306), Optional Application for Federal Employment (OF-612), cover letter, and resume.

Special requirements: Must pass a security background check.

Supervisory Information Technology Specialist

Salary: $59,231 to $91,263
Location: Washington, D.C.

Job description summary: Oversees the daily operation and support of the desktop PC environment. Performs and supervises several staff who perform technical workstation administration tasks to include: configure, test, and install PCs, other equipment, and desktop software; install hardware/software upgrades, system patches; provide troubleshooting, fault isolation, preventive maintenance and repair of desktop PCs; deliver hands-on user instruction, technical support, and problem solving advice and assistance to system users; and administer equipment maintenance contracts and equipment inventory.

Minimum qualifications required: Five years' user support experience, in a "Help Desk" type unit, with hands-on working-level knowledge of technology products, personal computer equipment, and desktop software. Working knowledge of the Windows 2000/XP operating systems and registry required. Experience performing hardware set-up and installation, fielding requests for assistance, documenting and responding to trouble calls, and providing hands-on user instruction. Project management or supervisory experience or other experience that demonstrates ability to manage and supervise staff performing technical tasks. Strong interpersonal communications skills, ability to communicate and understand technical information, comprehend technical instructions, evaluate problems, and assist automation users. Ability to remain calm and professional in high stress environment and interact in a courteous manner when confronted with demanding users, short timeframes, or other pressing and urgent demands.

Minimum application materials required: Fax a Declaration for Federal Employment (OF-306), Optional Application for Federal Employment (OF-612), cover letter, and resume.

Special requirements: Must pass a security background check.

Lower Courts

★ Web site: http://www.uscourts.gov/

★ Job vacancies: http://www.uscourts.gov/employment/vacancies.html

Article III of the Constitution declares, in section 1, that the judicial power of the United States shall be invested in one Supreme Court and in "such inferior Courts as the Congress may from time to time ordain and establish." The "inferior" or lower courts consist of the United States Courts of Appeals, the United States District Courts, Territorial Courts, the United States Court of International Trade, and the Judicial Panel on Multidistrict Litigation.

Job vacancies for all the lower courts are listed on the Web site noted at the bottom of the facing page, although additional vacancies may be listed on the Web sites of the individual courts.

Selected Lower Courts

The **United States Courts of Appeals** are intermediate appellate courts created to relieve the Supreme Court of considering all appeals in cases originally decided by the federal trial courts. They are empowered to review all final decisions and certain interlocutory decisions of district courts. They also are empowered to review and enforce orders of many federal administrative bodies. The decisions of the courts of appeals are final except as they are subject to review on writ of certiorari by the Supreme Court.

The United States is divided geographically into 12 judicial circuits, including the District of Columbia. Each circuit has a court of appeals. Each of the 50 states is assigned to one of the circuits. The territories and the Commonwealth of Puerto Rico are assigned variously to the first, third, and ninth circuits. In addition, the Court of Appeals for the Federal Circuit has nationwide jurisdiction to hear appeals in specialized cases, such as those involving patent laws and cases decided by the Court of International Trade and the Court of Federal Claims. Each of the twelve circuit courts posts job openings on its Web site.

★ Web site, federal circuit: http://www.fedcir.gov/

★ Job vacancies, federal circuit: http://fedcir.gov/mploymnt.html

★ Web site, first circuit: http://www.ca1.uscourts.gov/

★ Web site, second circuit: http://www.ca2.uscourts.gov/

★ Web site, third circuit: http://www.ca3.uscourts.gov/

★ Web site, fourth circuit: http://www.ca4.uscourts.gov/

★ Web site, fifth circuit: http://www.ca5.uscourts.gov/

★ Web site, sixth circuit: http://www.ca6.uscourts.gov/

★ Web site, seventh circuit: http://www.ca7.uscourts.gov/

★ Web site, eighth circuit: http://www.ca8.uscourts.gov/

★ Web site, ninth circuit: http://www.ca9.uscourts.gov/

★ Web site, tenth circuit: http://www.ca10.uscourts.gov/

★ Web site, eleventh circuit: http://www.ca11.uscourts.gov/

★ Web site, twelfth circuit: http://www.ca12.uscourts.gov/

The **United States District Courts** are the trial courts of general federal jurisdiction. Each state has at least one district court, while the larger states have as many as four. Altogether there are 89 district courts in the 50 states, plus the one in the District of Columbia. In addition, the Commonwealth of Puerto Rico has a district court with jurisdiction corresponding to that of district courts in the various states. Each district court has from 2 to 28 federal district judgeships, depending upon the amount of judicial work within its territory. Each district court has one or more United States magistrate judges and bankruptcy judges, a clerk, a United States attorney, a United States marshal, probation officers, court reporters, and their staffs. Cases from the district courts are reviewable on appeal by the applicable court of appeals.

★ Web site, Alabama Middle DC: http://www.almd.uscourts.gov/

★ Web site, Alabama Northern DC: http://www.alnd.uscourts.gov/

★ Web site, Alabama Southern DC: http://www.alsd.uscourts.gov/

★ Web site, Alaska DC: http://www.akd.uscourts.gov/

★ Web site, Arizona DC: http://www.azd.uscourts.gov/

★ Web site, Arkansas Eastern DC: http://www.are.uscourts.gov/default.html

★ Web site, Arkansas Western DC: http://www.arwd.uscourts.gov/

★ Web site, California Central DC: http://www.cacd.uscourts.gov/

★ Web site, California Eastern DC: http://www.caed.uscourts.gov/

★ Web site, California Northern DC: http://www.cand.uscourts.gov/

★ Web site, California Southern DC: http://www.casd.uscourts.gov/

★ Web site, Colorado DC: http://www.co.uscourts.gov/dindex.htm

★ Web site, Connecticut DC: http://www.ctd.uscourts.gov/

★ Web site, Delaware DC: http://www.ded.uscourts.gov/

★ Web site, Florida Middle DC: http://www.flmd.uscourts.gov/

★ Web site, Florida Northern DC: http://www.flnd.uscourts.gov/

★ Web site, Florida Southern DC: http://www.flsd.uscourts.gov/

★ Web site, Georgia Middle DC: http://www.gamd.uscourts.gov/

★ Web site, Georgia Northern DC: http://www.gand.uscourts.gov/

★ Web site, Georgia Southern DC: http://www.gasd.uscourts.gov/

★ Web site, Hawaii DC: http://www.hid.uscourts.gov/

★ Web site, Idaho DC: http://www.id.uscourts.gov/

★ Web site, Illinois Central DC: http://www.ilcd.uscourts.gov/

★ Web site, Illinois Northern DC: http://www.ilnd.uscourts.gov/

★ Web site, Illinois Southern DC: http://www.ilsd.uscourts.gov/

★ Web site, Indiana Northern DC: http://www.innd.uscourts.gov/

★ Web site, Indiana Southern DC: http://www.insd.uscourts.gov/

★ Web site, Iowa Northern DC: http://www.iand.uscourts.gov/

★ Web site, Iowa Southern DC: http://www.iasd.uscourts.gov/

★ Web site, Kansas DC: http://www.ksd.uscourts.gov/

★ Web site, Kentucky Eastern DC: http://www.kyed.uscourts.gov/

★ Web site, Kentucky Western DC: http://www.kywd.uscourts.gov/

★ Web site, Louisiana Eastern DC: http://www.laed.uscourts.gov/

★ Web site, Louisiana Middle DC: http://www.lamd.uscourts.gov/

★ Web site, Louisiana Western DC: http://www.lawd.uscourts.gov/

★ Web site, Maine DC: http://www.med.uscourts.gov/

★ Web site, Maryland DC: http://www.mdd.uscourts.gov/

★ Web site, Massachusetts DC: http://www.mad.uscourts.gov/default2.html

★ Web site, Michigan Eastern DC: http://www.mied.uscourts.gov/

★ Web site, Michigan Western DC: http://www.miwd.uscourts.gov/

★ Web site, Minnesota DC: http://www.mnd.uscourts.gov/

★ Web site, Mississippi Northern DC: http://www.msnd.uscourts.gov/

★ Web site, Mississippi Southern DC: http://www.mssd.uscourts.gov/

★ Web site, Missouri Eastern DC: http://www.moed.uscourts.gov/

★ Web site, Missouri Western DC: http://www.mowd.uscourts.gov/

★ Web site, Montana DC: http://www.mtd.uscourts.gov/

★ Web site, Nebraska DC: http://www.ned.uscourts.gov/

★ Web site, Nevada DC: http://www.nvd.uscourts.gov/

★ Web site, New Hampshire DC: http://www.nhd.uscourts.gov/

★ Web site, New Jersey DC: http://pacer.njd.uscourts.gov/

★ Web site, New Mexico DC: http://www.nmcourt.fed.us/web/index.htm

★ Web site, New York Eastern DC: http://www.nyed.uscourts.gov/

★ Web site, New York Northern DC: http://www.nynd.uscourts.gov/

★ Web site, New York Southern DC: http://www.nysd.uscourts.gov/

★ Web site, New York Western DC: http://www.nywd.uscourts.gov/

★ Web site, North Carolina Eastern DC: http://www.nced.uscourts.gov/

★ Web site, North Carolina Middle DC: http://www.ncmd.uscourts.gov/

★ Web site, North Carolina Western DC: http://www.ncwd.uscourts.gov/

★ Web site, North Dakota DC: http://www.ndd.uscourts.gov/

★ Web site, Ohio Northern DC: http://www.ohnd.uscourts.gov/

★ Web site, Ohio Southern DC: http://www.ohsd.uscourts.gov/

★ Web site, Oklahoma Eastern DC: http://www.oked.uscourts.gov/

★ Web site, Oklahoma Northern DC: http://www.oknd.uscourts.gov/

★ Web site, Oklahoma Western DC: http://www.okwd.uscourts.gov/

★ Web site, Oregon DC: http://www.ord.uscourts.gov/

★ Web site, Pennsylvania Eastern DC: http://www.paed.uscourts.gov/

★ Web site, Pennsylvania Middle DC: http://www.pamd.uscourts.gov/

★ Web site, Pennsylvania Western DC: http://www.pawd.uscourts.gov/

★ Web site, Rhode Island DC: http://www.rid.uscourts.gov/

★ Web site, South Carolina DC: http://www.scd.uscourts.gov/

★ Web site, South Dakota DC: http://www.sdd.uscourts.gov/

★ Web site, Tennessee Eastern DC: http://www.tned.uscourts.gov/

★ Web site, Tennessee Middle DC: http://www.tnmd.uscourts.gov/

★ Web site, Tennessee Western DC: http://www.tnwd.uscourts.gov/

★ Web site, Texas Eastern DC: http://www.txed.uscourts.gov/

★ Web site, Texas Northern DC: http://www.txnd.uscourts.gov/

★ Web site, Texas Southern DC: http://www.txsd.uscourts.gov/

★ Web site, Texas Western DC: http://www.txwd.uscourts.gov/

★ Web site, Utah DC: http://www.utd.uscourts.gov/

★ Web site, Vermont DC: http://www.vtd.uscourts.gov/

★ Web site, Virginia Eastern DC: http://www.vaed.uscourts.gov/

★ Web site, Virginia Western DC: http://www.vawd.uscourts.gov/

★ Web site, Washington Eastern DC: http://www.waed.uscourts.gov/

★ Web site, Washington Western DC: http://www.wawd.uscourts.gov/

★ Web site, West Virginia Northern DC: http://www.wvnd.uscourts.gov/

★ Web site, West Virginia Southern DC: http://www.wvsd.uscourts.gov/

★ Web site, Wisconsin Eastern DC: http://www.wied.uscourts.gov/

★ Web site, Wisconsin Western DC: http://www.wiwd.uscourts.gov/

★ Web site, Wyoming DC: http://www.ck10.uscourts.gov/wyoming/district/index.html

* Web site, District of Columbia DC: http://www.dcd.uscourts.gov/

* Web site, Commonwealth of Puerto Rico DC: http://www.prd.uscourts.gov/ USDCPR/index.htm

Other Lower Courts

Territorial Courts
Guam DC: http://www.gud.uscourts.gov/
Virgin Islands DC: http://www.vid.uscourts.gov/
Northern Mariana Islands DC: http://www.nmid.uscourts.gov/

United States Court of International Trade
http://www.cit.uscourts.gov/

Judicial Panel on Multidistrict Litigation
http://www.jpml.uscourts.gov/

Sample Job Vacancies

Case Manager
Agency: U.S. Court of Appeals for the Second Circuit
Salary: $28,445 to $56,670
Location: New York, New York

Job description summary: Reviews, routes, and prepares legal documents and correspondence pertaining to appellate cases. Enters case information in the Court's computer database, advises counsel and the public on court procedures and federal and local rules, and applies the rules as needed to appeals.

Minimum qualifications required: Must be computer literate and have excellent organizational and communication skills. Must possess a minimum of two years of work experience which relates to the processing of legal documents or the application of regulations or the use of technical terminology. Education above the high school level may be credited toward work experience.

Minimum application materials required: Submit a cover letter and resume.

Clerk of Court
Agency: U.S. District Court for the District of Massachusetts
Salary: $119,972 to $145,600
Location: Boston, Massachusetts

Job description summary: Serves as the chief executive officer of the nonjudicial functions of the court. Duties include personnel management, budget preparation, procurement management, training, statistical reporting, records management, and jury operations.

Minimum qualifications required: Must have a bachelor's degree; a postgraduate degree in law, business, or judicial administration is preferred. Must have a minimum of 10 years of leadership experience in complex public or private sector organizations that exhibits a thorough understanding of organizational, procedural, financial, and personnel management.

Minimum application materials required: Submit a letter of application, resume, and salary requirements via regular mail.

Special requirements: Must undergo a full FBI background investigation if selected.

Court Reporter
Agency: U.S. District Court, District of New Mexico
Salary: $62,563 to $75,076
Location: Albuquerque, New Mexico

Job description summary: Performs court reporting services for all judicial proceedings. The position requires the ability to record verbatim testimony of court proceedings, to read back any or all portions of the court record, to work well under pressure, and to produce transcripts within required time limitations. Realtime proficiency is required.

Minimum qualifications required: Must have at least four years of prime court reporting experience in the freelance field of service, in other courts, or a combination thereof; AND have qualified by testing for listing on the registry of professional reporters of the National Shorthand Reporters Association, or passed an equivalent qualifying examination. Should be mature; responsible; poised; possess tact, good judgment, and initiative (the average reporter produces more than 15,000 pages per year); be able to work harmoniously with others and communicate effectively, both orally and in writing.

Minimum application materials required: Submit letter of interest and resume directly to the court.

Special requirements: Successful applicant may be required to undergo National Crime Information Center background check and FBI National Name Check Program and Fingerprint Check.

Desktop Support Specialist
Agency: United States Court of International Trade
Salary: $38,329 to $62,306
Location: New York, New York

Job description summary: Provides technical and end-user support for PC-based systems in a help desk environment, and support for the following functions: system account registration and creation, Web updates, end-user training on Court-supported software, report requests, and courtroom technology equipment (video conferencing and digital court recording equipment).

Minimum qualifications required: Bachelor's degree in computer science. Three years of progressively responsible experience related to the support and use of data processing, office automation, and desktop applications and hardware; knowledge of Web design or HTML;

knowledge of Windows 2000/XP, word processing applications, Lotus Notes, and basic fundamentals of data communication networks. Understanding of operational processes in a Court environment is highly desirable.

Minimum application materials required: In a cover letter accompanying a detailed resume, specify how you satisfy the qualifications. Any resume without the required cover letter addressing those qualifications will not be considered.

Special requirements: Subject to the FBI National Name Check Program records check.

Jury/File Clerk

Agency: United States District Court, Middle District of Florida
Salary: $32,363 to $40,454
Location: Ft. Myers, Florida

Job description summary: Assists in the operations of the automated Jury Management System. Summons jurors and maintains attendance records. Processes all jury correspondence. Conducts juror orientation. Maintains records and ensures that juror payments are properly made. Prepares monthly jury statistical reports. Maintains in-house statistics necessary to monitor juror usage by division, judge, and nature of case. Provides judges with information as necessary to demonstrate compliance with the district's jury plan and federal statutes, monitoring compliance with same. Prepares initial appeal package for submission to the U.S. Court of Appeals and conducts appeal management and tracking to include docketing of transcript information sheets, court reporter acknowledgments, notifications, transcripts, and appellate orders/judgments. Handles all requests from the U. S. Court of Appeals. Processes incoming and outgoing mail. Delivers files to and from the clerk's office to judges' chambers. Places orders for general office supplies. Coordinates maintenance of general office equipment. Coordinates interpreter assignments.

Minimum qualifications required: High school graduate or equivalent and a minimum of three years of administrative work experience involving the routine use of specialized terminology, keyboard skills, and demonstrated ability to apply a body of rules, regulations, directives, or laws. Must present a professional demeanor, be extremely detail-oriented, and possess strong organizational and communication skills. Must be a self-starter with the ability to work alone yet be a constructive member of a team.

Minimum application materials required: Apply by mail with cover letter and resume.

Law Clerk

Agency: United States District Court for the District of Colorado
Salary: $61,712 to $112,737
Location: Denver, Colorado

Job description summary: Conducts legal research, prepares bench memos, drafts orders and opinions, proofreads the judge's orders and opinions, verifies citations, communicates with counsel regarding case management and procedural requirements, and assists the judge during courtroom proceedings.

Minimum qualifications required: Law School graduate; Bar membership; Minimum two years' legal work experience in the practice of law or in legal research (following graduation from law school); Westlaw experience, aptitude in computer applications, excellent legal writing and proofreading skills; state or federal experience in Habeas Corpus matters; writing experience in prisoner civil rights, motions for summary judgment, motions to dismiss, and discovery motions; previous federal law clerk experience is highly desirable. Experience in case management/electronic case filing (CM/ECF) highly desirable.

Minimum application materials required: Apply by mail. Send resume, two writing samples, and at least two letters of professional reference.

Legal Secretary

Agency: Office of the Federal Public Defender, Central District of California
Salary: $34,900 to $38,700
Location: Santa Ana, California

Job description summary: Prepares correspondence and legal papers such as summonses, complaints, motions, responses, and subpoenas under the supervision of an attorney or paralegal. Reviews legal journals and assists with legal research.

Minimum qualifications required: Must have a minimum of three years' experience, be proficient in WordPerfect, and have great organizational skills.

Minimum application materials required: Apply by mail. Send a cover letter, resume, salary history, and the names of at least three references.

Staff Attorney

Agency: United States Court of Appeals for the Eleventh Circuit
Salary: $49,702
Location: Atlanta, Georgia

Job description summary: The Staff Attorneys' Office is a central legal staff, serving the Court at large rather than individual judges. The principal task of the office is to assist in the disposition of appeals through the preparation of legal memoranda. The types of cases the office presently handles include 1) direct criminal appeals involving sentencing guidelines and guilt/innocence issues; 2) social security and black lung appeals; 3) all pro se appeals; and 4) employment discrimination cases.

Minimum qualifications required: Must have a Juris Doctor from a law school accredited by the American Bar Association and have excellent academic credentials. Must also have superior analytical, research, and writing skills and be proficient in computer-assisted research and WordPerfect. Good communication and interpersonal skills are essential.

Minimum application materials required: Apply by mail. Send a resume, cover letter, official law school transcript, unedited writing sample, and a list of at least three professional references.

Administrative Office of the United States Courts

One Columbus Circle NE
Washington, D.C. 20544
202-502-2600

★ Web site: http://www.uscourts.gov/

★ Job vacancies: http://www.uscourts.gov/employment/opportunities.html

★ USAJOBS By Phone: 912-757-3000

★ Federal law clerk information system: https://lawclerks.ao.uscourts.gov/

★ Judicial fellows program: http://www.fellows.supremecourtus.gov/index.html

★ Court links: http://www.uscourts.gov/links.html

The Administrative Office is the administrative arm of the federal judiciary devoted to serving the courts in fulfilling the federal judicial system's critical mission, which is providing justice to the citizens of the country. The agency provides service to the federal courts in three essential areas: administrative support, program management, and policy development. It is charged with implementing the policies of the Judicial Conference of the United States and supporting the network of Conference committees. It is also the focal point for judiciary communication, information, program leadership, and administrative reform.

The agency is a unique entity in government. Neither the executive branch nor the legislative branch has any one comparable organization that provides the broad range of services and functions that the Administrative Office does for the judicial branch. The agency's lawyers, public administrators, accountants, systems engineers, analysts, architects, statisticians, and other staff provide a broad array of professional services to meet the needs of judges and others working in federal courts nationwide.

Sample Job Vacancies

Accountant
Agency: Administrative Office of the United States Courts
Salary: $30,762 to $55,743
Location: Washington, D.C.

Job description summary: Applies knowledge of specialized areas of accounting to solve complex problems in financial reporting. Advises managers on broad complex accounting problems with no previous precedent. Provides assistance to managers at all levels on the most efficient use of financial data produced by the accounting system to meet the AO's mission. Reviews and analyzes data recorded in the AO's accounting system and works with program offices and courts to ensure data integrity. Assists in the reconciliation of treasury accounts to the AO accounting system; and provides ongoing assistance to district and bankruptcy courts to resolve accounting issues and problems.

Minimum qualifications required: Bachelor's degree in accounting or a related field. Must have one year of specialized experience in accounting operations which includes knowledge and application of accounting theories and practices as recognized in public and private sector accounting.

Minimum application materials required: Mail or hand deliver application, resume, and narrative answers to the following KSAs: 1) knowledge of and experience in applying federal accounting practices, procedures, and regulations; 2) experience with automated financial systems in the federal sector; 3) ability to communicate ideas, findings, and recommendations both orally and in writing.

Information Technology Specialist

Agency: Administrative Office of the United States Courts
Salary: $49,479 to $94,092
Location: Washington, D.C.

Job description summary: Assists with planning, design, and implementation of the CJA Trial Advocacy Workshop, a skills development program based on the use of the latest courtroom technology. Serves as faculty at local and regional training programs on the use of courtroom technology. Assists with development and preparation of materials for training programs including compiling and converting written materials for distribution at local and regional training programs on CD-ROM and posting online. Develops and maintains a CJA faculty and topics database, and maintains software programs and associated updates for use in developing and presenting CJA training materials. Assesses and coordinates procurement technology needs for training programs. Provides technical assistance with publication, online posting, and distribution of quarterly newsletter. Maintains Web sites.

Minimum qualifications required: Bachelor's degree in a related field. Must have one year of specialized experience which is in or directly related to the line of work of this position.

Minimum application materials required: Mail or hand deliver application, resume, and narrative answers to the following KSAs: 1) experience in analyzing, designing, developing, and maintaining information systems using modern tools and Web technology; 2) experience in the development and maintenance of informational and instructional Web sites and the use of associated Web tools; 3) ability to communicate technical information both orally and in writing.

CHAPTER 6

Executive Branch

The White House Office

1600 Pennsylvania Avenue NW
Washington, D.C. 20500
202-456-1414

★ Web site: http://www.whitehouse.gov/

★ Job vacancies: http://www.usajobs.opm/gov/

★ USAJOBS By Phone: 912-757-3000

★ Internship information: http://www.whitehouse.gov/government/wh-intern.html

★ Fellows program: http://www.whitehouse.gov/fellows/

★ Contact information: http://www.whitehouse.gov/contact/

The White House Office serves the president in the performance of the many detailed activities incident to his immediate office. The staff of the president facilitates and maintains communication with the Congress, the individual members of the Congress, the heads of executive agencies, the press and other information media, and the general public. The various assistants to the president assist the president in such matters as he may direct. The White House Office employs about 90 people, according to the Office of Personnel Management.

Office of Administration

725 Seventeenth Street NW
Washington, D.C. 20503
202-456-2891

★ Web site: http://www.whitehouse.gov/oa/

★ Job vacancies: http://www.whitehouse.gov/oa/jobs/oa.html

★ USAJOBS By Phone: 912-757-3000

The Office of Administration was established by Executive Order on December 12, 1977. The organization's mission is to provide administrative services to all entities of the Executive Office of the President (EOP), including direct support services to the president of the United States. The services include financial management and information technology support, human resources management, library and research assistance, facilities management, procurement, printing and graphics support, security, and mail and messenger operations. The director of the organization oversees the submission of the annual EOP Budget Request and represents the organization before congressional funding panels. The Office of Administration employs about 200 people, according to the Office of Personnel Management.

Office of Management and Budget

Executive Office Building
Washington, D.C. 20503
202-395-3080

★ Web site: http://www.whitehouse.gov/omb/

★ Job vacancies: http://jobsearch.usajobs.opm.gov/

★ USAJOBS By Phone: 912-757-3000

★ Internship information: http://www.whitehouse.gov/omb/recruitment/internships.html

★ Contact information: http://www.whitehouse.gov/omb/contact.html

★ How to apply: http://www.whitehouse.gov/oa/jobs/howtoapply.html

★ Organization chart: http://www.whitehouse.gov/omb/omb_org_chart.pdf

The mission of the Office of Management and Budget (OMB) is to assist the president in overseeing the preparation of the federal budget and to supervise its administration in executive branch agencies. In helping to formulate the president's spending plans, OMB evaluates the effectiveness of agency programs, policies, and procedures; assesses competing funding demands among agencies; and sets funding priorities. OMB ensures that agency reports, rules, testimony, and proposed legislation are consistent with the president's budget and with administration policies. In addition, OMB oversees and coordinates the administration's procurement, financial management, information, and regulatory policies. In each of these areas, OMB's role is to help improve administrative management, to develop better performance measures and coordinating mechanisms, and to reduce any unnecessary burdens on the public.

OMB is a small agency of fewer than 550 professional and administrative staff. Over 90 percent of the staff hold career, rather than political, appointments. Over 70 percent of the staff are professionals, most with graduate degrees in economics, business and accounting, public administration and policy, law, engineering, and other disciplines. The OMB career staff provide analyses on a full range of policy options to be considered by decision-makers. OMB's staff interact daily with high-level officials throughout government. OMB's work requires sharp analytical and quantitative skills; the ability to effectively present ideas and analyses both orally and in writing; and the ability to interact constructively with others, often under high pressure and tight deadlines. The environment in which OMB operates is fast-paced. Issues are diverse, cross-cutting, complex, politically sensitive, and frequently involve billions

of dollars in resources. OMB's major occupations include policy analyst, program examiner, budget preparation specialist, and legislative analyst.

Selected Agencies Within OMB

The **Office of Federal Financial Management** (OFFM) is responsible for the financial management policy of the federal government. OFFM responsibilities include implementing the financial management improvement priorities of the president and establishing government-wide financial management policies of executive agencies.

★ Web site: http://www.whitehouse.gov/omb/financial/index.html

★ Financial Standards and Grants Branch:
http://www.whitehouse.gov/omb/financial/fin_branch.html

★ Financial Integrity and Analysis Branch:
http://www.whitehouse.gov/omb/financial/fia_branch.html

★ Federal Financial Systems Branch:
http://www.whitehouse.gov/omb/financial/ffs_branch.html

Other OMB Agencies

Office of E-Government and Information Technology
http://www.whitehouse.gov/omb/egov/index.html

Office of Federal Procurement Policy
http://www.whitehouse.gov/omb/procurement/index.html

Office of Information and Regulatory Affairs
http://www.whitehouse.gov/omb/inforeg/

Sample Job Vacancy

Policy Analyst
Agency: Natural Resources Division, Office of Management and Budget
Salary: $41,815 to $78,826
Location: Washington, D.C.

Job description summary: Formulates and reviews the budget, reviews and clears legislative proposals and testimony, reviews regulations, and analyzes policy, program, and management issues in assigned areas. Continually reviews and oversees assigned environmental programs in order to stimulate program efficiency and effectiveness.

Minimum qualifications required: Master's degree in a related field. Must have a minimum of one year of specialized experience directly related to the work of the position. Must have training or experience in applying analytical techniques to public policy issues, as well as experience in working on natural resources or energy issues and either legislative or regulatory issues.

Minimum application materials required: Submit a resume or Optional Application for Federal Employment (OF-612). Include narrative answers to the following KSAs: 1) ability to conduct analyses and evaluations using quantitative and other techniques and to implement recommendations; 2) knowledge of the details of the budget, legislative, and regulatory processes; 3) experience in working on or significant knowledge of natural resource or energy issues; 4) ability to communicate effectively both orally and in writing.

Special requirements: Must be 18 and a U.S. citizen. Must pass a drug test and obtain a security clearance. Males born after December 31, 1959, must have registered with the Selective Service System.

Office of National Drug Control Policy

Executive Office of the President
Washington, D.C. 20503
202-395-6700

* Web site: http://www.whitehousedrugpolicy.gov/

* Job vacancies: http://www.usajobs.opm.gov/

* USAJOBS By Phone: 912-757-3000

* Internship information: http://www.whitehousedrugpolicy.gov/about/intern.html

The Office of National Drug Control Policy assists the president in establishing policies, priorities, and objectives in the National Drug Control Strategy. It also provides budget, program, and policy recommendations on the efforts of National Drug Control Program agencies.

Office of the United States Trade Representative

600 Seventeenth Street NW
Washington, D.C. 20508
202-395-3230

* Web site: http://www.ustr.gov/

* Job vacancies: http://jobsearch.usajobs.opm.gov/

* USAJOBS By Phone: 912-757-3000

* Internship information:
  http://www.ustr.gov/Who_We_Are/USTR_Student_Internship_Program.html

* Contact information: http://www.ustr.gov/Who_We_Are/Contact_Us/Section_Index.html

The Office of the U.S. Trade Representative (USTR) is responsible for developing and coordinating U.S. international trade, commodity, and direct investment policy, and overseeing negotiations with other countries. The head of USTR is the U.S. Trade Representative, a cabinet member who serves as the president's principal trade advisor, negotiator, and spokesperson on trade issues. USTR is part of the Executive Office of the President. Through an interagency structure, USTR coordinates trade policy, resolves disagreements, and frames issues for presidential decision. USTR also serves as vice chairman of the Overseas Private Investment Corporation (OPIC), is a nonvoting member of the Export-Import Bank, and a member of the National Advisory Council on International Monetary and Financial Policies.

Sample Job Vacancy

Policy Analyst

Agency: Offices of Services, Investment, & Intellectual Property,
Office of the U.S. Trade Representative
Salary: $72,108 to $130,305
Location: Washington, D.C.

Job description summary: Formulates and develops U.S. policy positions on international trade and intellectual property issues. Chairs or serves on trade-related subcommittees as appropriate. Initiates the development of trade policy for consideration by higher level policy makers in the interagency trade policy making process. Participates in the planning and formulation of negotiating positions and tactics to be taken by the U.S. government on trade issues during negotiations. Prepares Congressional testimony, briefing materials, summary statements, and speeches for the USTR, deputy USTRs, and other senior executives on major trade issues. Explains and defends the administration's trade policies to foreign governments, the public, the press, and the Congress.

Minimum qualifications required: Bachelor's degree in a related field. Must have one year of related experience. Must have knowledge of U.S. trade and investment policy, including provisions under existing trade legislation, and thorough knowledge of Intellectual Property Rights laws.

Minimum application materials required: Submit online or by FAX an Optional Application for Federal Employment (OF-612), a resume, an Application for Federal Employment (SF-171), or any other written application, ensuring that all required information shown in Applying for a Federal Job (OF-510) is included in your application. Must include narrative answers to the following KSAs: 1) ability to work with private sector stakeholders; 2) skill in developing strategies and tactics for negotiations; 3) ability to work effectively with other agencies in developing common goals and objectives to successfully implement U.S. trade policy; 4) ability to communicate effectively through oral presentations and in writing.

Executive Branch Agencies and Departments

Department of Agriculture

1400 Independence Ave. SW
Washington, D.C. 20250
202-720-2791

★ Web site: http://www.usda.gov

★ Job vacancies: http://jobsearch.usajobs.opm.gov/a9ag.asp

★ USAJOBS By Phone: 912-757-3000

★ Internship information: http://www.usda.gov/da/employ/intern.htm

★ Links to USDA agencies and offices: http://www.usda.gov; then click Agencies & Offices

★ Job categories by USDA agency: http://www.usda.gov/da/employ/careergr.pdf

★ Mailing addresses for USDA agencies: http://www.usda.gov/da/employ/director.htm

★ Basic employment information: http://www.usda.gov/USDAEmployeeServices

★ Employee directory: http://dc-directory.hqnet.usda.gov/DLSNew/Phone.aspx

As its name makes clear, the Department of Agriculture (USDA) primarily focuses on farming—but the agency has a huge range of programs that go far beyond traditional farming issues. Through 17 agencies and more than 200 programs, the USDA works to improve farm income, seeks to develop and expand markets in foreign countries for U.S. agricultural products, helps develop rural areas, assists Americans in rural areas rent or buy housing through loan and guarantee programs, helps feed hungry Americans by providing Food Stamps and free or reduced-cost school meals, and inspects meat, poultry, and egg products for safety.

The USDA also serves as steward of the nation's 192 million acres of national forests and rangelands through the Forest Service, encourages voluntary efforts to protect natural resources on land that is privately owned, conducts research on everything from human nutrition to new crop technologies, and publishes the Dietary Guidelines for Americans in conjunction with the Department of Health and Human Services.

Jobs should be plentiful at USDA in coming years. "USDA anticipates the retirement or the eligibility for retirement of a substantial portion of its almost 100,000 employees within the next few years," the department said in a recent publication.

The USDA offers careers in dozens of areas, including agricultural business, agricultural marketing, agronomy, animal sciences, archaeology, chemistry, consumer safety, economics, engineering, food program management, food technology, forestry, geology and hydrology, international trade economics, landscape architecture, mathematics and statistics, nutrition, plant pathology and physiology, soil sciences and conservation, veterinary medicine, and wildlife biology, among others. The administrative side of USDA offers opportunities in areas such as accounting and auditing, computer sciences, contracting procurement, criminal justice, management and program analysis, personnel management, and public affairs.

In a typical year, USDA employees 7,500 or more students in a variety of work and internship positions. Most students are paid between $10 and $11 per hour. Selected positions can lead directly into full-time federal employment, and in some cases new graduates are reimbursed for tuition, books, and incidental educational if they agree to work at USDA for a certain period of time. The Forest Service employs more students and interns than any other agency at USDA.

Selected Agencies Within USDA

The **Agricultural Marketing Service** provides standardization, grading, and market news for six commodity programs: cotton, dairy, fruit and vegetable, livestock and seed, poultry, and tobacco. It also purchases commodities for federal food programs, collects and analyzes data about pesticide residue levels in agricultural commodities, and helps solve problems affecting U.S. and world agricultural transportation.

★ Web site: http://www.ams.usda.gov

★ Job vacancies: http://www.ams.usda.gov/human/vacancy.htm

★ Headquarters contacts: http://www.ams.usda.gov/admin/amsorg.htm

★ Details about student employment programs: http://www.ams.usda.gov/lsg/scep/scep.htm

The **Agricultural Research Service** is the main in-house scientific research agency for the Department of Agriculture. It conducts research in areas such as protecting crops and livestock from pests and disease, improving the quality and safety of agricultural products, determining the best nutrition for people of all ages, and sustaining soil and other natural resources. With 2,100 scientists and 6,000 other employees, the ARS conducts 1,200 research projects within 22 national programs. It has Area Offices in Albany, California; Fort Collins, Colorado; Athens, Georgia; Peoria, Illinois; Beltsville, Maryland; Stoneville, Mississippi; Philadelphia, Pennsylvania; and College Station, Texas.

★ Web site: http://www.ars.usda.gov

★ Job vacancies: http://www.ars.usda.gov/careers

★ Receive new job vacancies by e-mail: http://www.ars.usda.gov/Careers/docs.htm?docid=1358

★ Recruitment office contacts: http://www.ars.usda.gov/Careers/docs.htm?docid=1356

★ Details about student employment programs: http://www.ars.usda.gov/Careers/docs.htm?docid=1345

The **Farm Service Agency** has offices across the country that offer marketing loans, price support programs, financial incentives for farmers and ranchers to employ sound land conservation practices, and disaster assistance for farmers and ranchers whose crops and livestock are harmed by the weather.

★ Web site: http://www.fsa.usda.gov

★ Job vacancies: http://jobsearch.usajobs.opm.gov/a9agfsa.asp

★ Descriptions of services provided: http://www.fsa.usda.gov/pas/services.htm

★ List of offices nationwide:
   http://oip.usda.gov/scripts/ndisapi.dll/oip_agency/index?state=us&agency=fsa

★ Agency directories: http://hr.ffas.usda.gov/about/directories.htm

The **Food and Nutrition Service** administers federal food assistance programs that serve one in six Americans, primarily low-income people and children. It provides Food Stamps to buy food at retail stores, free or reduced-price school breakfasts and lunches for children from low-income families, commodities for distribution to food banks and soup kitchens, cash and commodities for food delivered to senior citizens through senior citizen centers or meals-on-wheels programs, and nutritious food supplements for low-income women who are pregnant or postpartum and their infants and children up to five years of age. The FNS also supports nutrition education efforts and coordinates nutrition policy within USDA.

★ Web site: http://http://www.fns.usda.gov/fns

★ Job vacancies: http://jobs.quickhire.com/scripts/fns.exe

★ Descriptions of careers: http://fns.usda.gov/hr/careers.htm

★ List of offices nationwide: http://www.fns.usda.gov/cga/Contacts/FieldOffices/default.htm

★ Information about applying online: http://www.fns.usda.gov/hr/online.htm

The **Forest Service** manages 51,000 square miles of the nation's forests and grasslands. It employs more than 30,000 people in careers that include forestry, biology, education, fire-fighting, accounting, computer science, law enforcement, recreation, geographic information, and more. Many temporary employees are required for seasonal work such as fighting wildfires and conducting recreation programs. The Forest Service also employs more students and interns than any other agency in the Department of Agriculture. The Forest Service has Field Offices in Juneau, Alaska; Albany, California; San Francisco, California; Fort Collins, Colorado; Lakewood, Colorado; Atlanta, Georgia; St. Paul, Minnesota; Missoula, Montana; Albuquerque, New Mexico; Asheville, North Carolina; Portland, Oregon; Radnor, Pennsylvania; Ogden, Utah; Madison, Wisconsin; Milwaukee, Wisconsin; and Rio Piedras, Puerto Rico.

★ Web site: http://www.fs.fed.us

★ Job vacancies: http://www.fs.fed.us/fsjobs/openings.html

★ Links to Forest Service employment information: http://www.fs.fed.us/fsjobs

★ Descriptions of employee benefits: http://www.fs.fed.us/fsjobs/benefits.html

★ Details about student employment programs: http://www.fs.fed.us/fsjobs/employ.html

★ Employee directories: http://www.fs.fed.us/intro/directory

Other USDA Agencies

Animal and Plant Health Inspection Service
http://www.aphis.usda.gov

Center for Nutrition Policy and Promotion
http://www.usda.gov/cnpp

Cooperative State Research, Education, and Extension Service
http://www.csrees.usda.gov

Economic Research Service
http://www.ers.usda.gov

Food Safety and Inspection Service
http://www.fsis.usda.gov

Foreign Agricultural Service
http://www.fas.usda.gov

Grain Inspection, Packers, and Stockyards Administration
http://www.usda.gov/gipsa

National Agricultural Library
http://www.nalusda.gov

National Agricultural Statistics Service
http://www.usda.gov/nass

Natural Resources Conservation Service
http://www.nrcs.usda.gov

Risk Management Agency
http://www.rma.usda.gov

Rural Development
http://www.rurdev.usda.gov

Sample Job Vacancies

Agricultural Commodity Grader–Fresh Fruits and Vegetables
Agency: Agricultural Marketing Service
Salary: $49,110 to $63,841
Location: St. Louis, Missouri

Job description summary: Serves as Officer-in-Charge at a terminal market office that is responsible for grading and inspecting 30 to 40 different types of fresh fruits and vegetables. Schedules and assigns work, maintains relationships with area producers and wholesalers of fresh fruits and vegetables, prepares monthly reports on work performed and trade activity in the area, resolves disputes on grade determinations, explains proposals to amend or revise standards to wholesalers and receivers, and examines and evaluates fresh fruits and vegetables to determine their official U.S. grade in terms of quality and condition based on representative samples from product lots.

Minimum qualifications required: One year of specialized experience in grading commodities that included final responsibility for certifying the condition and grade and applying official U.S. Grade Standards; OR three years of higher level graduate education or a Ph.D. in agriculture, mathematics, engineering, science, business, or economics; OR a combination of specialized experience and graduate education.

Minimum application materials required: Completion of an online application at a specified URL, and mailing of a college transcript OR a copy of your college diploma OR a copy of a current license or certificate of membership in a professional organization that indicates you have met the educational requirements.

Special requirements: The selected candidate must complete a one-year probationary period, obtain and maintain an appropriate security clearance, sign a statement indicating willingness to accept a reassignment to other locations throughout the United States, and undergo a post-employment medical examination.

Agricultural Economist
Agency: Farm Service Agency
Salary: $60,638 to $93,742
Location: Washington, D.C., metro area

Job description summary: Develops and maintains national databases and conducts highly complex and comprehensive economic studies, analyses, and appraisals of current and proposed conservation and resource protection programs and policies involving the environment, commodity supplies, agricultural prices, producer incomes, and government spending. Provides advice on agricultural land conservation issues to top policy officials in the FSA and the Department of Agriculture.

Minimum qualifications required: A degree in economics that includes at least 21 semester hours in economics and 3 semester hours in statistics, accounting, or calculus and specialized experience in the field.

Minimum application materials required: Complete an online occupational questionnaire, plus mail college transcripts and a federal-style resume or Optional Application for Federal Employment (OF-612).

Archeologist
Agency: Forest Service
Salary: $48,947 to $63,629
Location: Clayton, Idaho

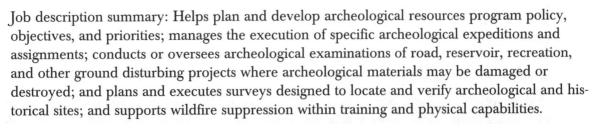

Job description summary: Helps plan and develop archeological resources program policy, objectives, and priorities; manages the execution of specific archeological expeditions and assignments; conducts or oversees archeological examinations of road, reservoir, recreation, and other ground disturbing projects where archeological materials may be damaged or destroyed; and plans and executes surveys designed to locate and verify archeological and historical sites; and supports wildfire suppression within training and physical capabilities.

Minimum qualifications required: A bachelor's degree in archeology that included specified courses OR a bachelor's degree in anthropology, history, American studies, or a related discipline as long as it included archeological field school OR four years of archeological work experience that demonstrated a thorough knowledge of the fundamental principles and theories of professional archeology. In addition, three years of higher level graduate education leading to a Ph.D. or equivalent doctoral degree in an area related to the position or one year of high-level specialized experience. Education and experience can be combined to meet the requirement.

Minimum application materials required: Completion of an online application or a questionnaire that can be scanned, along with mailing of transcripts, diplomas, or certificates of training if education is used to meet the basic qualification requirements

Special requirements: Must possess and maintain a valid state driver's license.

Community Development Assistant/Technician
Agency: Rural Housing Service
Salary: $26,699 to $42,993
Location: Butler, Missouri

Job description summary: Provides information and technical assistance for the Rural Housing Service's Single-Family Housing program. Counsels borrowers on financial management and home ownership, provides outreach for program services, performs all loan origination functions up to the point of approval, reviews documents submitted by loan closer for accuracy and compliance with program requirements, and conducts construction, site, and dwelling inspections.

Minimum qualifications required: A bachelor's degree OR one year of progressively responsible clerical/technical, office, or other work experience indicating the applicant can learn the specialized knowledge and skills needed for the position or a combination of

Minimum application materials required: Submit a resume, an Optional Application for Federal Employment (OF-612), or an Application for Federal Employment (SF-171), along with a copy of your college transcript. Include narrative responses to the following KSAs: 1) knowledge of financial/mortgage loan making and loan serving procedures; 2) skill in planning, coordinating work schedules, and establishing priorities; 3) ability to research, interpret, and apply regulatory material; 4) ability to communicate orally; and 5) ability to communicate in writing.

Special requirement: The selected candidate must be able to obtain and maintain a security clearance.

Contract Specialist

Agency: Forest Service
Salary: $50,620 to $65,803
Location: Sandy, Oregon

Job description summary: Solicits and procures a variety of products and services, monitors outstanding contracts to ensure satisfactory performance and identify problems that threaten contractor performance, negotiates contract modifications and the terms and costs of contract changes.

Minimum qualifications required: A bachelor's degree with a major in any field or at least 24 semester hours in any combination of fields that include accounting, business, finance, law, contracts, purchasing, economics, industrial management, marketing, quantitative methods, or organization and management. In addition, one year of specialized experience with contracting methods, cost and price analysis techniques, negotiation techniques, preparing and issuing solicitations, and performing other contract administration functions OR three years of higher level graduate education in one or a combination of the fields listed previously in this paragraph or an appropriate combination of education and experience.

Minimum application materials required: Completion of an online application or a questionnaire that can be scanned, along with mailing of transcripts, diplomas, or certificates of training if education is used to meet the basic qualification requirements.

Special requirements: Must complete a one-year probationary period.

Ecologist

Agency: Forest Service
Salary: $48,947 to $63,629
Location: Alturas, California

Job description summary: Evaluates, manages, classifies, interprets, and maps ecosystems; analyzes biological components and processes in the context of ecosystems; assesses a wide range of scientific, legal, environmental protection, and natural resource and environmental management issues; identifies opportunities and problems associated with public land uses and their impact on the environment; conducts studies of the interrelationships of organisms with each other, their physical and chemical environment, and society; conducts studies of the effects of proposed development projects on an area and identifies the applicable regulatory compliance issues and requirements.

Minimum qualifications required: A bachelor's degree with a major in biology or a related field of science underlying ecological research that included at least 9 semester hours in ecology and 12 semester hours in physical and mathematical sciences. In addition, three years of higher level graduate education leading to a Ph.D. or equivalent doctoral degree in an area related to the position or one year of high-level specialized experience. Education and experience can be combined to meet the requirement.

Minimum application materials required: Completion of an online application or a questionnaire that can be scanned, along with mailing of transcripts, diplomas, or certificates of training if education is used to meet the basic qualification requirements.

Special requirements: Must possess and maintain a valid state driver's license.

Information Technology Specialist

Agency: Natural Resources Conservation Service
Salary: $60,834
Location: Fort Worth, Texas, at the National Cartography & Geospatial Center

Job description summary: Provides Geographic Information Systems (GIS) computer programming and analysis for software and database evaluation, design, development, and maintenance throughout the lifecycle for technology automation projects used throughout the Natural Resources Conservation Service; uses enterprise GIS development environments such as ESRI ArcGIS, ArcObjects, ArcGIS server, and ArcIMS server to create applications that use and manipulate spatially based natural resource data; uses high-level programming languages and environments such as VS.NET, C, and JAVA to develop enterprise geospatial applications and tools; provides analysis and system design documentation; researches, develops, and applies solutions for technical problems relating to the underlying structure of an information system; monitors the effectiveness of GIS and graphics programming and analytical procedures being used on NCGC projects; and performs quality assurance reviews on technical and user documentation.

Minimum qualifications required: At least one year of experience as a high-level information technology specialist. An example of the required experience is work that required you to use one or more high-level programming languages such as VS.NET, C, and JAVA to develop enterprise geospatial applications and tools. Credit is given for qualifying unpaid experience or volunteer work.

Minimum application materials required: A federal-style resume or an Optional Application for Federal Employment (OF-612), copies of all college transcripts, and narrative responses to the following KSAs are 1) skill in using one or more high-level programming languages such as VS.NET, C, and JAVA to develop enterprise geospatial applications and tools; 2) skill in using GIS development environments to create applications that use and manipulate spatially based natural resource data; 3) knowledge of computer operating systems such as UNIX, DOS, Windows, and NT and relational DBMSs to identify problems with the design and development of application systems and recommending solutions; and 4) ability to communicate effectively.

Special requirements: The selected candidate must certify the accuracy of all information in the application, authorize a background security investigation, and complete a one-year probationary period.

Information Technology Specialist (Database Management)

Agency: Farm Service Agency
Salary: $52,080 to $59,776
Location: Salt Lake City, Utah

Job description summary: Serves as a technical specialist with the Aerial Photography Field Office, which involves monitoring database performance and file growth, developing and tuning databases, performing database backup and verification, and preparing for forward recovery.

Minimum qualifications required: At least three years of graduate education leading to a Ph.D. or equivalent graduate degree in computer science, information science, information systems management, mathematics, statistics, operations research, or engineering OR experience that required a range of knowledge of computer requirements and techniques, including experience in developing modifications to parts of a system that required significant revisions in the logic or techniques used in the original development.

Minimum application materials required: Complete an online occupational questionnaire, plus mail college transcripts and a federal-style resume or Optional Application for Federal Employment (OF-612).

Soil Conservation Technician

Agency: Natural Resources Conservation Service
Salary: $23,863 to $38,693
Location: Four vacancies available in South Dakota at Murdo, Huron, Lake Andes, and De Smet.

Job description summary: Surveys, designs, and lays out engineering practices that are normally used in the work area; assists with application of agronomic and engineering practices; gathers preliminary data for use by a conservationist in preparing resource management systems for conservation planning; prepares work schedules and timekeeping reports; assists with implementation of current conservation programs; and assists with the information program.

Minimum qualifications required: Two years of college that included at least 12 semester hours in courses such as forestry, agriculture, crop or plant science, wildlife management, watershed management, soil science, or outdoor recreation management OR four seasons of professional work such as installing and maintaining conservation measures on parks, shoreline, refuse waste sites, dams and reservoir areas, water and sewer sites, forests, wildlife habits, farms, ranches, or agricultural land. Credit is given for qualifying unpaid work experience or volunteer work.

Minimum application materials required: A federal-style resume or an Optional Application for Federal Employment (OF-612), college transcripts, and narrative responses to the following KSAs: 1) knowledge of natural resource conservation principles, techniques, methods, and practices; 2) knowledge of agronomic and engineering practices; 3) knowledge of current conservation programs in which the Natural Resources Conservation Service is involved; 4) knowledge of field office operations, and 5) ability to communicate with others and to maintain cooperative relationships.

Special requirements: The selected candidate must certify the accuracy of all information in the application, authorize a background security investigation, and complete a one-year probationary period.

Wildlife Biologist

Agency: Natural Resources Conservation Service
Salary: $42,373 to $66,647
Location: Escondido, California

Job description summary: Provides biological, technical, and habitat program assistance to field staff in a multi-county area that covers San Diego, Imperial, Riverside, and Orange counties; provides assistance and guidance to landowners, state and federal agencies, and special interest groups regarding programs administered by the Natural Resources Conservation Service; develops and implements wildlife habitat restoration and management plans and practices; conducts monitoring and status reviews; develops compatible use permits, habitat management plans, and environmental assessments; works with partnering groups and agencies to develop ranking and eligibility criteria, complete field rankings, and provide general program support; and plans and conducts studies and assessments for developing new procedures and management techniques.

Minimum qualifications required: A bachelor's degree with a major in biological science that includes at least 9 semester hours in wildlife subjects; at least 12 semester hours in zoology; and at least 9 semester hours in botany or related plant sciences OR a combination of education and experience that is equivalent to a major in biological science. Credit is given for qualifying unpaid work experiences or volunteer work.

Minimum application materials required: A federal-style resume or an Optional Application for Federal Employment (OF-612), college transcripts, and narrative responses to the following KSAs: 1) knowledge of wildlife biology and natural resource systems; ability to communicate orally, in writing, and through computers; and 2) knowledge of agricultural and community land use operations.

Special requirements: The selected candidate must certify the accuracy of all information in the application, authorize a background security investigation, complete a one-year probationary period, and possess a valid state driver's license because travel is required approximately five percent of the time.

Department of Commerce

Fourteenth Street and Constitution Avenue NW
Washington, D.C. 20230
202-482-2000

- ★ Web site: http://www.doc.gov/

- ★ Job vacancies: http://www.jobs.doc.gov/

- ★ USAJOBS By Phone: 912-757-3000

- ★ Senior Executive Service vacancies: http://ohrm.doc.gov/fjob/vacancies.htm

- ★ Internship information: http://ohrm.doc.gov/Intern/internwebsite.htm

★ Student employment opportunities:
http://ohrm.doc.gov/handbooks/student_empl/empl_opp.htm

★ Career information: http://ohrm.doc.gov/about/career.htm

★ Links to DOC offices: http://www.commerce.gov/statemap2.html

★ Basic employment information: http://ohrm.doc.gov/employees/employees.htm

The Department of Commerce (DOC) promotes the nation's international trade, economic growth, and technological advancement. The department provides a wide variety of programs: It offers assistance and information to increase America's competitiveness in the world economy; administers programs to prevent unfair foreign trade competition; provides social and economic statistics and analyses for business and government planners; provides research and support for the increased use of scientific, engineering, and technological development; works to improve our understanding and benefits of the Earth's physical environment and oceanic resources; grants patents and registers trademarks; develops policies and conducts research on telecommunications; provides assistance to promote domestic economic development; and assists in the growth of minority businesses.

The Commerce Department employed just over 37,000 civilians in 2004, 20,000 of them in the Washington, D.C., metropolitan area, according to the U.S. Office of Personnel Management. The DOC employs a wide variety of people, including accountants, agriculture engineers, attorneys, auditors, budget analysts, business development specialists, cartographers, chemical or material engineers, chemists, computer hardware and software engineers, computer scientists, computer specialists, criminal investigators, economists, electrical engineers, electronic engineers, engineering technicians, export compliance specialists, financial analysts, fishery or wildlife biologists, geodesists, geographers, geophysicists, international trade specialists, mathematicians, mechanical engineers, metallurgy engineers, meteorologists, oceanographers, physical scientists, physicists, program analysts and management analysts, statisticians, telecommunications policy analysts, textile engineers, and transportation and construction engineers.

Selected Agencies Within DOC

The **Economics and Statistics Administration** advises the government on matters relating to economic developments and forecasts and on the development of macroeconomic and microeconomic policy. This agency includes the Bureau of the Census and the Bureau of Economic Analysis.

The Bureau of the Census compiles and disseminates current statistics on population, housing, U.S. foreign trade, state and local governments, manufacturers, and transportation, among others.

The Bureau of Economic Analysis is the nation's economic accountant, integrating and interpreting a variety of source data to draw a complete picture of the U.S. economy. It provides information on such key issues as economic growth, regional development, and the nation's position in the world economy.

★ Web site: https://www.esa.doc.gov/

★ Job vacancies at ESA: https://www.esa.doc.gov/employment.cfm

★ USAJOBS By Phone: 912-757-3000

★ Details about student employment programs: https://www.esa.doc.gov/employment.cfm

★ Web site of Bureau of Economic Analysis: http://www.bea.gov/

★ Web site of Census Bureau: http://www.census.gov/

★ Job vacancies at the Bureau of Economic Analysis: http://www.bea.gov/bea/beajobs.htm

★ Job vacancies at the Census Bureau: http://www.census.gov/hrd/www/jobs/emp_opp.html

★ Details about student employment programs at the Census Bureau: http://www.census.gov/hrd/www/jobs/student.html

★ List of offices nationwide for the Census Bureau: http://www.census.gov/field/www/

★ Descriptions of employee benefits at the Census Bureau: http://www.census.gov/hrd/www/benefits/ben_comp.html

The **National Oceanic and Atmospheric Administration** conducts research, collects data, and makes predictions about our environment. NOAA works on a global scale, over a wide spectrum of disciplines. It also serves as the steward of the nation's oceans and coasts while assisting their economic development.

Unknown to many, NOAA has its own commissioned officer corps, NOAA Corps, the smallest of the seven uniformed services. NOAA Corps officers operate ships, fly aircraft, lead mobile field parties, conduct diving operations, manage research projects, and serve in staff positions throughout NOAA. Sea duty is common, and there is a two-year service obligation after successful completion of a Basic Officer Training Class.

★ Web site: http://www.noaa.gov/

★ Job vacancies: http://jobsearch.usajobs.opm.gov/a9noaa.asp

★ NOAA Corps: http://www.noaacorps.noaa.gov/corpsrecruiting/

★ Descriptions of employee benefits: http://www.rdc.noaa.gov/~hrmo/benefits.htm

★ NOAA Marine Operations opportunities: http://www.moc.noaa.gov/emp_ops.htm

★ Career opportunities in the Atlantic fleet: http://www.easc.noaa.gov/hrd/wmjobs_v2.htm

★ Career opportunities in the Pacific fleet: http://www.wasc.noaa.gov/services/hrd/wmjobs.htm

★ NOAA law enforcement career opportunities: http://www.nmfs.noaa.gov/ole/employment.html

Other DOC Agencies

Economic Development Administration
http://www.eda.gov/

Bureau of Industry and Security
http://www.bis.doc.gov/

International Trade Administration
http://www.ita.doc.gov/

Minority Business Development Agency
http://www.mbda.gov/

National Telecommunications and Information Administration
http://www.ntia.doc.gov/

U.S. Patent and Trademark Office
http://www.uspto.gov/

Technology Administration
http://www.technology.gov/

Sample Job Vacancies

Able-Bodied Seaman

Agency: National Oceanic and Atmospheric Administration
Salary: $26,677
Location: Norfolk, Virginia

Job description summary: Small boat handling; ship maintenance and upkeep; line handling and warping during berthing and departing movement of vessels; and handling of deck equipment and supplies.

Minimum qualifications required: Must have one year of experience aboard a research vessel, OR two years of college.

Minimum application materials required: Must submit a Commerce Opportunities On-Line (COOL) Application form that includes written responses to the following KSAs: 1) experience working aboard commercial, government, or research vessels; 2) experience deploying and recovering small boats/launches, oceanographic equipment, and other gear over the side; 3) experience performing watch standing duties aboard a ship; 4) experience in ship maintenance and repair, including painting, wood and metal surface preservation, and general cleaning; 5) experience handling small boats/launches; 6) experience in splicing wire rope and line; 7) been on duty alone, or completed non-routine assignments with minimal or no close supervision; 8) worked on a team with people from different occupations or diverse backgrounds; 9) done work that required you to live with others 24 hours a day while working with them toward a common goal.

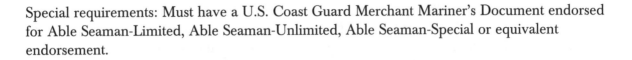

Special requirements: Must have a U.S. Coast Guard Merchant Mariner's Document endorsed for Able Seaman-Limited, Able Seaman-Unlimited, Able Seaman-Special or equivalent endorsement.

Accountant

Agency: Bureau of Economic Analysis
Salary: $28,090 to $39,996
Location: Washington, D.C.

Job description summary: Edits and reviews survey forms that cover data identification information about new investments in U.S. companies by foreigners. Determines whether the data are consistent, complete, and comply with all reporting requirements; resolves data problems by contacting the reporting company; follows up with delinquent survey respondents; and responds to inquiries from the public concerning the survey form and related data. Also conducts research using the Internet, business periodicals, and other available sources to locate information about new foreign investments in the United States.

Minimum qualifications required: Degree in accounting or a related field such as business administration, finance, or public administration that included or was supplemented by 24 semester hours in accounting, OR at least four years of experience in accounting, OR an equivalent combination of accounting experience, college-level education, and training that provided professional accounting knowledge.

Minimum application materials required: Must submit a Commerce Opportunities On-Line (COOL) Application form that includes written responses to the following KSAs: 1) knowledge of generally accepted accounting principles; 2) ability to communicate orally and in writing; 3) ability to set priorities and achieve objectives within a scheduled time frame.

Budget Analyst

Agency: Patent and Trademark Office
Salary: $34,184 to $44,439
Location: Alexandria, Arlington, & Falls Church, Virginia

Job description summary: Analyses budget data for a variety of programs and projects in the Office of Corporate Planning. Participates in budget formulation, presentation, execution, and reporting. Specific functions may include analyzing budget estimates in relation to performance results, analyzing resource requirements at different funding levels, drafting justifications, monitoring spending and performance against plan, and reporting. Work environment is corporate in nature requiring a business approach toward fee receipts, funds accountability, coordination with program counterparts, and an integrated approach to performance and budget within a fee-funded organization.

Minimum qualifications required: Must be a college graduate with a GPA of 3.5 or higher based on a 4.0 scale for ALL undergraduate courses completed toward a baccalaureate degree from an accredited college or university, or must be in the upper 10 percent of baccalaureate graduating class from an accredited college or university. Class standing is determined only on the basis of certification from the applicant's college or university. Must be a U.S. citizen.

Minimum application materials required: Candidates may submit a resume or Optional Application for Federal Employment (OF-612). Vacancy announcement number, position title and grade level you are applying for must be recorded on the application submitted. A copy of your college transcript from all undergraduate schools attended is required to verify your GPA. If you graduated in the upper 10 percent of your undergraduate class, then you must provide a copy of a letter from your educational institution stating your class rank. Graduates of foreign schools must have their academic credentials evaluated through a recognized credential evaluating institution.

High Voltage Electrician

Agency: National Institute of Standards and Technology
Salary: $21.55 to $25.17/hour
Location: Gaithersburg, Maryland

Job description summary: Performs a wide variety of assignments in connection with inspecting, testing, analyzing, repairing, and calibrating primary 13,200/7200 volt transformers, circuit breakers, underground cables, relays, 4160/2400 volt contractors with associated equipment for refrigeration units at the Steam and Chilled Water Generation Plant, secondary low voltage distribution switchgear, network protectors, supervisory circuits, and other associated equipment installed in the buildings, distribution system, and substation.

Minimum qualifications required: Applicant's overall background of experience, education, and training must clearly demonstrate the ability to perform journeyman level high voltage electrician duties, such as inspecting, testing, analyzing, repairing and calibrating primary 13,800/4160 volt transformers, circuit breakers, underground cables, relays, 4160/2400 volt contactors, etc. without more than normal supervision.

Minimum application materials required: Must submit a Commerce Opportunities On-Line (COOL) Application form that includes written responses to the following KSAs: 1) knowledge in High Voltage Safety; 2) knowledge in Network Protector or Circuit Breaker Maintenance; 3) ability to test, repair and maintain high voltage (600+) electric power controlling equipment and/or distribution lines; 4) knowledge applying electrical principles, materials and safety standards in the Electrical trade; 5) skill reading and interpreting circuit diagrams and electronic schematics and using test equipment to diagnose problems to determine corrective action; 6) ability to work with electrical distribution systems with voltage up to 480V; 7) ability to conduct safety meetings; 8) skills assembling, dismantling, repairing and cleaning the following electrical equipment; 9) ability to make emergency cutouts and substitutions of power lines and equipment and working on distribution systems when they are hot.

Hydrographic Junior Survey Technician

Agency: National Oceanic and Atmospheric Administration
Salary: $25,598
Location: Seattle, Washington

Job description summary: Serves on a ship, launch, small boat, or field party conducting survey operations. Assists in the operation and monitoring of instruments and equipment. Assists with data acquisition, data annotation, copying, filing, caring for field records and samples, data review, and data processing in support of operations. Assists in the maintenance and care of oceanographic and survey instruments and equipment. Recognizes and reports instrument and equipment problems to supervisor. May operate computer software programs for data acquisition and data processing. Recognizes and reports data acquisition and data processing problems; recognizes and reports computer software or system problems to supervisor. Maintains department work and storage areas, including cleaning, organizing, sweeping, swabbing, and other duties as assigned. Assists in the preparation of equipment and supplies for tide or horizontal control field work and sound velocity data acquisition. Stands watches including security watch and lookout watch as required. Handles mooring lines and assists with mooring details and small boat operations. Performs other mission-related duties as assigned, including duties related to the safety of the vessel and personnel.

Minimum qualifications required: No license is required for this position. No experience necessary; however, successful completion of a high school curriculum that included four half-year courses in any combination of the following subjects is required for any position within the Survey Department: mathematics (algebra, geometry, trigonometry, etc.), surveying, chemistry, physics, computer science or earth sciences.

Minimum application materials required: Must submit a Commerce Opportunities On-Line (COOL) Application form that includes written responses to the following KSAs: 1) hydrographic, and/or fishery research surveying or other scientific data acquisition, analysis and presentation experience; 2) experience using UNIX-based computer systems; 3) experience using Windows-based (95, 98, NT, etc.) computer systems; 4) experience using hydrographic, fishery research or other scientific data acquisition analysis and presentation software; 5) experience working independently or with small groups in isolated conditions; 6) experience using GIS software.

Special requirements: Selected candidates will be required to undergo a thorough medical and dental exam and meet specific standards.

Mathematical Statistician
Agency: Bureau of Economic Analysis
Salary: $38,767 to $59,862
Location: Washington, D.C.

Job description summary: Analyzes, develops, and implements systems to process and disseminate time series data from the National Income and Product Accounts (NIPAs). Identifies and documents methodological requirements and algorithms used to process NIPA estimates. Researches and evaluates the efficiency and accuracy of current and proposed methods used to prepare estimates, and develops recommendations for processing improvements. Analyzes program requirements to formulate processing algorithms for new systems. Develops, tests, and implements applications to process time series data and works with information technology specialists to integrate new applications into the current production environment. Reviews NIPA data products and supports and maintains new and existing NIWD processing systems.

Minimum qualifications required: Completion of a degree that included 24 semester hours of mathematics and statistics, of which at least 12 semester hours were in mathematics and

6 semester hours were in statistics. Must have at least one year of specialized experience developing, testing, and implementing application programs; OR one year of progressively higher-level graduate education; OR superior academic achievement. If you are qualifying for this position based on Superior Academic Achievement (SAA), you must be in the upper third of the graduating class; OR have a grade-point average of 2.9 or higher based on four years of education (or as computed based on courses completed during the final two years of the curriculum) OR have a grade-point average of 3.5 or higher based on the average of the required courses completed in the major field (or the required courses in the major field completed during the final two years of the curriculum); OR election to membership in a national scholastic honor society recognized by the Association of College Honor Societies.

Minimum application materials required: Must submit a Commerce Opportunities On-Line (COOL) Application form that includes written responses to the following KSAs: 1) knowledge of time series data; 2) knowledge of techniques used to formulate and analyze statistical estimates; 3) knowledge of the use of numerical methods such as interpolation, extrapolation, smoothing of data, approximation by function, etc., in computer applications; 4) skill in writing computer programs; 5) skill in developing, testing, and executing application programs to process time series data; 6) skill in writing programs with any of the following: MATLAB, APL, AREMOS, FAME, or SAS; 7) skill with computer programming using one or more of the following programming languages: FORTRAN, COBOL, C, C++, or BASIC; 8) skill in preparing technical documentation to communicate process algorithms such as requirements documents, screen templates, flow charts, or data flow diagrams; 9) skill in preparing written reports or technical memoranda.

Meteorologist

Agency: National Oceanic and Atmospheric Administration
Salary: $50,593 to $78,826
Location: Silver Spring, Maryland

Job description summary: Serves as a meteorologist on the Atmospheric Team within the Office of Scientific Support (OSS), Office of Oceanic and Atmospheric Research (OAR) and supports the Atmospheric Team Lead. Responsible for helping to coordinate OAR research contributions in meteorology, atmospheric chemistry, hydrology, and air quality monitoring systems. Assists the Atmospheric Team Lead in OAR initiative preparation and coordination with an emphasis on issues related to meteorology and atmospheric science. Additional responsibilities include serving as technical liaison to selected OAR laboratories and programs. Prepares program and budget materials for the Assistant Administrator, Deputy Assistant Administrator, Senior Research Council, Director of the Office of Weather and Air Quality, and OSS Director. Assists guiding labs and programs in the development and implementation of program goals and objectives including those with U.S. and international federal and state agencies; organizes meetings and workshops; participates in evaluations of OAR laboratories, programs and Joint Institutes; coordinates and reviews OSS response to controlled correspondence, congressional testimony, technical proposals and other requests from NOAA/Department of Commerce on scientific and/or policy issues. Collaborates with the OAR External Affairs and Outreach Team on atmospheric research and policy issues; engages OAR Budget staff on financial aspects of OAR programs; supports OAR Representatives to the NOAA Strategic Planning teams; and coordinates as appropriate with other NOAA line offices.

Minimum qualifications required: Degree in meteorology, atmospheric science, or other natural science major that included at least 24 semester hours in meteorology/atmospheric science, 6 semester hours of physics, 3 semester hours of ordinary differential equations, and at least 9 semester hours of course work appropriate for a physical science major in any combination of three or more of the following: physical hydrology, statistics, chemistry, physical oceanography, physical climatology, radiative transfer, aeronomy, advanced thermodynamics, advanced electricity and magnetism, light and optics, and computer science. Appropriate experience can substitute for some of the course requirements. Must also have one year of specialized experience providing policy guidance to labs and programs in the development and implementation of program goals and objectives including those with U.S. and international Federal and state agencies.

Minimum application materials required: Must submit a college transcript and a Commerce Opportunities On-Line (COOL) Application form that includes written responses to the following KSAs: 1) knowledge of science and technology research and development related to weather and/or water, prediction, including shipboard or airborne scientific research; 2) ability to develop, implement, and utilize operational numerical environmental prediction systems, data assimilation and modeling, and/or systems related to predicting and observing weather; 3) ability to analyze, evaluate, and prioritize science and technology requirements, needs, and opportunities especially with respect to numerical prediction systems, air quality, radar, satellites, forecasting, or solar weather; 4) ability to deal with constituencies among agencies and private sector industry or associations concerned with cross-cutting social science and technical impacts of weather & water, and/or prediction; 5) knowledge of weather/water product development and transition to operations, e.g. numerical weather prediction, models, radar or satellite data integrated into forecast guidance or operations; 6) ability to lead, organize, facilitate, or participate in integrated work teams and committees; 7) ability to develop and deliver oral and written presentations, reports, peer-reviewed scientific publications, briefs for technical and non-technical audiences, and/or senior decision makers; 8) ability to respond to requests and needs by formulating, developing, and coordinating science & technology plans and initiatives including budget proposals, resource requests, and schedules; 9) knowledge of field operations and customer interactions, e.g., operational forecasting, research, consulting or similar service program; 10) knowledge of performance-based management and quality systems, including data management, developing science and technology performance measures, and assessing outcomes; 11) knowledge of the academic research community as evidenced by having a leadership role in multi-disciplinary research programs or projects involving academic researchers, involvement with national or regional level planning, policy or review committees dealing with atmospheric issues, or leadership roles in scientific societies.

Research Fishery Biologist

Agency: National Oceanic and Atmospheric Administration
Salary: $37,276 to $65,278
Location: Auke Bay, Alaska

Job description summary: Assists in planning, logistics, and onboard sampling for research cruises, particularly involving acoustics, remotely operated vehicles (ROVs), and scuba. Must work effectively at sea aboard research vessels for extended periods, be familiar with the biology and life history of groundfish and forage species in the North Pacific, participate in a variety of technical working groups, and work cooperatively with others. Specific tasks will include identifying and sampling marine fish, invertebrates, and habitat types using trawl, longline, vidographic, and acoustic methods; sampling benthic organism using scuba, ROVs, and occupied submersibles; processing acoustic and survey catch data, and coauthoring reports

Minimum qualifications required: Degree in biology, zoology, or biological oceanography that included at least 30 semester hours in biological and aquatic science and 15 semester hours in the physical and mathematical sciences. Must have one year of specialized experience, such as experience processing acoustic data and classifying species or competency with computer software such as EXCEL, Echo View, Arc View, Noble Tec. Must have worked effectively for extended periods at sea aboard research vessels in the North Pacific. Training in the operation and maintenance of remotely operated underwater vehicles and NOAA scientific diver certification or equivalent highly desirable.

Minimum application materials required: Must submit a Commerce Opportunities On-Line (COOL) Application form that includes written responses to the following KSAs: 1) familiar with identification of marine fish; 2) familiar with marine fish life histories; 3) familiar with the measurement and preservation of marine fish; 4) familiar with using trawl gear for sampling marine fish; 5) familiar with acoustics gear used for sampling marine fish; 6) worked effectively on a fisheries research vessel or chartered fishing vessel on the open ocean; 7) acted as chief scientist/field party chief during field research; 8) familiar with using spreadsheets to manage data; 9) familiar with preparing tables for professional reports; 10) familiar with classification of echo sounder data using mid-water trawl data; 11) certified scuba diver; 12) familiar with the operation and maintenance of remote underwater vehicles (ROVs) used for fisheries work at sea. Additional supporting documents to be faxed as directed.

Senior Level Patent Attorney

Agency: Patent & Trademark Office
Salary: $117,927 to $144,600
Location: Alexandria, Arlington, & Falls Church, Virginia

Job description summary: Serves as the recognized technical and legal expert within the United States Patent and Trademark Office (USPTO) in the field of domestic and international industrial property rights protection covering the fields of patents, industrial designs, and related areas of law. Assists the Under Secretary and Director, the Deputy Under Secretary and Deputy Director, and the Director of the Office of International Relations (OIR) by rendering advisory legal and technical opinions relative to patents on a wide range of complex domestic and international industrial property issues, drafting legislative proposals which involve significant new technologies which can have a significant impact on a wide variety of industries, and representing the United States in delicate, highly sensitive international negotiations. Assists the Director by providing guidance to the industrial property functions of OIR.

Minimum qualifications required: Must possess a technical degree, a law degree, and membership in good standing of the Bar of any state, District of Columbia, Puerto Rico, or any territorial court under the Constitution. Additionally, must have significant work experience with technological and legal issues concerned with domestic and international industrial property rights protection covering the fields of patent, industrial design, and related areas of law, which provided a comprehensive knowledge of the laws, rules, policies, regulations, and practices related to the industrial property field.

Minimum application materials required: Submit an Application for Federal Employment (SF-171), an Optional Application for Federal Employment (OF-612), or a resume along with letters of reference. Include narrative responses to the following KSAs: 1) knowledge of patent, industrial design and related areas of law, both domestically and internationally; 2) knowledge of complex, emerging patent technology over a broad spectrum of arts; 3) knowledge of the U.S. legislative process; 4) knowledge of the procedures and responsibilities of U.S. trade agencies as well as international organizations having activities concerning industrial property law matters.

Statistical Clerk (bilingual)

Agency: Bureau of the Census
Salary: $23,863 to $31,020
Location: Jeffersonville, Indiana

Job description summary: Conducts telephone interviews for a wide variety of surveys for the National Processing Center. Obtains and records the data on a questionnaire or computer. Assures accurate and completed answers to all questions insofar as possible. May conduct "cold contact" interviews. Contacts previous refusals to persuade the individual to cooperate by providing a thorough explanation of the confidentiality and uses of the survey data. Does screening and interviewing of special places and may conduct interviews in English and Spanish.

Minimum qualifications required: Must have one year of general experience which is progressively responsible, clerical, office, or other work which indicates the ability to acquire the particular knowledge and skills needed to perform the duties of the position to be filled. Successful completion of two full years of study in an accredited business or technical school, college, or university may be substituted for the required experience. Equivalent combinations of successfully completed post high school education and experience may be used to meet total experience requirements.

Minimum application materials required: Submit a resume, the Optional Application for Federal Employment (OF-612), or an Application for Federal Employment (SF-171). Include written responses to the following KSAs: 1) skill in communication techniques for professional telephone interviewing and data collection including: probing, handling reluctant and irate respondents, promoting surveys, gaining cooperation, and maintaining open lines of communication with the public; 2) Ability to perform telephone interviewing and data collection while simultaneously operating a computer; 3) ability to handle stressful situations and pressure associated with conducting continuous telephone interviewing for entire workday/shifts; 4) experience conducting telephone interviews and entering the information in the CenCati or I-Cati system such as that used in the Jeffersonville Telephone Center.

Special requirements: Must be proficient in Spanish.

Department of Defense

Office of the Secretary
The Pentagon
Washington, D.C. 20301-1155
703-545-6700

★ Web site: http://www.defenselink.mil

★ Job vacancies (separating service members): http://dod.jobsearch.org/

★ Job vacancies (Human Resources Service Center): https://storm.psd.whs.mil/cgi-bin/apply.pl

★ USAJOBS By Phone: 912-757-3000

★ DoD job kit: http://persec.whs.mil/hrsc/instruct.html

★ Online resume builder: www.dfas.mil/careers/nonstatus/

★ Resume format: http://persec.whs.mil/hrsc/resume.html

★ Student career experience internship program: http://persec.whs.mil/hrsc/student.html

The Department of Defense (DoD) is responsible for providing the military forces needed to deter war and protect the security of our country. The major elements of these forces are the Army, Navy, Marine Corps, and Air Force, consisting of about 1.5 million men and women on active duty. They are backed, in case of emergency, by the 1.5 million members of the Reserve and National Guard. In addition, there are about 800,000 civilian employees in the Defense Department. Under the president, who is also commander in chief, the secretary of defense exercises authority, direction, and control over the Department, which includes the separately organized military departments of Army, Navy, and Air Force, the Joint Chiefs of Staff providing military advice, the combatant commands, defense agencies, and field activities established for specific purposes.

Selected Agencies Within DoD

The **Combatant Commands** are nine military commands with broad continuing missions maintaining the security and defense of the United States against attack; supporting and advancing the national policies and interests of the United States and discharging U.S. military responsibilities in their area of responsibility; and preparing plans, conducting operations, and coordinating activities of the forces assigned to them in accordance with the directives of higher authority. The operational chain of command runs from the president to the secretary of defense to the commanders of the combatant commands. The chairman of the Joint Chiefs of Staff serves as the spokesman for the commanders of the combatant commands, especially on the operational requirements of their commands.

★ Central Command: http://www.centcom.mil/

★ Pacific Command: http://www.pacom.mil/

★ Southern Command: http://www.southcom.mil/home/

★ Northern Command: http://www.northcom.mil/

★ European Command:
http://www.eucom.mil/index.htm?http://www.eucom.mil/Navigation_Frames/
Homepage_nf.htm&1

★ Joint Forces Command: http://www.jfcom.mil/

★ Special Operations Command: http://www.socom.mil/

★ Strategic Command: http://www.stratcom.mil/

★ Transportation Command: http://www.transcom.mil/

The **Department of Defense Education Activity** (DoDEA) is a civilian agency of the
U.S. Department of Defense. It is headed by a director who oversees all agency functions
from DoDEA headquarters in Arlington, Virginia. DoDEA's schools are divided into three
areas, each of which is managed by an area director. Within each of these three areas, schools
are organized into districts headed by superintendents. DoDEA's schools serve the children of
military service members and Department of Defense civilian employees throughout the
world. Children of enlisted military personnel represent 85 percent of the total enrollment in
DoDEA schools. DoDEA operates 222 public schools in 15 districts located in 13 foreign
countries, seven states, Guam, and Puerto Rico. All schools within DoDEA are fully accredited by U.S. accreditation agencies. Approximately 8,785 teachers serve DoDEA's 102,600
students. The DoDEA instructional program provides a comprehensive prekindergarten
through twelfth grade curriculum that is competitive with that of any school system in the
United States. DoDEA maintains a high school graduation rate of approximately 97 percent.

★ Web site: http://www.odedodea.edu/

★ Job vacancies: http://www.dodea.edu/pers/employment/

★ Application for Employment with DDESS:
http://www.ddess.org/Pages/Employment/DDESSApplication2004%20Feb.pdf

★ Schools: http://www.dodea.edu/data/allsites.cfm

Other DoD Agencies

American Forces Information Service
http://www.defenselink.mil/afis/

Defense Human Resources Activity
http://www.dhra.osd.mil/dhra/owa/go

Defense Prisoner of War/Missing Personnel Office
http://www.dtic.mil/dpmo/

The Joint Chiefs of Staff
http://www.dtic.mil/jcs/

Office of Economic Adjustment
http://emissary.acq.osd.mil/oea/home.nsf

Office of Inspector General
http://www.dodig.osd.mil/

Office of the Secretary of Defense
http://www.defenselink.mil/osd/

Tricare Military Health System
http://www.tricare.osd.mil/

Washington Headquarters Services
http://www.whs.pentagon.mil/

Sample Job Vacancies

Administrative Support Assistant
Agency: Office of the Inspector General
Salary: $26,750 to $43,074
Location: Indianapolis, Indiana

Job description summary: Provides centralized clerical and administrative support work. Assists in mission-related report development and preparation and in training, payroll, personnel, property, and records management. Maintains a variety of manual and automated databases systems, inputs data and queries the database to obtain audit information. Assists the audit staff in report processing. Processes approved procurement and acquisition requests for goods and services and inputs the data. Processes approved requests for training with the appropriate training coordinators. Inputs time and attendance information. Makes payroll adjustments that were identified by payroll reconciliation. Assists in conducting property inventories and in reconciling property records and inventories on hand.

Minimum qualifications required: One year of specialized experience that included maintaining database systems, report processing, processing procurement and acquisition requests, processing training requests, inputting time and attendance information, and conducting property inventories.

Minimum application materials required: Only resumes submitted via the Defense Finance and Accounting Service Designated Examining Unit online resume builder or resumes formatted and submitted in compliance with instructions contained in the most current DFAS DEU Job Kit will be accepted.

Special requirements: Must be a U.S. citizen and pass a drug test. Must be able to type 40 words per minute.

Autism Consultant
Agency: Domestic Dependent Elementary and Secondary Schools, Defense Education Activity
Salary: $59,570 to $77,437
Location: Peachtree City, Georgia

Job description summary: Serves as the principle consultant for Autism. Stays abreast of the latest theories and techniques for instruction of students with ASD. Confers with the DDESS Supervisory Instructional Systems Specialist for Special Education every six weeks to review area needs and concerns related to area of responsibility. Conducts on-site staff assistance visits to schools, advising administrators, special education teachers, and others as appropriate on specific student issues and methods and techniques for the provision of services to children with autism. Advises district special education coordinator of situations that appear to be controversial and that require conferencing with school, parent, or other community agency. Advises the district special education coordinator of potential mediation situations. Collaborates with military- and community-based programs that serve children with autism, including but not limited to EDIS teams, CDCs, and after-school programs. Provides staff development services to service providers involved in educating children with Autism/PDD to include general and special education teachers, paraprofessionals, administrators, school psychologists, and EDIS personnel. Identifies need for staff development services in assigned program areas.

Minimum qualifications required: Masters degree in education or a related field with a concentration in special education, speech and language, child development, social work, or psychology. A minimum two years of direct work with individuals having autism or related developmental disabilities.

Minimum application materials required: Submit a DDESS application for employment, an Optional Application for Federal Employment (OF-612), a resume, or an Application for Federal Employment (SF-171). Include narrative responses to the following KSAs: 1) knowledge of current theories, current developments, principles, methods, practices, techniques of education, and learning in individuals with autism spectrum disorders; 2) knowledge of laws, policies, regulations, restrictions, and standard operating procedures governing special education services; 3) knowledge of a wide repertoire of behavioral intervention strategies and techniques for working with children with Autism and ASD; 4) ability to effectively and tactfully communicate orally and in writing.

Communications Specialist

Agency: Defense Education Activity
Salary: $72,108 to $93,742
Location: Alexandria, Virginia

Job description summary: Plans, designs, and develops the DoDEA worldwide Web presence to convey information concerning DoDEA's programs, policies, and activities. Creates and manages Web content for the director and other members of the cabinet. Designs and produces the DoDEA headquarters Web site and content architecture. Works closely with the chief of communications and the Education Directorate Office to develop and deploy specific Web-oriented campaigns. Manages existing and new contacts with vendors to supply products and services for developing or maintaining Web sites, databases, and establishes processes for Internet file transfer to and from the vendors.

Minimum qualifications required: Must possess one full year of specialized experience that has equipped you with the particular knowledge, skills, and abilities to successfully perform the duties of this position.

Minimum application materials required: Submit a resume, Optional Application for Federal Employment (OF-612), or Application for Federal Employment (SF-171). Include narrative answers to the following KSAs: 1) knowledge of electronic and visual communications and product creation; 2) ability to develop project schedules and deliver high quality products on time and within budget; 3) ability to design information and content for effective and efficient distribution via the Internet; 4) ability to communicate, via interpersonal contact and presentation format, in technical and nontechnical terms about Internet implementations to a wide range of technical and nontechnical customers, including agency leadership; 5) knowledge of multimedia streaming software design, implementation, configuration, and maintenance; 6) knowledge of Internet technologies, including IP networks; multiprotocol networking and routing; server platforms (UNIX, Mac, Windows); Web server software (iPlanet, IIS, Apache) including configuration, operations, and maintenance; 7) knowledge of configuration and use of the common gateway interface (CGI/asp), hyper text markup language and its derivatives such as DHTML, Web search engines and Web site security; 8) experience with server-side scripting.

Special requirements: Males born after December 12, 1959, are required to register with the Selective Service.

Nurse

Agency: Domestic Dependent Elementary and Secondary Schools, Defense Education Activity
Salary: $31,991 to $51,957
Location: Guam

Job description summary: Conducts school programs as necessary for health screenings. Observes students on a regular basis to detect health needs. Instructs teachers on screening students for health defects. Systematically maintains accurate health information and documents health services in the student's "Cumulative School Health Record" and in other appropriate records. Administers medication and treatments authorized by physician. Reports to parents, school personnel, physicians, clinics, and other agencies on student health matters. Visits student homes when necessary. Administers emergency care for illness of occupational and nonoccupational origin and injuries that occur at the work place. Administers first aid. Implements Board policy on exclusion and readmission of students in connection with infectious and contagious diseases. Assists in in-service training programs regarding current health issues and serves as a resource person in health education for school personnel. Assists school personnel in maintaining sanitary standards in schools.

Minimum qualifications required: Must be a Registered Nurse and have an active, current registration.

Minimum application materials required: Submit an Application for DDESS employment, an Application for Federal Employment (SF-171), an Optional Application for Federal Employment (OF-612), or a resume, along with a copy of your current registration as a Professional Nurse. Include narrative answers to the following KSAs: 1) knowledge of established nursing principles and practices pertaining to a school environment; 2) ability to provide treatment for minor care and during emergencies; 3) knowledge in mental health and behavioral science; 4) ability to provide health instruction to help elementary school pupils understand how to prevent disease conditions and maintain good health; 5) ability to communicate effectively with children, both individually and in groups.

Professor of Financial Management

Agency: Defense Acquisition University
Salary: $64,586 to $113,981
Location: San Diego, California

Job description summary: Presents and facilitates instruction both in classroom and through Web-based or virtual learning modes. Develops and conducts lectures, cases, simulations, workshops and field trips; prepares course material (student and instructor) according to current instructional systems design technology; develops course schedules and arrange for guest speakers; develops and analyzes student assessments and provide student counseling to insure the highest degree of learning. Also provides performance support through consulting efforts to Defense Department, military services, and other federal agencies providing technical guidance and assistance on various matters including those of unusual complexity or without precedence. Participates in professional research, publishes papers in professional journals, and participates in proceedings, presentations at professional meetings, conferences, symposia, and seminars.

Minimum qualifications required: Master's degree in financial management or in a relating area. Must have at least six years of experience in the field and at least one year of specialized experience directly relating to the specific duties of the position.

Minimum application materials required: Submit a resume, Optional Application for Federal Employment (OF-612), or Application for Federal Employment (SF-171). Include narrative answers to the following KSAs: 1) knowledge and experience in financial management of DoD systems acquisition (defense or defense industry) programs; 2) ability to develop, direct, conduct, and evaluate courses of instruction using the fundamentals of adult learning theory as well as contemporary education theory; 3) ability to plan and conduct research in areas related to systems acquisition management and communicate (oral & written) results.

Special requirements: Must pass a background investigation. If selected for this position you will be required to become a member of the Acquisition Corps and to sign a written agreement requiring you to remain in the Federal Service and in this position for at least three years.

Public Affairs Specialist

Agency: American Forces Information Service
Salary: $100,231 to $130,305
Location: Arlington, Virginia

Job description summary: Provides expert advice to the deputy assistant secretary of defense and Office of the Assistant Secretary of Defense (OASD) on matters pertaining to the OSD Web Communications Program. Designs, develops, and produces Web material in support of the OSD Web Communications Program. Manages the OSD Web development team. Develops and maintains a strong working relationship with and acts as a primary liaison for the deputy secretary of defense to appropriate offices and organizations of Military Services.

Oversees the implementation of sound, integrated, and secure information management and information technology programs.

Minimum qualifications required: Must have one year of specialized experience, including information technology and associated technologies, especially as applied to the dissemination of information to both internal and public audiences.

Minimum application materials required: Submit a resume that identifies your work experience, education, and skills. Use the sample format to structure your resume and identify the job announcement number.

Special requirements: Males born after December 12, 1959, are required to register with the Selective Service. Must pass a personnel security investigation. Must test negative for the presence of illegal drugs.

Social Science Analyst
Agency: Defense Logistics Agency, Defense Human Resources Activity
Salary: $48,451 to $89,774
Location: Arlington, Virginia

Job description summary: Plans, designs, and conducts personnel surveys of military personnel to determine attitudes and opinions on specified topics. Develops survey questions. Revises sampling plan, pretests survey instruments, and coordinates the administration of surveys. Analyzes survey response data utilizing bivariate and multivariate statistical techniques as appropriate. Prepares reports and presents oral briefings. Performs statistical analysis of survey data as requested by DoD and other government agencies. Consults with researchers and analysts to determine the most efficient means of satisfying their information needs. Develops specifications for senior technical personnel and prepares computer programs for storing survey data in a computerized survey data bank

Minimum qualifications required: Bachelor's degree in behavioral or social science; OR a combination of education and experience; OR four years of appropriate experience that demonstrated that the applicant has acquired knowledge of one or more of the behavioral or social sciences equivalent to a major in the field. Must also have one year of specialized experience planning, designing, and conducting personnel surveys.

Minimum application materials required: Submit a resume and the completed Occupational Questionnaire from the vacancy announcement. Questionnaire includes more than 20 KSAs, including the following: 1) ability to analyze data from large-scale, probability-based sample surveys to determine attitudes and opinions; 2) ability to plan, design, and conduct large-scale, probability-based sample surveys of military personnel, military spouses, and/or federal civilians to determine attitudes and opinions on specified topics; 3) ability to develop survey questions by reviewing relevant literature in economics, sociology, psychology, or other related fields; 4) knowledge of personnel research methodology and techniques; 5) experience planning and supervising/monitoring probability-based sample survey data collection operations for surveys mailed to at least 1,000 persons; 6) ability to write programming code for statistical analysis packages (running on mainframe or desktop computers) to do survey data analysis for research on personnel programs; 7) experience in formatting questionnaire computer administrations.

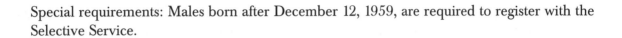

Special requirements: Males born after December 12, 1959, are required to register with the Selective Service.

Speech Pathologist

Agency: Domestic Dependent Elementary and Secondary Schools, Defense Education Activity
Salary: $31,059 to $75,351
Location: Fort Campbell, Kentucky

Job description summary: Develops, manages, and coordinates speech language services at the school(s) where assigned. Serves as a consultant to teachers and school staff in the development of a balanced speech-language program for eligible students with communication disorders. Provides in-service training to faculty members as needed, on topics concerning speech and language development and improvement. Evaluates three-year-olds, preschoolers, and students in the school population with suspected or identified communication disorders. Assists and guides teachers in observing, describing, and referring suspected and identified speech and language impairments. Serves on teacher assistance teams as needed. Provides thorough evaluations, diagnosis, and interpretation of assessment, results of suspected speech, voice, fluency, hearing, and language impairments. Provides therapy for a variety of hearing impairments including severe handicapping conditions which may be in addition to other mental or physical impairments.

Minimum qualifications required: Must have appropriate education from an accredited institution, and must possess a valid certificate for the appropriate area of work.

Minimum application materials required: Submit an Application for Employment with DDESS along with a copy of your current educational teaching certificate, and copies of college transcripts.

Staff Accountant

Agency: Office of the Secretary of Defense
Salary: $85,210 to $130,305
Location: Arlington, Virginia

Job description summary: Develops, promulgates, and reviews Department-wide policies to improve the management, control, and productivity of financial resources and associated organizations and systems. Conducts evaluations of DoD-wide issues to support management decision-making. Reviews, develops, and coordinates recommendations to improve and strengthen controls over operations and programs. Manages efforts to resolve complex issues identified by other DoD or non-DOD elements. Directs, arranges, develops, monitors, and presents analyses of financial management data and trends, and performs other in-depth professional analyses or special projects as required. Develops oral and written presentations for delivery by the applicable Director or other higher-level official, on policies and current or proposed developments within areas of responsibility and expertise.

Minimum qualifications required: Bachelor's degree in accounting or a related field; OR a combination of education and experience. Must have one year of specialized experience in developing and reviewing the execution of department-wide policies to improve the management, control, and productivity of financial resources and associated organizations and systems. Must be a Certified Public Accountant or a Certified Internal Auditor.

Minimum application materials required: Submit a resume that identifies your work experience, education, and skills. Use the sample format to structure your resume and identify the job announcement number. Submission of a resume MUST be in accordance with the instructions contained in our job kit.

Special requirements: Males born after December 12, 1959, are required to register with the Selective Service. Must pass a drug test.

Teacher

Agency: Domestic Dependent Elementary and Secondary Schools, Defense Education Activity
Salary: $31,991 to $100,895
Location: Fort Benning, Georgia

Job description summary: Plans, organizes, and presents information and instruction which helps students learn subject matter and skills that will contribute to their educational and social development; has an instructional plan which is compatible with the school and system-wide curricular goals; interacts effectively with students, coworkers, and parents; carries out noninstructional duties as assigned or as needed; adheres to established laws, policies, rules, and regulations; and follows a plan for professional development.

Minimum qualifications required: Bachelor's degree and a current (valid) professional teacher certificate appropriate for the position being filled.

Minimum application materials required: Submit an Application for Employment with DDESS. Include a handwritten statement on your philosophy of education, a copy of your college transcripts, and a copy of your teacher's certificate.

Department of the Air Force

1670 Air Force Pentagon
Washington, D.C. 20330-1670
703-697-6061

- ★ Web site: http://www.af.mil/

- ★ Job vacancies: http://jobsearch.usajobs.opm.gov/a9af.asp

- ★ USAJOBS By Phone: 912-757-3000

- ★ Internship information: http://www.afpc.randolph.af.mil/cp/recruit/default.htm

- ★ National Security Personnel System: https://www.dp.hq.af.mil/dpp/dppn/nsps/

- ★ Air Force Personnel Center: http://www.afpc.randolph.af.mil/default.htm

- ★ Air Force job kit: https://ww2.afpc.randolph.af.mil/resweb/. Then click on Air Force Job Kit.

- ★ Air Force resume writer: https://ww2.afpc.randolph.af.mil/resweb/resume/resume.htm

- ★ Receive job information via e-mail: https://ww2.afpc.randolph.af.mil/resweb/cans.htm

★ PALACE Acquire Intern Program: http://www.afpc.randolph.af.mil/cp/recruit/paq.htm

★ COPPER Cap Intern Program: http://www.afpc.randolph.af.mil/cp/CCP/copperc.htm

★ Summer employment: https://ww2.afpc.randolph.af.mil/resweb/summer/summer.htm

The Department of the Air Force is responsible for defending the United States through control and exploitation of air and space.

The United States Air Force employs over 150,000 civilians in a full range of occupations, including financial management, information management, public affairs, engineering, computers/communications, sports/fitness recreation management, contracting, logistics, education, human resource management, child development, scientist, technical training, lodging management, community planning, architect, manpower management, safety, security, occupational health, family matters, history, and special investigation.

Selected Agencies Within the Air Force

The **Air Education and Training Command** recruits, trains, and educates quality people for the aerospace force and the nation. It provides basic military training, initial and advanced technical training, flying training, and professional military and degree-granting professional education. It also conducts joint, medical service, readiness, and Air Force security assistance training.

★ Web site: http://www.aetc.randolph.af.mil/default.htm

★ Air Force Academy: http://www.academyadmissions.com/home.htm?flash=yes

★ Air Force ROTC: http://www.afrotc.com/home.htm?flash=yes

★ Community College of the Air Force: http://www.au.af.mil/au/ccaf/index.htm

★ AETC base directory: http://www.aetc.randolph.af.mil/organizational_links.htm

Air Force Special Operations Command is America's specialized air power. The command provides combat search and rescue, agile combat support, information warfare, precision aerospace fires, psychological operations, specialized aerospace mobility, and refueling to unified commands and delivers special operations power anytime, anywhere.

★ Web site: http://www.afsoc.af.mil/index2.shtml

Other Air Force Agencies

Air Combat Command
http://www2.acc.af.mil/

Air Force Materiel Command
http://www.afmc-pub.wpafb.af.mil/

Air Force Space Command
http://www.peterson.af.mil/hqafspc/

Air Mobility Command
http://public.amc.af.mil/

Air National Guard
http://www.ang.af.mil/

Air Force Reserve
http://www.afreserve.com/home1.asp

Pacific Air Forces
http://www2.hickam.af.mil/pacaf/

U.S. Air Forces in Europe
http://www.usafe.af.mil/home.html

Sample Job Vacancies

Auditor

Agency: Air Force Audit Agency
Salary: $24,704 to $63,436
Location: Worldwide

Job description summary: Performs a variety of duties designed to provide training necessary for the systematic examination and appraisal of financial records, reports, management controls, policies, and practices affecting or reflecting the financial condition and operating results of Air Force activities.

Minimum qualifications required: Bachelor's degree in accounting, OR at least four years of experience in accounting, or an equivalent combination of accounting experience, college-level education, and training that provided professional accounting knowledge. Must be a Certified Public Accountant or a Certified Internal Auditor. Must have one year of specialized experience as an auditor or a closely related field.

Minimum application materials required: Submit a resume, Optional Application for Federal Employment (OF-612), or an Application for Federal Employment (SF-171). Include narrative answers to the following KSAs: 1) knowledge of the theory, concepts, and practices of professional accounting and auditing techniques, and methodologies; 2) knowledge of internal auditing requirements and procedures applicable to financial systems and management; 3) ability to apply auditing techniques and methodology when planning audit phases; 4) skill in applying professional auditing techniques during internal audit evaluations.

Special requirements: Males over the age of 18 born after December 31, 1959, must be registered with the Selective Service System. Must be a U.S. citizen.

Child Development Program Technician

Agency: U.S. Air Forces, Europe
Salary: $12,037
Location: Bury St Edmunds, Suffolk, England

Job description summary: Provides specialized developmental care and instruction for children in the Child Development Center.

Minimum qualifications required: One year of specialized experience that has equipped you with the knowledge, skills, and ability to perform the duties of the position, OR a bachelor's degree in a related field.

Minimum application materials required: Submit a resume and a completed Occupational Questionnaire from the vacancy announcement. Questionnaire includes the following KSAs: 1) knowledge of child development techniques; 2) knowledge of child development and behavior sufficient to notice, aid, and tailor program to help children with disabilities, behavioral problems, gifted children, etc.; 3) skill in conducting appropriate activities to meet the children's needs; 4) ability to closely observe children's development level and convey to supervisor suggested improvements; 5) knowledge of guidelines and instructions relating to child safety; 6) ability to deal with coworkers and subordinates as a close working team; 7) knowledge of general office techniques sufficient to write accurate reports, order supplies, and answer telephones.

Special requirements: Males over the age of 18 born after December 31, 1959, must be registered with the Selective Service System. Must be a U.S. citizen. Food Handler's Certificate required.

Electronics Engineer
Agency: Air Force Materiel Command
Salary: $63,505 to $98,174
Location: Edwards Air Force Base, California

Job description summary: Performs test and evaluation of state-of-the-art sensor systems employed on the United States Air Force Global Hawk (RQ-4) unmanned aerial vehicle. Leads a team of engineers to plan and execute complex collection campaigns and mission scenarios to test and evaluate advanced Imagery Intelligence, Signals Intelligence, and Measurements & Signatures Intelligence packages. Assists in the development, maturation, and refinement of sensors as they are integrated into one of the most unique military aircraft in the world. Designs test methods and conditions, writes test plans, evaluates, and reports on system performance. Produces and delivers written and oral reports to local management and other agencies, participates in aircrew briefings, and works in the mission control room, outside test facilities, and the field to orchestrate and carry out test missions.

Minimum qualifications required: Bachelor's degree in engineering technology, OR a combination of education and experience that furnished a knowledge of the physical and mathematical sciences underlying professional engineering and an understanding of the engineering sciences and techniques and their applications to engineering. Must be currently registered as a Professional Engineer or have passed the Engineer-in-Training (EIT) examination. Must have at least one year of specialized engineering experience in Intelligence Community, Military ISR Community, or Civilian Remote Sensing Community. In addition, must have knowledge of tasking, processing, exploitation, and dissemination systems architectures, including some exposure to mission/collection planning functions, data analysis/exploitation tools, and dissemination methodologies; and system test or scientific research experience.

Minimum application materials required: Submit a resume and a completed Occupational Questionnaire from the vacancy announcement. Questionnaire includes the following KSAs: 1) experience testing, evaluating, and reporting results on manned or unmanned air vehicle avionics or military electronic systems or subsystems; 2) experience leading teams in accomplishing complex projects on schedule and within resource constraints; 3) ability to communicate orally and in writing.

Special requirements: Males over the age of 18 born after December 31, 1959, must be registered with the Selective Service System. Must be a U.S. citizen.

Hazardous Material Packer

Agency: Air Combat Command
Salary: $15.35/hour
Location: Beale Air Force Base, Marysville, California

Job description summary: Packs items and equipment, including hazardous materials, for storage and shipment; prepares and verifies shipping documents; maintains packaging and preservation equipment.

Minimum qualifications required: There is no specific length of training of experience required. However, your written application materials must clearly demonstrate, by appropriate experience or training in the trade, that you possess sufficient knowledge, skills, and abilities in order to perform the duties of the positions without more than normal supervision.

Minimum application materials required: Submit a resume and a completed Occupational Questionnaire from the vacancy announcement. Questionnaire includes more than 30 KSAs.

Special requirements: Males over the age of 18 born after December 31, 1959, must be registered with the Selective Service System. Must be a U.S. citizen. You must be able to obtain and maintain a Secret or Top Secret Clearance. Must pass a physical examination.

Human Resource Analyst

Agency: Air Force Personnel Center
Salary: $51,635 to $67,123
Location: Bedford and Hanscom Air Force Base, Massachusetts

Job description summary: Manages functional manpower and personnel to ensure cost, performance, and schedule objectives are met and that resources are used effectively and efficiently. Provides database management support, including designing, developing, integrating, and maintaining database structures. Conducts complicated analytical studies of organizations or programs to develop functional strategies. Maintains functional management related information using a number of different tools including Unit Manning Documents, internal relational databases, as well as civilian and military personnel information. Maintains, monitors, and updates resource management database.

Minimum qualifications required: Experience: Master's degree in related field. One year of specialized experience in or related to the work of the position.

Minimum application materials required: Submit a resume and a completed Occupational Questionnaire from the vacancy announcement. Questionnaire includes the following KSAs: 1) knowledge and skill to gather, assemble and analyze facts, draw conclusions, devise solutions to problems, and identify changes and trends; 2) skill in conducting interviews with supervisors and employees to obtain information about organizational missions, function, and work procedures; 3) knowledge of a full range of database management concepts, operations, design principles, methodologies, and approaches; 4) ability to use a personal computer and software programs; 5) knowledge of functional management policies and practices; 6) skill in application of analytical and evaluative methods and procedures to resolve complex and difficult problems.

Special requirements: Males over the age of 18 born after December 31, 1959, must be registered with the Selective Service System. Must be a U.S. citizen. Must obtain and maintain a secret clearance.

Lifeguard
Agency: Air Force Space Command
Salary: $20,587 to $29,195
Location: Fort MacArthur, San Pedro, California

Job description summary: Assists water safety instructors in conducting swimming lessons. Rescues and resuscitates swimmers in danger of drowning, and renders first aid to injuries. Participates in required in-service training and maintains currency, capability and certification to perform lifesaving and water rescue, and to administer basic first aid and CPR. Checks and documents pool water chemistry; cleans and maintains bathrooms, decks, locker rooms, showers, pool, etc in safe, sanitary conditions.

Minimum qualifications required: High school graduate, OR three full months of general experience in any type of progressively responsible clerical, office, or other work that demonstrated your ability to acquire the particular knowledge and skills needed to perform recreational-related work. Must possess the following current and valid nationally recognized certifications at the time you enter on duty: Lifeguard Certificate, CPR Certificate (which includes adult, child and infant procedures), Basic First Aid Certificate, and Water Safety Instructor Certificate.

Minimum application materials required: Submit a resume and a completed Occupational Questionnaire from the vacancy announcement. Questionnaire includes more than 30 KSAs.

Special requirements: Males over the age of 18 born after December 31, 1959, must be registered with the Selective Service System. Must be a U.S. citizen. Must pass a preemployment screening for swimming ability, rescue skills, and CPR skills. Must pass a criminal background check and a physical. Must be able to lift and carry at least 45 pounds. Must be at least 16 years of age at the time you enter on duty.

Pharmacist
Agency: Air Force Space Command
Salary: $69,143 to $82,382
Location: Peterson Air Force Base, Colorado Springs, Colorado

Job description summary: Serves as Pharmacist-in-Charge at the Base Commissary and/or the Outpatient Pharmacy at the Main Clinic. Manages all aspects of the daily operation of the Refill Pharmacy. Establishes procedures, schedules workload, and integrates the work of the Refill Pharmacy with the overall pharmacy program. Serves as consultant on pharmaceutical matters for professional staff of the Refill pharmacy and the outpatient pharmacy services at the main Clinic. Ensures compliance with state and federal regulations. Maintains accurate quality control data. Develops and provides technical pharmacy training/instruction to supervisors, employees, and/or clinical department on a wide range of work operations such as pharmacology, chemistry, pharmaceutical calculations and compounding, pharmaceutical storage and handling, and pharmacy regulations and policies.

Minimum qualifications required: Bachelor's degree in pharmacy. Must be licensed to practice pharmacy. Must have one year of specialized experience in or related to the position to be filled.

Minimum application materials required: Submit a resume and a completed Occupational Questionnaire from the vacancy announcement. Questionnaire includes the following KSAs: 1) knowledge of pharmacy; 2) knowledge of legally required records, record keeping and reports as they pertain to pharmacy operations; 3) knowledge of state and federal regulations governing receiving, safeguarding, and issuing of controlled drugs; 4) knowledge of standard training techniques, methods, and materials; 5) ability to keep abreast of the latest developments affecting the field; 6) ability to plan, organize, and direct the functions and staff of the Refill and main Pharmacy; 7) ability and skill to communicate orally and in writing and to deal effectively with others.

Special requirements: Males over the age of 18 born after December 31, 1959, must be registered with the Selective Service System. Must be a U.S. citizen. Must pass a drug test.

Telecommunications Specialist

Agency: Air Force Materiel Command
Salary: $63,505 to $82,554
Location: Edwards Air Force Base, California

Job description summary: Provides electromagnetic spectrum management and frequency control to the Air Force Flight Test Center (AFFTC), USAF Plant 42, the National Test Range R-2508, and five special DoD-contracted test facilities operating in the region. Plans and coordinates during all phases of research, development, operational testing and evaluation. Resolves spectrum conflicts on numerous integrated systems. Acts as technical advisor on the selection of new radiating devices and systems and contract specifications. Develops frequency plans. Reviews all incoming AFFTC programs introduction documents and provides technical advice to AFFTC/XR on possible availability of spectrum and potential interference to existing programs.

Minimum qualifications required: Bachelor's degree in related field. Must have at least one year of specialized experience in evaluating, analyzing, developing, managing, or improving communications systems, procedures, and requirements that demonstrated knowledge of current developments and trends in communications concepts and technology.

Minimum application materials required: Submit a resume and a completed Occupational Questionnaire from the vacancy announcement. Questionnaire includes the following KSAs: 1) knowledge of all aspects of the principles, policies, concepts, methodology, operations, products, services, needs, and goals of the program and the organization studied or served, to perform the supervisory and administrative duties of the position; 2) ability to research, analyze, interpret and apply policies, rules, regulations, and procedures; 3) ability to plan and execute complex, multifaceted projects simultaneously; 4) ability to communicate orally and in writing; 5) ability to use a personal computer to create and update databases and create quality productivity indicators and graphic presentations.

Special requirements: Males over the age of 18 born after December 31, 1959, must be registered with the Selective Service System. Must be a U.S. citizen.

Work/Life Consultant
Agency: Pacific Air Forces
Salary: $36,478 to $47,422
Location: Misawa Air Base, Japan

Job description summary: Assesses individual and family needs and provides continuing work/life services to eligible populations. Participates in implementing, maintaining, and providing installation work/life services that meet community needs. Conducts and implements marketing and public relations campaigns to ensure target populations are informed of services and activities. Ensures availability of technology-based resources to maximize customer access to a full spectrum of resources to meet life-cycle needs.

Minimum qualifications required: Bachelor's degree in behavioral or social science, AND one year of specialized experience planning, implementing, administering, and counseling on career, transition, relocation, family, and other work/life services; OR a master's degree.

Minimum application materials required: Submit a resume and a completed Occupational Questionnaire from the vacancy announcement. Questionnaire includes the following KSAs: 1) knowledge of social services delivery systems and concepts, principles, and theories and practices relating to one or more of the social or behavior science fields; 2) knowledge of personal financial management practices and techniques; 3) skill in conducting interviews; 4) skill in establishing and maintaining effective working relationships.

Special requirements: Males over the age of 18 born after December 31, 1959, must be registered with the Selective Service System. Must be a U.S. citizen.

Department of the Army

The Pentagon
Washington, D.C. 20310
703-695-6518

★ Web site: http://www.army.mil/

★ Job vacancies: https://cpolwapp.belvoir.army.mil/public/vabSelfNom/

★ USAJOBS By Phone: 912-757-3000

★ Civilian personnel homepage: http://cpol.army.mil/index.html

★ Civilian benefits: http://cpol.army.mil/library/benefits/

★ Army job application kit: http://cpol.army.mil/library/employment/jobkit/

★ Army Resume Builder: http://www.cpol.army.mil

★ Application/employment FAQs:
   http://cpol.army.mil/library/employment/faq_resumix.html

The mission of the Department of the Army is to organize, train, and equip active duty and reserve forces for the preservation of peace, security, and the defense of the country. As part of the national military team, the Army focuses on land operations; its soldiers must be trained with modern arms and equipment and be ready to respond quickly. The Army also administers programs aimed at protecting the environment, improving waterway navigation, flood and beach erosion control, and water resource development. It provides military assistance to federal, state, and local government agencies, including natural disaster relief assistance.

The Army conducts both operational and institutional missions. The operational Army consists of numbered armies, corps, divisions, brigades, and battalions that conduct full-spectrum operations around the world. The institutional Army supports the operational Army. Institutional organizations provide the infrastructure necessary to raise, train, equip, deploy, and ensure the readiness of all Army forces. The training base provides military skills and professional education to every soldier as well as members of sister services and allied forces. It also allows the Army to expand rapidly in time of war. The industrial base provides world-class equipment and logistics, and Army installations provide the power-projection platforms required to deploy land forces promptly to support combatant commanders. Once those forces are deployed, the institutional Army provides the logistics needed to support them.

Selected Agencies Within the Army

The **United States Army Corps of Engineers** (USACE) is made up of approximately 34,600 civilian and 650 military men and women—engineers, scientists and other specialists—who work hand in hand as leaders in engineering and environmental matters. Its diverse workforce of biologists, engineers, geologists, hydrologists, natural resource managers, and other professionals provide quality responsive engineering services to the country, including planning, designing, building, and operating water resources and other civil works projects (Navigation, Flood Control, Environmental Protection, Disaster Response, etc.); designing and managing the construction of military facilities for the Army and Air Force; and providing design and construction management support for other defense and federal agencies.

★ Web site: http://www.usace.army.mil/

★ Links to Civilian Personnel Advisory Centers and Web sites (nationwide job vacancies):
   http://www.usace.army.mil/employment/cpacjoblst.htm

★ Types of jobs: http://www.usace.army.mil/employment/careers.html

★ Descriptions of employee benefits: http://www.usace.army.mil/employment/benefits.html

U.S. Army Europe and 7th Army (USAREUR) is the U.S. European Command's primary land component. It monitors armed conflicts and potential flashpoints throughout a 98-nation area. The U.S. Army's largest forward-deployed command, USAREUR supports NATO and U.S. bilateral, multinational, and unilateral objectives. It supports U.S. Army forces in the European Command area; receives and assists in the reception, staging, and onward movement and integration of U.S. forces; establishes, operates, and expands operational lines of communication; and supports U.S. combat commanders and joint and combined commanders.

★ Web site: http://www.hqusareur.army.mil/

★ Civilian Human Resource Management Agency: http://www.chrma.hqusareur.army.mil/

The **United States Military Academy** is located at West Point, New York. The course is of four years' duration, during which the cadets receive, besides a general education, theoretical and practical training as junior officers. Cadets who complete the course satisfactorily receive the degree of Bachelor of Science and a commission as second lieutenant in the Army.

★ Web site: http://www.usma.edu/

★ Job vacancies: http://www.usma.edu/cpac/Jobs/jobs.htm

★ Contact information: http://www.usma.edu/agencies.asp

Other Army Agencies

Army National Guard
http://www.arng.army.mil/

8th U.S. Army, Korea
http://8tharmy.korea.army.mil/

Surface Deployment and Distribution Command
http://www.mtmc.army.mil/

U.S. Army Criminal Investigation Command
http://www.cid.army.mil/

U.S. Army Forces Command
http://www.forscom.army.mil/default.htm

U.S. Army Intelligence and Security Command
http://www.inscom.army.mil/

U.S. Army Military District of Washington
http://www.mdw.army.mil/

U.S. Army Reserve
http://www4.army.mil/USAR/home/index.php

U.S. Army South
http://www.usarso.army.mil/

U.S. Army Special Operations Command
http://www.soc.mil/

U.S. Army Space and Missile Defense Command
http://www.smdc.army.mil/

U.S. Army Materiel Command
http://www.amc.army.mil/

U.S. Army Medical Command
http://www.armymedicine.army.mil/default2.htm

U.S. Army Pacific
http://www.usarpac.army.mil/home.asp

U.S. Army Training and Doctrine Command
http://www-tradoc.army.mil/index.html

Sample Job Vacancies

Civil Engineering Technician
Agency: Army Corps of Engineers
Salary: $36,626 to $57,914
Location: Duck, North Carolina

Job description summary: Maintains field notes and writes detailed methods manuals, trip reports, and sections for papers describing survey methods with figures of data obtained. Selects and maintains surveying equipment. Assists in the planning, mobilization, and execution of other data collection programs pertaining to the problem under study, including conducting geotechnical surveys using interferometric side-scan sonars, sub-bottom profilers, and multibeam survey systems.

Minimum qualifications required: Bachelor's degree in a related field. One year of experience directly related to this occupation. Graduate education or an internship meets the experience required when it is directly related to the work of the position.

Minimum application materials required: This position will be filled from the Army Centralized Resumix database using an automated recruitment and referral system. Your resume must be on file with the Army Centralized Resumix database.

Special requirements: Must pass a security investigation. Must be a U.S. citizen. Male applicants born after December 31, 1959, must have registered with the Selective Service.

Editorial Assistant
Agency: Armed Forces Command
Salary: $26,699 to $34,714
Location: Fort Hood, Texas

Job description summary: Edits technical documents and text. Ensures correctness of formats; grammar, punctuation, spelling, etc. Provides assistance to directive authors, explaining requirements of publication guidelines and inadequacies or errors in document. Advises on proper treatment of data and facts within the document, how to treat questionable information and exclusions of extraneous text, inconsistency of information, proper organization of directive, proper treatment of deviations from standard format, etc. Maintains an audit trail on directive from the date it is initially received until it is published. Uses an electronic publishing system.

Minimum qualifications required: Bachelor's degree in a related field. One year of specialized experience editing a variety of text, technical documents, directives, circulars, pamphlets, regulations, and supplements; ensuring the proper format; verifying references; and converting text from a computer software program to an electronic desktop publishing system.

Minimum application materials required: This position will be filled from the Army Centralized Resumix database using an automated recruitment and referral system. Your resume must be on file with the Army Centralized Resumix database.

Special requirements: Must be a U.S. citizen. Male applicants born after December 31, 1959, must have registered with the Selective Service.

Environmental Protection Specialist

Agency: U.S. Army, Pacific
Salary: $44,136 to $57,375
Location: Wheeler AAF, Hawaii

Job description summary: Reviews and provides comments on environmental assessments and environmental impact statements and NEPA documentation. Drafts environmental assessments and environmental impact statements. Participates in environmental committee meetings. Determines appropriate authorization for proposed projects; evaluates permit applications and proposed modifications. Monitors compliance with permits and conducts investigation of unauthorized work; recommends resolution of enforcement actions. Coordinates legal issues; prepares environmental assessments, factual photographic litigation materials, and recommendations for legal action.

Minimum qualifications required: Bachelor's degree in a related field and one year of experience directly related to the position, OR Ph.D. or three years of progressively higher-level graduate education. Extensive knowledge of environmental sciences and related disciplines. Knowledge of pertinent federal, state, and local laws, regulations, licensing/permitting requirements, policies, and precedents which affect programs and related issues. Knowledge of environmental protection program principles and procedures applicable to a variety of program and functional areas. Comprehensive knowledge of management practice. Skill in applying analytical and evaluative methods and techniques to issues or studies. Ability to communicate orally and in writing. Must be able to type 40 words per minute.

Minimum application materials required: This position will be filled from the Army Centralized Resumix database using an automated recruitment and referral system. Your resume must be on file with the Army Centralized Resumix database.

Special requirements: Must pass a security investigation. Must be a U.S. citizen. Male applicants born after December 31, 1959, must have registered with the Selective Service.

Geographer

Agency: Army Corps of Engineers
Salary: $48,947 to $63,629
Location: New Orleans, Louisiana

Job description summary: Applies advanced working knowledge of computer aided drafting/design (CADD), GIS, relational databases, and related computer software to assist technical staff in the design, modification, and completion of various civil works projects. Plans, coordinates, and develops digital data and mapping products. Generates three-dimensional digital terrain models, topographic contours and cross-sections from topographic survey or photogrammetric data. Coordinates and develops computer applications software to aid in the data collection, editing, manipulating, and generating of digital data for CAD, GIS, or related products.

Minimum qualifications required: Bachelor's degree in a related field. Must have one year of specialized experience with civil works projects, assisting in the development and implementation of civil engineering, geographic, or cartographic automation tools; experience developing and applying flood plain or terrain modeling; and experience creating three-dimensional automated visualization or digital mapping tools.

Minimum application materials required: This position will be filled from the Army Centralized Resumix database using an automated recruitment and referral system. Your resume must be on file with the Army Centralized Resumix database.

Special requirements: Must pass a security investigation. Must be a U.S. citizen. Male applicants born after December 31, 1959, must have registered with the Selective Service.

Intelligence Specialist

Agency: U.S. Army Communications Electronics Command
Salary: $35,573 to $68,443
Location: Fort Monmouth, New Jersey

Job description summary: Assists analysts in the review and maintenance of existing security programs. Assists with implementation of policies and procedures on physical security and crime prevention. Maintains various automated systems to track requests for security clearance requests and current clearances for all Center employees and visitors. Safeguards national security information with emphasis on classified or other sensitive information originated within or controlled by the Center or support activities. Monitors or reviews classification, marking, transportation, reproduction, and control.

Minimum qualifications required: Bachelor's degree in a related field, OR one year of specialized experience related to the field.

Minimum application materials required: This position will be filled from the Army Centralized Resumix database using an automated recruitment and referral system. Your resume must be on file with the Army Centralized Resumix database.

Special requirements: Top security clearance required. Must pass a drug test. Must be a U.S. citizen. Male applicants born after December 31, 1959, must have registered with the Selective Service.

Recreation Assistant

Agency: U.S. Army Europe & Seventh Army
Salary: $24,075 to $31,302
Location: Wiesbaden, Germany

Job description summary: Applies a practical knowledge of recreational sports activities, rules, procedures, and skill in the use and maintenance of various sports equipment, playing fields, and courts. Assists the sports program director in conducting a variety of sports activities.

Minimum qualifications required: One year of experience directly related to this occupation, OR a four year course of study above the high school level leading to a bachelor's degree with courses related to this occupation, or a combination of experience and education.

Minimum application materials required: This position will be filled from the Army Centralized Resumix database using an automated recruitment and referral system. Your resume must be on file with the Army Centralized Resumix database.

Special requirements: Must pass a security investigation. Must be a U.S. citizen. Male applicants born after December 31, 1959, must have registered with the Selective Service.

Safety and Occupational Health Specialist

Agency: Army Corps of Engineers
Salary: $52,899 to $68,766
Location: Iraq

Job description summary: Develops, writes, and reviews policies, guidelines, and regulations concerning explosive ordnance, chemical agents, and other toxic and hazardous materials. Provides technical recommendations and answers a variety of questions from a broad customer base. Formulates and executes safety and occupational health policies for assuring safe handling and disposal of ordnance. Constructs effective comprehensive plans for removal and disposal of ordnance consistent with agency missions. Reviews and updates existing policies and guidelines. Performs field work which includes investigation, plans for disposal and disposal of explosive ordnance, chemical agents and other toxic and hazardous materials from contaminated sites.

Minimum qualifications required: Must have specialized experience in developing, writing, and reviewing policies, guidelines, and regulations concerning ordnance, chemical agents, and other toxic and hazardous materials; experience in formulating and executing safety and occupational health policies for assuring safe handling and disposal of ordnance; and experience in development of safety policies and procedures associated with clean-up activities of ordnance and explosive waste sites.

Minimum application materials required: This position will be filled from the Army Centralized Resumix database using an automated recruitment and referral system. Your resume must be on file with the Army Centralized Resumix database.

Special requirements: Must be able to obtain and maintain a Secret security clearance. Must pass a medical examination. Must be a U.S. citizen. Male applicants born after December 31, 1959, must have registered with the Selective Service.

Sewing Machine Operator

Agency: U.S. Military Academy
Salary: $11.42 to $14.65/hour
Location: West Point, New York

Job description summary: Operates standard high speed industrial sewing machine to perform a number of operations in the manufacture of items in the Cadet Uniform Factory by section work. May occasionally perform related nonsewing work depending on the workload. Identifies completed garments according to size and lot by marking and attaching bar-code tickets using a nylon tagging gun. Cleans basting threads, clips long threads on completed garments. Folds and bundles or boxes completed items. Positions fusible reinforcements onto cut parts and feeds into automatic fusing machine. Operates portable steam ironing machine to open seams and press parts of items in process.

Minimum qualifications required: Must have the following skills and knowledges: 1) ability to do the work of a sewing machine operator without more than normal supervision; 2) knowledge of equipment assembly, installation, and repair; 3) ability to interpret instructions, specifications; 4) ability to measure and layout; 5) ability to use and maintain tools and equipment.

Minimum application materials required: This position will be filled from the Army Centralized Resumix database using an automated recruitment and referral system. Your resume must be on file with the Army Centralized Resumix database.

Special requirements: Must pass a medical examination. Must be a U.S. citizen. Male applicants born after December 31, 1959, must have registered with the Selective Service.

Department of the Navy

The Pentagon
Washington, D.C. 20350
703-545-6700

- ★ Web site: http://www.navy.mil/

- ★ Job vacancies: http://chart.donhr.navy.mil/jobsearch/searchjobs.asp

- ★ USAJOBS By Phone: 912-757-3000

- ★ Human resources service centers: http://www.donhr.navy.mil/HRSC/default.asp

- ★ How to apply: http://www.donhr.navy.mil/Jobs/default.asp

- ★ Civilian human resources manual: http://www.donhr.navy.mil/donchrm/default.asp

- ★ National Security Personnel System: http://www.donhr.navy.mil/NSPS/default.asp

- ★ Employee benefits: http://www.donhr.navy.mil/Jobs/Benefits.asp

The primary mission of the Department of the Navy is to protect the United States, as directed by the president or the secretary of defense, by the effective prosecution of war at sea including, with its Marine Corps component, the seizure or defense of advanced naval bases; to support, as required, the forces of all military departments of the United States; and to maintain freedom of the seas.

The Department of the Navy has three principal components: The Navy Department, consisting of executive offices mostly in Washington, D.C.; the operating forces, including the Marine Corps, the reserve components, and, in time of war, the U.S. Coast Guard (in peace, a component of the Department of Homeland Security); and the shore establishment.

The operating forces report to the Chief of Naval Operations and provide, train, and equip naval forces. As units of the Navy enter the area of responsibility for a particular Navy area commander, they are *operationally* assigned to the appropriate numbered fleet. All Navy units also have an administrative chain of command with the various ships reporting to the appropriate *Type Commander*. All ships are organized into categories by type. Aircraft carriers, aircraft squadrons, and air stations are under the administrative control of the appropriate Commander Naval Air Force. Submarines come under the Commander Submarine Force. All other ships fall under Commander Naval Surface Force. Normally, the type command controls the ship during its primary and intermediate training cycles and then it moves under the operational control of a fleet commander.

The shore establishment provides support to the operating forces (known as "the fleet") in the form of: facilities for the repair of machinery and electronics; communications centers; training areas and simulators; ship and aircraft repair; intelligence and meteorological support; storage areas for repair parts, fuel, and munitions; medical and dental facilities; and air bases.

Selected Agencies Within the Navy

The mission of the **Space and Naval Warfare Systems Command** is to provide the warfighter with knowledge superiority by developing, delivering, and maintaining effective, capable and integrated command, control, communications, computer, intelligence and surveillance systems. SPAWAR is an integral part of the San Diego Community and is located near the fleet customer, academia, and the Southern California High-Tech Industry.

★ Web site: http://enterprise.spawar.navy.mil/

The largest of the Navy's five systems commands, the **Naval Sea Systems Command** (NAVSEA) engineers, builds and supports America's Fleet of ships and combat systems. Accounting for nearly one-fifth of the Navy's budget (approximately $20 billion), NAVSEA manages more than 130 acquisition programs, which are assigned to six affiliated Program Executive Officers (PEOs) and various Headquarters elements. The nearly 50,000 NAVSEA team members serve the Fleet in four shipyards, the undersea and surface warfare centers, nine supervisors at major shipbuilding locations and the headquarters, currently located at the Washington Navy Yard, in Washington, D.C. America's Fleet operates throughout the world.

★ Web site: http://www.navsea.navy.mil/

★ Job vacancies: http://www.navsea.navy.mil/navseajobs/

The **Naval Special Warfare Command** is the Naval component to the United States Special Operations Command headquartered in Tampa, Florida. NSW provides a versatile, responsive and offensively focused force with continuous overseas presence. The major operational components of Naval Special Warfare Command include Naval Special Warfare Groups ONE and THREE in San Diego, California, and Naval Special Warfare Groups TWO and FOUR in Norfolk, Virginia. These components deploy SEAL Teams, SEAL Delivery Vehicle Teams and Special Boat Teams worldwide to meet the training, exercise, contingency and wartime requirements of theater commanders.

★ Web site: http://www.navsoc.navy.mil/

★ Job vacancies: http://www.navsoc.navy.mil/navsoc_employment.asp

★ Headquarters contacts: http://www.navsoc.navy.mil/navsoc_address.asp

The **United States Marine Corps** is the only forward-deployed force designed for expeditionary operations by air, land or sea. The Marine Corps has a civilian workforce totaling some 25,000 employees.

★ Web site: http://www.usmc.mil/

★ Job vacancies: https://lnweb1.manpower.usmc.mil/CCLD/employment_opps_main.htm

★ Employment application tools: https://lnweb1.manpower.usmc.mil/CCLD/employment/employment_opportunities_employee_applicant_tools.htm

★ Career communities:
https://lnweb1.manpower.usmc.mil/CCLD/career_communities_main.htm

The **U.S. Naval Observatory** is one of the oldest scientific agencies in the country. Established in 1830 as the Depot of Charts and Instruments, its primary mission was to care for the U.S. Navy's chronometers, charts and other navigational equipment. Today, the U.S. Naval Observatory is the preeminent authority in the areas of Precise Time and Astrometry, and distributes Earth Orientation parameters and other Astronomical Data required for accurate navigation and fundamental astronomy.

★ Web site: http://www.usno.navy.mil/

★ Job vacancies: http://www.usno.navy.mil/jobs.html

Other Navy Agencies

Bureau of Medicine and Surgery
http://navymedicine.med.navy.mil/

Military Sealift Command
http://www.msc.navy.mil/

Naval Air Systems Command
http://www.navair.navy.mil/

Naval Education and Training Command
https://www.cnet.navy.mil/

Naval Facilities Engineering Command
https://portal.navfac.navy.mil/portal/page?_pageid=34,1&_dad=ptl&_schema=PTLP

Naval Network Warfare Command
https://ekm.netwarcom.navy.mil/netwarcom/nnwc-nipr/index.htm

Naval Reserve
http://reserves.navy.mil/Public/Staff/WelcomeAboard/default.htm

Naval Safety Center
http://www.safetycenter.navy.mil/

Naval Strike and Air Warfare Center
http://www.fallon.navy.mil/nsawc.htm

Naval Supply Systems Command
http://www.navsup.navy.mil/npi/

Navy Installations Command
http://www.cni.navy.mil/

Operational Test and Evaluation Forces
http://www.cotf.navy.mil/

U.S. Fleet Forces Command
http://www.cffc.navy.mil/

U.S. Marine Corps
http://www.usmc.mil/

U.S. Naval Academy
http://www.usna.edu/

U.S. Naval Forces Central Command and 5th Fleet
http://www.cusnc.navy.mil/

U.S. Pacific Fleet
http://www.cpf.navy.mil/

Sample Job Vacancies

Instructor (Physics)

Agency: Academic Department of the Naval Academy Preparatory School,
United States Naval Academy
Salary: $42,676 to $55,479
Location: Newport, Rhode Island

Job description summary: Serves as a supplemental instructor in the three-tiered science (chemistry and physics) program in the Science Department. Provides assistance to students in physics as a supplement to the faculty after the class day. Conducts extra instruction, study skills, and time management. Meets with students one-on-one or in small groups to address learning development in physics. Provides assistance for other learning tools such as computer applications software. Keeps abreast of modern methods of teaching physics and maintains currency in study skills development and time management. Independently diagnoses problem solving and reading comprehension impediments, prescribes corrective measures, and advises the physics faculty on the status of student development. Assists in the training of new faculty on physics principles and instructional aids.

Minimum qualifications required: Bachelor's degree in physics or a related field, OR a combination of education and experience. Must have one year of specialized experience as a physics instructor or tutor teaching college-level physics using computer-assisted programs.

Minimum application materials required: Apply online using the Navy's resume builder. Application includes the following KSAs: 1) knowledge of physics sufficient to teach or tutor introductory college-level physics; 2) knowledge of varied methods of instruction including group discussions, programmed instructions, self-paced work, and computer-assisted programs; 3) ability to incorporate physics, learning skills, and information technology to develop new instructional aids and to modify exiting ones.

Special requirements: Must be a U.S. citizen.

Industrial Hygienist

Agency: Naval Medical Command
Salary: $42,066 to $79,301
Location: Willow Grove, Pennsylvania

Job description summary: Makes recommendations that include controls for physical and chemical agents, and environmental stresses where work processes are highly technical and complex. Assesses work processes to identify populations at risk and detect violations of published health standards. Researches and evaluates toxicity data on new and rare chemicals. Recommends engineering controls to correct deficiencies where feasible. Investigates occupational health hazards. Conducts studies and surveys to determine needs for medical surveillance. Prepares reports and briefings for upper level command information.

Minimum qualifications required: Bachelor's degree in industrial hygiene. Knowledge of industrial hygiene principles and practices gained from IH work demonstrating skills such as collecting environmental monitoring data or information to assist senior hygienists to evaluate relatively specialized or simple operations (such as asbestos/lead abatement, office environments and warehouses) involving few hazards (such as asbestos, lead, noise, computer workstation ergonomics and carbon monoxide/forklift emissions). Some experience in the use of basic IH equipment such as noise meters, light meters, air sampling pumps, and carbon monoxide meters. Some experience using computers for reporting.

Minimum application materials required: Apply online using the Navy's resume builder.

Special requirements: Must be a U.S. citizen.

Photographer

Agency: Navy Field Offices
Salary: $33,026 to $42,935
Location: Honolulu, Manoa, Ft. Ruger, Ft. Derussy, Diamond Head, Hawaii

Job description summary: Provides photographic support with responsibility for all aspects of photographic documentation of the Center's events and activities. Maintains up-to-date schedule of photography requirements. Identifies, articulates, coordinates, and obtains required photographic equipment and supplies. Shoots, edits, prints, and distributes photos. Transfers photos to CDs and internal network. Posts, updates, and removes photos from APCSS Web site and maintains photo/video archives. Produces and video tapes documenting Center events. Researches and drafts articles for various communication products. Assists with the design and layout of brochures, agendas, fact sheets, trifolds, papers and reports. Assists with maintaining the static display and escorts media.

Minimum qualifications required: One year specialized experience in operating standard and specialized camera and film processing equipment related to the position to be filled.

Minimum application materials required: Apply online using the Navy's resume builder. Application includes the following KSAs: 1) knowledge of journalism, photojournalism, and public affairs practices; 2) skill in operating a variety of photographic equipment including conventional and digital imaging systems, photographic processing printers, photographic and video editing software; 3) knowledge of Asia-Pacific region issues and concerns, including an awareness of and sensitivity to the various cultural difference exhibited by different Asia-Pacific nations; 4) skill in using various computer programs and applications, information databases and the internet; 5) skill in writing and public speaking in a public affairs environment.

Special requirements: Must be a U.S. citizen.

Machinist

Agency: Puget Sound Naval Shipyard, U.S. Pacific Fleet
Salary: $41,990 to $52,885
Location: Bangor, Bremerton, Washington

Job description summary: Performs work at the worker or journey level, which involves the manufacture of parts and items of equipment from castings, forgings, and raw stocks made of various metals, metal alloys, and other materials, and/or machining operations required in the repair of such items.

Minimum qualifications required: Ability to do the work of the position with no more than normal supervision. The work requires the use of various types of conventional and computer numerical control (CNC) machine tools and their attachments to perform machining operations in the repair and manufacture of parts from raw stock; knowledge of the makeup of blueprints and drawings and the skill necessary to interpret them; and skill in working from other types of specifications such as sketches, models of parts to be manufactured, or work orders. The work performed by machine tool operators requires basic knowledge of machining processes and skill in performing machining operations such as boring, drilling, planning, milling, and turning on milling machines, radial, or multiple spindle drill presses, shaper, planers, lathes, or equivalent types of conventional and/or CNC machine tools.

Minimum application materials required: Apply online using the Navy's resume builder. Application includes the following KSAs: 1) ability to use shop equipment and tools safely; 2) knowledge of technical practices in the trade.

Special requirements: Must be a U.S. citizen.

Firefighter

Agency: Systems Management Activity
Salary: $20,855 to $36,097
Location: various locations in the Southeast Region

Job description summary: Firefighters combat fires resulting from aircraft (including ships and industrial plants), structures and their contents and other operational accidents; or from the storage and/or handling of large quantities of special fuels and propellants related to the operation of aircraft. They rescue persons endangered from crashed or burning aircraft or from structures. They may be required to drive motorized fire fighting vehicles and/or operate pumping and ladder equipment. Operates and maintains fire fighting equipment and administers emergency medical care, recognizes fire hazards, and write reports documenting findings.

Minimum qualifications required: One year of related education or training in an accredited college or university in Fire Training, Fire Science, or other related fields of study. Six months of general experience that demonstrates the ability to follow directions and to read, understand, and retain a variety of instructions, regulations, and procedures and that otherwise demonstrates the ability to perform or learn to perform the duties of the position. At an entry level, firefighters must successfully complete any and all required training, to include becoming certified at DoD Firefighter I and II levels and Airport Firefighter level, if applicable, within a maximum of 12 months.

Minimum application materials required: Apply online using the Navy's resume builder. Application includes the following KSAs: 1) knowledge of firefighting techniques; 2) skill in operating firefighting equipment; 3) ability to work as a team member.

Special requirements: Must be a U.S. citizen.

Defense Agencies

The Defense Agencies constitute a separate department within the Department of Defense. There are 16 defense agencies, and they serve under the authority of the various undersecretaries for defense.

Selected Defense Agencies

The **Defense Advanced Research Projects Agency** (DARPA) is the central research and development organization of the Department of Defense (DoD), charged with maintaining U.S. technological superiority over potential adversaries. Its research programs include advanced technology, defense sciences, information processing and exploitation, microsystems, tactical technology, and unmanned combat air systems.

DARPA has job opportunities for scientists and engineers as well as security, administrative, budget, and management professionals.

★ Web site: http://www.darpa.mil/

★ Job vacancies: http://www.usajobs.opm.gov/

★ Employment opportunities: http://www.darpa.mil/hrd/

The **Defense Commissary Agency** (DCA) provides a worldwide system of nearly 280 commissaries for selling groceries and household supplies to members of the military services, their families, and other authorized patrons. It employs more than 17,000 people throughout 14 countries.

★ Web site: http://www.commissaries.com/

★ Job vacancies: http://www.usajobs.opm.gov/

★ Human resources: http://www.commissaries.com/inside_deca/HR/index.htm

The **Defense Contract Audit Agency** (DCAA) performs all contract audit functions for DoD and provides accounting and financial advisory services to all DoD components responsible for procurement and contract administration. In addition to its headquarters, DCAA has five regional offices and more than 300 field audit offices and suboffices throughout the United States and overseas. DCAA employs more than 4,000 people, almost 3,500 of them auditors.

★ Web site: http://www.dcaa.mil/

★ Job vacancies: http://www.usajobs.opm.gov/

★ DCAA Career Center: http://www.dcaa.mil/

The **Defense Information Systems Agency** (DISA) is responsible for planning, developing, fielding, operating, and supporting command, control, communications, and information systems that serve the needs of the president, vice president, the secretary of defense, the Joint Chiefs of Staff, the combatant commanders, and other DoD components under all conditions of peace and war. DISA employs about 8,200 people, of which 6,200 are civilians.

★ Web site: http://www.disa.mil/

★ Job vacancies: http://jobopps.disa.mil/careers.html

★ USAJOBS By Phone: 912-757-3000

★ General employment information: http://www.disa.mil/main/joa.html

★ Internship information: http://www.disa.mil/mps/intern/pages/default.html

The mission of the **Defense Intelligence Agency** (DIA) is to provide timely, objective, all-source military intelligence to policymakers, warfighters, and force planners. DIA collects and produces foreign military intelligence; coordinates DoD intelligence collection requirements; operates the Central Measurement and Signature Intelligence Organization; manages the Defense Human Intelligence Service and the Defense Attache System; and operates the Joint Intelligence Task Force for Combatting Terrorism and the Joint Military Intelligence College.

Most of DIA's activities are performed at the Defense Intelligence Analysis Center at Bolling Air Force Base in Washington, D.C. The Agency's headquarters are located at the Pentagon. There are additional locations in Arlington, Virginia, Fort Detrick in Frederick, Maryland, and Redstone Arsenal in Huntsville, Alabama. DIA has over seven thousand military and civilian employees worldwide.

★ Web site: http://www.dia.mil/

★ Job vacancies: http://www.dia.mil/Careers/Vacancies/index.html

★ USAJOBS By Phone: 912-757-3000

The **Defense Logistics Agency** (DLA) is DoD's largest combat support agency, providing worldwide logistics support in both peacetime and wartime to the military services as well as several civilian agencies and foreign countries. According to the DLA Web site, if America's forces eat it, wear it, maintain equipment with it, or burn it as fuel, DLA probably provides it.

★ Web site: http://www.dla.mil/

★ Job vacancies: http://www.usajobs.opm.gov/

★ USAJOBS By Phone: 912-757-3000

★ General employment information: http://www.hr.dla.mil/

★ Business and service area sites: http://www.dla.mil/about.asp

The **Defense Security Service** (DSS), formerly the Defense Investigative Service, conducts background investigations on individuals being considered for a security clearance, a sensitive position, or entry into the U.S. Armed Forces; ensures the safeguard of classified information used by contractors under the defense portion of the National Industrial Security Program; protects conventional arms, munitions, and explosives in custody of DoD contractors; protects and assures DoD's private sector critical assets and infrastructures throughout the world; and provides security education, training, and awareness programs. DSS also has a counter-intelligence office to support the national counterintelligence strategy.

★ Web site: http://www.dss.mil

★ Job vacancies (main): http://www.usajobs.opm.gov/

★ Job vacancies (other): https://storm.psd.whs.mil/cgi-bin/apply.pl

★ USAJOBS By Phone: 912-757-3000

★ Application and job vacancy information: http://www.dss.mil/employment/index.htm

The mission of the **Defense Threat Reduction Agency** (DTRA) is to reduce the threat posed by weapons of mass destruction (WMD). DTRA reduces the threat of WMD by implementing arms control treaties and executing the Cooperative Threat Reduction Program. It uses combat support, technology development, and chemical-biological defense to deter the use and reduce the impact of such weapons. It prepares for future threats by developing the technology and concepts needed to counter the new weapons of mass destruction threats and adversaries.

DTRA employs approximately 2,100 military and civilian personnel, and most of the agency's employees work in the National Capital Region; other locations are Albuquerque, New Mexico; Darmstadt, Germany; Moscow, Russia; and Yokota Air Base, Japan. DTRA employees have a variety of skills and include nuclear physicists; policy analysts and treaty experts; mechanical, civil, electrical, and computer engineers; chemists; biologists; linguists; accountants; program analysts; and financial and logistics management specialists.

★ Web site: http://www.dtra.mil

★ Job vacancies: https://storm.psd.whs.mil/cgi-bin/apply.pl

★ Job vacancies: http://www.usajobs.opm.gov/

★ USAJOBS By Phone: 912-757-3000

★ Summer employment/internships: http://www.dtra.mil/employment_opp/civilian/summer_prog.cfm

★ General employment information: http://www.dtra.mil/employment_opp/civilian/index.cfm

The **National Security Agency** (NSA) and the **Central Security Service** (CSS) together make up the country's cryptologic organization. It employs the country's premier codemakers and codebreakers and ensures an informed, alert, and secure environment for U.S. warfighters and policymakers.

NSA/CSS employs individuals in the following career fields: acquisition and business management, computer/electrical engineering, computer science, cryptanalysis, foreign languages, human resources, intelligence analysis, mathematics, occupational health, research security (police), and signals analysis.

★ Web site: http://www.nsa.gov/

★ Job vacancies: http://jobsearch.usajobs.opm.gov/

★ USAJOBS By Phone: 912-757-3000

★ Career homepage: http://www.nsa.gov/programs/employ/homepage.cfm

★ Career FAQs: http://www.nsa.gov/programs/employ/faq.cfm

Other Defense Agencies

Defense Contract Management Agency
http://www.dcma.mil/

Defense Finance and Accounting Service
http://www.dfas.mil/

Defense Legal Services Agency
http://www.defenselink.mil/dodgc/

Defense Security Cooperation Agency
http://www.dsca.mil

Missile Defense Agency
http://www.acq.osd.mil/mda/

National Geospatial-Intelligence Agency
http://www.nima.mil/portal/site/nga01/

Pentagon Force Protection Agency
http://www.pfpa.mil/

Sample Job Vacancies

Automotive Mechanic Helper
Agency: Defense Logistics Agency
Salary: $15.45 to $18.03/hour
Location: San Joaquin, California

Job description summary: Lubricates and cleans Material Handling Equipment (MHE) and GSA vehicles. Drains and refills crankcases, transmissions, differentials, gear cases, etc. Refills, tests, and charges batteries. Replaces andrepairs tires and tubes on MHE/GSA equipment. Makes roadside tire repairs. May drive warehouse tractor with retriever to retrieve forklifts and small equipment to the maintenance shop.

Minimum qualifications required: Experience, education, and training must show enough of the knowledge, skills and abilities to demonstrate the potential to successfully perform the duties of the position, such as work that represents your ability to perform physically strenuous duties successfully or completion of a related vocational technical program.

Minimum application materials required: Submit an Occupational Questionnaire along with a resume or Optional Application for Federal Employment (OF-612). Include narrative answers to the following KSAs: 1) reliability and dependability as an automotive mechanic helper; 2) ability to follow directions in a shop; 3) ability to handle weights and loads; 4) dexterity and safety; 5) knowledge of preventative maintenance and servicing.

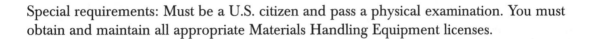

Special requirements: Must be a U.S. citizen and pass a physical examination. You must obtain and maintain all appropriate Materials Handling Equipment licenses.

General Engineer

Agency: Missile Defense Agency
Salary: $60,638 to $93,742
Location: Arlington, Virginia

Job description summary: Engages in the design, development, integration, and verification of the Ballistic Missile Defense System (BMDS). Employs classical and innovative engineering processes required for the engineering of large systems of systems. Engages in all phases of the defense acquisition process. Serves as the system engineering authority on technical alternatives and conducts extensive coordination with: BMDS system, element, and component engineers; DOD agencies, the military services, defense contractors, and participating allied nations to facilitate the development of the BMDS.

Minimum qualifications required: Bachelor's degree in professional engineering or a combination of college-level education, training or technical experience that furnished a thorough knowledge of the physical and mathematical sciences underlying professional engineering and a good understanding, both theoretical and practical, of the engineering sciences and techniques and their applications to one of the branches of engineering. Expert system engineering knowledge and skills to perform in-depth analysis of complex problems to formulate and execute technical research projects.

Minimum application materials required: Submit resume and application following the instructions in MDAs online Jobkit. KSAs are those that demonstrate performance of the duties and responsibilities as outlined under minimum qualifications.

Special requirements: Must be a U.S. citizen. Must pass a personnel security investigation and a drug test.

Geospatial Intelligence Analyst

Agency: National Geospatial-Intelligence Agency
Salary: $44,136 to $101,593
Location: Macdill Airforce Base, Florida

Job description summary: Researches, assesses, integrates, manipulates, exploits, extracts, and analyzes digital imagery, geospatial databases, intelligence databases, and various ancillary sources. Uses understanding of remote sensing, spatial analysis, GIS, intelligence issues, and background in the social or physical sciences to characterize events, discover relationships and trends, infer conclusions, enable descriptive and predictive behavior, and communicate the meaning and significance of these results as multisource geospatial intelligence. The analytical focus may be functional, regional, or technical, supporting Imagery and Geospatial Community (IGC) internal and external, DOD, and national policy customers.

Minimum qualifications required: Bachelor's degree in one of the following or a closely related disciplines, with a desired emphasis in GIS: geography (physical, demographic), civil engineering (photogrammetry, geodesy), remote sensing, information science, geology, hydrology, meteorology, cartography, mathematics, statistics, philosophy (logic), cognitive science (perception and visual communication), or targeted social science; OR a combination of education and experience. Must have skill in data and statistical analysis; organizational representation; process improvement; customized product generation; research and information gathering; visualization; spatial analysis; geographic network analysis.

Minimum application materials required: Must use NGA's online eRecruit System to complete an online application and submit a resume. Applicants are requested to submit a two-page narrative on the following KSAs: 1) practical experience with. GIS applications (ESRI, ERDAS and other applications); 2) system administration (UNIX, XP and/or NT); 3) direct customer interaction (in a primarily military environment), verbal and written, with minimal supervision; 4) knowledge of NGA products, including imagery (especially digital products).

Special requirements: Must be a U.S. citizen. Must pass a top secret security clearance and a polygraph test. Physical examination and color vision required.

Human Resources Specialist
Agency: Defense Finance and Accounting Service
Salary: $49,040 to $63,749
Location: Indianapolis, Indiana

Job description summary: Advises managers and supervisors regarding position management and the efficient use of civilian positions. Performs position audits and writes position descriptions and evaluation statements. Analyzes and applies Office of Personnel Management classification standards and principles derived from significant classification appeal decisions. Also analyzes and documents Fair Labor Standards Act and competitive level determinations. Advises and counsels managers and supervisors regarding employee relations, labor relations, performance management, leave administrations, and incentive and performance awards. Develops case work on disciplinary actions, adverse actions, performance actions, and so on by analyzing applicable laws and regulations, reviewing adjudications, coordinating with officials, obtaining documentary evidence and writing proposing and decision memoranda.

Minimum qualifications required: One year of specialized experience that included a wide range of human resources experience including one or more of the following: staffing, recruitment, placement, position management and classification, human resource case-law, and principles and regulations pertaining to employee and labor relations issues. A Ph.D. (or equivalent doctoral degree) or three full academic years of progressively higher-level graduate education leading to a Ph.D. may be substituted for the specialized experience requirement.

Minimum application materials required: Complete and submit an online application.

Special requirements: You must be a U.S. citizen.

Intelligence Officer (Targeting)
Agency: Defense Intelligence Agency
Salary: $72,108 to $93,742
Location: Alexandria, Arlington, and Falls Church, Virginia

Job description summary: Conducts all-source, multidisciplined targeting research and analysis on counter terrorism issues. Develops comprehensive targeting packages based on national priorities for tasking through unit referents to field collectors. Develops detailed targeting guidance and defines specific, quantifiable, and obtainable collection objectives.

Minimum qualifications required: Must have one year of specialized experience at a level close to the work of this job that has given you the particular knowledge, skills, and abilities required to successfully perform.

Minimum application materials required: Submit an online application. Include narrative answers to the following KSAs: 1) familiarity with DoD and national directives and other guidance on HUMINT; 2) knowledge and understanding of a variety of classified, governmental, and commercial databases and how they are used to support HUMINT; 3) knowledge of DoD and intelligence community organizational missions and functions and interrelationship of the national and DoD HUMINT structures; 4) knowledge of defense collection management systems and procedures; 5) knowledge of all-source analysis; 6) demonstrated oral and written communications skills.

Special requirements: Must be a U.S. citizen. Designated and random drug testing and background and security investigation required.

International Relations Specialist
Agency: Defense Threat Reduction Agency
Salary: $41,815 to $93,742
Location: Fort Belvoir, Virginia

Job description summary: Responsible for initiating and developing office program plans and monitoring, coordinating, and facilitating implementation and compliance program plans and activities. Initiates and develops full range of continuous and frequent action items which include point/issue papers, essential office reports, memoranda, and position papers regarding resource programming actions and requirements. Provides advice and recommendations. Monitors and develops solutions on treaty program matters. Conducts original research, conceptualizes alternative solutions, and develops, staffs, and presents program positions and documents. Participates in internal DoD working and ad hoc groups that resolve issues related to DoD planning, preparation, and execution.

Minimum qualifications required: Bachelor's degree in international law and international relations, political science, economics, history, sociology, geography, social or cultural anthropology, law, statistics, or the humanities; OR a combination of education and experience; OR four years of appropriate experience in one or more of the fields listed above in work associated with international organizations, problems, or other aspects of foreign affairs.

Minimum application materials required: Submit a resume that identifies work experience, education, and skills. Resume MUST be submitted in accordance with the instructions contained in DTRA's job kit. KSAs are those that demonstrate performance of the duties and responsibilities as outlined above.

Special requirements: must be able to obtain and maintain a top secret (TS)/Sensitive Compartmented Information (SCI) security clearance. Must pass a drug test.

Military Pay Technician

Agency: Defense Finance and Accounting Agency
Salary: $24,075 to $38,767
Location: Cleveland, Ohio

Job description summary: Responsible for ensuring the privacy and accuracy of payroll information for military personnel. Establishes, maintains, reviews, and closes payroll accounts for active, reserve, or retired armed forces personnel and their annuitants. Reviews pay actions from automated systems, audits a wide variety of difficult pay actions, and compiles information regarding the causes of incorrect pay entitlements.

Minimum qualifications required: Bachelor's degree in any field or one year of experience which involved establishing, maintaining, correcting, and closing pay accounts for active, reserve, or retired armed forces personnel and their annuitants. Qualifying specialized experience may include authorizing payments, auditing and reconsidering previous pay determinations, responding to pay inquires, reviewing military pay debts, and processing adjustment actions.

Minimum application materials required: Submit an online application and resume at the DFAS DEU online resume builder Web site.

Special requirements: Must be a U.S. citizen.

NSA Historian

Agency: National Security Agency/Central Security Service
Salary: $60,638 to $85,210
Location: Anne Arundel County, Maryland

Job description summary: Must become familiar with the entire range of cryptologic history with primary emphasis on American cryptology during the twentieth century, and will develop specialized expertise in several aspects of this field. Conducts major research projects, publishes articles and monographs, responds to historical inquiries from NSA's senior leadership, and interacts with historians and personnel from other government agencies and universities. Makes public presentations, teaches at the National Cryptologic School, and participates in a variety of history outreach programs as necessary. Manages projects such as NSA's biennial Cryptologic History Symposium, history-related hallway displays, crisis documentation efforts, and daily historical features on internal Web pages.

Minimum qualifications required: A Ph.D. in history is highly desirable, with a preference for the modern period and specialization in military or diplomatic history. Strong written and oral communication skills are a must. Related military or intelligence experience is preferred. A publication record in the field of military or intelligence history is a plus.

Minimum application materials required: Submit an online resume and application through NSA's eRecruit Web site.

Special requirements: Must be a U.S. citizen. A security clearance must be granted prior to employment, and you will be required to undergo extensive pre-employment processing that includes: aptitude testing; an interview with a psychologist and a security interview conducted

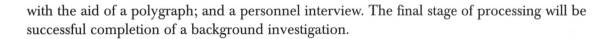

with the aid of a polygraph; and a personnel interview. The final stage of processing will be successful completion of a background investigation.

Office Automation Assistant
Agency: Defense Contract Audit Agency
Salary: $28,719 to $32,013
Location: New York, New York

Job description summary: Provides a wide range of support duties to the audit staff including updating and maintaining the DCAA Integrated Information System (DIIS), inputting audit management data, and producing reports from the DCAA Management Information System (DMIS). Provides a variety of systems maintenance and updates, security, user support, and related functions for DIIS. Adds and deletes temporary users, maintains public, common, and private directories, and updates LAN and subsystem applications including debugging "patches" as scheduled or as directed by Regions DIIS System Analyst. Assists users in accessing and utilizing the various DIIS applications, routines, and printer configurations. Resolves operational problems, referring more complex problems and questions regarding specific audit-related uses of the subsystem routines to the DIIS Systems Analyst, a technical specialist, or other staff specialist as appropriate

Minimum qualifications required: Must be a qualified typist with a minimum typing speed of 40 words per minute; have experience or training using word processors, microcomputers, or computer terminals using a standard typewriter style keyboard with additional function keys; and have skill in operating related equipment such as printers and modems. Must have one year of specialized experience providing clerical/administrative support utilizing advanced and varied office automation software and hardware; OR a bachelor's degree in any field; OR a combination of specialized experience and education.

Minimum application materials required: Submit resume and completed online Occupational Questionnaire. Questionnaire includes the following KSAs: 1) ability to organize and maintain file systems; 2) knowledge of the capabilities and operating characteristics of a variety of office software; 3) knowledge of clerical practices and office procedures.

Special requirements: Must be a U.S. citizen.

Staff Officer
Agency: National Geospatial-Intelligence Agency
Salary: $50,593 to $82,868
Location: Bethesda, Maryland

Job description summary: Executes the Human Development Resource Program. Provides guidance on all HD-related programs, works with HD and PE staff to manage the office billet structure, tracks staffing needs, monitors compliance with performance management requirements, and establishes and maintains career development processes. Plans and prepares manpower/personnel briefing materials for management and attends meetings. Provides direct administrative support to the Customer and Program Oversight Division.

Minimum qualifications required: Must have skill in oral communication, briefing, and presentation. Must have knowledge of planning and scheduling; of NGA products and services; of problem-solving processes and techniques; of customer service principles; and of NGA organizational units' missions and functions.

Minimum application materials required: Must use NGA's online eRecruit System to complete an online application and submit a resume.

Special requirements: Must be a U.S. citizen. Must pass a top secret security clearance and a polygraph test. Physical examination and color vision required.

Store Worker
Agency: Defense Commissary Agency
Salary: $11.93 to $15.12/hour
Location: Orote Commissar, Guam

Job description summary: Performs a variety of tasks, such as price marking, shelf-stock replenishment, segregating, rotating, receiving, and displaying items for sale. Processes/price marks subsistence items and segregates damaged or unacceptable merchandise. Unloads incoming stock, transports to warehouse storage location, and stores merchandise. Uses cardboard baler and electric hydraulic/hand-operated pallet jacks. Assists with maintaining adequate standards of sanitation throughout the store.

Minimum qualifications required: Must show the ability to perform the duties of the position, including the ability to prepare and arrange items together safely and neatly.

Minimum application materials required: Submit resume and completed Occupational Questionnaire.

Special requirements: Must pass a preemployment investigation. Work requires frequently lifting up to 50 pounds, and long periods of standing, bending, and walking.

Telecommunications Specialist
Agency: Defense Information Systems Agency
Salary: $52,899 to $68,766
Location: Vaihingen, Germany

Job description summary: Serves as Operations Manager for the European DISN Video Services hub, supporting customers in the USEUCOM and USCENTCOM theaters. Responsible for operations, implementation, testing, operation, and scheduling of DISA-EUR VTC systems. Reviews and evaluates performance of, and registers, tests, and troubleshoots theater VTC systems. Implements and operates new VTC user and hub equipment and conducts interoperability/interface testing between various systems.

Minimum qualifications required: Expertise in video teleconferencing (VTC) codes, suites, and peripheral equipment as well as cryptographic equipment, transmission media, IP and ISDN interfaces, and telephone switches. Must have specialized experience in management of VTC equipment and the implementation, operation, and troubleshooting of VTC systems and networks.

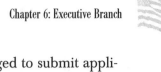

Minimum application materials required: Applicants are strongly encouraged to submit applications and supplemental paperwork via DISA's online Resume Builder. Include narrative answers to the following KSAs: 1) knowledge of VTC hub and user-end equipment; 2) skill in performing video/communications systems analysis; 3) skill in Network/Voice Systems troubleshooting; 4) knowledge of INDX and ATM Transmissions Systems.

Special requirements: Must be able to obtain and maintain a Secret clearance. Must pass a drug test.

Joint Service Schools

The Joint Service Schools constitute a separate department within the Department of Defense. There are four joint service schools, open to students from all branches of the armed forces, that train students in acquisition, technology, and logistics; military intelligence; national security, regional and information strategy and defense; and public health.

The **Defense Acquisition University** is a corporate university serving the Department of Defense Acquisition, Technology, and Logistics workforce, a total of more than 134,000 people. It provides basic, intermediate, and advanced certification training, assignment-specific training, performance support, job-relevant applied research, and continuous learning opportunities. It has six campuses nationwide, including its headquarters in Fort Belvoir, Virginia.

★ Web site: http://www.dau.mil/

★ Job vacancies: http://www.dau.mil/about-dau/jobs.aspx

★ Regions and campuses: http://www.dau.mil/basedocs/regionsandcampuses.asp

The **Joint Military Intelligence College** serves the intelligence community and operates under the authority of the Director of the Defense Intelligence Agency. Its mission is to educate military and civilian intelligence professionals and conduct and disseminate relevant intelligence research. The College awards the Bachelor of Science in Intelligence (BSI) and Master of Science of Strategic Intelligence (MSSI) degrees and also offers two diploma intelligence programs, at the undergraduate and postgraduate levels. Evening and weekend programs are available as well, one of which is specifically for military reservists and is taught by reserve faculty.

★ Web site: http://www.dia.mil/Jmic/index.html

★ Job vacancies: http://www.usajobs.opm.gov/

The **National Defense University** incorporates the following colleges: the Industrial College of the Armed Forces, the National War College, the Joint Forces Staff College; and the Information Resources Management College. The mission of the National Defense University is to educate military and civilian leaders through teaching, research, and outreach in national security, military, and national resource strategy; joint and multinational operations; information strategies, operations, and resource management; acquisition; and regional defense studies.

★ Web site: http://www.ndu.edu/

★ Job vacancies: http://www.ndu.edu/info/employment.cfm

★ Regional centers: http://www.ndu.edu/centers.cfm

★ Contact telephone numbers: http://www.ndu.edu/info/contact_us.cfm

★ National War College: http://www.ndu.edu/nwc/index.htm

★ Information Resources Management College: http://www.ndu.edu/irmc/

★ Industrial College of the Armed Forces: http://www.ndu.edu/icaf/

★ Joint Forces Staff College: http://www.jfsc.ndu.edu/

★ School for National Security Executive Education: http://www.ndu.edu/snsee/index.cfm

The **Uniformed Services University of the Health Sciences** educates career-oriented medical officers for the military departments and the Public Health Service. The University currently incorporates the F. Edward Hébert School of Medicine (including graduate and continuing education programs) and the Graduate School of Nursing. Medical school matriculants must be commissioned officers in one of the uniformed services. They must meet the physical and personal qualifications for such a commission and must give evidence of a strong commitment to serving as a uniformed medical officer. The graduating medical student is required to serve for seven years, excluding graduate medical education. Students of the Graduate School of Nursing must be commissioned officers of the Army, Navy, Air Force, or Public Health Service prior to application. Graduate nursing students must serve a commitment determined by their respective service.

★ Web site: http://www.usuhs.edu/

★ Job vacancies: http://www.usuhs.mil/chr/vacancies.htm

★ F. Edward Hébert School of Medicine: http://www.usuhs.mil/medschool/fehsom.html

★ Graduate School of Nursing: http://cim.usuhs.mil/gsn/

Sample Job Vacancies

Education Technician
Agency: Uniformed Services University of the Health Sciences
Salary: $30,762 to $39,996
Location: Bethesda, Maryland

Job description summary: Performs educational and administrative support duties for the Third Year Psychiatry Clerkship, with five teaching hospitals and involving 160 medical students per year. Schedules seminars and didactic programs and preceptor assignments. Ensures that all course materials are in the appropriate format, to include typing, editing, proofreading, copying, collating, filing, records management, etc. Assembles student evaluations, assists in data entry of grading components, and compilation of final student evaluations and evaluation summary packets for each clinical rotation. Coordinates course orientation packets. Provides administrative assistance to department faculty involving research or special projects, such as preparing and assembling bibliographies, cross-checking references, using library resources for literature review, preparing presentation materials, etc. Establishes and maintains course-related and office files.

Minimum qualifications required: Must have one year of experience independently performing a full range of standard and nonstandard clerical assignments using word processing software, as well as experience in the following areas: receiving visitors and answering/transferring telephone calls; organizing and maintaining official files; and proofreading documents for grammar and spelling.

Minimum application materials required: Submit resume and application online. Include written responses to the following KSAs: 1) skill in operating a personal computer and its software to produce a variety of products such as general correspondence, educational materials, manuscripts, bibliographies, spreadsheets and grade reports, and PowerPoint presentations; 2) knowledge of correct spelling, grammar, and punctuation, including scientific and medical terminology; 3) ability to compose letters, memoranda, reports, bulletins, and electronic communication of a general nature; 4) ability to organize and maintain files; 5) ability to receive visitors, answer and transfer phone calls, and communicate clearly to provide information and answer questions concerning department programs and activities.

Special requirements: Must be able to type at least 40 words per minute.

Lead Training Technician

Agency: Defense Acquisition University
Salary: $40,866 to $64,277
Location: Kettering, Ohio

Job description summary: Documents and updates course class schedules. Assists with the development of annual projections of teaching assignments and faculty teaching loads. Monitors faculty professional development, leaves, research, and consultations. Prepares requests for professional development courses, conferences, and seminars. Maintains metrics on Department performance and prepares periodic reports and briefings on the Department status. Recommends basic formats and layouts of course materials and develops samples of such formats for review and approval. Plans and oversees the production of course materials, tests, visual aids and student handouts. Provides assistance and research to faculty in the planning and management of curriculum development. Prepares drafts and final versions of education materials, course modules, student guides, and project planning and management documentation. Edits and reformats electronic drafts of educational documents prepared by staff members.

Minimum qualifications required: Two years of higher-level graduate education OR a master's degree. Must be able to lift, move, and arrange course materials and equipment that weigh up to 50 pounds.

Minimum application materials required: Submit resume or Optional Application for Federal Employment (OF-612) or Application for Federal Employment (SF-171). Application must include narrative statements addressing each of the following KSAs: 1) ability to manage the Educational and Training Program; 2) ability to manage and analyze data; 3) ability to formulate plans, policies, and procedures.

Special requirements: Before hiring, this agency will ask you to complete a declaration for federal employment to determine your suitability for federal employment and to authorize a background investigation.

Professor, Civil-Military Relations

Agency: Africa Center for Strategic Studies
Location: Washington, D.C.

Job description summary: Develops the curriculum for the civil-military relations module of the ACSS academic program, organizes seminars, conducts research, represents the Africa Center in policy discussions, prepares for outside lectures, serves as facilitator, and publishes scholarly works.

Minimum qualifications required: Advanced degree in Civil-Military Relations, Security Studies, or African Area Studies and familiarity with civil-military issues as they relate to African security issues; evidence of a record of research and contributions within the civil-military relations field and publications of books, monographs, and pieces in recognized professional journals. Outstanding reputation as a teacher and recognition within the academic or research community; and experience in graduate-level education desirable. Experience either in the federal government or a national security–related institution highly desirable. Well-versed on U.S. policy in Africa.

Minimum application materials required: Submit an Optional Application for Federal Employment (OF-612), an Application for Federal Employment SF-171), a resume, a Curriculum Vitae, or any other written format you choose provided it includes sufficient information to support your qualifications for this position.

Department of Education

400 Maryland Avenue SW
Washington, D.C. 20202
800-USA-LEARN

- ★ Web site: http://www.ed.gov/index.jhtml

- ★ Job vacancies: http://web99.ed.gov/hrg

- ★ USAJOBS By Phone: 912-757-3000

- ★ EdHIRES: http://www.ed.gov/about/jobs/open/edhires/index.html

- ★ Internship application: http://www.ed.gov/students/prep/job/intern/index.html

- ★ Links to state contacts: http://www.ed.gov/about/contacts/state/index.html?src=sm

- ★ DOE staff and organization: http://www.ed.gov/about/offices/list/index.html?src=sm

- ★ Regional DOE offices: http://www.ed.gov/about/contacts/gen/regions.html

- ★ Benefits: http://www.ed.gov/about/jobs/work/benefits.html

★ Hispanic employment: http://www.ed.gov/about/jobs/work/RHhispanics.html

★ Employment of people with disabilities:
http://www.ed.gov/about/jobs/work/Disabilities.doc

The Department of Education (DOE) establishes policy, administers, and coordinates most federal funding to education; collects data on America's schools and disseminates research; focuses national attention on key education issues; and enforces federal statutes prohibiting discrimination in programs and activities receiving federal funds and ensures equal access to education for everyone.

DOE has almost 5,000 employees and a budget of more than $54 billion. The majority of the staff work at the various DOE buildings in Washington, D.C. Additionally, there are about 1,300 employees who work in 10 regional offices around the country.

The DOE's online application tool is called EdHIRES, which stands for the Department of Education Hiring Information/Recruiting Enhancement System. Through the EdHIRES Web site, you can quickly and easily prepare and submit applications to the DOE. It provides access to all DOE job openings for which you are eligible, access via e-mail to the status of your application, and it will notify you of positions that match your profile as they become available.

Selected Agencies Within DOE

The **Institute of Education Sciences** is DOE's main research arm. It compiles statistics, conducts and funds research, and provides guidance to others researching education policy and practice. Its three operational divisions are the National Center for Education Research, the National Center for Education Evaluation and Regional Assistance, and the National Center for Education Statistics.

The National Center for Education Research researches topics in education related to teaching methods, the impact of technology, and the way children learn. Within it are two divisions. The division of Teaching and Learning researches topics related to literacy, math and science, readiness, and socialization. The division of Policy and Systems researches topics related to rural and distance schooling, school reform, assessment and accountability, education workforce, and adult and postsecondary education.

The National Center for Education Evaluation and Regional Assistance evaluates and disseminates information on educational studies, especially those relating to reading, mathematics, and science; closing the achievement gap; educational practices; and education technology. It also manages the National Library of Education.

The National Center for Education Statistics collects and analyses data related to education in the United States and other countries.

★ Web site: http://www.ed.gov/about/offices/list/ies/index.html?src=oc

★ Job vacancies: http://web99.ed.gov/hrg

★ Web site for NCER: http://www.ed.gov/about/offices/list/ies/ncer/index.html

★ Web site for NCEERA: http://www.ed.gov/about/offices/list/ies/ncee/index.html

★ Web site for NCES: http://www.ed.gov/about/offices/list/ies/nces/index.html

★ Headquarters contacts: http://www.ed.gov/about/offices/list/ies/contacts.html

The **Office of Elementary and Secondary Education** directs, coordinates, and recommends policy for programs designed to improve student achievement and ensures equal access to such programs. It also provides grants to state and local education agencies for both public and private preschool, elementary, and secondary education. Some of its programs include Academic Improvement and Teacher Quality, Impact Aid, Migrant Education, School Support and Technology, and Student Achievement and School Accountability.

★ Web site: http://www.ed.gov/about/offices/list/oese/index.html?src=oc

★ Job vacancies: http://www.ed.gov/about/jobs/open/edjobs.html?src=ln

★ Headquarters contacts: http://www.ed.gov/about/offices/list/oese/contacts.html

The **Office of Vocational and Adult Education** works to ensure that all Americans have the knowledge and technical skills necessary to succeed in postsecondary education, the workforce, and life. Through the Preparing America's Future initiative's comprehensive policies, programs, and activities, OVAE is helping reform America's high schools, supporting America's community colleges, and expanding America's adult education programs.

★ Web site: http://www.ed.gov/about/offices/list/ovae/index.html?src=oc

★ Job vacancies: http://www.ed.gov/about/jobs/open/edjobs.html?src=ln

★ Headquarters contacts: http://www.ed.gov/about/offices/list/ovae/contactus.html

Other DOE Agencies

Office for Civil Rights
http://www.ed.gov/about/offices/list/ocr/index.html

Office of English Language Acquisition, Language Enhancement, and Academic Achievement for Limited English Proficient Students
http://www.ed.gov/about/offices/list/oela/index.html?src=oc

Office of Federal Student Aid
http://www.ed.gov/about/offices/list/fsa/index.html?src=oc

Office of Innovation and Improvement
http://www.ed.gov/about/offices/list/oii/index.html?src=oc

Office of Postsecondary Education
http://www.ed.gov/about/offices/list/ope/index.html?src=oc

Office of Safe and Drug-Free Schools
http://www.ed.gov/about/offices/list/osdfs/index.html?src=oc

Office of Special Education and Rehabilitative Services
http://www.ed.gov/about/offices/list/osers/index.html?src=oc

Center for Faith-Based and Community Initiatives
http://www.ed.gov/about/inits/list/fbci/index.html

Office of the White House Initiative on Historically Black Colleges and Universities
http://www.ed.gov/about/inits/list/whhbcu/edlite-index.html

Office of the White House Initiative on Tribal Colleges and Universities
http://www.ed.gov/about/inits/list/whtc/edlite-index.html

Office of the White House Initiative on Educational Excellence for Hispanic Americans
http://www.yic.gov/

Office of International Education
http://www.ed.gov/about/offices/list/ous/international/edlite-index.html

Sample Job Vacancies

Associate Research Scientist
Agency: Institute of Education Sciences
Salary: $50,000 to $80,000
Location: Washington, D.C.

Job description summary: Assists in implementing and managing research, evaluation, and statistics activities and programs carried out or funded by the agency, by grantees, and contractors; conducting scientific reviews of research, evaluation, and statistics plans and products; analyzing data and synthesizing information from education research and related areas; preparing written products to convey research-based knowledge and information to a variety of audiences; conducting evaluations of agency activities; and dissemination and outreach activities.

Minimum qualifications required: Doctorate in cognitive, developmental, educational, or social psychology; economics; education; or statistics. Must have experience conducting research in education-related fields or topics.

Minimum application materials required: Submit a Curriculum vitae or resume, along with a letter of interest.

Special requirements: Must be a U.S. citizen.

Attorney Adviser
Agency: Office for Civil Rights
Salary: $100,231 to $130,305
Location: Washington, D.C.

Job description summary: Responsible for the management of one of OCR's four enforcement divisions. Provides leadership and direction to OCR's core business, the enforcement of civil rights laws in federally funded education programs, including the resolution of approximately one-fourth of the agency's caseload, proactive compliance activities, and technical assistance/educational outreach. Ensures that the Division's enforcement activities are conducted consistent with agency policies and procedures. Consults directly with the enforcement director and the deputy assistant secretary for enforcement on critical management and leadership issues of national importance. Provides leadership and direction to the field office directors in regional/divisional enforcement planning and other proactive compliance activities.

Minimum qualifications required: Must show proof of admission to the Bar. Must possess the following skills: 1) ability to manage staff and projects; 2) knowledge in applying laws, policies, procedures, etc. to determine compliance; 3) skill in analyzing and resolving problems that concern difficult legal and extremely complex concepts; 4) knowledge of investigative, analytical, dispute resolution, negotiation, and mediation techniques; 5) knowledge of legal standards for litigation in federal courts and before administrative tribunals; 6) skill in litigation techniques, preparing legal documents for litigation, and all matters related to evidentiary trials and subsequent appeals; 7) skill in ensuring legal quality; 8) skill in oral and written communications.

Minimum application materials required: Submit a resume, an Application for Federal Employment (SF-171), an Optional Application for Federal Employment (OF-612) along with a letter of reference. Application must include narrative answers tot the following KSAs: 1) knowledge of federal laws, regulations, and policies, including civil rights law; 2) ability to apply leadership and manage a program; 3) ability to apply laws and regulations to make sound decisions to resolve complex law enforcement issues; 4) ability to establish and maintain effective relationships with high-level officials; 5) knowledge of litigation techniques, preparation of legal documents for litigation, and other matters related litigation.

Special requirements: Must be a U.S. citizen.

Program Support Assistant

Agency: Office of Management
Salary: $27,597 to $35,881
Location: Washington, D.C.

Job description summary: Performs a variety of clerical and administrative duties and responsibilities. Explains resources, services, and administrative processes to clients using the appropriate form(s) and making appropriate referrals following established procedures. Provides limited technical answers to inquiries related to the organization's mission. Utilizes Microsoft Word, Outlook, Excel, and Access sufficient to enter and retrieve data, produce documents and reports, and update databases. Maintains financial records and transaction logs.

Minimum qualifications required: Bachelor's degree OR one year of specialized experience related to the duties of the position.

Minimum application materials required: Apply online through EdHIRES. Include narrative responses to the following KSAs: 1) knowledge of Washington, D.C., area roads, landmarks, Federal buildings and traffic patterns to determine the most appropriate route for reaching one location from another; 2) ability to maintain financial records and transaction logs; 3) ability to interact professionally with high-level officials, equivalent to federal agency secretaries and chief executive officers; 4) ability to interact professionally and courteously with customers; 5) skill in using Microsoft Word, Outlook, Excel, and Access sufficient to enter and retrieve data, produce documents and reports, and update databases.

Special requirements: Must have a valid driver's license; pass drug test; and be a U.S. citizen.

Vocational Rehabilitation Program Specialist
Agency: Office of Special Education and Rehabilitation Service
Salary: $72,108 to $93,742
Location: Washington, D.C.

Job description summary: Serves as national expert in American Indian vocational rehabilitation. Leads in the preparation and promulgation of program regulations and revisions and related policy and procedures relating to the American Indian Vocational Rehabilitation Services (AIVRS) Program. Formulates and interprets AIVRS Program policies; develops and coordinates activities under the AIVRS Program with the State Vocational Rehabilitation Services Program. Provides technical assistance to other offices; provides leadership and guidance in the provision of rehabilitation services to American Indians and other native people with significant disabilities. Develops application kits and operates discretionary grant competitions.

Minimum qualifications required: Bachelor's degree in behavioral or social science; OR a combination of education and experience; OR four years of appropriate experience. Must have one year of specialized experience, such as work with program planning and development in areas of social welfare, health, and rehabilitation; or research work in organizations concerned with social, psychological, vocational, or economic aspects of programmed services; and demonstrated knowledge of laws, regulations and policies governing Vocational Rehabilitation programs.

Minimum application materials required: Apply online through EdHIRES.

Special requirements: Must be a U.S. citizen.

Department of Energy

1000 Independence Avenue SW
Washington, D.C. 20585
202-586-5000

★ Web site: http://www.energy.gov

★ Job vacancies: http://chris.inel.gov/jobs/index.cfm?fuseaction

★ USAJOBS By Phone: 912-757-3000

★ Internship information: http://www.ma.mbe.doe.gov/pers/Cip/index.htm

★ Corporate Human Resource Information System (CHRIS): http://chris.inel.gov/

★ How to apply: http://chris.inel.gov/jobs/index.cfm?fuseaction=howtoapply&public=true

★ Benefits: http://www.ma.mbe.doe.gov/pers/benefits.htm

★ Student employment: http://www.ma.mbe.doe.gov/pers/SPEM/Stuindex.htm

★ DOE laboratories and technology centers:
http://www.energy.gov/engine/content.do?BT_CODE=OF_NLTC

★ Power Marketing Administrations:
http://www.energy.gov/engine/content.do?BT_CODE=OF_PMA

★ DOE Operation Offices and field organizations:
http://www.energy.gov/engine/content.do?BT_CODE=OF_OO

★ DOE employee Work Life Center: http://worklifecenter.doe.gov/

★ Links to DOE major operating locations: http://www.ma.mbe.doe.gov/pers/usmap.htm

The Department of Energy's (DOE) mission is to foster a secure and reliable energy system that is environmentally and economically sustainable; to be a responsible steward of the nation's nuclear weapons; to clean up the Department's facilities; to lead in the physical sciences and advance the biological, environmental, and computational sciences; and to provide premier scientific instruments for the nation's research enterprise.

In addition to its headquarters in Washington, D.C., DOE has nine operations offices located throughout the country which oversee activities in support of two or more of the four missions assigned to the Department. DOE's 24 laboratories and technology centers house world-class facilities where more than 30,000 scientists and engineers perform cutting-edge research.

Power produced at federal water projects in excess of project needs is marketed by the Power Marketing Administrations to consumers. Each of the four power marketing administrations is a distinct and self-contained entity within the Department of Energy, much like a wholly owned subsidiary of a corporation.

DOE Jobs ONLINE is the Department of Energy's automated recruitment system that allows applicants to apply for certain DOE jobs online. By using DOE Jobs ONLINE, applicants can choose to receive e-mail notifications of job openings as well as get notification of the status of each job for which they have applied.

Selected Agencies Within DOE

The **Office of Fossil Energy** is made up of about 1,000 scientists, engineers, technicians, and administrative staff. Its headquarters offices are in downtown Washington, D.C., and in Germantown, Maryland. The organization also has field offices in Morgantown, West Virginia; Pittsburgh, Pennsylvania; Tulsa, Oklahoma; New Orleans, Louisiana; Casper, Wyoming; and Albany, Oregon.

The Office of Fossil Energy is responsible for several high-priority presidential initiatives including implementation of the administration's $2 billion, 10-year initiative to develop a new generation of environmentally sound clean coal technologies, the $1 billion *FutureGen* project to develop a pollution-free plant to co-produce electricity and hydrogen, and the nation's Strategic Petroleum Reserve and Northeast Home Heating Oil Reserve, both key

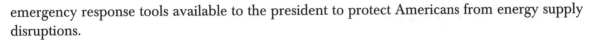

emergency response tools available to the president to protect Americans from energy supply disruptions.

★ Web site: http://www.fossil.energy.gov/

★ Job vacancies: http://fossil.energy.gov/aboutus/jobs/index.html

★ Contact information: http://fossil.energy.gov/aboutus/contactus/index.html

★ Labs and facilities: http://fossil.energy.gov/facilities/index.html

★ Student employment and grants: http://fossil.energy.gov/education/index.html

The **Office of Nuclear Energy, Science, and Technology's** Nuclear Energy Program represents the core of the U.S. government's expertise in nuclear engineering and technology. Its activities benefit the American people by helping to maintain the nation's access to diverse and environmentally responsible sources of energy, and by advancing the country's economic and technological competitiveness.

★ Web site: http://www.ne.doe.gov/

★ Job vacancies: http://www.ne.doe.gov/admin/jobs1.html

★ Program offices: http://www.ne.doe.gov/programoffices.html

The **Office of Science** manages fundamental research programs in basic energy sciences, biological and environmental sciences, and computational science. In addition, the Office of Science is the federal government's largest single funder of materials and chemical sciences, and it supports unique and vital parts of U.S. research in climate change, geophysics, genomics, life sciences, and science education.

★ Web site: http://www.science.doe.gov/

★ Job vacancies: https://jobsonline.doe.gov/scripts/qhwebdoe.exe

★ Contact information: http://phonebook.doe.gov/callup.html

★ National laboratories and user facilities:
   http://www.sc.doe.gov/sub/organization/map/national_labs_and_userfacilities.htm

★ Field organizations:
   http://www.sc.doe.gov/sub/organization/field_organizations/field_organizations.htm

★ Program offices:
   http://www.sc.doe.gov/sub/organization/program_offices/program_offices.htm

★ Workforce development for students and teachers:
   http://www.scied.science.doe.gov/scied/sci_ed.htm

★ Internship information: http://www.science.gov/internships/

Other DOE Agencies

Energy Information Administration
http://www.eia.doe.gov/

Environmental Management Program
http://www.em.doe.gov/

National Nuclear Security Administration
http://www.nnsa.doe.gov/

Office of Civilian Radioactive Waste Management
http://www.ocrwm.doe.gov/

Office of Electric Transmission and Distribution
http://www.electricity.doe.gov/

Office of Energy Efficiency and Renewable Energy
http://www.eere.energy.gov/

Office of Environment, Safety, and Health
http://www.eh.doe.gov/

Office of Legacy Management
http://www.lm.doe.gov/

Office of Worker and Community Transition
http://www.wct.doe.gov/

Sample Job Vacancies

Criminal Investigator

Agency: Office of Inspector General, Office of Investigations
Salary: $39,428 to $49,864
Location: Denver, Colorado

Job description summary: Conducts investigations in alleged violations of law that impact DOE programs, operations, facilities, and personnel. Generally involves the investigation of Department personnel, contractors, and others receiving DOE funds. Special Agents have the authority to conduct criminal, civil, and administrative investigations, to apply for and execute search warrants, to make arrests, to carry firearms, and to utilize a range of specialized investigative techniques.

Minimum qualifications required: Candidates must be between the ages of 21 and 37 years old to be considered for initial appointment to a law enforcement position.

Minimum application materials required: Must apply online through the DOE jobs Web site. Additional materials may be faxed.

Special requirements: Must pass a background investigation and a preemployment physical. Must pass a drug test. Those selected must successfully complete the 10-week Federal Law Enforcement Training Center's Basic Criminal Investigator Training Program.

General Engineer/Physical Scientist

Agency: National Nuclear Security Administration
Salary: $82,438 to $131,879
Location: Los Alamos, New Mexico

Job description summary: Serves as a technical expert and consultant for quality program activities. Performs oversight activities, monitors and maintains surveillance of the Los Alamos National Laboratory (LANL) and various vendor facilities to ensure that product generating processes and quality control operations for nuclear weapons, and nuclear and nonnuclear weapon components are adequate and will result in acceptable product quality and program support.

Minimum qualifications required: Professional engineering degree OR college-level education, training, or technical experience that furnished 1) a thorough knowledge of the physical and mathematical sciences underlying professional engineering, and 2) a good understanding, both theoretical and practical, of the engineering sciences and techniques and their applications to one of the branches of engineering. The adequacy of such background must be demonstrated by either current registration as a professional engineer or evidence of having passed the Engineer In Training exam. In addition you must have at least one year of specialized experience in or directly related to the line of work of the position.

Minimum application materials required: Must apply online through the DOE jobs Web site. Include narrative answers to more than 20 KSAs, including the following: 1) ability to assess overall effectiveness of quality assurance program implementation; 2) skill in planning and developing inspection checklists and in evaluating results of inspections of large complex nuclear, waste treatment, storage and disposal, or large chemical processing facilities as a lead quality control inspector; 3) experience providing trending of deficiencies to identify areas where corrective actions have not minimized recurrence; 4) served as member or leader on evaluation or inspection teams; 5)skill in applying quality principles and programs to achieve continuous improvement across diverse organizations; 6) ability to review quality plans, test procedures, specifications, production methods, processes, and equipment relating to quality and reliability to ensure their adequacy; 7) ability to evaluate contractor's inspection methods, techniques, and practices for destructive and nondestructive testing; 8) skill in performing verification inspection of nonnuclear weapon components and subassemblies; 9)ability to assess overall effectiveness of quality assurance, weapons surveillance, and program implementation; 10) knowledge of quality assurance issues specifically related to product acceptance.

Special requirements: Must obtain a "Q" level security clearance/access authorization, pass a drug test, and be a U.S. citizen. Males born after December 31, 1959, must have registered with the Selective Service.

Industry Economist

Agency: Energy Information Administration
Salary: $41,815 to $78,826
Location: Washington, D.C.

Job description summary: Performs segments of economic analyses projects using standard techniques. Participates in evaluations of impacts of new technologies, systems, and policies;

prepares reports and charts to document study purposes, methods, premises, and conclusions, and participates in briefing officials on progress and conclusions of studies. Acquires sufficient parametric knowledge of subjects studied to perform sound economic analyses reflective of real world environments.

Minimum qualifications required: Bachelor's degree in economics. Must have one year of specialized experience that equipped you with the particular knowledge, skills and abilities to perform the duties of this position.

Minimum application materials required: Must apply online through the DOE jobs Web site. Include narrative answers to the following KSAs: 1) ability to do research using library research tools, the Internet, primary sources; 2) ability to evaluate sources for reliability and usefulness; 3) ability to compile, organize, and quantify economic information and data; 4) ability to use econometric tools and techniques and perform quantitative analysis of complex economic data; 5) ability to relate macro-economic statistics to industry statistics; 6) skill in analyzing factual economic statistics, trends in commodity production, consumption, and prices, and trends in capitalization, investment, and taxation; 7) skill in interpreting economic findings and synthesizing complex, multifaceted economic information; 8) knowledge of linear and nonlinear programming; 9) knowledge of PERT, CPM, or Network Analysis; 10) knowledge of Monte Carlo Methods, Curve Fitting, Delphi, and Time Series Analysis; 11) knowledge of spreadsheet and personal computer software, as well as statistical or econometric software, other database software, and HTML JSP, and ASP.

Special requirements: Must be a U.S. citizen

Microbiologist

Agency: Life Sciences Division, Office of Biological and Environmental Research, Office of Science
Salary: $100,231 to $130,305
Location: Germantown, Maryland

Job description summary: Serves as the Division's senior environmental microbiologist with responsibility for planning, managing, implementing, and overseeing all environmental microbiology, microbial physiology, and metabolic pathway analysis and modeling research conducted in the OBER Genomics: Genomes to Life (GTL) and Microbial Genome Program (MGP). Responsible for the microbial physiology modeling and simulation research within the GTL and MGP that is applied to issues of importance to DOE and OBER's subdivisions. Conceives, justifies, plans, initiates, manages, and coordinates all aspects of the programs related to understanding how living systems function in order to address important issues such as energy production, carbon sequestration, subsurface bioremediation of energy-related pollutants, and development of advanced biotechnology options. Monitors and evaluates the current status of information in relevant databases (e.g., Protein Data Bank, GenBank, and SwisProt) and reports findings relevant to DOE programs and missions.

Minimum qualifications required: Bachelor's degree in microbiology or a related field. One year of specialized experience that equipped you with the particular knowledge, skills, and abilities to perform the duties of this position.

Minimum application materials required: Must apply online through the DOE jobs Web site.

Include narrative answers to the following KSAs: 1) experience in microbiology research activities; 2) experience in publishing and presenting results of environmental microbiology research activities; 3) skill in establishing program goals and objectives, and examining and ascertaining the research needs and opportunities of a basic research program; 4) experience preparing, justifying, and supporting budgets for a basic research and development program; 5) management and oversight of environmental microbiology and technology research and development performed by multiple or single-industry institutions, universities, or national laboratories at geographically disparate locations; 6) participate in and represent the organization at briefings, meetings, or conferences; 7) contact with varying levels of management and science officials; 8) fundamental scientific research experience that has led to publications in peer-reviewed archival scientific journals or appropriate professional journals; 9) performed long-range strategic program planning for an organization; 10) presented papers and research results before national, international, and open-forum scientific conferences; 11) served on scientific committees; 12) written publications for peer-reviewed archival scientific journals.

Special requirements: Must be a U.S. citizen.

Power System Dispatcher

Agency: Western Area Power Administration
Salary: $79,116 to $96,158
Location: Folsom, California

Job description summary: Balances control area generation and load. Maintains adequate control area reserves and regulates margin in compliance with North American Electric Reliability Council and applicable regional council policies. Monitors the net total hourly tie-line schedule verifying its suitability with the transmission scheduling and security dispatcher; tracks hourly and daily control area inadvertent interchange, validating the data collected. Responds to changes in availability and capacity of control area generating resources and requests for emergency assistance from other control areas within the interconnection. Maintains logs and records of the activities and procedures carried out by the AGC dispatcher.

Minimum qualifications required: Must be one of the following: 1) a power system operator with centralized SCADA/EMS control of power system equipment with 115-kV or higher voltage transmission lines and substations; 2) an operations or maintenance journeyman that has written and issued switching for clearances or similar protective actions on power system equipment at 115-kV or above voltage level; 3) an energy merchant or NERC balancing authority/interchange authority with responsibility for matching generation and energy purchases/sales to real-time total load requirements; 4) an electrical engineer with at least one year of engineering experience in design, planning, maintenance, construction, or operation of the power system; OR 5) a power plant or control center operator with direct SCADA control over multiple remotely operated power plants.

Minimum application materials required: Must apply online through the DOE jobs Web site. Include narrative answers to the following KSAs: 1) experience with the operation of energy management systems for high voltage power systems; 2) experience as a control area operator; 3) experience implementing interchange schedules; 4) experience with the operation of interconnected high voltage power systems; 5) experience with initiating emergency actions related to power system generation; 6) experience as a power system operator, operating an AGC system with interconnections with two or more control areas; 7) skill in developing and implementing control area operations control performance indicators such as Control Performance Standard 1 and Control Performance Standard 2; 8) skill in providing assistance to power systems operations/control area management personnel (e.g., dispatchers, schedulers); 9) knowledge of NERC Operating Policies; 10) knowledge of WECC Minimum Operating Reliability Criteria.

Special requirements: You must become certified as a power system operator by the North American Electric Reliability Council and the Western Electricity Coordinating Council, and maintain certification during your employment. Must pass a drug test.

Department of Health and Human Services

200 Independence Avenue SW
Washington, D.C. 20201
202-619-0257

* ★ Web site: http://www.hhs.gov/

* ★ Job vacancies: http://jobsearch.usajobs.opm.gov/a9hhs.asp

* ★ USAJOBS By Phone: 912-757-3000

* ★ Student employment information: http://www.hhs.gov/careers/students.html

* ★ Contact information: http://www.hhs.gov/ContactUs.html

* ★ Links to regional offices: http://www.hhs.gov/about/regionmap.html

* ★ Emerging leaders program: http://www.hhs.gov/careers/elp.html

* ★ Presidential management fellows program: http://www.hhs.gov/careers/pmi.html

* ★ Benefits: http://hhs.gov/jobs/benefits.htm

The Department of Health and Human Services is the cabinet-level department of the federal executive branch most involved with the nation's human concerns. In one way or another, it touches the lives of more Americans than any other federal agency. It is a department of people serving people, from newborn infants to persons requiring health services to our most elderly citizens.

Selected Agencies Within HHS

The **Centers for Disease Control and Prevention** (CDC) provides a system of health surveillance to monitor and prevent disease outbreaks (including bioterrorism), implement disease prevention strategies, and maintain national health statistics. Provides for immunization services, workplace safety, and environmental disease prevention. Working with the World Health Organization, CDC also guards against international disease transmission, with

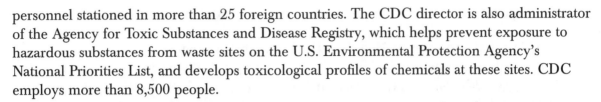

personnel stationed in more than 25 foreign countries. The CDC director is also administrator of the Agency for Toxic Substances and Disease Registry, which helps prevent exposure to hazardous substances from waste sites on the U.S. Environmental Protection Agency's National Priorities List, and develops toxicological profiles of chemicals at these sites. CDC employs more than 8,500 people.

★ Web site: http://www.cdc.gov/

★ Job vacancies: http://www2.cdc.gov/hrmogb/vsearch.asp

★ Headquarters contacts: http://www.cdc.gov/doc.do?id=0900f3ec80093d70

★ Details about student employment programs: http://www.cdc.gov/hrmo/intern.htm

★ Centers, Institutes, Offices: http://www.cdc.gov/cio.do

★ General employment information: http://www.cdc.gov/hrmo/emplopt.htm

Centers for Medicare & Medicaid Services (CMS) administers the Medicare and Medicaid programs, which provide health care to about one in every four Americans. Medicare provides health insurance for more than 41 million elderly and disabled Americans. Medicaid, a joint federal-state program, provides health coverage for some 44 million low-income persons, including 19 million children, and nursing home coverage for low-income elderly. CMS also administers the State Children's Health Insurance Program that covers more than 4.2 million children. It employs more than 4,500 people.

★ Web site: http://www.cms.gov/

★ Job vacancies: http://www.cms.hhs.gov/careers/rns/default.asp

★ Headquarters contacts: http://www.cms.hhs.gov/about/agency/visiting/

★ Details about student employment programs: http://www.cms.hhs.gov/careers/programs/default.asp

★ Regional offices: http://www.cms.hhs.gov/about/regions/professionals.asp

★ Descriptions of employee benefits: http://www.cms.hhs.gov/careers/worklife/benefits.asp

Health Resources and Services Administration (HRSA) provides access to essential health care services for people who are low-income, uninsured, or who live in rural areas or urban neighborhoods where health care is scare. HRSA-funded health centers provide medical care to more than 13 million patients each year at more than 3,600 sites nationwide. The agency helps prepare the nation's health care system and providers to respond to bioterrorism and other public health emergencies, maintains the National Health Service Corps, and helps build the health care workforce through many training and education programs. HRSA administers a variety of programs to improve the health of mothers and children and serves people living with HIV/AIDS through the Ryan White CARE Act programs. HRSA also oversees the nation's organ transplantation system. HRSA employs more than 1,800 people.

★ Web site: http://www.hrsa.gov/

★ Job vacancies: http://www.hrsa.gov/jobs/jobs.htm#public

★ Regional offices: http://www.hrsa.gov/staff.htm#HRSA%20Field%20Coordinators

The **National Institutes of Health** (NIH) is the world's premier medical research organization, supporting some 35,000 thousand research projects nationwide in diseases including cancer, Alzheimer's, diabetes, arthritis, heart ailments and AIDS. NIH includes 27 separate health institutes and centers. It employs more than 17,000 people.

* Web site: http://www.nih.gov

* Job vacancies: http://www.jobs.nih.gov/current.htm

* Headquarters contacts: http://www.nih.gov/about/Faqs.htm#aboutnih

* Details about student employment programs: http://www.jobs.nih.gov/student.htm

* Institutes, Offices, and Centers: http://www.nih.gov/icd/

* Descriptions of employee benefits: http://www.jobs.nih.gov/Benefits/default.htm

Other HHS Agencies

Administration for Children and Families
http://www.acf.gov/

Administration on Aging
http://www.aoa.dhhs.gov/

Agency for Healthcare Research and Quality
http://www.ahrq.gov/

Agency for Toxic Substances and Disease Registry
http://www.atsdr.cdc.gov/

Food and Drug Administration
http://www.fda.gov/

Indian Health Service
http://www.ihs.gov/

Substance Abuse and Mental Health Services Administration
http://www.samhsa.gov/

U.S. Public Health Service Commissioned Corps
http://www.usphs.gov/

Sample Job Vacancies

Children and Families Program Specialist
Agency: Administration for Children and Families
Salary: $50,593 to $65,769
Location: Washington, D.C.

Job description summary: Participates in on-site review of state Child and Family Service programs–including Child Protective Services, Foster Care, Adoption, Family Preservation, and Family Support and Independent Living–planning and coordinating all aspects of the review process with federal and state review team members. Analyzes and interprets complex data and qualitative information with regard to Child and Family Service program policy and practice, outcomes for children and families, and state or local agency functioning. Prepares preliminary assessments and reports, letters of notification, and other documents.

Minimum qualifications required: Bachelor's degree in the behavioral or social sciences OR a combination of education and experience. In addition, must have one year of specialized experience in or related to the work of the position to be filled OR a Ph.D.

Minimum application materials required: Complete an online application and resume through the HHS Careers Web site. Application includes the following KSAs: 1) ability to analyze and interpret complex data and qualitative information; 2) experience reviewing plans to determine compliance with regulations, performance standards, and financial guidelines; 3) knowledge of the principles, methods, and techniques of behavioral and social science as they relate to child welfare programs.

Special requirements: Must be a U.S. citizen.

Epidemiologist
Agency: Centers for Disease Control and Prevention
Salary: $74,335 to $113,674
Location: Abuja, Nigeria

Job description summary: Implements prevention program activities in the field of HIV infection as conducted by the Global AIDS Program (GAP) in Nigeria. Provides scientific and epidemiologic advice and consultation as a nationally and internationally recognized expert in HIV infection as it applies to adults and children. Serves as Chief of Party for all GAP activities in Nigeria. Supervises a staff of medical epidemiologists, public health advisors, medical research technicians, nurses, social workers, research assistants, and support staff. Provides leadership, direction, and technical expertise to universities, medical institutions, nongovernmental organizations, and Ministry of Public Health.

Minimum qualifications required: Bachelor's degree in the health sciences. Must have one year of specialized experience related to the position and which has equipped the you with the particular knowledge, skills, and abilities to perform the duties of the position.

Minimum application materials required: Complete an online application and resume through the HHS Careers Web site. Application includes the following KSAs: 1) conducted analytical studies related to epidemiology; 2) designed epidemiological research projects; 3) experience working with developing countries and international agencies on public health issues; 4) experience working with HIV/AIDS treatment or disease control programs; 5) ability to adapt to changing courses of action or work methods in response to new information, changing conditions, instructions or behavior or unexpected obstacles; 6) experience working successfully in and with a variety of international cultures and environments; 7) experience in making oral presentations or presenting scientific information and in preparing reports of scientific research studies.

Special requirements: Medical and security clearance required.

Grants Management Specialist

Agency: Centers for Disease and Prevention
Salary: $59,569 to $92,090
Location: Atlanta, Georgia

Job description summary: Serves as a technical authority in communicating with grantees and federal staff. Manages and coordinates a complex grant portfolio. Provides authoritative technical advice on all aspects of grant/financial mechanisms. Participates in grant review meetings; provides administrative and budgetary information; identifies need for development of new, or revisions of, existing policies and operating guidelines; develops and negotiates budgets with program staff and the grant community, and effectively presents and solicits information that is complex or controversial in nature.

Minimum qualifications required: Bachelor's degree. Must have one year of specialized experience related to the duties of the position.

Minimum application materials required: Complete an online application and resume through the HHS Careers Web site. Application includes the following KSAs: 1) experience preparing and awarding grant applications for complex programs; 2) experience providing technical assistance and advice to grantees; 3) interpersonal communication skills; 4) experience preparing cooperative agreement documents; 5) knowledge of statutes, regulations, HHS legislative mandates and authorities, grants policies, financial Management Policies; 6) participated in the entire grant-cycle from the preapplication and site visit to the final audit; 7) experience administering grants; 8) experience with interpreting regulations, policies and procedures related to grants and cooperative agreement management.

Special requirements: Must be a U.S. citizen.

Health Insurance Specialist

Agency: Centers for Medicare and Medicaid Services
Salary: $72,108 to $93,742
Location: Woodlawn, Maryland

Job description summary: Provides leadership in the development of guidelines and procedures for determining whether long-term-care-facility residents are being well cared for. Conducts and supervises special studies and develops comparative analyses to evaluate the effectiveness of the survey process. Plans, develops, executes, and distributes special studies designed to determine results of the application of the resident assessment process. Provides leadership and guidance to other professional staff both in central and regional offices.

Minimum qualifications required: Bachelor's degree. One year of specialized experience in or related to the work of the position.

Minimum application materials required: Complete an online application and resume through the HHS Careers Web site. Application includes the following KSAs: 1) experience in developing, interpreting, and applying policies related to nursing homes; 2) experience reviewing, analyzing, developing, and responding to inquiries regarding survey and certification or other

Medicare related policies; 3) experience in communicating technical and nontechnical information; 4) experience working as a project lead or team member in your organization's contracting or grant award process; 5) experience with federal and state health programs.

Medical Records Technician

Agency: Indian Health Service
Salary: $21,257 to $34,714
Location: Poplar, Montana

Job description summary: Maintains individual clinical records for all patients treated at the Service Unit. Operates the computer system to include patient registration, documentation, and printing. Interviews patients to obtain information, pulls charts, and fills out patient forms. Maintains notifiable disease roster for TBC, VD, RHD, etc. Assigns unit numbers to new charts, obtains social security numbers, assembles new charts, and types patient index cards. Obtains proper terminology for coding and routes charts that are deficient for providers to complete. Files laboratory reports and other pertinent data in charts. Annotates death and other changes in patients' records and sends charts of deceased patients to the Federal Records Center. Abstracts medical information from the medical records for other facilities with proper authorization. Operates and provides preventative maintenance for the addressograph, embossing machine, microfiche machine, and computer.

Minimum qualifications required: Six months of general experience that was progressively responsible clerical, office, or other work that indicates ability to acquire the particular knowledge and skills needed to perform the duties of the position.

Minimum application materials required: Complete an online application and resume through the HHS Careers Web site. Application includes the following KSAs: 1) experience complying with Privacy Act regulations or other privacy policies when dealing with personal information to maintain confidentiality; 2) experience using medical terminology; 3) experience using a computer.

Microbiologist

Agency: Laboratory of Persistent Viral Diseases, Rocky Mountain Laboratories,
Division of Intramural Research, National Institute of Allergy and Infectious Diseases,
National Institutes of Health
Salary: $40,454 to $63,629
Location: Hamilton, Montana

Job description summary: Serves as a laboratory support specialist. Participates in the design, planning, conduct, and evaluation of research experiments. Searches scientific literature for new methods and procedures; selects the appropriate methodology and procedures; maintains accurate, daily records; performs a wide variety of complex procedures and techniques; calibrates and operates a variety of laboratory instruments; writes reports of findings; interprets, evaluates, and discusses the results of each experiment with supervisors.

Minimum qualifications required: Bachelor's degree in microbiology, biology, chemistry, or basic medical science that included at least 20 semester hours in microbiology. Must have at least one year of specialized experience related to the work of the position.

Minimum application materials required: Complete an online application and resume through the HHS Careers Web site. Application includes the following KSAs: 1) experience working with microorganisms; 2) experience using scientific instruments; 3) knowledge of laboratory safety and biosafety procedures; 4) experience working with radioactive materials; 5) experience with ordering and stocking of laboratory supplies, reagents, etc.; 6) experience with laboratory hazardous waste storage and disposal procedures and protocols; 7) experience with infectious agents; 8) ability to work effectively with others to achieve a common goal and carry out duties.

Pharmacist

Agency: Food and Drug Administration
Salary: $60,638 to $110,775
Location: Washington, D.C.

Job description summary: Reviews and evaluates applications for pharmacologic drug products and reports of clinical trials and studies, as well as case reports of adverse reactions. Documents findings, incorporates the results of statistical reviews, weighs the effectiveness of the drug, and determines whether there exists a population for which the drug is adequately labeled. Evaluates plans and protocols to conduct clinical trials of Investigational New Drugs in humans and participates in the evaluation and determination of whether human subjects can be protected from unreasonable risk. Consults with other scientists and medical officers in other FDA organizations and with private industry and represents the organization in meetings with the drug pharmaceutical industry and other government agencies. Reviews the packaging and labeling components of products to assure that it meets all safety and efficacy requirements. Assures the product will be used by professionals and patients in a manner which will provide clear instructions to optimize proper use.

Minimum qualifications required: Bachelor's degree in pharmacy. Must have one year of specialized experience in or related to the work of the position.

Minimum application materials required: Complete an online application and resume through the HHS Careers Web site. Application includes the following KSAs: 1) involvement in pharmacotherapy; 2) experience with patients in the design of complex drug treatment plans; 3) experience with respect to the analysis and interpretation of clinical pharmacy studies; 4) developed patient education materials to teach patients on the proper administration, relevant side effects, and contraindications of prescribed drugs.

Special requirements: Must be able to distinguish colors.

Public Health Advisor

Agency: Centers for Disease Control and Prevention
Salary: $62,905 to $96,637
Location: Beijing, China

Job description summary: Serves as the assistant director for operations and functions as the principal management person for all Global AIDS Program (GAP) activities in China. Responsibilities include program planning and evaluation, formulation and implementation of policy and program, management of resources, property, contracts, memorandums of agreement, and procurement activities. Acts with full authority in the absence of the director on all matters involving nonscientific program operations and field activities. Provides program and operational support to the GAP initiative with particular emphasis on HIV/AIDS prevention program activities in China. Provides assistance on the implementation, direction, and evaluation of the management of program activities funded through collaborative agreements and contracts.

Minimum qualifications required: Must have one year of specialized experience that provided the following: 1) knowledge of organizational, operational, and programmatic concepts and practices applied organizations engaged in public health activities; 2) knowledge of the methods, processes, and techniques used to develop and deliver public health programs in state and local settings; 3) knowledge of a specialized public health program; 4) knowledge of the application of administrative or analytical methods and techniques necessary for working within the framework of a public health organization and carrying out specific program functions; 5) skill in oral and written communications.

Minimum application materials required: Complete an online application and resume through the HHS Careers Web site. Application includes more than 15 KSAs, including the following: 1) experience working with developing countries and international agencies on public health issues; 2) experience in establishing and maintaining effective working relationships with health officials and community representatives; 3) experience conducting prevention activities in public health specialties; 4) knowledge of HIV/AIDS prevention programs.

Special requirements: Must have a security clearance and a medical clearance.

Department of Homeland Security

Washington, D.C. 20528
202-282-8000

- ★ Web site: http://www.dhs.gov/
- ★ Job vacancies: http://www.usajobs.opm.gov/homeland.asp
- ★ USAJOBS By Phone: 912-757-3000
- ★ DHS organization: http://www.dhs.gov/dhspublic/display?theme=13

The job of the Department of Homeland Security (DHS) is to protect the country against terrorist attacks. Component agencies will analyze threats and intelligence, guard borders and airports, protect critical infrastructure, and coordinate the response of the country for future emergencies. Besides providing a better coordinated defense of the homeland, DHS is also dedicated to protecting the rights of American citizens and enhancing public services, such as natural disaster assistance and citizenship services, by dedicating offices to these important missions.

Selected Agencies Within DHS

On March 1, 2003, services formerly provided by the Immigration and Naturalization Service (INS) transitioned into the Department of Homeland Security (DHS) under **U.S. Citizenship & Immigration Services** (USCIS). In support of the DHS overall mission, the priorities of the USCIS are to promote national security, continue to eliminate immigration case backlogs, and improve customer services. This new Bureau includes approximately 15,000 employees and contractors. Through a network of local offices, application support centers, service centers, local area immigration services field offices, national customer service call (NCSC) centers, forms centers, and the Internet, USCIS processes all immigrant and nonimmigrant benefits provided to visitors of the United States.

★ Web site: http://uscis.gov/graphics/index.htm

★ Job vacancies: http://www.usajobs.opm.gov/homeland.asp

★ Field Offices: http://uscis.gov/graphics/fieldoffices/index.htm

★ Application Support Centers: http://uscis.gov/graphics/fieldoffices/ascs/asc.htm

★ Working for immigration programs: http://uscis.gov/graphics/workfor/index.htm

★ Core occupations, immigration: http://uscis.gov/graphics/workfor/careers/core.htm

★ Careers in customs enforcement: http://www.ice.gov/graphics/careers/index.htm

The **Emergency Preparedness and Response Directorate** oversees domestic disaster preparedness training and coordinates government disaster response. It brings together the Federal Emergency Management Agency (FEMA), the Strategic National Stockpile and the National Disaster Medical System (HHS), the Nuclear Incident Response Team (Energy), the Domestic Emergency Support Teams (Justice), and the Office for Domestic Preparedness (FBI).

★ Web site: http://www.dhs.gov/dhspublic/theme_home2.jsp

★ Job vacancies: http://www.usajobs.opm.gov/homeland.asp

★ Federal Emergency Management Agency: http://www.fema.gov/

★ Office for Domestic Preparedness: http://www.ojp.usdoj.gov/odp/

The **United States Coast Guard** is one of five branches of the U.S. Armed Forces. It is the country's oldest continuous seagoing service with responsibilities including Search and Rescue (SAR), Maritime Law Enforcement (MLE), Aids to Navigation (ATON), Icebreaking, Environmental Protection, Port Security, and Military Readiness. In order to accomplish these missions the Coast Guard's 38,000 active-duty men and women, 8,000 reservists, and 35,000 auxiliarists serve in a variety of job fields, ranging from operation specialists and small-boat operators and maintenance specialists to electronic technicians and aviation mechanics. In addition, the Coast Guard has over six thousand civilian positions in over 200 types of jobs in over 100 locations across the country.

★ Web site: http://www.uscg.mil/uscg.shtm

★ Job vacancies (civilian): http://jobsearch.usajobs.opm.gov/a9uscg.asp

★ Coast Guard FAQs: http://www.gocoastguard.com/faq.html

★ Benefits: http://www.uscg.mil/hq/cgpc/cpm/jobs/careerbenefits.htm

★ General civilian employment information: http://www.uscg.mil/hq/cgpc/cpm/home/geninfo.htm

★ Civilian Office of Human Resources:
http://www.uscg.mil/hq/cgpc/cpm/home/index1.htm

United States Customs and Border Protection (CBP) is the unified border agency within the Department of Homeland Security (DHS). CBP combines the inspectional workforces and broad border authorities of U.S. Customs, U.S. Immigration, Animal and Plant Health Inspection Service, and the entire U.S. Border Patrol. CBP includes more than 41,000 employees to manage, control, and protect the country's borders, at and between the official ports of entry.

★ Web site: http://www.customs.gov/xp/cgov/home.xml

★ Job vacancies: http://www.customs.gov/xp/cgov/careers/jobs/

★ Customs careers: http://www.customs.gov/xp/cgov/careers/customs_careers/

★ Study guides and preparation manuals:
http://www.customs.gov/xp/cgov/careers/study_guides/

★ Contact information: http://www.customs.gov/xp/cgov/toolbox/contacts/

The **United States Secret Service** protects the president and vice president, their families, heads of state, and other designated individuals; investigates threats against these protectees; protects the White House, vice president's residence, foreign missions, and other buildings within Washington, D.C.; and plans and implements security designs for designated national special security events. The Secret Service also investigates violations of laws relating to counterfeiting of obligations and securities of the United States; financial crimes that include access device fraud, financial institution fraud, identity theft, and computer fraud; and computer-based attacks on the country's financial, banking, and telecommunications infrastructure.

★ Web site: http://www.secretservice.gov/

★ Job vacancies: http://www.secretservice.gov/opportunities.shtml

★ Headquarters contact information: http://www.secretservice.gov/contact.shtml

★ Field offices: http://www.secretservice.gov/field_offices.shtml

★ Application forms: http://www.secretservice.gov/opportunities_forms.shtml

★ Career fairs: http://www.secretservice.gov/opportunities_fairs.shtml

Other DHS Agencies

Animal and Plant Health Inspection Service
http://www.aphis.usda.gov/

Federal Law Enforcement Training Center
http://www.fletc.gov/

Directorate of Border and Transportation Security
http://www.dhs.gov/dhspublic/display?theme=50

Directorate of Information Analysis and Infrastructure Protection
http://www.dhs.gov/dhspublic/theme_home6.jsp

Directorate of Science and Technology
http://www.dhs.gov/dhspublic/theme_home5.jsp

National Communications System
http://www.ncs.gov/

National Infrastructure Protection Center
http://www.nipc.gov/

Nuclear Incident Response Team
http://www.llnl.gov/nai/rdiv/nucinc.html

Office of Energy Assurance
http://www.ea.doe.gov/

Plum Island Animal Disease Center
http://www.ars.usda.gov/plum/

Transportation Security Administration
http://www.tsa.gov/public/index.jsp

United States Computer Emergency Readiness Team
http://www.us-cert.gov/federal/

Sample Job Vacancies

Architect

Agency: Federal Law Enforcement Training Center
Salary: $69,762 to $90,692
Location: Glynco, Georgia

Job description summary: Provides professional architectural duties in the planning, design, construction, operation, and maintenance of real properties, facilities, and assigned public services. Serves as the principal project manager of a broad program of development and coordinative functions relating to architectural design and construction of large complex and specialized training and support facilities. Develops long- and short-range plans; monitors and guides progress of projects; develops procedures and instructions for determining and presenting architectural compliance data; conducts joint studies; provides professional architectural advice and direction to organizations.

Minimum qualifications required: Bachelor's degree in architecture; OR a combination of education and experience. Must have at least one year of specialized experience in the design, construction, repair and renovation, restoration, rehabilitation, design, or construction of major commercial or industrial facilities, managing all or a large phase of a major design or construction project.

Minimum application materials required: Submit either a resume or Optional Application for Federal Employment (OF-612), along with a completed Occupational Questionnaire (19 questions) from the vacancy announcement.

Special requirements: Must be a U.S. citizen to. Male applicants born after December 31, 1959, must have registered with the Selective Service System.

Citizen & Immigration Services Clerk
Agency: U.S. Citizenship & Immigration Services
Salary: $28,719 to $37,340
Location: Newark, New Jersey

Job description summary: Evaluates various types of applicants and petitions for benefits under the Immigration and Nationality Act. Checks for completeness and consistency of statements. Prepares replies to applicants requesting additional information and follows through to obtain required documents from a variety of sources. Determines and annotates the most appropriate section of law under which application/petition can be processed. Explains basic eligibility requirements and provisions of law to applicants and interested parties. Provides nonroutine information and assistance on general aspects of CIS law. Performs general clerical work.

Minimum qualifications required: One year of specialized experience in explaining rules and regulations and providing accurate information to outside parties; working knowledge of various software programs and experience providing clerical support; OR a bachelor's degree. Must be able to type 40 words per minute.

Minimum application materials required: Submit either a resume or Optional Application for Federal Employment (OF-612). Include narrative answers to the following KSAs: 1) knowledge of record keeping systems; 2) ability to communicate effectively both orally and in writing; 3) ability to make independent decisions by using personal judgment.

Special requirements: Must be a U.S. citizen. Must pass a drug test Male applicants born in after December 31, 1959, must have registered with the Selective Service.

Fire Program Specialist
Agency: Federal Emergency Management Agency
Salary: $60,638 to $93,742
Location: Emmitsburg, Maryland

Job description summary: Responsible for a variety of program initiatives requiring coordination in such program areas as National Response Plan, National Incident Management

System, Emergency Medical Services, Arson, Hazardous Materials, and Incident Command. Assists in budgetary preparation, planning, implementation, monitoring, and analysis of various programs within the Response Branch. Evaluates emergency services and fire-related issues to develop policies that help to fulfill the Agency's mission. Evaluates proposals, recommends contracts or grants for funding, provides technical direction to contractor or grantee, and monitors work efforts to ensure that work meets quality and completion requirements. Coordinates the development of the content and design of specific programs and project goals, analyzing their effectiveness and determining their validity to the fire service.

Minimum qualifications required: Must have one year of specialized experience in or directly related to the line of work of the position.

Minimum application materials required: Submit either a resume or Optional Application for Federal Employment (OF-612). Include narrative answers to the following KSAs: 1) knowledge of National Response Plan, National Incident Management System, and Critical Infrastructure Protection initiatives and the impact of such initiatives to emergency services programs; 2) knowledge of program administration procedures and principles; 3) ability to review, analyze and interpret complex technical documents, legislation, or regulations prepare comprehensive responses or position papers; 4) ability to produce reports and other planning and strategic documents that render complex technical information into a form that is easily understood by various audiences.

Special requirements: Must be able to relocate to emergency sites with little advance notice and function under intense physical and mental stress. Males born after December 31, 1959, must have registered with the Selective Service. Must be a U.S. citizen. Must pass a drug test and a background investigation.

Intelligence Research Specialist

Agency: Office of Protective Research, Intelligence Division, U.S. Secret Service
Salary: $41,815 to $54,360
Location: Washington, D.C.

Job description summary: Assists in reviewing highly classified and sensitive incoming intelligence information to extract pertinent data for online data systems input; initiates or updates aspects of investigations of individuals or groups posing a threat to the physical security of Secret Service protectees; assists in the briefing and debriefing of investigative and protective personnel; searches intelligence information files, organizes information, and prepares information abstracts; performs name checks and other information retrieval searches related to individuals or groups suspected of posing a threat to protectees; and provides input to a variety of regular statistical and narrative reports.

Minimum qualifications required: Must have one year of specialized experience in or related to the work of the position, OR a master's degree.

Minimum application materials required: Submit either a resume or Optional Application for Federal Employment (OF-612). Include narrative answers to the following KSAs: 1) ability to abstract and summarize pertinent information from various types of materials; 2) ability to research and analyze information and to draw conclusions; 3) ability to work effectively with personnel at various levels.

Special requirements: Must be a U.S. citizen. Male applicants born after December 31, 1959, must have registered with the Selective Service System. Must qualify for a top secret clearance. Must pass a drug test and a polygraph examination.

Law Enforcement Communications Assistant

Agency: Security, Customs, and Border Protection
Salary: $26,699 to $47,615
Location: Nogales, Arizona

Job description summary: Provides information to aid officers in detaining, apprehending, and deporting aliens from the United States and facilitates officer safety by monitoring officers' radio transmissions. Searches, locates, and transmits to field agents/officers information and corresponding facts such as driver's license, criminal records, vehicle registration, immigration status, etc. Reads, decodes, and interprets electronic sensor intrusions using knowledge of terrain, local conditions, and traffic patterns; reviews and interprets automated enforcement data retrieved in response to specific requests from field personnel; files record copies of incoming and outgoing messages and determines proper routing; and makes daily inspections of equipment to ensure working order, making minor repairs as necessary.

Minimum qualifications required: One year of specialized experience in a similar or related position.

Minimum application materials required: Apply through CareerFinder, the Department of Homeland Security's online application system.

Special requirements: Must be a U.S. citizen. Must pass a background security investigation and a drug test. Must possess a valid driver's license.

Transportation Security Screener

Agency: Transportation Security Administration
Salary: $23,600 to $35,400
Location: Albuquerque, New Mexico

Job description summary: Responsible for identifying dangerous objects in baggage and cargo, and on passengers; and preventing those objects from being transported onto aircraft. Performs various tasks such as: wanding, pat down searches, operation of X-ray machines, lifting of baggage, and screening and ticket review using electronic and imaging equipment.

Minimum qualifications required: Must have a high school diploma or GED; OR at least one year of full-time work experience in security work, aviation screener work, or X-ray technician work. Must possess the following knowledge, skills, and abilities: 1) proficient in English; 2) observant; 3) courteous; 4) dependable; 5) responsible and honest; 6) able to lift and carry baggage up to 70 lbs.; 7) have good, color vision and hearing and joint mobility.

Minimum application materials required: Submit an online application. If you meet the minimum qualifications, you will be notified to schedule for a computerized test that will consist of: 1) a competency inventory (service orientation, work values, integrity, and dependability); 2) English proficiency; and 3) object recognition. If you pass the computerized test, you will be eligible to be scheduled to attend a further assessment sessions. During this assessment process, you will undergo: 1) an interview; 2) a color vision test; 3) a medical evaluation including a physical abilities test and a review of a medical questionnaire that will be provided at the assessment session; and 4) a drug test. If you successfully pass each of the above assessments, you will be considered further for employment.

Special requirements: Must be a U.S. citizen. Must pass a background investigation, a drug test, and a credit check. In addition, you must successfully complete required training, which includes: 56-72 hours of classroom training, 112-128 hours of on-the-job training, and a certification examination.

Transportation Security Specialist

Agency: Transportation Security Administration (TSA)
Salary: $54,100 to $83,900
Location: Herndon, Virginia

Job description summary: Serves in support of the Transportation Security Operations Center (TSOC) as a subject matter expert for 3D modeling, simulation, and Geospatial Information System (GIS) database development. Ensures that critical GIS data required for the TSA is collected, documented, and disseminated. Provides technical assistance and training in support of the Standardization and Exercise Section in the use of ESRI-ARC software programs and the use of GIS-developed information.

Minimum qualifications required: Bachelor's degree. Must have one year of specialized experience in or related to the work of the position to be filled. Such experience must include Geospatial Information System (GIS) experience with an emphasis on modeling and simulation.

Minimum application materials required: Submit either a resume or Optional Application for Federal Employment (OF-612). Include narrative answers to the following KSAs: 1) ability to develop, organize, and present technical data and information orally and in writing to a diverse audience; 2) knowledge of Geospatial Information System, ERSI, ArcView, and ArcInfo database design and management; 3) proficiency in the installation, maintenance, and application of multiple hardware/software systems and platforms; 4) ability to convert/extract metadata into scenario files in support of exercises or real-world applications and operations.

Special requirements: Must have a Secret Security Clearance and pass a background investigation. Must pass a drug and alcohol screening. Required to work full-time on a rotational 24-hour schedule, seven days per week and may be required to work outside of the standard workday/workweek on a rotating shift schedule on short notice. Will also be on call for 24 hours per day to cover emergency response needs. Required to carry a paging device and mobile telephone at all times.

Welder

Agency: U.S. Coast Guard
Salary: $20.57 to $23.98/hour
Location: San Pedro, California

Job description summary: Performs all kinds of journeyman welding tasks involved in the construction, repair, maintenance, overhaul, and conversion of a wide variety of types and sizes of marine craft and vessels, and in connection with miscellaneous manufacturing projects. Plans and lays out the work from blueprints, sketches, shop drawings, specifications, job/service orders, models, or supervisor's instructions. Operates welding tools and equipment. Welds are subject to X-ray analysis, magnaflux inspection, dye check, and water or gas tight pressure or other tests. Uses a variety of manual welding processes to weld commonly used metals and alloys of various sizes, shapes, and thickness, including dissimilar metals such as copper to steel.

Minimum qualifications required: There is no specific amount of education or experience needed to qualify for this position. However, applicants must be able to fully perform the duties as a welder at the journeyman level without more than normal supervision; possess knowledge of the welding trade practices and materials, including various welding processes, procedures and technical practices and metals/alloys; and be able to safely operate equipment and take precautionary measures to enhance personal safety.

Minimum application materials required: Submit either a resume or Optional Application for Federal Employment (OF-612), along with a completed Occupational Questionnaire (66 questions) from the vacancy announcement.

Special requirements: Must be a U.S. citizen. Males born after December 31, 1959, must have registered with the Selective Service System.

Department of Housing and Urban Development

451 Seventh Street SW
Washington, D.C. 20410
202-708-1422

★ Web site: http://www.hud.gov/

★ Job vacancies: http://jobsearch.usajobs.opm.gov/a9hudp.asp

★ USAJOBS By Phone: 912-757-3000

★ Internship information: http://www.hud.gov/offices/adm/jobs/internship.cfm

★ HUD local office directory: http://www.hud.gov/directory/ascdir3.cfm

The Department of Housing and Urban Development (HUD) is the principal federal agency responsible for programs concerned with the country's housing needs, fair housing opportunities, and improvement and development of the nation's communities. HUD's mission is to increase homeownership, support community development, and increase access to affordable housing free from discrimination. HUD is organized in 10 regions that oversee various field offices.

Selected Agencies Within HUD

The **Office of Housing** oversees the Federal Housing Administration (FHA), the largest mortgage insurer in the world, as well as regulates housing industry business. The mission of the Office of Housing is to contribute to building and preserving healthy neighborhoods and communities; maintain and expand homeownership, rental housing, and healthcare opportunities; and stabilize credit markets in times of economic disruption.

★ Web site: http://www.hud.gov/offices/hsg/

★ Job vacancies: http://jobsearch.usajobs.opm.gov/a9hudp.asp

★ Contact information: http://www.hud.gov/offices/hsg/contacts.cfm

★ Office of Multifamily Housing Assistance Restructuring:
http://www.hud.gov/offices/hsg/omhar/index.cfm

★ Federal Housing Administration: http://www.hud.gov/offices/hsg/fhahistory.cfm

The **Office of Public and Indian Housing** (PIH) ensures safe, decent, and affordable housing, creates opportunities for residents' self-sufficiency and economic independence, and assures the fiscal integrity of all program participants. It manages several programs, including the Capital Fund, which provides funds to Public Housing Agencies for the development, financing, and modernization of public housing developments and for management improvements; the HOPE VI Program, which addresses severely distressed public housing by helping with physical improvements, management improvements, and social and community services to address resident needs; and Housing choice vouchers, which allow very low-income families to choose and lease or purchase safe, decent, and affordable privately owned rental housing.

★ Web site: http://www.hud.gov/offices/pih/

★ Job vacancies: http://jobsearch.usajobs.opm.gov/a9hudp.asp

★ Links to offices, divisions, and centers: http://www.hud.gov/offices/pih/about/offices.cfm

★ Headquarters and staff directory: http://www.hud.gov/offices/pih/about/headquarters.cfm

Other HUD Agencies

Ginnie Mae
http://www.ginniemae.gov/

Faith-Based and Community Initiatives
http://www.hud.gov/offices/fbci/index.cfm

Office of Community Planning and Development
http://www.hud.gov/offices/cpd/

Office of Fair Housing and Equal Opportunity
http://www.hud.gov/offices/fheo/

Office of Federal Housing Enterprise Oversight
http://www.ofheo.gov/

Office of Healthy Homes and Lead Hazard Control
http://www.hud.gov/offices/lead/

Office of Policy Development and Research
http://www.huduser.org/

Real Estate Assessment Center
http://www.hud.gov/offices/reac/

Small and Disadvantaged Business Utilization
http://www.hud.gov/offices/osdbu/

Sample Job Vacancies

Field Office Director
Agency: Office of Field Policy and Management
Salary: $82,438 to $126,064
Location: New Orleans, Louisiana

Job description summary: Supervises the front office field staff and is responsible for coordinating outreach activities and program delivery to HUD customers and communities throughout the jurisdiction. Manages, coordinates, and administers authorities and responsibilities as delegated by the regional director. Represents the agency and has a comprehensive knowledge of the broad range of HUD programs and initiatives and how they are administered and funded, and explains their value and requirements to a full range of clients, including elected officials, governors, mayors, Congressional representatives, tenant groups, and other public interest groups concerned with HUD programs. Effects necessary coordination with HUD customers and HUD program managers, explains and resolves outstanding issues, and actively promotes HUD programs in various governmental, political, and social arenas.

Minimum qualifications required: One year of experience in or related to the work of this position, such as experience as a specialist, team leader, program manager, or other responsible position which encompassed duties, responsibilities or significant involvement in management practices such as developing or planning management systems, managing or monitoring organizational budgets, human resources management; OR experience as the senior staff-level person in the housing or community development area, responsible for reviewing an resolving issues involving large-scale residential construction projects, mortgage lending for multifamily projects, etc.

Minimum application materials required: Submit either an Optional Application for Federal Employment (OF-612) or a resume as long as it includes the information listed in the vacancy announcement. Include narrative answers to the following KSAs: 1) knowledge of management practices; 2) ability to effectively communicate, both in writing and orally; 3) knowledge of housing/community development programs; 4) ability to manage work relationships.

Special requirements: Must be a U.S. citizen.

Public Housing Revitalization Specialist

Agency: Office of Public and Indian Housing (PIH)
Salary: $72,108 to $93,742
Location: Cleveland, Ohio

Job description summary: Provides technical assistance and advice and performs work assignments which may involve the interpretation of policies and procedures related to facilities management (FM) aspects of PIH programs as they relate to the overall recovery efforts of troubled Public Housing Authorities (PHAs). May serve as a project management team member or team leader of assigned PHAs; as an internal consultant within the Recovery and Prevention Corps (RPC) on technical/facilities management-related problems involving PIH activities and projects when necessary; and, as a specialist in the area of facilities management, handling a wide variety of programs.

Minimum qualifications required: Must have one year of specialized experience related to the work of the position. Experience in reviewing building plans and specifications, contract proposals, requisitions, change order, construction or modernization implementation schedules and proposals, review of technical engineering matters related to maintenance activities and overall housing quality, as well as the ability to address compliance violations at troubled PHAs by developing tailored training packages or providing technical assistance in the facilities management functions.

Minimum application materials required: Submit either an Optional Application for Federal Employment (OF-612), a resume, or some other format as long as it includes the information listed in the vacancy announcement. Include narrative answers to the following KSAs: 1) ability to analyze complex PHA management problems and to present findings and recommendations; 2) knowledge of public and assisted-housing programs, policies, and procedures; 3) ability to provide technical assistance through effective communication of program knowledge to others; 4) ability to read and interpret architectural/engineering plans and specifications.

Special requirements: Male applicants born after December 31, 1959, must have registered with the Selective Service System. Must pass a background security investigation.

Clerk

Agency: Department of Housing and Urban Development
Salary: $24,666 to $32,063
Location: Washington, D.C.

Job description summary: Greets visitors and answers telephone calls, referring them to proper persons, or providing information requested. Maintains office files. Types a wide variety of material including memoranda, letters, and reports using word processing equipment. Prepares charts and spreadsheets.

Minimum qualifications required: Must have one year of general experience in or related to the work of the position OR an associate's degree. Must be able to type at least 40 words per minute.

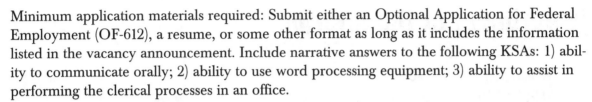

Minimum application materials required: Submit either an Optional Application for Federal Employment (OF-612), a resume, or some other format as long as it includes the information listed in the vacancy announcement. Include narrative answers to the following KSAs: 1) ability to communicate orally; 2) ability to use word processing equipment; 3) ability to assist in performing the clerical processes in an office.

Special requirements: Male applicants born after December 31, 1959, must have registered with the Selective Service System. Must pass a background security investigation.

Financial Engineer I
Agency: Office of Federal Housing Enterprise Oversight
Salary: $75,496 to $120,792
Location: Washington, D.C.

Job description summary: Provides assistance in conducting theoretical and applied research in the economics of housing finance markets related to economic capital adequacy issues. Provides assistance in developing and documenting prototype risk management models and measurements of risk and capital adequacy suggested by the OCS research program. Presents findings of research studies and analyses at departmental meetings and to other OFHEO offices. Participates on projects with other OCS and OFHEO staff members on issues relating to housing finance, capital, and modeling.

Minimum qualifications required: Master's degree or Ph.D. in finance, economics, mathematics, statistics, or computer science; OR at least four years of experience in the use of economic theory and econometric techniques to analyze technical issues, including two years' experience conducting qualitative or quantitative research in microeconomics, finance, or macroeconomic subject areas. Must be able to assist in analyzing residential mortgage default, loss severity, and prepayment patterns and models; term structure of interest rates; house price indexes; security and portfolio valuation; or options theory. Must be able to produce empirical economic studies and prepare written reports, papers, and summaries. Must be able to work as either team leader or team member in an interdisciplinary environment.

Minimum application materials required: Submit either an Optional Application for Federal Employment (OF-612), a resume, or some other format as long as it includes the information listed in the vacancy announcement. Include narrative answers to the following KSAs: 1) knowledge of financial engineering principles and computational finance principles and theories to conduct econometric research and analysis of financial and economic issues, implement model prototypes, and to develop models for risk evaluation and management; 2) ability to communicate technical information, both orally and in writing, to technical and nontechnical audiences; 3) knowledge and understanding of the mission and goals of a financial regulatory institution; 4) general knowledge of economics, finance, and risk management principles, theories, concepts, methods, and techniques.

Special requirements: Male applicants born after December 31, 1959, must have registered with the Selective Service System. Must pass a background security investigation.

Department of the Interior

1849 C Street NW
Washington, D.C. 20240
202-208-3100

★ Web site: http://www.doi.gov/

★ Job vacancies: http://www.doi.gov/doijobs/jobs.html

★ USAJOBS By Phone: 912-757-3000

★ Internship information: http://www.doi.gov/doijobs/employ5.html

★ DOI phone numbers: http://www.doi.gov/doiphone.html

★ Employee orientation: http://www.doiu.nbc.gov/orientation/

★ Benefits: http://www.doi.gov/doijobs/employ4.html

★ Contact information: http://www.doi.gov/contact.html

The Department of the Interior (DOI) manages the country's public lands and minerals, national parks, national wildlife refuges, and western water resources and upholds federal trust responsibilities to Indian tribes and commitments to island communities. It is responsible for migratory wildlife conservation; historic preservation; endangered species; surface-mined lands protection and restoration; mapping; geological, hydrological, and biological science; and assistance for the insular areas.

DOI is a large, decentralized agency with over 78,315 employees and 183,000 volunteers located at approximately 2,400 operating locations across the United States, Puerto Rico, U.S. territories, and freely associated states. It employs people in more than 90 career fields, including accounting, animal care, archaeology, biological sciences, cartography, chemistry, construction engineering, ecology, firefighting, geology, landscape architecture, curating, petroleum engineering, public affairs, surface mining reclamation, telecommunications, vocational training, and water management.

Selected Agencies Within DOI

The **Bureau of Land Management** (BLM) is responsible for managing 262 million acres of land—about one-eighth of the land in the United States—and about 300 million additional acres of subsurface mineral resources. The Bureau is also responsible for wildfire management and suppression on 388 million acres. Most of the lands the BLM manages are located in the western United States, including Alaska, and are dominated by extensive grasslands, forests, high mountains, arctic tundra, and deserts. The BLM manages a wide variety of resources and uses, including energy and minerals; timber; forage; wild horse and burro populations; fish and wildlife habitat; wilderness areas; archaeological, paleontological, and historical sites; and other natural heritage values. BLM employs more than 10,000 people who are assisted by 20,000 volunteers.

- ★ Web site: http://www.blm.gov

- ★ Job vacancies: http://jobsearch.usajobs.opm.gov/a9blm.asp

- ★ Contact information and links: http://www.blm.gov/nhp/directory/index.htm

- ★ Temporary and student employment: http://www.nc.blm.gov/jobs/

- ★ Volunteer information: http://www.blm.gov/volunteer/

- ★ Firefighting jobs: http://www.firejobs.doi.gov/

The **National Park Service** preserves unimpaired the natural and cultural resources and values of the national park system for the enjoyment, education, and inspiration of this and future generations. The Park Service cooperates with partners to extend the benefits of natural and cultural resource conservation and outdoor recreation throughout this country and the world. The National Park System of the United States comprises 384 areas covering more than 83 million acres in 49 states, the District of Columbia, American Samoa, Guam, Puerto Rico, Saipan, and the Virgin Islands.

- ★ Web site: http://www.nps.gov

- ★ Job vacancies: http://data2.itc.nps.gov/digest/usajobs.cfm

- ★ Headquarters and regional offices: http://www.nps.gov/legacy/regions.html

- ★ Volunteer information: http://www.nps.gov/volunteer/

- ★ Seasonal employment: http://www.sep.nps.gov/

The **United States Fish and Wildlife Service** manages more than 95 million acres of land and water consisting of more than 500 national wildlife refuges, thousands of small wetlands, and other special management areas. It also operates 70 national fish hatcheries, 64 fish and wildlife management assistance offices, 64 fishery resource offices, and 78 ecological services field stations. The Service is responsible for migratory birds, endangered species, certain marine mammals, and inland sport fisheries.

- ★ Web site: http://www.fws.gov

- ★ Job vacancies: http://jobs.fws.gov/

- ★ General employment information: http://hr.fws.gov/hr/index.htm

- ★ Office directory: http://offices.fws.gov/

- ★ National programs and functions: http://info.fws.gov/function.html

- ★ Details about student employment programs: http://jobs.fws.gov/studentjobs.htm

Other DOI Agencies

Bureau of Indian Affairs
http://www.doi.gov/bureau-indian-affairs.html

Bureau of Reclamation
http://www.usbr.gov

Minerals Management Service
http://www.mms.gov

Office of Surface Mining Reclamation and Enforcement
http://www.osmre.gov

United States Geological Survey
http://www.usgs.gov

Sample Job Vacancies

Biological Science Technician
Agency: National Park Service
Salary: $17.75/hour
Location: Point Reyes National Seashore, California

Job description summary: Responsible for data management, site prioritization, GIS map development, and report preparation; assists with completion of environmental compliance documents. This position will require strenuous physical activity including periods of standing, walking, climbing, and lifting and carrying heavy objects. The work performed will include both indoor tasks and fieldwork in steep, heavily vegetated terrain in all types of weather.

Minimum qualifications required: Bachelor's degree in a related field. One year of specialized experience related to the work of the position, OR one full year of graduate education directly related to the work of the position.

Minimum application materials required: Submit resume and supporting documentation (transcripts, etc.) along with completed Occupational Questionnaire. Questionnaire includes the following KSAs: 1) knowledge of and experience with plant species identification and experience with plant keys; 2) knowledge of and experience in aspects of Integrated Pest Management (IPM) related to invasive nonnative plant control; 3) ability to communicate orally and in writing; 4) knowledge of vegetation data management on computers.

Special requirements: Must be a U.S. citizen and have a valid driver's license. Male applicants born after December 31, 1959, must have registered with the Selective Service. Must pass a background security investigation.

Cartographic Technician
Agency: Water Resources Branch, Division of Engineering of the Fish and Wildlife Service
Regional Office, U.S. Fish and Wildlife Service
Salary: $34,202
Location: Portland, Oregon

Job description summary: Creates maps using mapping software. Maintains both hard and electronic water rights maps drawing databases. Plans, develops, and maintains spatial and nonspatial databases. Prepares neat, accurate, and easily understood graphs, forms, and drawings for technical reports, exhibits, and presentations. Performs necessary research to compile information required to produce defensible product. Collects, processes, and manages GPS data. Monitors the review process of maps and drawings. Operates electronic data processing equipment including a CAM (Computer Aided Mapping) system, digitizer, scanner, and plotter to digitize and produce water right maps.

Minimum qualifications required: Bachelor's degree in a related field. Must have one year of full-time specialized experience related to the duties of the position; OR at least one full year of progressively higher-level graduate education; OR a combination of graduate education and work experience.

Minimum application materials required: Submit resume and supporting documentation (transcripts, etc.) along with completed Occupational Questionnaire. Questionnaire has more than 30 KSAs, including the following: 1) operate a GIS workstation and related software; 2) systems maintenance of GIS personal computers and related software; 3) conduct systems maintenance on a shared computer network; 4) operate a Windows-based system, and ESRI GIS software; 5) develop and/or modify computer programs and software related to science, mathematics, statistical analysis, operating systems and/or information processing; 6) use GIS software such as ArcGIS, Arc View, Arc SDE, SQL server and related technology to design databases; 7) perform mapping tasks using GIS; 8) plan and conduct surveys or resurveys involving land survey problems of substantial variety and complexity.

Dam Tender

Agency: Bureau of Reclamation
Salary: $15.83/hour
Location: Arrowrock Field Station, Boise, Idaho

Job description summary: Operates and adjusts gates and valves to divert water, regulate reservoir and water flow to meet irrigation and domestic water needs. Takes and records readings of reservoir level, river flow, and reservoir releases. Operates equipment in connection with maintenance work. Performs painting, carpentry, plumbing, mechanical, and electrical maintenance work. Patrols and services telephone and electrical lines serving the dam. Removes debris from reservoir and surrounding area. Makes periodic inspections of all equipment, buildings, roads, grounds, and water, electrical and sewage systems.

Minimum qualifications required: Must be able to lift, carry, and hold objects heavier than 40 pounds; stand, bend and crawl for extended periods of time; work on scaffolding and objects above ground level; work in confined spaces; clearly communicate in high noise areas and/or with portable two-way radios; wear half-mask respirator. Must have a valid state driver's license.

Minimum application materials required: Submit resume or Optional Application for Federal Employment (OF-612) along with narrative answers to the following KSAs: 1) ability to work as a Dam Tender with normal supervision; 2) ability to perform dam operations and minor maintenance tasks; 3) ability to follow written and oral instructions; 4) ability to properly use common hand and power tools and equipment such as shovels, picks, brooms (hand and powered), vacuums, etc.; 5) knowledge of safety requirements.

Special requirements: Must have valid driver's license.

Geographic Information System Specialist
Agency: Bureau of Land Management
Salary: $40,454 to $48,947
Location: Shoshone, Idaho

Job description summary: Responsible for the acquisition and management of the wide range of spatial information required to support the management of public lands. Identifies requirements and implements advanced analytical techniques necessary to solve complex GIS issues. Develops and modifies GIS software applications and interfaces. Provides technical user support for all aspects of geo-spatial data and software. Works with a diverse group of resources specialists, planners, and managers to coordinate and implement GIS activities, to include development of project objectives, evaluation of adequacy of existing data sources, creation/modification of GIS coverage's and databases, analysis, preparation of final output products, and data storage.

Minimum qualifications required: Bachelor's degree in a related field. Must have one year of specialized experience in or related to the work of the position.

Minimum application materials required: Submit resume and supporting documentation (transcripts, etc.) along with completed Occupational Questionnaire.

Hydrologic Technician
Agency: U.S. Geological Survey
Salary: $21,257 to $34,714
Location: Charlotte, North Carolina

Job description summary: Collects and analyses streamflow and precipitation data. Collects, compiles, and analyzes water quality and sediment data, including calibration of instruments. Installs, maintains, and operates scientific instruments.

Minimum qualifications required: Bachelor's degree in a related field. One year of specialized experience related to the duties of the position.

Minimum application materials required: Submit resume and supporting documentation (transcripts, etc.) along with completed Occupational Questionnaire.

Special requirements: This position requires completion of a medical examination at Federal expense. If selected for this position, a background investigation is required.

Inspector
Agency: Minerals Management Service (MMS)
Salary: $48,947 to $63,629
Location: Jefferson, Louisiana

Job description summary: Performs safety and environmental inspections of oil, gas, and other mineral facilities on the outer-continental shelf of the United States. Inspections include production, drilling, workover/completion, measurement/verification, pipeline, and site security activities and operations and compliance with environmental quality regulations. As accidents occur, participates with investigative teams to determine the accident conditions; includes examining equipment for proper functioning, reviewing operator records of examination and, tests.

Minimum qualifications required: Must have three full years of progressively higher-level graduate education or Ph.D.; OR at least one year of specialized experience in conducting inspections or performing offshore accident investigations; OR a combination of education and experience. Must possess a technical knowledge of the facilities, processes, methods, and equipment commonly utilized in offshore oil and gas operations. Must have skill in analyzing or evaluating production process systems, SAFE Charts and Flow Diagrams, and technical information relative to drilling, workover, and completion equipment.

Minimum application materials required: Complete and submit an online resume and Occupational Questionnaire.

Special requirements: Frequent walking, bending, stooping, and climbing tall ladders during inspection of offshore oil and gas facilities; helicopter travel required. Must pass a physical examination.

Park Guide

Agency: National Park Service
Salary: $11.42/hour
Location: Cape Hatteras, North Carolina

Job description summary: Staffs a visitor and operates an information desk responding to visitor inquiries, requests, and needs. Develops and conducts interpretive talks and guided tours.

Minimum qualifications required: Combination of education and experience may qualify you for this position. Six months of general experience and six months of specialized experience, OR one year as a Guide, OR two years of college with 12 semester hours in American history, science, or public speaking.

Minimum application materials required: Apply online at the seasonal employees Web site.

Special requirements: Must have a valid driver's license.

Prescribed Fire Specialist

Agency: U.S. Fish and Wildlife Service
Salary: $40,454
Location: San Luis National Wildlife Refuge Complex, Los Banos, California

Job description summary: Provides technical advice and guidance to staff regarding prescribed fire activities. Integrates prescribed fire, smoke management, fuels modification principles and procedures, fire effects knowledge, and knowledge of scientific data collection and analysis principles into a comprehensive prescribed fire program for an individual station and/or a prescribed fire district (group of stations).

Minimum qualifications required: Bachelor's degree in the biological sciences, agriculture, natural resources management, or related disciplines. Must have one year prior wildland firefighting experience.

Minimum application materials required: Submit resume and supporting documentation (transcripts, etc.) along with completed Occupational Questionnaire. Questionnaire has more than 20 KSAs, including the following: 1) develop and execute presuppression and wildland fire suppression activities; 2) develop and recommend plans and schedules for prescribed burning and smoke management; 3) develop and execute a fuels inventory; 4) personally implement and direct prescribed burns; 5) develop and recommend long-term and annual schedule of burns; 6) develop and execute land-use planning and environmental coordination.

Special requirements: Must be a U.S. citizen. Must pass a physical and a drug test.

Wildlife Biologist

Agency: U.S. Fish and Wildlife Service
Salary: $33,071 to $52,591
Location: Tensas River National Wildlife Refuge, Tallulah, Louisiana

Job description summary: Makes recommendations to the Refuge Manager on numerous biological matters; conducts research and monitoring on the threatened Louisiana Black Bear and other endangered wildlife species using radio telemetry equipment; manipulates and enhances habitat for the benefit of waterfowl; manages moist soil units for the production of high value waterfowl foods; conducts wildlife population monitoring and other resource inventories, station banding/tagging activities, monitors population trends and interactions, analyzes data and recommends strategies; prepares/develops population and habitat management plans, environmental compliance documents, various reports and correspondence.

Minimum qualifications required: Bachelor's degree in biological sciences. Must have one year or specialized experience in or related to the work of the position.

Minimum application materials required: Submit resume and supporting documentation (transcripts, etc.) along with completed Occupational Questionnaire, which includes the following KSAs: 1) knowledge of theory, principles, and methods of wildlife biology, habitat, and population management specifically as it relates to the threatened Louisiana Black Bear; 2) knowledge of methods and procedures using radio telemetry and radio tracking equipment for threatened, endangered, and other wildlife; 3) knowledge of theory, principles, and methods of waterfowl ecology and conservation; 4) ability to recognize critical trends in wildlife resources; 5) skill in written communication relating specifically to wildlife management.

Department of Justice

950 Pennsylvania Avenue NW
Washington, D.C. 20530
202-514-2000

- ★ Web site: http://www.usdoj.gov/
- ★ Job vacancies: http://www.usdoj.gov/06employment/06_1.html
- ★ USAJOBS By Phone: 912-757-3000
- ★ Contact information: http://www.usdoj.gov/contact-us.html

★ Student employment: http://www.usdoj.gov/careers/student_programs.html

★ Student volunteer program: http://www.atf.gov/jobs/links/studentvol.htm

★ Basic employment information: http://www.usdoj.gov/06employment/index.html

★ Employee directory: http://www.usdoj.gov/cgi-bin/phonebook/db.cgi

The Department of Justice (DOJ) serves as counsel for its citizens. It represents them in enforcing the law in the public interest. Through its thousands of lawyers, investigators, and agents, DOJ plays the key role in protection against criminals and subversion, ensuring healthy business competition, safeguarding the consumer, and enforcing drug, immigration, and naturalization laws.

Selected Agencies Within DOJ

The **Bureau of Alcohol, Tobacco, Firearms, and Explosives** (ATF) is a law enforcement agency within the DOJ. Its unique responsibilities include protecting the public and reducing violent crime. ATF enforces the federal laws and regulations relating to alcohol and tobacco diversion, firearms, explosives, and arson. It works to suppress and prevent crime and violence through enforcement, regulation, and community outreach; ensure fair and proper revenue collection; provide fair and effective industry regulation; assist federal, state, local, and international law enforcement; and provide innovative training programs in support of criminal and regulatory enforcement functions.

ATF has employees at headquarters and in 23 field offices. In addition, the Office of Laboratory Services is staffed by over 120 chemists, document analysts, fingerprint specialists, firearm and toolmark examiners, firearm technicians, and administrative support personnel. Other types of jobs at ATF include: fingerprint identification, security administration, and intelligence, classification specialists, and administrative and support staff.

★ Web site: http://www.atf.gov/

★ Job vacancies: http://www.atf.gov/jobs/joblist.htm

★ Headquarters contacts: http://www.atf.gov/contact/hq.htm

★ Details about student employment programs:
  http://www.atf.gov/jobs/links/studentprog.htm

★ Field divisions nationwide: http://www.atf.gov/field/index.htm

★ Descriptions of employee benefits: http://www.atf.gov/jobs/links/benefits.htm

The **Criminal Division** develops, enforces, and supervises the application of all federal criminal laws except those specifically assigned to other divisions. The Division, and the 93 U.S. Attorneys, has the responsibility for overseeing criminal matters under more than 900 statutes as well as certain civil litigation. Criminal Division attorneys prosecute many nationally significant cases. In addition to its direct litigation responsibilities, the Division formulates and implements criminal enforcement policy and provides advice and assistance. For example, the Division approves or monitors sensitive areas of law enforcement such as participation in the

Witness Security Program and the use of electronic surveillance; advises the attorney general, Congress, the Office of Management Budget, and the White House on matters of criminal law; provides legal advice and assistance to federal prosecutors and investigative agencies; and provides leadership for coordinating international as well as federal, state, and local law enforcement matters.

★ Web site: http://www.usdoj.gov/criminal/criminal-home.html

★ Job vacancies: http://www.usdoj.gov/criminal/employment/vacancies.html

★ Headquarters contacts: http://www.usdoj.gov/criminal/contacts.html

The **Federal Bureau of Investigation** (FBI) is the investigative arm of the DOJ. Its priorities are to protect the U.S. from terrorist attacks, from foreign intelligence operations, and from cyber-based attacks and high-technology crimes; combat public corruption at all levels; protect civil rights; combat international and national organized crime, major white-collar crime, and significant violent crime; support law enforcement and intelligence partners; and upgrade FBI technology.

The best-known career at FBI is the special agent. Other positions include computer specialist, crime scene specialist, linguist, fingerprint expert, intelligence research specialist, laboratory tech, accounting professional, laborer, and secretary.

★ Web site: http://www.fbi.gov/

★ Job vacancies: https://www.fbijobs.com/joblist.asp

★ Special agent vacancies: https://www.fbijobs.com/jobdesc.asp?requisitionid=368

★ Intelligence analyst vacancies: https://www.fbijobs.com/Trans.asp

★ Headquarters contacts: http://www.fbi.gov/contactus.htm

★ Internships: https://www.fbijobs.com/intern.asp

★ Employment FAQs: https://www.fbijobs.com/Faq.htm

★ Links to field offices: http://www.fbi.gov/contact/fo/fo.htm

★ Career fairs: https://www.fbijobs.com/fairs.asp

The **Office of Justice** (OJP) provides federal leadership in developing the country's capacity to prevent and control crime, improve the criminal and juvenile justice systems, increase knowledge about crime and related issues, and assist crime victims. It is organized into five bureaus: the Bureau of Justice Assistance, the Bureau of Justice Statistics, the National Institute of Justice, the Office of Juvenile Justice and Delinquency Prevention, and the Office for Victims of Crime.

★ Web site: http://www.ojp.usdoj.gov/

★ Job vacancies: http://www.ojp.usdoj.gov/op/

★ Headquarters contacts: http://www.ojp.usdoj.gov/dir.htm

The **Tax Division** handles or supervises civil and criminal matters that arise under the internal revenue laws. The Tax Division strives to ensure consistent application and uniform enforcement of the internal revenue code in order to promote compliance with the tax laws and maintain confidence in the integrity of the tax system. Tax Division attorneys work closely with the Internal Revenue Service and U.S. Attorneys to develop tax administration policies; handle civil trial and appellate litigation in federal and state courts; pursue federal grand jury investigations; and handle criminal prosecutions and appeals.

★ Web site: http://www.usdoj.gov/tax/

★ Job vacancies: http://www.usdoj.gov/tax/vacancies.htm

★ Headquarters contacts: http://www.usdoj.gov/tax/contact.htm

★ Details about student employment programs: http://www.usdoj.gov/tax/students.htm

★ Legal intern program: http://www.usdoj.gov/oarm/arm/int/legalinternjq.htm

The **United States Marshals Service** is the nation's oldest and most versatile federal law enforcement agency. Since 1789, federal marshals have served the nation through a variety of vital law enforcement activities. Ninety-five U.S. marshals, appointed by the president or the U.S. attorney general, direct the activities of 94 district offices and personnel stationed at more than 350 locations throughout the country, Guam, Northern Mariana Islands, Puerto Rico, and the Virgin Islands.

The Marshals Service is involved in virtually every federal law enforcement initiative. Approximately 4,200 deputy marshals and career employees perform the following nationwide, day-to-day missions: protection of federal judicial officials, which includes judges, attorneys, and jurors; apprehension of federal fugitives; insurance of the safety of witnesses who risk their lives testifying for the government; transportation of prisoners and illegal aliens; management and disposal of seized and forfeited properties acquired by criminals through illegal activities; service to most federal court criminal process.

★ Web site: http://www.usdoj.gov/marshals/

★ Headquarters contacts: http://www.usmarshals.gov/contacts/index.html

★ Local contacts for recruitment information: http://www.usmarshals.gov/careers/dros.htm

★ Hiring process: http://www.usmarshals.gov/careers/exam.htm

★ Basic training: http://www.usmarshals.gov/careers/basic_training.htm

★ Descriptions of employee benefits: http://www.usmarshals.gov/careers/benefits.htm

The **U.S. Trustee Program** oversees the administration of bankruptcy cases and private trustees. It consists of 21 regional U.S. Trustee Offices nationwide and an executive office for U.S. Trustees in Washington, D.C. It works to secure the just, speedy, and economical resolution of bankruptcy cases; monitors the conduct of parties and takes action to ensure compliance with applicable laws and procedures; identifies and investigates bankruptcy fraud and abuse; and oversees administrative functions in bankruptcy cases.

★ Web site: http://www.usdoj.gov/ust/

★ Job vacancies: http://www.usdoj.gov/ust/vacancies/trusteevacs.htm

★ Headquarters contacts: http://www.usdoj.gov/ust/about_ustp.htm#contact

★ List of offices nationwide: http://www.usdoj.gov/ust/regional_links.htm

Other DOJ Agencies

Antitrust Division
http://www.usdoj.gov/atr/index.html

Attorney General
http://www.usdoj.gov/ag/index.html

Bureau of Prisons
http://www.bop.gov/

Civil Division
http://www.usdoj.gov/civil/home.html

Civil Rights Division
http://www.usdoj.gov/crt/crt-home.html

Environment and Natural Resources Division
http://www.usdoj.gov/enrd/

The Executive Office for Immigration Review
http://www.usdoj.gov/eoir/

The Executive Office for U.S. Attorneys
http://www.usdoj.gov/usao/eousa/

Drug Enforcement Administration
http://www.usdoj.gov/dea/

Foreign Claims Settlement Commission
http://www.usdoj.gov/fcsc/

Justice Management Division
http://www.usdoj.gov/jmd/

National Criminal Justice Reference Service
http://www.ncjrs.org/

National Drug Intelligence Center
http://www.usdoj.gov/ndic/index.htm

National Institute of Corrections
http://www.nicic.org/

The Office of Intelligence Policy and Review
http://www.usdoj.gov/oipr/

The Office of the Pardon Attorney
http://www.usdoj.gov/pardon/

The Office of the Solicitor General
http://www.usdoj.gov/osg/

The Office of Tribal Justice
http://www.usdoj.gov/otj/index.html

United States National Central Bureau of INTERPOL
http://www.usdoj.gov/usncb/

United States Parole Commission
http://www.usdoj.gov/uspc/

Sample Job Vacancies

Biologist (Forensic Examiner)
Agency: Federal Bureau of Investigation
Salary: $50,593 to $93,742
Location: Quantico, Virginia

Job description summary: Serves as a forensic examiner responsible for planning, coordinating, and directing forensic science activities. Inventories, examines, and performs comprehensive technical analysis of evidence such as DNA in body fluid stains and body tissues and forensic serology of blood and other body fluids. Prepares oral and written reports. Presents testimony in court. Locates, identifies, reconstructs, and preserves pertinent items of evidence for examinations from crime scenes.

Minimum qualifications required: Bachelor's degree in biology, chemistry, or forensic science along with course work in subjects which provide a basic understanding of the foundation of forensic DNA analysis and statistics. Must have one year of professional work experience in biochemistry, genetics, and molecular biology performed in a laboratory setting, which includes the successful analysis of a range of DNA samples. Must be able to identify colors and judge difference in colors, estimate size, and lift moderate to heavy objects up to 50 pounds or more.

Minimum application materials required: Applications (resume and application questions) for this vacancy must be received online via the FBIjobs Online Application System.

Special requirements: Must be a U.S. citizen and consent to a complete background investigation, urinalysis, and polygraph. If selected, must successfully complete a two-year training program necessary for certification as an FBI Forensic Examiner. Must sign a training agreement to remain a Forensic Examiner for three times the length it takes to be certified as an examiner.

Clinical Nurse

Agency: Health Services Department, Federal Medical Center, Bureau of Prisons
Salary: $52,962 to $66,201
Location: Devens, Massachusetts

Job description summary: Guides, directs and supervises patient care and the quality of work completed by nursing staff. Monitors and evaluates nursing practices to promote consistency in performance and ensure safe patient care. Serves as a resource person to other nursing staff. Provides health services along with other health professionals. The primary duties of this position require direct and frequent contact with inmates

Minimum qualifications required: Must be a registered nurse with three full years of progressively higher-level graduate education or a Ph.D. Must have one year of directly related experience.

Minimum application materials required: Submit a resume, Optional Application for Federal Employment (OF-612), or other written format of your choice. Include narrative responses to the following KSAs: 1) ability to communicate orally and in writing; 2) ability to interpret and apply policies and guidelines; 3) ability to make decisions in emergency situations; 4) ability to perform supervisory and administrative duties using principles and techniques of supervision.

Special requirements: All appointments are contingent upon successful completion of a three-week training course, "Introduction to Correctional Techniques" at the Federal Law Enforcement Training Center in Glynco, Georgia. Must pass a drug test, as well as a physical and a background investigation.

Historian

Agency: Criminal Division, Office of Special Investigations
Salary: $85,210 to $110,775
Location: Washington, D.C.

Job description summary: Responsible for the full range of research, development, and presentation of complex material in support of litigation pertaining to the perpetration of war crimes and crimes against humanity during World War II. Initiates research activities and prepares studies that are complex and typically include a variety of fields of history. Conducts analysis for current and long-term planning and policy deliberations.

Minimum qualifications required: Must have a Ph.D. in Russian, German, Hungarian, or East European History or completion of all requirements for a Ph.D. except the dissertation or equivalent demonstrated ability to conduct research in and analyze primary source material relating to Russian, German, Hungarian or East European history in the period 1919-1945. Must have one year of specialized experience related to the position. Must be either fluent in Russian, Ukrainian, or Hungarian and in English, and have excellent reading and speaking ability in German; OR fluent in German and English, and have excellent reading and speaking ability in an Eastern European language. Must have experience in conducting historical research in support of World War II war crimes litigation.

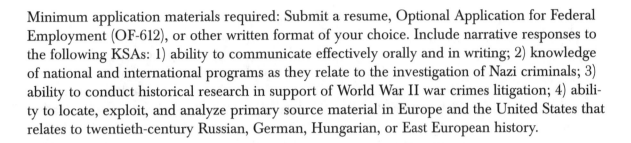

Minimum application materials required: Submit a resume, Optional Application for Federal Employment (OF-612), or other written format of your choice. Include narrative responses to the following KSAs: 1) ability to communicate effectively orally and in writing; 2) knowledge of national and international programs as they relate to the investigation of Nazi criminals; 3) ability to conduct historical research in support of World War II war crimes litigation; 4) ability to locate, exploit, and analyze primary source material in Europe and the United States that relates to twentieth-century Russian, German, Hungarian, or East European history.

Support Service Clerk
Agency: Federal Bureau of Investigation
Salary: $26,699 to $34,714
Location: Jackson, Mississippi

Job description summary: Operates the radio base station to support agents and other investigative personnel in the field. Serves as a Law Enforcement Communications Network (LECN) operator for the field office. Provides assistance to officers by conducting searches of databases and entering and modifying information stored within the LECN. Provides telecommunications equipment support for a variety of systems used throughout the office. Types and transcribes documents.

Minimum qualifications required: One year of education above high school. Must have six months of general experience performing clerical or office work such as duplicating documents; processing mail; keeping records; and compiling, maintaining, updating data, lists, and reports in support of an organization's operations.

Minimum application materials required: Submit an online applications and resume via the FBIjobs Online Application System.

Special requirements: Male applicants born after December 31, 1959, must have registered with the Selective Service System. Must be a U.S. citizen and consent to a complete background investigation, urinalysis, and polygraph.

Victim-Witness Specialist
Agency: Executive Office U.S. Attorneys and Office of U.S. Attorneys
Salary: $41,045 to $77,382
Location: Seattle, Washington

Job description summary: Serves as an advocate and point of contact for activities relating to victim-witness assistance programs. Establishes and maintains mutual communication between the U.S. Attorney's Office and federal, state, and local community organizations concerned with promoting the rights of victims and witnesses under applicable law, as well as providing direct services to crime victims and witnesses relevant to legal activities. Analyzes local district programs and audiences and identifies the informational needs of victims and witnesses; develops and disseminates information, ensuring that litigative activities are promoted through a comprehensive victim-witness program.

Minimum qualifications required: Must have one year of specialized experience in or related to the work of the position; OR a master's degree in a related field.

Minimum application materials required: Submit a resume, Optional Application for Federal Employment (OF-612), or other written format of your choice. Include narrative responses to the following KSAs: 1) knowledge of victim advocacy programs, policies, regulations, and procedures; 2) knowledge of crisis intervention, social service case management, or the provision of direct services to targeted groups; 3) knowledge of state and local law enforcement organizations to which applicable federal statues apply; 4) ability to communicate orally and in writing; 5) knowledge and ability to conduct workshops, seminars, and other meetings with a variety of groups both within and outside of the Office.

Special requirements: Males born after December 31, 1959, must have registered with the Selective Service System. Must be a U.S. citizen.

Writer-Editor

Agency: Bureau of Alcohol, Tobacco, Firearms, and Explosives
Salary: $43,209 to $65,769
Location: Washington, D.C.

Job description summary: Analyzes, develops, and edits various written materials including procedures, directives, reports, briefing papers, etc., essential to the Bureau's firearms enforcement effort. Conducts research projects involving firearms enforcement and related matters. Writes, edits, and finalizes manuscript copies of information documents (such as ATF orders), technical reports, forms etc. Maintains forms and directives catalogs and publications. Submits timely updates to the appropriate offices within the Bureau for publication.

Minimum qualifications required: Must have one year of specialized experience in researching and extracting data from numerous sources and in composing and editing a variety of manuscripts and other written materials.

Minimum application materials required: Submit a resume or Optional Application for Federal Employment (OF-612) by e-mail. Include narrative responses to the following KSAs: 1) ability to accurately compose and edit a variety of written materials; 2) ability to analyze and make sound judgments; 3) ability to conduct research and extract data from numerous sources; 4) ability to meet and deal with a variety of people at all levels.

Special requirements: Must be a U.S. citizen. Must be able to obtain and keep a secret security clearance. A preemployment background investigation is required.

Department of Labor

200 Constitution Avenue NW
Washington, D.C. 20210
202-693-5000

★ Web site: http://www.dol.gov/

★ Job vacancies: http://www.doors.dol.gov/index.asp

★ USAJOBS By Phone: 912-757-3000

★ Internship information: http://www.dol.gov/_sec/media/internprogram.htm

★ State Labor offices: http://www.dol.gov/esa/contacts/state_of.htm

★ Fellows programs:
http://www.dol.gov/oasam/doljobs/MBA_Outreach_Program/mba_outreach_page1.htm

★ Starting a career with DOL:
http://www.dol.gov/oasam/doljobs/what_you_should_know.htm

★ Benefits: http://www.dol.gov/oasam/doljobs/paybenefits.htm

★ Information about student employment: http://www.dol.gov/oasam/doljobs/
college-guide.htm

The purpose of the Department of Labor (DOL) is to foster, promote, and develop the wel-fare of the wage earners of the United States, to improve their working conditions, and to advance their opportunities for profitable employment. In carrying out this mission, DOL works to ensure safe and healthful working conditions, a minimum hourly wage and overtime pay, freedom from employment discrimination, unemployment insurance, and workers' com-pensation. DOL also protects workers' pension rights; provides for job training programs; helps workers find jobs; works to strengthen free collective bargaining; and keeps track of changes in employment, prices, and other national economic measurements.

Selected Agencies Within DOL

The **Bureau of International Labor Affairs** (ILAB) assists in formulating international eco-nomic, trade, and immigration policies affecting American workers. The Bureau represents the United States on delegations to multilateral and bilateral trade negotiations, and on such international bodies as the General Agreement on Tariffs and Trade (GATT), the International Labor Organization (ILO), the Organization for Economic Cooperation and Development (OECD), and other U.N. organizations. It also helps administer the U.S. labor attaché pro-gram at embassies abroad; carries out overseas technical assistance projects; monitors inter-nationally recognized worker rights; and conducts labor study programs for foreign visitors to the United States. ILAB has established itself as one of the most important and reliable sources of information on the exploitation of child labor around the world.

★ Web site: http://www.dol.gov/ilab/

★ Headquarters contacts: http://www.dol.gov/ILAB/contacts/main.htm

★ Links to offices: http://www.dol.gov/ILAB/programs/offices.htm

The **Bureau of Labor Statistics** is the principal fact-finding agency for the Federal Govern-ment in the broad field of labor economics and statistics. The BLS is an independent national statistical agency that collects, processes, analyzes, and disseminates essential statistical data to the American public, Congress, other federal agencies, state and local governments, business, and labor. The BLS also serves as a statistical resource to the Department of Labor. BLS hires economists, mathematical statisticians, and computer programmers.

★ Web site: http://www.bls.gov/

★ Job vacancies (Washington, D.C.): http://www.bls.gov/eop/home.htm#openings

★ Job vacancies (regional offices): http://www.bls.gov/roj/home.htm#openings

★ Headquarters contacts: http://www.bls.gov/bls/contact.htm

★ Summer employment programs: http://www.dol.gov/oasam/programs/summer2004/2004-summer-emp-prog.htm

The **Employment and Training Administration** (ETA) ensures that American workers get the employment and training services they need by providing grants to states for training programs, unemployment services, and services for laid-off workers. ETA provides information and services to help workers manage their careers and employers to find skilled workers. These services include a toll-free telephone help line and the online America's Career Kit, which includes America's Job Bank, America's Talent Bank, America's Career InfoNet, and America's Learning Exchange.

★ Web site: http://www.doleta.gov/

★ Job vacancies: http://www.doleta.gov/jobs/ETA_Jobs/vacstat.cfm

★ Headquarters contacts: http://www.dol.gov/dol/contact/index.htm

★ Regional offices: http://www.doleta.gov/regions/regoffices/

The **Mine Safety & Health Administration** enforces compliance with mandatory safety and health standards as a means to eliminate fatal accidents, to reduce the frequency and severity of nonfatal accidents, to minimize health hazards, and to promote improved safety and health conditions in the country's mines. MSHA hires mining, chemical, and electrical engineers; mine safety and health inspectors; and industrial hygienists, among others.

★ Web site: http://www.msha.gov/

★ Job vacancies: http://www.doors.dol.gov/

★ Headquarters contacts: http://www.msha.gov/programs/programs.htm

The **Occupational Safety & Health Administration's** (OSHA) mission is to save lives, prevent injuries, and protect the health of America's workers. To accomplish this, federal and state governments must work in partnership with more than 100 million working men and women and their six and a half million employers who are covered by the Occupational Safety and Health Act of 1970. OSHA's staff establishes protective standards, enforces those standards, and reaches out to employers and employees through technical assistance and consultation programs. **OSHA** hires industrial hygienists, safety engineers, and safety and health specialists, along with administrative and support staff.

★ Web site: http://www.osha.gov/index.html

★ Headquarters contacts: http://www.osha.gov/html/oshdir.html

★ Regional offices: http://www.osha.gov/html/RAmap.html

Other DOL Agencies

Administrative Review Board
http://www.dol.gov/arb/welcome.html

Benefits Review Board
http://www.dol.gov/brb/welcome.html

Center for Faith-Based and Community Initiatives
http://www.dol.gov/cfbci/

Employee Benefits Security Administration
http://www.dol.gov/ebsa/

Employees' Compensation Appeals Board
http://www.dol.gov/ecab/welcome.html

Employment Standards Administration
http://www.dol.gov/esa/

Office of Small Business Programs
http://www.dol.gov/osbp/welcome.html

Office of the Solicitor
http://www.dol.gov/sol/

Office of the 21st Century Workforce
http://www.dol.gov/21cw/welcome.html

Veterans' Employment and Training Service
http://www.dol.gov/vets/

Women's Bureau
http://www.dol.gov/wb/

Sample Job Vacancies

Economics Assistant
Agency: Bureau of Labor Statistics
Salary: $27,715 to $36,035
Location: Pullman, Washington

Job description summary: Collects primary data for the Consumer Price Index (CPI). Prices a wide variety of outlet and product types in establishments which provide retail goods and services to the public. Monitors and reports on local economic conditions affecting retail transactions and trends. Secures initial voluntary cooperation from housing unit inhabitants and reprices rental units for the CPI.

Minimum qualifications required: Must have one year of specialized experience that involved collecting, compiling, verifying, or reporting data.; OR a bachelor's degree with a major in economics. Must be able to communicate effectively orally, to collect and organize data, to plan and organize work independently, and have knowledge of consumer marketing practices.

Minimum application materials required: Submit an Optional Application for Federal Employment (OF-612), or a resume. Must include answers to the following KSAs: 1) ability to perform tasks using automated data processing equipment and supporting software; 2) knowledge of consumer products and services; 3) skill in investigating, analyzing, and resolving a variety of collection problems.

Special requirements: Must have a valid driver's license.

Equal Opportunity Specialist (Spanish Speaking)
Agency: Employment Standards Administration
Salary: $33,951 to $44,136
Location: Dallas, Texas

Job description summary: Conducts evaluation and complaint investigations. Develops strategies for investigation or data collection and analysis; discusses issues which are strongly contested; and negotiates with corporate officials, union officials, and their attorneys and writes reports of investigation. Prepares show-cause notices and recommendations for enforcement action. Analyzes various types of evidence for use in determining basis for administrative or other proceedings. Develops and presents evidence of systemic discrimination. Monitors reports and other activities of contractors to ensure compliance with terms of conciliation agreements and consent decrees. Provides compliance assistance in developing acceptable affirmative action programs to contractors.

Minimum qualifications required: One full year of graduate-level education OR one year of specialized experience in or related to employment programs or investigation processes.

Minimum application materials required: Submit an Optional Application for Federal Employment (OF-612), or a resume. Must include answers to the following KSAs: 1) knowledge of the concepts, principles, and methods of the equal opportunity area; 2) skill in fact finding, analysis, and problem solving; 3) skill in written and oral communication; 4) skill in working effectively with persons regardless of their socioeconomic background.

Special requirements: Must be fluent in Spanish.

International Relations Officer
Agency: Bureau of International Labor Affairs
Salary: $72,108 to $110,775
Location: Washington, D.C.

Job description summary: Develops and evaluates authoritative analysis of child labor issues through study, and monitoring of relevant legislation, bills, and proposed legislation. Develops and prepares in-depth analysis of exploitive child labor at national, regional, and global levels.

Conducts extensive research on exploitive child labor and consults with key agency staff in developing needed material as to the objectives to be achieved. Coordinates child labor policy and directives with other offices in ILAB, in the Department of Labor (DOL) and with other U.S. Government agencies.

Minimum qualifications required: Bachelor's degree in international law and international relations, political science, economics, history, sociology, geography, social or cultural anthropology, law, statistics, or in the humanities. Must have at least one year of specialized experience that included development and oversight of technical assistance/grants programs. Experience should also indicate research experience and knowledge of international child labor or basic education issues.

Minimum application materials required: Submit an Optional Application for Federal Employment (OF-612), or a resume. Must include answers to the following KSAs: 1) knowledge of International relations to serve as a recognized expert to undertake comprehensive analyses of a variety of complex international labor and economic issues, preferably child labor issues; 2) ability to develop or review technical assistance proposals, develop work plans, and monitor their implementation; 3) ability to demonstrate initiative, imagination and originality in the developing and using data and other materials essential to the successful completion of research responsibilities; 4) ability to communicate orally and in writing; 5) interpersonal and administrative skills sufficient to organize a variety of policy issues and initiatives and to coordinate major activities with other staff.

Special requirements: Must obtain and maintain a security clearance.

Manpower Development Specialist
Agency: Employment and Training Administration
Salary: $62,558 to $81,323
Location: Chicago, Illinois

Job description summary: Principal duties involve project manager activities relating to the administration and oversight of the regional Job Corps Program.

Minimum qualifications required: Bachelor's degree. Must have one year of specialized experience in or directly related to employment and training activities.

Minimum application materials required: Submit an Optional Application for Federal Employment (OF-612), or a resume. Must include answers to the following KSAs: 1) identifies rules, principles, or relationships that explain facts, data, or other information; 2) persuades others to accept recommendations, cooperate, or change their behavior; 3) encourages and facilitates cooperation, pride, trust, and group identity; 4) uses correct English grammar, punctuation, and spelling; 5) expresses information to individuals or groups effectively.

Special requirements: Must be a U.S. citizen.

Mathematical Statistician
Agency: Bureau of Labor Statistics
Salary: $28,803 to $69,099
Location: Washington, D.C.

Job description summary: Performs work involving the development and adaptation of mathematical statistical theory and methodology for a wide variety of statistical investigations. Develops and refines sample frames and defines and implements that sample. Designs surveys. Measures the quality of the data collected and improves the data collection and processing procedures. Derives or selects appropriate estimation procedures and prepares written systems requirements. Evaluates the results of surveys with respect to sample design and accuracy. Researches and develops statistical measures and procedures to improve surveys.

Minimum qualifications required: Bachelor's degree in statistics; OR a combination of education and four year's experience performing duties such as sampling, collecting, computing, and analyzing statistical data; applying known statistical techniques such as measurement of central tendency, dispersion, skewness, sampling error, and simple and multiple correlation; conducting analysis of variance; and conducting tests of significance.

Minimum application materials required: Submit an Optional Application for Federal Employment (OF-612), or a resume. Must include answers to the following KSAs: 1) develop programs and apply statistical applications using statistical packages such as SPSS, STATA, or SUDAAN; 2) use basic office software packages that include two of the following: word processors, spreadsheets, and graphics and presentation programs; 3) use database programs; 4) use Geographic Information Systems; 5) use symbolic manipulation software; 6) develop programs using programming languages; 7 use Web site tools and languages; 8) perform software testing; 9) develop software applications in a UNIX environment.

Special requirements: Must be a U.S. citizen. Male applicants born after December 31, 1959, must have registered with the Selective Service System.

Mining Engineer
Agency: Mine Safety and Health Administration
Salary: $27,287 to $60,317
Location: Bruceton, Pennsylvania

Job description summary: Serves as an investigator of roof-control problems and other ground-control problems. Performs field investigations of roof-control problems in underground mines using existing rock mechanics techniques and methods of evaluating the performance of roof supports. Conducts laboratory investigations to determine the effectiveness of new and existing roof support methods. Attends meetings and conferences with federal, state, and private organizations to obtain and provide information relative to roof control.

Minimum qualifications required: Bachelor's degree in professional mining engineering; OR a combination of education and experience. Must have one year of professional engineering experience performing nonroutine engineering.

Minimum application materials required: Submit an Optional Application for Federal Employment (OF-612), or a resume. Must include answers to the following KSAs: 1) knowledge of mining methods and roof control theories; 2) ability to work as a team member in the investigation and analysis of mining systems, materials, and equipment; 3) ability to communicate orally and in writing.

Special requirements: Must have a valid driver's license and pass a medical examination.

Safety and Occupational Health Specialist

Agency: Occupational Safety and Health Administration
Salary: $52,650 to $82,031
Location: Hasbrouck Heights, New Jersey

Job description summary: Performs a variety of safety inspections in workplaces. Documents case files, describes hazards in detail, cites the detailed provision of standards allegedly violated. Calculates penalties and proposes abatement action required. Provides testimony in cases under contest. Provides technical clarification of standards and explanations of agency policy, procedures and directives. Explains substance of agency programs to employers, employees, and general public. Provides assistance to the employers and employee representatives concerning recognition and correction of hazards. Participates in outreach activities.

Minimum qualifications required: Ph.D. in a related field; OR one year of specialized experience which demonstrates knowledge of OSHA standards or related codes; expertise in analyzing work processes and conditions and identifying and eliminating/controlling safety and occupational health hazards; OR broad knowledge in two or three industries as it applies to analyzing work processes and conditions, identifying and eliminating/controlling safety and occupational health hazards. Computer skills are desirable.

Minimum application materials required: Submit an Optional Application for Federal Employment (OF-612), or a resume. Must include answers to the following KSAs: 1) skill in enforcement of safety and occupational health standards or related codes; 2) skill in conducting reconstructive investigations or other complex investigations; 3) ability to prepare narrative reports of a technical or enforcement nature; 4) ability to communicate technical information and interact with individuals with diverse backgrounds and levels of understanding.

Special requirements: Must be fluent in Spanish. Must pass a medical examination. Must have a valid drivers license. Must pass a drug test.

Supervisory Physical Security Specialist

Agency: Office of Assistant Secretary, Administration and Management
Salary: $72,108 to $93,742
Location: Washington, D.C.

Job description summary: Initiates and develops policy and procedures, and ensures compliance with the physical security program; plans, organizes, develops, coordinates, and evaluates the DOL security program; prepares technical reports and briefings to record security issues and develops documentation and justification of implementation or procurement of those recommendations; conducts surveys, researches specific topics, and replies to correspondence and prepares briefings or information on topics relating to information security. Responds to requests for security guidance and assistance as required.

Minimum qualifications required: Bachelor's degree in a related field. One year of specialized experience in planning, organizing, developing, coordinating, and evaluating a security program; identifying risks, threats, and vulnerabilities; or physical protection of sensitive or classified information, personnel, facilities, installations, resources, or processes against criminal, terrorist, or hostile activities.

Minimum application materials required: Submit an Optional Application for Federal Employment (OF-612) or a resume. Must include answers to the following KSAs: 1) knowledge of physical security and creating secure environments using effective countermeasures, and experience with various security disciplines; 2) skill in developing and interpreting security legislation, department policies, and regulations and in the implementation of security awareness programs; 3) skill in the theory and operation of sophisticated protective systems (e.g., access controls, intrusion detection equipment, and protective personnel) and their application to building design; 4) skill in oral and written communication; 5) experience in supervising and managing security personnel.

Special requirements: This position requires a Top Secret security clearance and a supervisory/managerial probationary period.

Veterans' Employment Representative
Agency: Veterans Employment and Training Service
Salary: $40,454 to $63,629
Location: Madison, Wisconsin

Job description summary: Participates in the review and evaluation of services provided to veterans under job service program operations. Maintains current job market information and training opportunities for eligible veterans. Attends meetings with employers, program staff, and veterans' organizations. Advises State Employment Security Agency staff on requirements and limitations of programs. Accompanies specialists to meetings with veterans and employers where Uniformed Services Employment and Reemployment Rights Act (USERRA) problems are discussed. Assists the state director with the Transition Assistance Program, providing liaison within the state, coordinating and monitoring the presentation of program information to members of the armed forces.

Minimum qualifications required: One year of specialized experience in or directly related to the line of work of the position; OR a master's degree.

Minimum application materials required: Submit an Optional Application for Federal Employment (OF-612), or a resume. Must include answers to the following KSAs: 1) knowledge of recruitment, selection, placement, or occupational training involving public relations or personnel administration with employers, employment offices, veterans organizations or trade associations; 2) ability to maintain effective working relationship with potential employers, civic groups and Veteran agencies; 3) knowledge of the federal grant process, applicable statues and policies; 4) knowledge of federal and state laws regarding Veterans' employment and reemployment rights; 5) ability to communicate effectively in writing with individuals, agencies, and organizations concerning employment matters.

Special requirements: Must be a U.S. citizen.

Workers' Compensation Claims Examiner
Agency: Employment Standards Administration
Salary: $33,739 to $53,653
Location: Cleveland, Ohio

Job description summary: Develops and adjudicates claims under the Federal Employees' Compensation Act. Obtains witness statements, medical evidence, employment records, etc., from claimant, employing agency, and other sources. Provides technical information to interested parties. Resolves conflicts, weighs evidence, and prepares Statement of Accepted Facts. Authorizes medical treatment and compensation payments and is responsible for case management, including vocational rehabilitation.

Minimum qualifications required: Bachelor's degree. One year of specialized experience in the line of work of the position.

Minimum application materials required: Submit an Optional Application for Federal Employment (OF-612), or a resume. Must include answers to the following KSAs: 1) ability to comprehend complex, legal, medical procedural information; 2) ability to communicate effectively orally and in writing; 3) ability to analyze and identify rules, principles, and relationships that explains facts and draw conclusions; 4) ability to set well-defined and realistic personal goals.

Special requirements: Must be a U.S. citizen.

Department of State

2201 C Street NW
Washington, D.C. 20520
202-647-4000

★ Web site: http://www.state.gov/

★ Job vacancies: http://jobsearch.usajobs.opm.gov/a9st00.asp

★ USAJOBS By Phone: 912-757-3000

★ Student employment information: http://www.careers.state.gov/student/

★ Benefits, civil service: http://www.careers.state.gov/civil/benefits.html

★ Job categories, civil service: http://www.careers.state.gov/civil/c_search.html

★ Links to offices and programs worldwide: http://www.careers.state.gov/abt_where.html

★ How to apply: http://www.careers.state.gov/civil/c_steps.html

★ Steps to Becoming a Foreign Service Specialist: http://careers.state.gov/specialist/apply.html

★ Employment FAQs: http://www.careers.state.gov/faqs.html

★ Job information via e-mail: http://www.careers.state.gov/informed.html

★ Contact information: http://www.careers.state.gov/contact.html

The Department of State (DOS) advises the president in the formulation and execution of foreign policy and promotes the long-range security and well-being of the United States. DOS determines and analyzes the facts relating to American overseas interests, makes recommendations on policy and future action, and takes the necessary steps to carry out established policy. DOS engages in continuous consultations with the American public, the Congress, other U.S. departments and agencies, and foreign governments; negotiates treaties and agreements with foreign nations; speaks for the United States in the U.N. and other international organizations in which the United States participates; and represents the United States at international conferences.

The United States maintains diplomatic relations with nearly 180 of the 191 countries in the world, as well as with many international organizations. DOS maintains nearly 265 diplomatic and consular posts around the world, including embassies, consulates, and missions to international organizations. The Foreign Service and the Civil Service for the U.S. Department of State represent the American people, working together to achieve the goals and implement the initiatives of American foreign policy. The Foreign Service employs nine thousand people. A Foreign Service career is a way of life that offers unique rewards, opportunities, and sometimes hardships. Members of the Foreign Service can be sent to any embassy, consulate, or other diplomatic mission anywhere in the world, to serve the diplomatic needs of the United States. The Foreign Service selection process is lengthy, multistaged, and highly competitive. For detailed information about the process, see the link "Steps to becoming a Foreign Service Specialist."

There are about 65,000 Civil Service employees, headquartered primarily in Washington D.C., who are involved in virtually every area of the Department—from human rights to narcotics control to trade to environmental issues. They also are the domestic counterpart to consular officers abroad, issuing passports and assisting U.S. citizens in trouble overseas.

Selected Agencies Within DOS

The **Bureau of Diplomatic Security** (DS) is responsible for providing a safe and secure environment for the conduct of U.S. foreign policy. Every diplomatic mission in the world operates under a security program designed and maintained by Diplomatic Security. In the United States, DS investigates passport and visa fraud, conducts personnel security investigations, and protects the secretary of state and high-ranking foreign dignitaries and officials visiting the United States. DS trains foreign civilian law enforcement officers in disciplines designed to reduce the threat and repercussions of terrorism throughout the world. Through the Office of Foreign Missions, the bureau manages reciprocity and immunity issues for foreign diplomats in the United States.

★ Web site: http://www.state.gov/m/ds/

★ Career opportunities: http://www.state.gov/m/ds/career/

★ Headquarters contacts: http://www.state.gov/m/ds/contact/

The **Bureau for International Narcotics and Law Enforcement Affairs** (INL) advises the president, secretary of state, other bureaus in the Department of State, and other departments and agencies within the U.S. government on the development of policies and programs to combat international narcotics and crime.

★ Web site: http://www.state.gov/g/inl/

★ International Law Enforcement Academies: http://www.state.gov/g/inl/ilea/

★ International Civilian Police Program: http://www.state.gov/g/inl/civ/

The **Bureau of International Organization Affairs** (IO) develops and implements U.S. policy in the UN, the UN's specialized agencies, and other international organizations. IO works to advance U.S. policies and interests through multilateral diplomacy and to ensure that the UN and other international organizations remain viable and effective.

★ Web site: http://www.state.gov/p/io/

★ Job vacancies: http://www.state.gov/p/io/empl/

★ U.S. Mission to the United Nations: http://www.un.int/usa/

The **Bureau of Population, Refugees, and Migration** formulates policies on population, refugees, and migration, and administers U.S. refugee assistance and admissions programs.

★ Web site: http://www.state.gov/g/prm/

★ Junior professional officer program: http://www.state.gov/g/prm/c7977.htm

The **Foreign Service Institute** (FSI) is the federal government's primary training institution for officers and support personnel of the U.S. foreign affairs community, preparing American diplomats and other professionals to advance U.S. foreign affairs interests overseas and in Washington. At the George P. Shultz National Foreign Affairs Training Center, FSI provides more than 450 courses, including some 70 foreign languages, to more than 50,000 enrollees a year from the State Department and more than 40 other government agencies and the military service branches.

★ Web site: http://www.state.gov/m/fsi/

★ Transition center: http://www.state.gov/m/fsi/tc/

The **Health, Space and Science Directorate** includes the Office of International Health Affairs which works with U.S. Government agencies to facilitate policy-making regarding international bioterrorism, infectious disease, surveillance and response, environmental health, and health in postconflict situations. The Office of Space and Advanced Technology handles issues arising from our exploration of space to assure global security regarding this new frontier, and the Office of Science & Technology Cooperation promotes the interests of the U.S. science and technology communities in the international policy arena.

★ Web site: http://www.state.gov/g/oes/

The **Office of Protocol** directly advises, assists, and supports the president of the United States, the vice president, and the secretary of state on official matters of national and international protocol, and in the planning, hosting, and officiating of related ceremonial events and activities for visiting heads of state. The Office also is the administrator of Blair House, the president's official guesthouse. The Office of Protocol serves as the coordinator within and between the Department and the White House on all protocol matters for presidential or vice presidential travel abroad. The chief of protocol, the deputy chief, and four assistant chiefs share responsibility for officiating the swearing in of senior State Department officials, selection boards, and incoming Foreign Service and Civil Service employees.

★ Web site: http://www.state.gov/s/cpr/

Other DOS Agencies

Bureau of Administration
http://www.state.gov/m/a/

Bureau of African Affairs
http://www.state.gov/p/af/

Bureau of Arms Control
http://www.state.gov/t/ac/

Bureau of Consular Affairs
http://travel.state.gov/

Bureau of Democracy, Human Rights, and Labor
http://www.state.gov/g/drl/

Bureau of East Asian and Pacific Affairs
http://www.state.gov/p/eap/

Bureau of Economic and Business Affairs
http://www.state.gov/e/eb/

Bureau of European and Eurasian Affairs
http://www.state.gov/p/eur/

Bureau of Intelligence and Research
http://www.state.gov/s/inr/

Bureau of International Information Programs
http://www.state.gov/r/iip/

Bureau of Near Eastern Affairs
http://www.state.gov/p/nea/

Bureau of Nonproliferation
http://www.state.gov/t/np/

Bureau of Oceans and International Environmental and Scientific Affairs
http://www.state.gov/g/oes/

Bureau of Overseas Buildings Operations
http://www.state.gov/obo/

Bureau of Political-Military Affairs
http://www.state.gov/t/pm/

Bureau of South Asian Affairs
http://www.state.gov/p/sa/

Bureau of Verification and Compliance
http://www.state.gov/t/vc/

Bureau of Western Hemisphere Affairs
http://www.state.gov/p/wha/

Sample Job Vacancies

Audio-Visual Production Specialist
Agency: Office Facilities Branch, Interiors and Furnishings Division, Office of Project Execution, Overseas Building Operations
Salary: $50,593 to $78,826
Location: Washington, D.C.

Job description summary: Serves as an Interior Design Computer Aided Design and Drafting (CADD) Specialist. Works with an in-house technical team to facilitate the planning, design, and management of government-owned and operated buildings overseas. Designs and produces design documentation, graphics and artwork for publication and distribution; provides CADD technical expertise and support; coordinates CADD operational standards, procedures, and drafting techniques for the interior architectural design, space planning, and furnishing layouts of buildings and compounds; provides three-dimensional modeling and rendering for use in a variety of presentation types; and provides drafting support as required to support the Division's project workload.

Minimum qualifications required: One year of experience communicating designs and developing detailed drawings for interior architectural design, space planning, and furnishings layouts, primarily through use of a Computer-Aided Design and Drafting (CADD) system; providing three-dimensional modeling and rendering for use in a variety of presentation types; producing slides, transparencies, photographs, line art and illustrations, charts, pamphlets, booklets, and brochures in terms of objectives and time frames; and designing and displaying creative visual products utilizing print and electronic dissemination media; OR a Ph.D. in visual communication, commercial art, or another field directly related to this position.

Minimum application materials required: Submit a resume or Application for Federal Employment (OF-612), and a completed Occupational Questionnaire from the vacancy announcement. Include a narrative response to the following statement: Tell us about your experience related to the above minimum qualifications.

Special requirements: Males born after December 31, 1959, must have registered with the Selective Service System.

Foreign Service Construction Engineer
Agency: Office of Foreign Buildings Operations
Salary: $36,703 to $66,519
Location: Worldwide

Job description summary: Oversees, evaluates, approves, prepares, and coordinates a variety of construction activities, such as oversees contractor activities on new or existing properties used by the Department of State and other oversees agencies; inspects construction work for contract compliance; renders technical interpretations of plans and specifications; reviews and approves contractor submittals; evaluates, negotiates and approves change order proposals; evaluates and participates in settlement of contractor claims and disputes.

Minimum qualifications required: Bachelor's degree in architecture, architectural engineering, construction engineering, construction management, civil/structural engineering, electrical engineering, or mechanical engineering Must have one year of specialized experience that shows that you have an in-depth knowledge of your field and can be expected to perform engineering or architectural duties related to construction at Department of State projects worldwide.

Minimum application materials required: Submit an Application for Federal Employment (DS-1950), supplementary material (college transcripts, current licenses), a two-page autobiography, and the completed Supplementary Questionnaire from the vacancy announcement addressing the following questions: 1) ability to work toward a common goal; 2) skill in organizing and planning in accomplishing complex tasks according to a firm schedule; 3) ability to think logically and objectively, to analyze problems, and to apply sound judgment in assessing the practical implications of alternative solutions; 4) ability to communicate effectively and persuasively both orally and in writing; 5) skill in using computer software in managing construction-related projects; 6) summarize your knowledge, skills, and abilities which would apply to a career as a Foreign Service Construction Engineer.

Foreign Service English Language Officer

Agency: Bureau of Educational and Cultural Affairs
Salary: $57,410 to $84,309
Location: Worldwide and Washington, D.C.

Job description summary: Foreign Service English Language Officers (ELOs) provide professional expertise and program support to U.S. embassies and consulates around the world through a variety of responsibilities, such as counseling U.S. mission officials in the most effective use of English language programs to meet the post's Public Diplomacy and Mission goals; establishing contacts with host country education officials and academic institutions involved in delivering English language programs; evaluating and reporting to Washington on the English language programs in the geographic area of regional responsibility and recommending new programs; providing academic and programmatic guidance for Embassy-sponsored English Teaching Programs for certain embassies in Africa, the Near East, and East Asia.

Minimum qualifications required: Master's degree in Teaching English as a Foreign Language. Must have five years of TEFL experience, two of which must be overseas; two year's experience in program administration; and two year's experience in teacher training. The ability to draft an essay demonstrating a strong command of English grammar, spelling and punctuation is essential. A passing grade on the written essay allows the applicant to proceed to the personal interview and oral assessment portion of the candidate selection process, all to be carried out in Washington, D.C.

Minimum application materials required: Submit an Application for Federal Employment (DS-1950), supplementary material (college transcripts), and a completed Supplementary

Questionnaire from the vacancy announcement addressing the following two questions:
1) Describe a specific example or examples of your leadership and managerial abilities in an English language program; evaluate the impact of this action and project how these experiences might apply to your job as an English Language Officer. 2) Describe specific examples which demonstrate your experience in planning and implementing significant English language programs in teacher training, curriculum design, or materials development. Describe how you evaluated the success of the program and assess the long-term effects, if any, of the program.

Foreign Service Health Practitioner

Agency: Foreign Health Service
Salary: $55,901 to $82,093
Location: Worldwide

Job description summary: Provides primary health care at home posts and regional posts to authorized patients. Recommends and facilitates medical/dental evacuation as necessary. Evaluates the quality of local and regional health care providers and facilities. Establishes and maintains professional relationships with local providers and other health care facilities. Monitors environmental health and safety conditions and acts as liaison with local and U.S. authorities. Assures sanitation surveys and monitors inspection of post food facilities. Provides a proactive disease prevention and health education program at home and regional posts. Prepares Health and Information Booklet. Administers the Health Unit and supervises support staff.

Minimum qualifications required: Must be a Nurse Practitioner (NP) or Physician Assistant (PA). Must have minimum of four years of recent experience providing direct patient care, which includes at least two years' experience as a NP or PA. Must have experience providing primary care. Must have specialized experience in chronic and emergency care, in an independent family or general practice setting. Must demonstrate the ability to manage administrative aspects of a health unit as well as the ability to cope with extraordinary medical crisis, often in remote and isolated settings. Experience in providing long-distance triage and care via electronic communications such as telephone, radio, telegram and e-mail is important. Must understand the unique cultural differences related to health care delivery in varied countries and address these differences in a positive manner. Must be able to write and communicate clearly. Must be computer literate.

Minimum application materials required: Submit an Application for Federal Employment (DS-1950), supplementary material (college transcripts, current license as nurse practitioner or physician's assistant), and a completed Supplementary Questionnaire from the vacancy announcement addressing the following KSAs: 1) experience working with well and acutely ill infants, children, adolescents, and women; 2) ability to care for and stabilize multiple trauma patients prior to a medical evacuation; 3) skill in organizing patient problems and solutions; 4) skill in planning and organizing a multidisciplinary practice; 5) ability to participate as a team member working toward a common goal; 6) skill in public speaking and teaching.

Interior Designer

Agency: Office Facilities Design Branch
Salary: $50,593 to $78,826
Location: Washington, D.C.

Job description summary: Plans for open, closed and executive offices, layout of health and food service delivery areas, communication and mail distribution centers, and library and conference facilities. Highly skilled in all aspects of the design continuum and able to execute all supporting documentation including scopes of work, cost estimates, conceptual and working drawings, schedules and details (both free-hand and CADD-based), background research, calculations and written reports; product specifications for bid and justifications for purchase; written, oral and graphic presentations; and postoccupancy reporting.

Minimum qualifications required: One year of experience developing and implementing interior designs for offices and multiuse commercial facilities being constructed, leased, or refurbished; assisting in establishing architectural guidelines relative to interior designs; coordinating portions of activities to ensure timely completion of projects; researching local markets and manufacturers; estimating costs; developing plans and specifications; ensuring that plans and specifications comply with codes; and assisting in coordinating deliveries and installations, OR a Ph.D. in interior design.

Minimum application materials required: Submit a resume or Optional Application for Federal Employment (OF-612), a completed Occupational Questionnaire from the vacancy announcement, and a narrative response to the following: Please tell us about your experience working on various overseas and domestic office facilities and multiuse commercial facilities being constructed, leased, or refurbished. Describe your responsibilities and the types of buildings for which you have performed interior design.

Special requirements: Males born after December 31, 1959, must have registered with the Selective Service System. Must be able to obtain a Top Secret security clearance.

Physical Scientist

Agency: Bureau of Verification and Compliance, Office of Technology and Assessments
Salary: $72,108 to $110,775
Location: Washington, D.C.

Job description summary: Provides substantive review, evaluation, coordination, and analysis of information related to U.S. arms control and nonproliferation policy objectives in foreign chemical and biological program assessments; extends and refines existing methods and develops new approaches to the analysis of critical policy issues; and conducts detailed technical analyses of biological and chemical weapons issues to determine options with respect to arms control treaty compliance policy areas. Develops and provides recommendations for external research projects, and serves as a representative of the Bureau to Intelligence Community meetings on foreign chemical and biological weapons programs and activities.

Minimum qualifications required: Bachelor's or master's degree in the physical sciences, engineering, or mathematics; OR a combination of education, training, and technical experience. Must have one year of specialized experience in a related position.

Minimum application materials required: Submit a resume or Application for Federal Employment (OF-612), and a completed Occupational Questionnaire from the vacancy announcement. Questionnaire has more than 30 KSAs, includes the following: 1) provide expert review, evaluation, coordination, and analysis of information related to U.S. arms control and nonproliferation policy objectives in foreign chemical and biological program assessments; 2) extend and refine existing assessment methods used to analyze chemical and biological weapons compliance; 3) develop new approaches to the analysis of critical policy issues related to the nonproliferation of chemical and biological weapons; 4) conduct probing technical analyses to determine options and alternatives in broad and complex arms control treaty compliance policy areas.

Special requirements: Must be a U.S. citizen. Must be able to obtain a Top Secret security clearance. Subject to random drug testing.

Department of Transportation

400 Seventh Street SW
Washington, D.C. 20590
202-366-4000

★ Web site: http://www.dot.gov/

★ Job vacancies: http://jobsearch.usajobs.opm.gov

★ USAJOBS By Phone: 912-757-3000

★ Headquarters contacts: http://www.dot.gov/contact.html

★ How to apply: http://careers.dot.gov/js_apply.html

★ Internships: http://careers.dot.gov/stu_intern.html

★ Co-op program: http://careers.dot.gov/stu_coop.html

★ Career entry-level programs: http://careers.dot.gov/stu_entryprog.html

★ Benefits: http://careers.dot.gov/benefits.html

★ Career opportunities overview: http://careers.dot.gov/js_oppareas.html

The U.S. Department of Transportation (DOT) establishes the country's overall transportation policy. Under its umbrella there are 11 administrations whose jurisdictions include highway planning, development, and construction; motor carrier safety; urban mass transit; railroads; aviation; and the safety of waterways, ports, highways, and oil and gas pipelines. Decisions made by the DOT in conjunction with the appropriate state and local officials strongly affect other programs such as land planning, energy conservation, scarce resource utilization, and technological change. DOT employs more than 60,000 people across the country.

Selected Agencies Within DOT

The **Federal Aviation Administration** (FAA) is responsible for the safety of civil aviation. The FAA's major roles include: regulating civil aviation to promote safety; encouraging and developing civil aeronautics, including new aviation technology; developing and operating a system of air traffic control and navigation for both civil and military aircraft; researching and developing the National Airspace System and civil aeronautics; developing and carrying out programs to control aircraft noise and other environmental effects of civil aviation; and regulating U.S. commercial space transportation. In addition to its headquarters in Washington, D.C., the FAA has nine geographical regions and two major centers, the Mike Monroney Aeronautical Center in Oklahoma City, Oklahoma, and the William J. Hughes Technical Center in Atlantic City, New Jersey. The FAA employs aviation professionals such as air traffic controllers, airway transportation specialists, aerospace engineers, aviation safety inspectors, and civil aviation security specialists, as well as administrators, support staff, and technical specialists.

★ Web site: http://www.faa.gov/

★ Job vacancies: http://jobs.faa.gov/announcement_summary.asp

★ Headquarters contacts: http://www.faa.gov/aboutfaa/Headquarters.cfm

★ Regional offices and centers: http://www.faa.gov/aboutfaa/Regional.cfm

★ General employment information: http://www.faa.gov/careers/employment/jobinfo.htm

★ FAA Academy: http://www.academy.jccbi.gov/

★ FAA education offices and events: http://www.faa.gov/education/Education_Offices.cfm

The **National Highway Traffic Safety Administration** is responsible for reducing deaths, injuries, and economic losses resulting from motor vehicle crashes; regulating the motor vehicle industry; investigating safety defects in motor vehicles; setting and enforcing fuel economy standards; helping states an local communities reduce the threat of drunk drivers; promoting the use of safety belts, child safety seats and air bags; investigating odometer fraud; establishing and enforcing vehicle antitheft regulations; and providing consumer information on motor vehicle safety topics. The Agency employs 600 people and has 10 regional offices.

★ Web site: http://www.nhtsa.dot.gov/

★ Job vacancies: http://www.nhtsa.dot.gov/nhtsa/announce/jobs/

★ List of offices nationwide:
    http://www.nhtsa.dot.gov/nhtsa/whatis/regions/Index.cfm?Fitting=No

The mission of the **Saint Lawrence Seaway Development Commission** is to serve the marine transportation industries by providing a safe, secure, reliable, efficient, and competitive deep draft international waterway, in cooperation with the Canadian St. Lawrence Seaway Management Corporation.

★ Web site: http://www.seaway.dot.gov/

★ Job vacancies: http://www.greatlakes-seaway.com/en/aboutus/slsdc_employment.html

★ Contact information: http://www.greatlakes-seaway.com/en/aboutus/slsdc_contacts.html

Other DOT Agencies

Bureau of Transportation Statistics
http://www.bts.gov/

Federal Highway Administration
http://www.fhwa.dot.gov/

Federal Motor Carrier Safety Administration
http://www.fmcsa.dot.gov/

Federal Railroad Administration
http://www.fra.dot.gov/

Federal Transit Administration
http://www.fta.dot.gov/

Maritime Administration
http://www.marad.dot.gov/

Office of the Inspector General
http://www.oig.dot.gov/

Office of the Secretary of Transportation
http://www.dot.gov/ost/index.html

Research and Special Programs Administration
http://www.rspa.dot.gov/

Surface Transportation Board
http://www.stb.dot.gov/

Sample Job Vacancies

Aviation Safety Inspector
Agency: Federal Aviation Administration
Salary: $52,899 to $68,766
Location: Anchorage, Alaska

Job description summary: Serves as a resource and technical authority in an assigned field office on cabin safety requirements as they relate to work activities affecting civil aviation. Provides technical support regarding cabin safety for assigned air carriers and air operators. Ensures assigned operators comply with applicable Federal Aviation Regulations, FAA policy, and guidance and approved programs

Minimum qualifications required: High school graduate or equivalent. Three years of experience in a passenger carrying multiengine aircraft over 12,500 pounds gross takeoff weight, which provided specific experience in a wide range of cabin safety policies, procedures, duties, practices, and equipment, as well as experience managing, supervising, and training air craft personnel in cabin safety. Specialized experience described above must have been gained in more than one kind (e.g., make, model, series, variant) of aircraft and must have been gained within the last three years.

Minimum application materials required: Submit an Application for Federal Employment (SF-171), an Optional Application for Federal Employment (OF-612), or a resume. Application must include narrative answers to the following KSAs: 1) ability to interpret and apply cabin safety and flight attendance certification procedures, policies, and regulations; 2) ability to evaluate programs, analyze data, and identify trends; 3) skill in writing a significant document, report, or presentation; 4) ability to work as an effective team member; 5) ability to work with both small and large air carriers as it relates to flight attendant safety procedures and emergency equipment.

Special requirements: Valid driver's license. Must have good distant vision in each eye and be able to read without strain printed materials the size of typewritten characters (glasses and contact lenses permitted). Must have the ability to hear the conversational voice (hearing aid permitted).

Community Planner

Agency: Office of Planning, Environmental, and Realty, Federal Highway Administration
Salary: $85,210 to $110,775
Location: Washington, D.C.

Job description summary: Leads the development and execution of a comprehensive research, training, and technical assistance program for FHWA on transportation, land use, livability, and community issues. Serves as spokesperson for FHWA on transportation and land use programs and initiatives. Provides advice and leadership on transportation, land use, and livability issues.

Minimum qualifications required: Bachelor's degree in community planning. One year of specialized experience in a related position.

Minimum application materials required: Apply online through the DOT's Careers in Motion Web site by submitting a resume an Occupational Questionnaire. Application must include narrative answers to the following KSAs: 1) experience with transportation modeling and forecasting; 2) experience in developing and using travel models within the transportation planning process; 3) knowledge of transportation planning and the application of planning theories to transportation program development; 4) ability to apply knowledge of transportation planning to transportation program development; 5) experience in the planning and development of transportation projects involving local projects; 6) experience working with federal, state and local officials in the development and administration of local and statewide transportation plans; 7) skill level as an instructor for training and technology deployment; 8) experience conducting, managing or developing training courses; 9) wide variety of communication skills, both oral and written.

Emergency Operations Coordinator

Agency: Office of Operations, Office of Transportation Operations, Federal Highway Administration
Salary: $72,108 to $93,742
Location: Washington, D.C.

Job description summary: Establishes a communications network and process between Headquarters and field offices for reporting of significant events. Responsible for operational readiness of Agency Headquarters and field offices by assuring capability for the continuation of essential functions in periods of national emergencies. Assures preparedness of Headquarters' alternate sites. Assists the Lead EOC in planning, staff preparation, and participation in exercises; in organizing, preparing, training, and deploying agency personnel to staff agency desk in departmental crisis management center during crisis periods.

Minimum qualifications required: Master's degree in a field related to the position, plus one year of specialized experience related to the duties of the position.

Minimum application materials required: Apply online through the DOT's Careers in Motion Web site by submitting a resume and an Occupational Questionnaire. Application must include narrative answers to the following KSAs: 1) ability to work cooperatively with other team members and contribute to group solutions; 2) ability to work independently; 3) skill in negotiating difficult situations; 4) experience motivating others; 5) ability to develop and present briefings; 6) experience in authoring, modifying, or implementing a Continuity of Operations (COOP) plan for an organization; 7) experience activities to support (COOP) plans; 8) contracting-related actions that you have performed independently as a regular part of your job; 9) experience assessing progress relative to goals, plans, and changing needs; 10) experience managing, directing, or administering an important program or significant program segments; 11) experience in developing detailed work plans for identifying customer needs and addressing product delivery challenges

Special requirements: Must pass a background investigation and a drug test. This position is subject to 24-hour on call in the event of an emergency, or exercise, or other related duties.

Highway Safety Specialist

Agency: National Highway Safety Administration
Salary: $50,593 to $78,826
Location: Washington, D.C.

Job description summary: Develops and promotes new programs, provides technical guidance and support, and coordinates program activities relative to traffic safety involving state, municipal, and county law enforcement agencies. Focuses on internal and external networking in the area of accident and injury prevention, improving public information and education efforts for traffic safety, and providing technical assistance on an array of traffic safety issues to NHTSA regional offices, states, and communities.

Minimum qualifications required: Bachelor's degree in accounting, business administration, business or commercial law, commerce, economics, engineering, finance, industrial management, statistics, traffic management, transportation, motor mechanics, public administration, hazardous materials management, or other fields related to the position; OR one year of specialized experience in or directly related to the line of work of the position.

Minimum application materials required: Apply online through the DOT's Careers in Motion Web site by submitting a resume and an Occupational Questionnaire. Application must include narrative answers to the following KSAs: 1) skill in oral and written communication; 2) experience in analyzing projected safety data; 3) experience with the development and implementation of Highway Safety Programs; 4) experience with the implementation of traffic law enforcement programs; 5) experience developing traffic safety programs for law enforcement; 6) experience with providing technical assistance in the development and implementation of Highway Safety Programs, regulations, and legislation; 7) experience in developing and implementing outreach and public information activities to promote highway safety programs; 8) knowledge of a variety of traffic safety program contracts.

Maintenance Mechanic

Agency: Airway Facilities Division, Federal Aviation Administration
Salary: $21.78 to $26.42/hour
Location: Las Vegas, Nevada

Job description and summary: Performs carpentry, electrical, painting, plumbing, maintenance, and hazardous material handling in the repair, maintenance, and construction of facilities serviced by the Airway Facilities Division.

Minimum qualifications required: Applicant must have a minimum of six months of experience which demonstrates the ability to perform electrical, painting, plumbing, carpentry, and masonry work.

Minimum application materials required: Submit an Application for Federal Employment (SF-171), an Optional Application for Federal Employment (OF-612), or a resume. Application must include narrative answers to the following KSAs: 1) ability to work independently; 2) knowledge and certification in hazardous material handling; 3) knowledge of carpentry, electrical, painting, plumbing, and maintenance work.

Special requirements: Position requires extensive and frequent travel. Must pass a drug test.

Motor Carrier Safety Specialist

Agency: Federal Motor Carrier Safety Administration
Salary: $27,966 to $45,032
Location: Otay Mesa, California

Job description summary: Prepares and carries out recurring assignments according to established procedures and guidelines. Plans and conducts inspections of carrier equipment, driver documentation, insurance, and economic permitting during highway operations to ascertain compliance with safety and permitting standards. Performs routine inspections at ports of entry on commercial type vehicles (trucks and buses) to determine if they comply with authority, registration, safety, and equipment system requirements. Inspects vehicles transporting hazardous materials for compliance with all applicable shipping and handling requirements.

Minimum qualifications required: One full year of graduate-level education or one year of specialized experience in or directly related to the line of work of the position.

Minimum application materials required: Apply online through the DOT's Careers in Motion Web site by submitting a resume and an Occupational Questionnaire. Application has more than 20 KSAs, including the following: 1) experience performing and conducting safety compliance audits; 2) knowledge of commercial motor vehicle systems and regulations; 3) ability to comprehend information pertaining to the components of commercial vehicle mechanical systems; 4) ability to inspect trucks or buses for safety hazards; 5) ability to promote and enforce motor carrier safety regulations; 6) knowledge of conventional fact-finding, auditing, or investigative techniques; 7) ability to review and analyze documents and data to determine compliance with regulations.

Special requirements: Must have a valid State driver's license. Must pass a drug test. You will be required to travel to Mexico to carry out work assignments. Must be able to speak and write fluently in English and Spanish. Selected candidates must successfully complete the FMCSA's Training Academy Program.

Spatial Data Analyst

Agency: Geographic Information Program Team, Bureau of Transportation Statistics
Salary: $41,815 to $68,766
Location: Washington, D.C.

Job description summary: Provides mapping and spatial analysis support. Develops procedures for, and monitors the production and maintenance of, geospatial data to support DOT spatial analysis and cartographic requirements. Improves geospatial data using standardized methodologies. Manipulates geospatial data, performs geospatial analyses, documents geospatial processes, and creates geographic information from geographic data. Assists other geographic information professionals in developing services related to the creation, maintenance, or dissemination of geographic information.

Minimum qualifications required: Three years of progressively higher-level graduate education leading to a Ph.D., OR a Ph.D. One year of specialized experience related to the work of the position.

Minimum application materials required: Apply online through the DOT's Careers in Motion Web site by submitting a resume and an Occupational Questionnaire. Application must include narrative answers to the following KSAs: 1) skill in using information technology related to spatial analysis; 2) experience with the application of geographic information systems technology; 3) ability to identify and analyze problems, make logical decisions and provide solutions to problems; 4) skill in using software to accomplish day-to-day office functions; 5) produced a variety of written products on a regular and recurring basis; 6) ability to communicate in person; 7) experience in communicating technical and programmatic information to individuals or audiences; 8) experience developing effective internal and external working relationships; 9) experience detailing geospatial analyses performed and the results, cartographic production, development of geospatial data, or any programs created to perform geospatial tasks.

Special requirements: Males born after December 31, 1959, must have registered with the Selective Service.

Department of the Treasury

1500 Pennsylvania Avenue NW
Washington, D.C. 20220
202-622-2000

★ Web site: http://www.treas.gov/

★ Job vacancies: http://www.usajobs.opm.gov/

★ USAJOBS By Phone: 912-757-3000

★ Contact information: http://www.treas.gov/contacts.html

★ Treasury offices: http://www.treas.gov/offices/

★ Treasury bureaus: http://www.treas.gov/bureaus/

The Department of the Treasury performs four basic functions: formulating and recommending economic, financial, tax, and fiscal policies; serving as financial agent for the U.S. Government; enforcing the law; and manufacturing coins and currency. It employs more than 100,000 people.

Apply for Treasury jobs through its CareerConnector Web site. CareerConnector allows you to complete an online resume and questionnaire and receive e-mails of job openings you qualify for.

Selected Agencies Within DOT

The **Bureau of Engraving & Printing** designs and manufactures U.S. currency, many stamps, securities, and other official certificates and awards. BEP is the largest producer of security documents in the United States, producing a wide range of documents at both its Washington, D.C., and Fort Worth, Texas, facilities. Production ranges from banknotes, postage stamps, and Treasury Securities to identification cards, naturalization certificates, and special security documents such as White House Invitations. Employment opportunities include administrative support, police officers, security specialists, chemists, engineers, and attorneys.

★ Web site: http://www.moneyfactory.com/

★ Job vacancies (Washington, D.C.):
http://www.moneyfactory.com/hr/document.cfm/95/248/2132

★ Job vacancies: (Fort Worth): http://www.moneyfactory.com/hr/document.cfm/95/249/

★ Headquarters contacts: http://www.moneyfactory.com/section.cfm/16

★ Benefits: http://www.moneyfactory.com/hr/section.cfm/241

The **Internal Revenue Service** (IRS) is the largest of Treasury's bureaus. It is responsible for determining, assessing, and collecting internal revenue in the United States. The IRS employs more than 99,000 people and has an operating budget of more than $10 billion. In 2003, the IRS collected nearly $2 trillion in revenue and processed more than 222 million tax returns. It cost taxpayers 48 cents for each $100 collected by the IRS.

★ Web site: http://www.irs.gov/

★ Job vacancies: http://www.usajobs.opm.gov/

★ Contact information: http://www.irs.gov/contact/index.html

★ How to apply: http://www.jobs.irs.gov/mn-student1.html

★ Details about student employment programs: http://www.jobs.irs.gov/mn-Students.html

★ Links to local offices: http://www.irs.gov/localcontacts/index.html

★ Descriptions of employee benefits: http://www.jobs.irs.gov/mn-working-beneflts.html

The **U.S. Mint** designs and manufactures domestic, bullion, and foreign coins as well as commemorative medals and other items. The Mint also distributes U.S. coins to the Federal Reserve banks as well as maintains physical custody and protection the country's silver and gold assets. There are Mint facilities in Washington, D.C.; Philadelphia, Pennsylvania; Fort Knox, Kentucky; Denver, Colorado; San Francisco, California; and West Point, New York.

★ Web site: http://www.usmint.gov/index.cfm?flash=yes

★ Job vacancies: https://jobs.usmint.gov/scripts/mint.exe

★ Contact information: http://www.usmint.gov/email/

★ Internships: http://www.usmint.gov/careers/index.cfm?headID=87

★ List of offices nationwide:
http://www.usmint.gov/about_the_mint/index.cfm?action=mint_facilities

★ Descriptions of employee benefits: http://www.usmint.gov/careers/index.cfm?headID=78

Other DOT Agencies

Alcohol and Tobacco Tax and Trade Bureau
http://www.ttb.gov/

Bureau of the Public Debt
http://www.publicdebt.treas.gov/

Community Development Financial Institution Fund
http://www.cdfifund.gov/

Financial Crimes Enforcement Network
http://www.fincen.gov/

Financial Management Service
http://www.fms.treas.gov/

Inspector General
http://www.treas.gov/inspector-general/

Treasury Inspector General for Tax Administration
http://www.treas.gov/tigta/

Office of the Comptroller of the Currency
http://www.occ.treas.gov/

Office of Thrift Supervision
http://www.ots.treas.gov/

Sample Job Vacancies

Auditor

Agency: Alcohol and Tobacco Tax and Trade Bureau
Salary: $27,730 to $67,786
Location: Sacramento County, California

Job description summary: Conducts assigned excise tax audits at alcohol and tobacco industry members. Provides excise tax assistance to federal and state officials, as well as to members of associated industries. Assists other auditors and/or investigators in the audits or reviews of regulated industries. Prepares reports and disseminates findings and disclosures developed during excise tax audits or reviews. Interprets general policy guidelines and provides specific technical guidance as requested.

Minimum qualifications required: Bachelor's degree in accounting or auditing.

Minimum application materials required: Submit a resume or Optional Application for Federal Employment (OF-612), along with the Occupational Questionnaire from the vacancy announcement. Include narrative answers to the following KSAs: 1) knowledge of auditing and accounting concepts, standards, principles, internal controls and practices to conduct audits; 2) knowledge of a variety of computer software packages, including electronic audit management system software; 3) ability to research and apply laws, regulations or procedures to conduct audit tests; 4) ability to communicate effectively orally and in writing.

Special requirements: Daily and overnight travel on a regular and recurring basis will be required, as well as regular and recurring overtime work.

Industrial Equipment Operator

Agency: Financial Management Service
Salary: $12.44 to $16.73/hour
Location: Austin, Texas

Job description summary: Operates a check wrapping machine and makes adjustments required to maintain proper operation. Removes enclosed checks and places them in mail trays; monitors quality of adhesive, printed information and proper construction of envelopes; assists the repairer with minor adjustments and repairs; makes web changes; performs preventive maintenance.

Minimum qualifications required: Must be willing and able to work for long periods of time standing in one place; work in the presence of strong odors; work where noise is very loud; follow strict safety regulations. Good distant vision in at least one eye; near vision sufficient to read the size of typewritten characters, glasses permitted; and the ability to hear the conversational voice. Must be emotionally and mentally stable.

Minimum application materials required: Submit a resume or Optional Application for Federal Employment (OF-612), along with the Occupational Questionnaire accompanying the vacancy announcement. Include narrative answers to the following KSAs: 1) ability to do the work of an industrial equipment operator; 2) skill in using measuring instruments, hand tools, and devices; 3) ability to interpret instructions and specifications; 4) ability to meet deadlines under pressure; 5) ability to troubleshoot and make adjustments; 6) knowledge of work practices relating to control procedures.

Special requirements: Males born after December 31, 1959, must have registered with the Selective Service System. Must pass a background/security investigation, which includes a credit check.

Internal Revenue Officer
Agency: Internal Revenue Service
Salary: $33,071 to $37,041
Location: Nationwide

Job description summary: Conducts research, interviews and investigations. Analyzes financial statements and contacts third parties for information. Collects delinquent taxpayer accounts and secures delinquent returns. Files extensions to statutes of limitations for collection. Determines the accuracy of assessed liabilities and adjusts or abates erroneous liabilities. Participates in agency compliance programs. Has extensive face-to-face personal contacts with taxpayers, attorneys, accountants, and other representatives, and spends a major portion of time performing fieldwork. Conducts preliminary analyses of cases, schedules appointments, consults with group managers, prepares administrative reports, and assembles files for closure.

Minimum qualifications required: Bachelor's degree in a curriculum related to this position with a GPA of at least 3.0; OR at least one full year of graduate-level education with a major that demonstrates the competencies necessary for successful job performance; OR at least one year of combined graduate education and experience.

Minimum application materials required: Submit a resume or Optional Application for Federal Employment (OF-612), along with the Occupational Questionnaire accompanying the vacancy announcement. Include narrative answers to the following KSAs: 1) knowledge of business organization and commercial practices; 2) knowledge of investigative techniques and methods, and the ability to apply such techniques to the analysis of business and financial matters; 3) knowledge of business law; 4) knowledge of delinquent loan collection processes and techniques; 5) knowledge of accounting principles and practices; 6) knowledge of Internal Revenue Code and related federal tax regulations and procedures.

Special requirements: Must be a U.S. citizen. Males born after December 31, 1959, must have registered with the Selective Service System. Must be fingerprinted. Must pass a background investigation. During the first year, all selectees will receive approximately 3 weeks of orientation, 10 weeks of classroom training and 40 weeks of on-the-job training.

Tax Examiner
Agency: Internal Revenue Service
Salary: $26,195 to $34,052
Location: Ogden, Utah

Job description summary: Reviews case files, prepares closing documents, and verifies tax liability on tax returns. Examines tax returns for accuracy and completeness, codes tax returns for computer processing, resolves errors or corresponds with taxpayers to obtain missing information.

Minimum qualifications required: Bachelor's degree OR one year of specialized experience in or related to this position.

Minimum application materials required: Submit a resume, Optional Application for Federal Employment (OF-612), or other written application format of your choice, along with the Occupational Questionnaire accompanying the vacancy announcement.

Tax Specialist

Agency: Internal Revenue Service
Salary: $26,195 to $46,828
Location: Vernon Hills, Illinois

Job description summary: Provides technical tax guidance and accounting consultation to tax-payers. Conducts surveys, studies, and focus groups to determine the effectiveness of existing agency tax-specific products and services and serves as a liaison in conducting compliance education and outreach activities, and other volunteer programs.

Minimum qualifications required: Bachelor's degree in accounting and certification as a Certified Public Accountant, OR at least three years of general experience, one year of which demonstrated a general knowledge of business practices and basic accounting principles.

Minimum application materials required: Submit a resume or Optional Application for Federal Employment (OF-612), along with the Occupational Questionnaire (156 questions) accompanying the vacancy announcement.

Special requirements: Fingerprints will be required as part of the preemployment process. Applicants will be required to pass a structured oral interview to demonstrate their oral communication and customer service skills.

Writer

Agency: Financial Management Service
Salary: $60,638 to $78,826
Location: Prince George County, Maryland

Job description summary: Composes brochures, articles, speeches, presentations, and other written products that explain, interpret, support, and enhance the agency's programs and activities. Assists senior specialists in the development of documentation related to personal computer inter/intranet applications. Uses desktop publishing technology to finalize text and prepare layouts. Designs visual aspects of the publication, and coordinates with other design specialists to select or develop graphic and other illustrative materials as necessary.

Minimum qualifications required: Bachelor's degree. One year of specialized experience in work related to the position.

Minimum application materials required: Submit a resume or Optional Application for Federal Employment (OF-612), along with the Occupational Questionnaire accompanying the vacancy announcement. Include narrative answers to the following KSAs: 1) knowledge of

English syntax and composition, including skills in editing technical or functional documents, and the ability to translate technical material general audiences; 2) ability to understand the basic elements of personal computer and mainframe hardware, software, and applications, and Internet applications and Internet telecommunications; 3) skills using word processing software and other standard computer software to produce reports; 4) ability to communicate effectively both orally and in writing.

Special requirements: Must pass a security check, which may include a credit check.

Department of Veterans Affairs

810 Vermont Avenue NW
Washington, D.C. 20420
202-273-4800

★ Web site: http://www.va.gov/

★ Job vacancies: http://jobsearch.usajobs.opm.gov/a9va.asp

★ USAJOBS By Phone: 912-757-3000

★ Central offices: http://www1.va.gov/directory/guide/hq_flsh.asp

★ Facility and leadership directory:
   http://www1.va.gov/directory/guide/home.asp?isFlash=1

★ How to apply: http://www.va.gov/jobs/apply.htm

★ Benefits: http://www.va.gov/jobs/benefits.htm

The Department of Veterans Affairs (VA) operates programs to benefit veterans and members of their families. Benefits include compensation payments for disabilities or death related to military service; pensions; education and rehabilitation; home loan guaranty; burial; and a medical care program incorporating nursing homes, clinics, and medical centers. The Department of Veterans Affairs comprises three organizations that administer veterans programs: the Veterans Health Administration, the Veterans Benefits Administration, and the National Cemetery Administration. Each organization has field facilities and a central office component. VA is the second largest of the 14 Cabinet departments, with over 220,000 employees.

Selected Agencies Within VA

The **Veterans Health Administration** is responsible for the operation of the nation's largest integrated health care system. It serves the needs of America's veterans by providing primary care, specialized care, and related medical and social support services. It operates more than 160 hospitals, with at least one in each of the 48 contiguous states, Puerto Rico, and the District of Columbia. It conducts more than 10,000 research projects at 115 VA medical centers, and its career development program provides young scientists an opportunity to develop skills as clinician-researchers. It manages the largest medical education and health professions training program in the United States. More than half of the physicians practicing in the Unites States have had part of their professional education in the VA health care system.

★ Web site: http://www1.va.gov/Health_Benefits/

★ Facility directory: http://www1.va.gov/directory/guide/division_flsh.asp?divisionId=1

Other VA Agencies

Veterans Benefits Administration
http://www.vba.va.gov/

National Cemetery Administration
http://www.cem.va.gov/index.htm

Sample Job Vacancies

Biomedical Engineer Technician
Agency: Veterans Health Administration
Salary: $29,821 to $38,767
Location: San Juan, Puerto Rico

Job description summary: Services and troubleshoots complex electronic equipment, which includes all laundry electronic equipment, electronic surveillance equipment, electromagnetic surveillance equipment, Radiographic/Fluoroscopic equipment, as well as cardio and physiological monitors, defibrillators, EKG, etc. Assures that all complex electronic equipment meets electrical safety standards. Performs preventive maintenance that includes operational checks, adjustments, and calibrations.

Minimum qualifications required: One or more years of specialized experience working with electronic equipment and systems, identifying system failures, hazards, etc., OR one full year of graduate education or an internship that included courses directly related to the work of this position.

Minimum application materials required: Submit a resume or Optional Application for Federal Employment (OF-612), along with a completed Occupational Questionnaire from the vacancy announcement. Questionnaire contains more than 15 KSAs, including the following: 1) evaluates and makes recommendations on electronic instrumentation prior to purchase or issue; 2) inspects electronic equipment to ensure compliance with manufacturing specifications and safety; 3) recommends that a system is to be removed from service, allowed to remain in service, or restored to service; 4) maintains a competence level in the state-of-the-art technology through contacts with factory, private and in-house training, current texts, electronic, and medical publications, seminars, etc.

Special requirements: Must be a U.S. citizen. Male applicants born after December 31, 1959, must have registered with the Selective Service. Must be able to stoop, reach, kneel, crouch in confined spaces, and maintain intense concentration for long periods of time under most adverse conditions, such as repairing and/or calibrating electronic equipment while it is supporting the medical staff and hospital staff. Acceptable hearing, visual accuracy, field of vision, and color perception are required for working on minute circuit. Moderate lifting is necessary.

Vocational Rehabilitation Counselor

Agency: Veterans Health Administration
Salary: $49,935 to $64,914
Location: Cleveland, Ohio

Job description summary: Provides a wide range of rehabilitation and personal adjustment counseling and case management services, including coordination of rehabilitation, training, and employment services to disabled veterans. Assesses data received from medical, psychological, and vocational evaluations, and develops individualized rehabilitation plans. Networks with local employers to develop transitional work, employment, or other therapeutic work opportunities for veterans.

Minimum qualifications required: Master's degree in rehabilitation counseling, including an internship; or a master's degree in counseling psychology or a related field. Must have one year of professional vocational rehabilitation counseling experience.

Minimum application materials required: Submit a resume or Optional Application for Federal Employment (OF-612), along with a completed Occupational Questionnaire from the vacancy announcement. Questionnaire has more than 15 KSAs, including the following: 1) motivated clients to pursue rehabilitation services; 2) developed individualized rehabilitation plans; 3) determined the vocational goals and objectives of the client based on a referral from a professional staff member or by interviewing the client; 4) collaborated with treatment teams and clients in selection of rehabilitation services; 5) analyzed mental and physical disabilities or other handicaps in terms of the practical effects of such handicaps on motivations, adjustment to training, and difficulty in employment placement.

Special requirements: Must be a U.S. citizen. Males born after December 31, 1959, must have registered with the Selective Service System.

Medical Records Technician

Agency: Veterans Health Administration
Salary: $23,863 to $31,020
Location: Las Vegas, Nevada

Job description summary: Monitors and controls the accurate and timely release and administrative information to authorized requesters. Completes all aspects of the Tort Claim process with regard to paginating, copying, and forwarding copies to Regional Counsel within time and accuracy standards. Prepares and submits weekly productivity reports to supervisor, and maintains an accurate and complete system of requests in order to monitor and assure timely responses.

Minimum qualifications required: One and one half years of general experience and one half year of specialized experience.

Minimum application materials required: Submit a resume or Optional Application for Federal Employment (OF-612), along with a completed Occupational Questionnaire from the vacancy announcement. Respond in narrative form to the following KSAs: 1) knowledge of procedures for assembling patient charts and integrating X-ray reports, test results, consultations and progress notes, etc.; 2) knowledge of the VISTA computer system; 3) knowledge of proper interviewing techniques to talk with staff or patients when necessary in locating misplaced medical records; 4) knowledge of the Privacy Act and Freedom of Information Act to accurately release medical information; 5) skill in operating bar code machine, scanner, and copy and fax machines.

Special requirements: This position requires completion of a one-year probationary period. Must pass a preemployment medical examination and a background security investigation.

Cemetery Caretaker

Agency: National Cemetery Administration
Salary: $13.15/hour
Location: Fort Meade, South Dakota

Job description summary: Performs duties related to interments (such as preparing interment building for committal services and preparing gravesites; lowering caskets; backfilling graves using shovels, rakes and tamper; operating pickup, van and industrial tractor with front end loader); grounds maintenance; facility maintenance; and maintenance on all vehicles and equipment used by the cemetery.

Minimum qualifications required: Must be able to perform heavy manual labor, including heavy lifting.

Minimum application materials required: Submit a resume or Optional Application for Federal Employment (OF-612), along with a completed Occupational Questionnaire from the vacancy announcement. Respond in narrative form to the following KSAs: 1) ability to do work of the position without more than normal supervision; 2) ability to perform the technical practices related to the duties of a cemetery caretaker; 3) ability to interpret instructions and directives; 4) ability to use and maintain tools and equipment.

Special requirements: A physical examination may be required. Must possess a valid driver's license.

Claims Assistant

Agency: Veterans Benefits Administration
Salary: $24,666 to $39,996
Location: Washington, D.C.

Job description summary: Maintains the claims folders. Analyzes claim and determines if disposition of claim and control action has been appropriately identified. Establishes or updates control action. Generates various types of correspondence and prepares reports of contact on all telephone calls or inquiries needed to complete the development of claims. Inputs requests for VA examinations into the CAPRI system. Receives, opens, reviews and date stamps all incoming correspondences, (claims and miscellaneous mail). Analyzes mail for appropriate routing. Forwards claim folders to appropriate team member for review and/or action. Greets all visitors and reviews claim files and VA electronic records for the completeness of VA exams. Associates completed exams with files for review. Monitors, tracks, and ensures timely responses for files temporarily sent to VA Medical Center.

Minimum qualifications required: Must have one year of general experience, OR an associate's degree.

Minimum application materials required: Submit a resume or Optional Application for Federal Employment (OF-612), along with a completed Occupational Questionnaire from the vacancy announcement. Questionnaire includes more than 40 KSAs, including the following: 1) responds to requests or complaints from potentially hostile individuals; 2) follows-up on requests or complaints verbally or in writing relaying information on rules and regulations of programs; 3) corrects mistakes in written or computer documents or records; 4) obtains facts for making decisions or recommendations as it pertains to rules, regulations or laws; 5) searches files, documents, or other sources for information as it relates to claims, rules, regulations or laws; 6) identifies needs or problems and determines corrective action in the application of rules, regulations or laws.

Special requirements: Must be a U.S. citizen.

Senior Appraiser
Agency: Veterans Benefits Administration
Salary: $48,947 to $76,261
Location: Albuquerque, New Mexico

Job description summary: Fields reviews of appraisals of residential properties for both origination and liquidation of loans; fields reviews of Notices of Value issued under the Lender Appraisal Processing Program (LAPP); fields reviews of liquidation cases in which there was a 20 percent or more loss in value during the past two years; fields reviews of compliance inspection reports on new construction; fields reviews on construction complaint cases where direct intervention is deemed necessary.

Minimum qualifications required: Three full years of progressively higher-level graduate education, OR Ph.D.; OR a combination of education and experience. Must have one year of specialized experience in a related position.

Minimum application materials required: Submit a resume or Optional Application for Federal Employment (OF-612), along with a completed Occupational Questionnaire from the vacancy announcement. Respond in narrative form to the following KSAs: 1) ability to determine financial capability based on established standards and good judgement; 2) experience in accounting; 3) ability to communicate information to individuals with varied backgrounds; 4) knowledge of construction; 5) knowledge of, appraising principles and techniques; 6) ability to analyze and interpret the effects of unstable social, economic, and political trends on property uses and values; 7) knowledge of the valuation approaches and appraisal techniques; 8) skill to detect differences in comparable properties and adjust data to make defensible value estimates; 9) knowledge of pertinent laws, regulations, policies and procedures which affect the use of the specially adapted housing program and related support services.

Special requirements: Must be a U.S. citizen.

Independent Establishments and Government Corporations

Central Intelligence Agency

Washington, D.C. 20505
703-482-1100

- ★ Web site: http://www.cia.gov/

- ★ Job vacancies: http://www.cia.gov/employment/viewall.html

- ★ USAJOBS By Phone: 912-757-3000

- ★ Career information: http://www.cia.gov/employment/index.html

- ★ Student opportunities: http://www.cia.gov/employment/student.html

- ★ How to apply for a job at CIA: http://www.cia.gov/employment/apply.html

- ★ Career Director work preference tool: http://www.cia.gov/employment/cardir.html

- ★ Employee benefits: http://www.cia.gov/employment/benefits.html

- ★ Working for the CIA: http://www.cia.gov/employment/about.html

The Central Intelligence Agency (CIA) collects, evaluates, and disseminates vital information on political, military, economic, scientific, and other developments abroad needed to safe-guard national security. Under the direction of the president or the National Security Council, the CIA advises the National Security Council in matters concerning intelligence activities and conducts counterintelligence activities outside the United States. The Agency has no police, subpoena, or law enforcement powers or internal security functions.

In addition to "spies" (clandestine service) the CIA employs a wide variety of professionals and support staff, including attorneys, auditors, bookbinders, cartographers, cost analysts, counterterrorism analysts, crime and counternarcotics analysts, digital imaging technicians, electrical engineers, electronics specialists, fitness specialists, foreign language instructors, foreign media analysts, geographers, graphic designers, librarians, materials engineers, medical officers, multimedia designers, polygraph examiners, prepress specialists, psychologists, security professionals, software specialists, and video production specialists.

Selected Agencies Within CIA

The **Directorate of Intelligence** is the analytical branch of the CIA and is responsible for the production and dissemination of all source intelligence analysis on key foreign issues.

- ★ Web site: http://www.cia.gov/cia/di/index.html

★ Job vacancies: http://www.cia.gov/employment/viewall.html

The **Directorate of Operations** is responsible for the clandestine collection of foreign intelligence. It does not have a Web site.

★ Job vacancies: http://www.cia.gov/employment/viewall.html

The **Directorate of Science and Technology** creates and applies innovative technology in support of the intelligence collection mission.

★ Web site: http://www.cia.gov/cia/dst/index.html

★ Job vacancies: http://www.cia.gov/employment/viewall.html

Other CIA Agencies

Center for the Study of Intelligence
http://www.cia.gov/csi/index.html

Office of General Counsel
http://www.cia.gov/ogc/index.htm

Office of Public Affairs
http://www.cia.gov/cia/public_affairs/pas.html

Sample Job Vacancies

Materials Engineer
Agency: Central Intelligence Agency
Salary: $50,000 to $65,000
Location: Washington, D.C.

Job description summary: Responsible for designing, fabricating, and assembling all forms of complex polymeric, co-polymeric, and composite devices from initial concept through deployment.

Minimum qualifications required: Degree in materials science or plastic engineering, as well as knowledge and understanding of thermoset and thermoplastic materials and manufacturing processes used to develop and produce devices. Must be able to recognize and duplicate surface finishes and textures; understand color analysis for the purpose of color matching paints and pigments using a spectrophotometer; be well versed in adhesive technology, and familiar with various sealant and potting compounds; and be familiar with various rapid prototyping systems (SLA, FDM, etc.). Hands-on experience with silicone mold making and various plastics part processing machinery (injection molding machines, thermoforming, rotational casting machines, etc.) is also required, as is travel, both domestic and foreign.

Minimum application materials required: Submit resume online through CIA's resume builder as directed from job listing. CIA recruiters will match your skills against their needs. If there is a fit, a recruiter will contact you by telephone or e-mail.

Special requirements: Must successfully complete a thorough medical and psychological exam, a polygraph interview, and an extensive background investigation. U.S. citizenship is required.

Graphic Designer

Agency: Central Intelligence Agency
Salary: $35,000 to $40,000
Location: Washington, D.C.

Job description summary: Provides traditional printing, Web, and multimedia support to the CIA's intelligence efforts. Supports Agency customers with hard and soft copy products, such as Web sites, publications, brochures, covers, posters, briefings and multimedia presentations, illustrations, logos, and exhibits.

Minimum qualifications required: An associate's or bachelor's degree in fine art or graphic design, or equivalent experience with a strong background in graphic design. Knowledge of Adobe Photoshop and Illustrator, PowerPoint, QuarkXPress, PageMaker, Flash, Director and InDesign is required. Familiarity with digital file formats and comprehensive knowledge of graphic design principles and a wide variety of media and production methods is also required. Must possess basic knowledge of black-and-white and color photographic processes and conventional and digital print processes.

Minimum application materials required: Submit resume online through CIA's resume builder as directed from job listing. CIA recruiters will match your skills against their needs. If there is a fit, a recruiter will contact you by telephone or e-mail.

Special requirements: Must successfully complete a thorough medical and psychological exam, a polygraph interview, and an extensive background investigation. U.S. citizenship is required.

Textile Designer

Agency: Central Intelligence Agency
Salary: $50,000 to $55,000
Location: Washington, D.C.

Job description summary: Entry-level and experienced Functional Textile Products Designer to fabricate materials for specific end use.

Minimum qualifications required: Bachelor of science in textile engineering or science, apparel design, textile product design or a related field, or equivalent experience. The ability to design and produce textiles and to lay out patterns for functional apparel using CAD software is required, along with experience in operating industrial sewing machines, knowledge of fiber, yarn, and textile structures and their physical performance properties. Must have mechanical aptitude and an affinity for problem-solving, as well as familiarity with basic hand and machine tools.

Minimum application materials required: Submit resume online through CIA's resume builder as directed from job listing. CIA recruiters will match your skills against their needs. If there is a fit, a recruiter will contact you by telephone or e-mail.

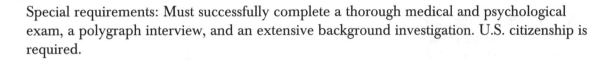

Special requirements: Must successfully complete a thorough medical and psychological exam, a polygraph interview, and an extensive background investigation. U.S. citizenship is required.

Middle Eastern Language Specialist

Agency: Central Intelligence Agency
Salary: $45,000 to $70,000
Location: Washington, D.C.

Job description summary: Reads and translates Arabic, Dari and/or Pashtu into English.

Minimum qualifications required: Bachelor's degree in international relations, regional studies, or a related field is a plus, but not required. As part of the screening process, selected applicants may be required to take a language proficiency test. Candidates must possess native- or near native-level fluency in the language, as well as fluency in English.

Minimum application materials required: Submit resume online through CIA's resume builder as directed from job listing. CIA recruiters will match your skills against their needs. If there is a fit, a recruiter will contact you by telephone or e-mail.

Special requirements: All applicants must successfully complete a thorough medical and psychological exam, a polygraph interview, and an extensive background investigation. U.S. citizenship is required.

Operations Officer (trainee)

Agency: Clandestine Service
Salary: $47,390 to $65,769
Location: Washington, D.C.

Job description summary: Participates in the Clandestine Service Trainee Program, with the potential to serve abroad.

Minimum qualifications required: Bachelor's degree and an excellent academic record, with a strong interest in international affairs and solid interpersonal and communications skills. Foreign travel, foreign language proficiency, prior residency abroad, military experience, a background in Central Eurasian, East Asian, and Middle Eastern languages, and degrees and experience in international economics and business, as well as in the physical sciences, are preferred. Maximum age for entrance into this program is 35.

Minimum application materials required: Submit resume online through CIA's resume builder as directed from job listing. CIA recruiters will match your skills against their needs. If there is a fit, a recruiter will contact you by telephone or e-mail.

Special requirements: Must successfully complete a thorough medical and psychological exam, a polygraph interview, and an extensive background investigation. U.S. citizenship is required for both applicant and spouse.

Analytic Methodologist

Agency: Central Intelligence Agency
Salary: $37,900 to $78,800
Location: Washington, D.C.

Job description summary: Develops and applies new or established analytic methodologies that include statistics; operations research; and econometric, mathematical, and geospatial modeling to add rigor and precision to intelligence analysis and collection.

Minimum qualifications required: Advanced degree and experience in fields involving statistics, mathematics, econometrics, GIS/remote sensing, operations research, computer or mathematical programming, survey research, design, and analysis or gaming. Must have a grade point average of at least 3.2, along with good oral expression and strong writing skills, including the ability to write concise prose. Must also possess a strong interest in international affairs and the ability to work in a team environment. Foreign language ability, particularly in Arabic, Chinese (any dialect), Russian, or Spanish, is a plus, as is familiarity with database creation and manipulation.

Minimum application materials required: Submit resume online through CIA's resume builder as directed from job listing. CIA recruiters will match your skills against their needs. If there is a fit, a recruiter will contact you by telephone or e-mail.

Special requirements: All applicants must successfully complete a thorough medical and psychological exam, a polygraph interview, and an extensive background investigation. U.S. citizenship is required.

Counterterrorism Analyst

Agency: Central Intelligence Agency
Salary: $37,900 to $78,800
Location: Washington, D.C.

Job description summary: Assesses developments related to terrorism worldwide in support of U.S. policymakers. Monitors and assesses the leadership, motivations, plans, and intentions of foreign terrorist groups and their state and nonstate sponsors. Produces a range of current and longer-term intelligence products, briefs key U.S. policymakers, and provides tactical analytic support to law enforcement and intelligence operations.

Minimum qualifications required: Bachelor's or master's degree in international affairs, national security studies, or related subjects, preferably with a strong Middle East or South Asia focus. Strong skills in written and oral English and excellent analytical ability, solid interpersonal skills, and the ability to work under tight deadlines are also required, as is a minimum grade point average of 3.2. Foreign language proficiency and foreign area knowledge gained through study, travel or work abroad are desired.

Minimum application materials required: Submit resume online through CIA's resume builder as directed from job listing. CIA recruiters will match your skills against their needs. If there is a fit, a recruiter will contact you by telephone or e-mail.

Special requirements: Must successfully complete a thorough medical and psychological exam, a polygraph interview, and an extensive background investigation. U.S. citizenship is required.

Science, Technology, and Weapons Analyst
Agency: The Directorate of Intelligence
Salary: $49,100 to $81,000
Location: Washington, D.C.

Job description summary: Analyzes challenging national security issues, such as foreign weapons development, weapons proliferation, information warfare and emerging technologies. Serves as professional intelligence officer, applying scientific and technical knowledge to solving complex intelligence problems, and presenting assessments to senior policymakers.

Minimum qualifications required: Bachelor's or master's degree in aerospace, chemical, mechanical, electrical, computer, or nuclear engineering; computer science; physics, mathematics, or chemistry; biotechnology and microbiology; physical sciences; or remote sensing/GIS. Applicants must also possess strong written and oral English communications skills and a grade point average of 3.0 or better.

Minimum application materials required: Submit resume online through CIA's resume builder. CIA recruiters will match your skills against their needs. If there is a fit, a recruiter will contact you by telephone or e-mail.

Special requirements: Must successfully complete a thorough medical and psychological exam, a polygraph interview, and an extensive background investigation. U.S. citizenship is required.

Commodity Futures Trading Commission

1155 Twenty-first Street NW
Washington, D.C. 20581
202-418-5000

- ★ Web site: http://www.cftc.gov/cftc/cftchome.htm

- ★ Job vacancies: http://www.cftc.gov/ohr/ohrvacsum.htm

- ★ USAJOBS By Phone: 912-757-3000

- ★ Job vacancies by phone: 202-418-5009

- ★ Headquarters and regional offices addresses: http://www.cftc.gov/cftc/cftccontacts.htm

- ★ Job descriptions: http://www.cftc.gov/ohr/ohrprofopps.htm

- ★ Employee benefits: http://www.cftc.gov/ohr/ohrempbenefits.htm

The Commodity Futures Trading Commission (CFTC) is the Federal regulatory agency for futures trading. The Commission oversees the rules under which contract markets and derivatives transaction execution facilities operate and monitors enforcement of those rules. It reviews the terms of futures contracts and registers companies and individuals who handle customer funds or give trading advice. The Commission also enforces rules that require that customer funds be kept in bank accounts separate from accounts maintained by firms for their own use, and that such customer accounts be marked to present market value at the close of trading each day.

The Commission has six major operating components: the Divisions of Market Oversight, Clearing and Intermediary Oversight, and Enforcement, and the Offices of the Executive Director, General Counsel, and Chief Economist. CFTC has one large regional office in Chicago and another in New York City, where many of the country's futures exchanges are located. Additional regional offices are located in Kansas City, Missouri, and Minneapolis, Minnesota. CFTC employs about 500 people as attorneys, auditors, economists, futures trading specialists and investigators, and management professionals.

Consumer Product Safety Commission

East-West Towers
4330 East-West Highway
Bethesda, Maryland 20814
301-504-7908

★ Web site: http://www.cpsc.gov/

★ Job vacancies: http://www.cpsc.gov/about/personnel.html

★ USAJOBS By Phone: 912-757-3000

★ Headquarters and regional contact information: http://www.cpsc.gov/about/contact.html

★ Student volunteer information: http://www.cpsc.gov/about/volunteer.html

★ How to apply: http://www.cpsc.gov/about/howto.html

★ Employment benefits: http://www.cpsc.gov/about/recruit.html

★ Receive new job vacancies by e-mail: http://www.cpsc.gov/about/hrlist.asp

The Consumer Product Safety Commission (CPSC) protects the public against unreasonable risks of injury from consumer products; assists consumers in evaluating the comparative safety of consumer products; develops uniform safety standards for consumer products and minimizes conflicting state and local regulations; and promotes research and investigation into the causes and prevention of product-related deaths, illnesses, and injuries.

CPSC employs about 1,000 people as engineers, compliance officers, toxicologists/chemists, mathematicians/statisticians, product safety investigators, pharmacologists, attorneys, computer specialists, and administrative and support staff. Its product testing laboratory is in Gaithersburg, Maryland; in addition to the headquarters, there are three regional offices: in New York, New York; Chicago, Illinois; and Oakland, California.

Sample Job Vacancy

Product Safety Investigator
Agency: Consumer Product Safety Commission
Salary: $37,041 to $71,265
Location: San Francisco County, California

Job description summary: Conducts inspections of manufacturers, distributors, wholesalers, and retailers who produce, assemble, distribute, and sell consumer products. Travels to on-site locations, such as production plants, company offices, and distribution facilities. Examines production methods, product specifications, manufacturer's testing and quality control procedures, product certification, and labeling. Identifies and evaluates products for potential, substantial, and imminent hazards. Determines compliance with CPSC regulations, laws, and product standards. Conducts investigations by interviewing consumers, fire and police officials, as well as other knowledgeable officials and witnesses. Conducts interviews of responsible management personnel. Obtains affidavits and documents and prepares concise, factual reports. Conducts media interviews and responds to inquiries from the local media. Conducts information and education campaigns that promote consumer safety. Maintains contact with local Congressional offices, coroners, and medical examiners.

Minimum qualifications required: Must have one year of specialized experience that has equipped you with the knowledge, skills, and abilities to conduct product safety investigations, fire investigations and death investigations; OR Superior Academic Achievement (SAA). Equivalent combinations of education and experience are qualifying.

Minimum application materials required: Submit an Optional Application for Federal Employment (OF-612), an Application for Federal Employment (SF-171), or a resume. Include narrative responses to the following KSAs: 1) ability to conduct oral presentations; 2) ability to prepare concise written reports; 3) ability to establish and maintain effective work relationships at all levels; 4) ability to develop and maintain a network of contacts in order to market an issue, idea, or strategy.

Special requirements: Telecommuting is a condition of employment. Must reside in or relocate to the area in which the vacancy is listed. Must live in an area that has high-speed cable or DSL and possess a valid state motor vehicle operator's license. Use of a privately owned motor vehicle may be required. Moderate physical exertion is required, such as lifting and carrying, as well as intermittent strenuous activity, such as climbing ladders, crawling, kneeling, and bending. Frequent travel required, inside and outside the geographic area of responsibility.

Corporation for National and Community Service

1201 New York Avenue NW
Washington, D.C. 20525
202-606-5000

★ Web site: http://www.nationalservice.org/

★ Job vacancies: http://www.nationalservice.org/jobs/jobopenings/index.html

★ USAJOBS By Phone: 912-757-3000

★ Internship information: http://www.nationalservice.org/jobs/internships/index.html

★ How to apply: http://www.nationalservice.org/jobs/jobopenings/jobs_how_to.html

★ Links to CNCS state offices:
http://www.nationalservice.org/about/family/state_offices_pick.html

★ Links to CNCS state commissions: http://www.nationalservice.org/about/family/commissions_pick.html

★ USA Freedom Corps: http://www.usafreedomcorps.gov/

The Corporation for National and Community Service (CNCS) engages Americans of all ages and backgrounds in community-based service. CNCS oversees three major service initiatives–AmeriCorps, Learn and Serve America, and the National Senior Service Corps–and is part of USA Freedom Corps, a White House initiative designed to foster a culture of citizenship, service, and responsibility.

Selected Agencies Within CNCS

AmeriCorps, the domestic Peace Corps, engages more than 50,000 Americans in intensive results-oriented service. Most AmeriCorps members are selected by and serve with local and national organizations like Habitat for Humanity, the American Red Cross, Big Brothers/Big Sisters, and Boys and Girls Clubs. Others serve in AmeriCorps*VISTA (Volunteers in Service to America) and AmeriCorps*NCCC (the National Civilian Community Corps). After their term of service, AmeriCorps members receive education awards that help finance college or pay back student loans.

★ Web site: http://www.americorps.org/

★ Job vacancies: http://www.nationalservice.org/jobs/

★ Volunteering for Americorps: https://recruit.cns.gov/

Other CNCS Agencies

Learn and Serve America
http://www.learnandserve.org/

National Senior Service Corps
http://www.seniorcorps.org/

Sample Job Vacancy

State Program Specialist
Agency: AmeriCorps
Salary: $33,581 to $46,787
Location: Atlanta, Georgia

Job description summary: Provides technical assistance to support AmeriCorps*VISTA and Senior Corps project sponsors and ensures operational accountability. This includes: assisting project sponsors in planning, design, and submission of a grant application; reviewing and evaluating project operations (including on-site monitoring and progress report review and feedback); and assisting project sponsors with administrative requirements. Acts as a Corporation representative with national service and other entities working to promote volunteerism, and develops collaborative partnerships to address community needs. Assists in marketing and promotion of national service programs. Supports the effectiveness of state office operations and activities to ensure adherence to Corporation initiatives, deadlines, and requirements.

Minimum qualifications required: Those applications showing experience which is in, or related to, the line of work of this position and demonstrating the possession of the KSAs described below will be referred to the selecting official for further evaluation to determine the best qualified candidates.

Minimum application materials required: Submit a resume, including salary history, and written responses to the following KSAs: 1) experience in establishing and supporting successful partnerships with a variety of private and public sector organizations; 2) ability to work independently and to manage and prioritize deadline requirements; 3) experience in program development, monitoring, or grants management; 4) ability to communicate strongly and clearly orally and in writing, preferably with a diverse audience; 5) ability to form and maintain effective and cordial working relationships at all levels; 6) ability to function as a team member and to assume leadership; 7) competency in the use of Microsoft Office and Web-based programs; 8) demonstrated track record in community service as a volunteer or with an organization that uses service and volunteering to meet community needs.

Special requirements: Frequent travel. Work with projects and community organizations will occur primarily within Georgia, but will also include activities in the region or around the country. A valid driver's license is required.

Environmental Protection Agency

1200 Pennsylvania Avenue NW
Washington, D.C. 20460-0001
202-260-2090

* Web site: http://www.epa.gov/

* Job vacancies: http://www.epa.gov/ezhire/

* USAJOBS By Phone: 912-757-3000

* Internships, fellowships, and student information:
  http://www.epa.gov/epahome/intern.htm

* Links to EPA regional offices and labs: http://www.epa.gov/epahrist/located.htm

* Research Triangle Park, North Carolina: http://www.epa.gov/rtp/

* Employee benefits: http://www.epa.gov/epahrist/benefits.htm

* Human resources offices nationwide: http://www.epa.gov/epahrist/hroffices.htm

The mission of the Environmental Protection Agency (EPA) is to protect human health and to safeguard the natural environment–air, water, and land–upon which life depends. EPA develops and enforces regulations that implement environmental laws enacted by Congress; supports state environmental programs through grants; performs environmental research at laboratories around the country; sponsors voluntary environmental partnerships and programs that work to prevent pollution and conserve energy; and works to further environmental education.

EPA employs 18,000 people across the country, including its headquarters offices in Washington, D.C., 10 regional offices, and more than a dozen labs. Its staff are highly educated and technically trained; more than half are engineers, scientists, and policy analysts. In addition, a large number of employees are legal, public affairs, financial, information management, and computer specialists.

Ezhire is EPA's Web-based recruitment and application system. Applicants can browse, register, receive electronic notification of vacancies, and apply to EPA jobs by using ezhire@EPA. Paper applications are not accepted unless hardship circumstances can be demonstrated.

Selected Agencies Within EPA

The **American Indian Environmental Office** coordinates the Agency-wide effort to strengthen public health and environmental protection in Indian Country, with a special emphasis on building tribal capacity to administer their own environmental programs.

★ Web site: http://www.epa.gov/indian/

★ Job vacancies: http://www.epa.gov/ezhire/

★ Headquarters contacts: http://www.epa.gov/indian/staff.htm

★ Program offices and tribal programs: http://www.epa.gov/indian/programs.htm

★ Regional offices: http://www.epa.gov/indian/map.htm

★ Tribal contacts: http://www.epa.gov/indian/tcont.htm

The **Office of Prevention, Pesticides and Toxic Substances** (OPPTS) plays an important role in protecting public health and the environment from potential risk from toxic chemicals. It promotes pollution prevention and the public's right to know about chemical risks. It evaluates pesticides and chemicals to safeguard people and animals. Top priorities include dealing with emerging issues like endocrine disruptors and lead poisoning prevention.

★ Web site: http://www.epa.gov/oppts/

★ Job vacancies: http://www.epa.gov/ezhire/

★ Headquarters contacts: http://www.epa.gov/opptsmnt/comments.htm

The **Office of Solid Waste and Emergency Response** (OSWER) provides policy, guidance, and direction for the Agency's solid waste and emergency response programs. It develops guidelines for the land disposal of hazardous waste and underground storage tanks; provides technical assistance to the government to establish safe practices in waste management; and administers the Brownfields program, which supports state and local governments in redeveloping and reusing potentially contaminated sites. It also manages the Superfund program, designed to respond to abandoned and active hazardous waste sites and accidental oil and chemical releases as well as encourage innovative technologies to address contaminated soil and groundwater.

★ Web site: http://www.epa.gov/swerrims/

★ Job vacancies: http://www.epa.gov/ezhire/

★ Headquarters contacts: http://www.epa.gov/swerrims/comments.htm

The mission of the **Office of Water** is to ensure that drinking water is safe and to restore and maintain oceans, watersheds, and their aquatic ecosystems in order to protect human health, support economic and recreational activities, and provide a healthy habitat for fish, plants, and wildlife.

★ Web site: http://www.epa.gov/OW/

★ Job vacancies: http://www.epa.gov/ezhire/

★ Headquarters contacts: http://www.epa.gov/water/comments.html

Other EPA Agencies

History Office
http://www.epa.gov/history/

Office of Administration and Resources Management
http://www.epa.gov/oarm/

Office of Air and Radiation
http://www.epa.gov/oar/

Office of Enforcement & Compliance Assurance
http://www.epa.gov/compliance/

Office of Environmental Information
http://www.epa.gov/oei/

Office of Environmental Justice
http://www.epa.gov/compliance/environmentaljustice/index.html

Office of International Affairs
http://www.epa.gov/oia/

Office of Research and Development
http://www.epa.gov/ORD/

Science Policy Council
http://www.epa.gov/osa/spc/

Sample Job Vacancies

Environmental Health Scientist
Agency: National Health and Environmental Effects Research Laboratory
Salary: $82,438 to $107,170
Location: Research Triangle Park, North Carolina

Job description summary: Provides guidance, leadership, and expertise to the laboratory in matters related to human research ethics and subject safety. Provides advice and recommendations which may serve as a basis for policy decisions in areas related to the ethical study of human research subjects. Extramural resources management duties comprise less than 25 percent of the duties and consist of contracts management, grants/cooperative agreements, and interagency agreements.

Minimum qualifications required: Bachelor's degree with major in a field related to the health sciences or allied sciences appropriate to the work of the position. Must have one year of specialized experience, such as experience with applying the Common Rule, Belmont Report, or other relevant requirements and guidelines related to the ethical treatment of human research subjects; or scientific research with respect to design, conduct, analysis, and evaluation of clinical research, operational research activities, and epidemiologic research projects.

Minimum application materials required: Submit an online resume, application, and college transcript through Ezhire@EPA. Respond in narrative form to the following KSAs: 1) member of an Institutional Review Board or a comparable panel that reviews human studies for at least three years; 2) chair of an IRB or held a similar position which entailed an oversight or review of the ethical implications of human studies other than my own research; 3) five years of hands-on experience as an independent investigator in performing human epidemiology or clinical studies in which I prepared and submitted protocols to an IRB or comparable review committee; 4) five peer reviewed publications describing my epidemiology or human clinical study research; 5) experience in communicating information orally as evidenced by at least five presentations at local, regional, or national meetings; 6) knowledge of the Common Rule, the Belmont Report and other related documents on ethics related to human studies; 7) experience training researchers in the ethics related to human studies; 8) experience working in a team environment including both being a team member and being a team leader.

Special requirements: Must undergo successful review by the NHEERL Technical Qualification Board. Male applicants born after December 31, 1959, must certify that they have registered with the Selective Service System, or are exempt from having to do so under Selective Service law.

Environmental Protection Specialist
Agency: Office of Environmental Information and Analysis
Salary: $41,815 to $65,769
Location: Washington, D.C.

Job description summary: Conducts outreach efforts to identify Agency constituencies, assess their needs, and solicit feedback on information policies and tools. Provides administrative and procedural support to stake-holders to design and implement the Agency's public access interface, encouraging effective integration of public access concerns and public involvement in Agency activities. Works on program-related federal, state, and local policy development and rules, documentation, and reporting requirements. Serves as a project/team member to provide critical analyses and recommendations for studies, program plans, and proposals. Provides administrative and procedural support for management of extramural funding activities. Provides support to higher-level program specialist for development of technical and policy analyses.

Minimum qualifications required: Must have one year of specialized experience; OR a Ph.D. or equivalent doctoral degree; OR three full years of progressively higher-level graduate education; OR an LL.M.; OR a combination of experience and education. Specialized experience includes knowledge of environmental protection principles and procedures applicable to a wide range of duties requiring a high level of skill in assisting in solving complex problems involving diverse aspects of environmental protection (e.g., of a new program or a program that is being redefined, where procedures require frequent modification and change in order to incorporate revised theories and techniques). The work requires knowledge of statutes, regulations, and precedent decisions.

Minimum application materials required: Submit an online resume and application through Ezhire@EPA. Application should include answers to the following KSAs: 1) negotiate with others to reach consensus; 2) communicate with a variety of individuals and managers; 3) experience in preparing issue papers on environmental policies; 4) prepare summaries of complex technical, regulatory, or scientific materials for nontechnical audiences; 5) prepare research papers or position documents which present environmental policy analyses, summaries, or recommendations for both technical and nontechnical audiences; 6) experience in developing or reviewing content for Web sites; 7) contribute to the development of marketing and branding strategies.

Interdisciplinary Biologist/Chemist

Agency: Office of Research and Development, National Risk Management Research Laboratory
Salary: $60,871 to $94,102
Location: Cincinnati, Ohio

Job description summary: Develops an in-house computational toxicology research program. The results of this research will include in silico methods or techniques that can be used in risk management approaches, such as minimizing, eliminating, or replacing harmful chemicals. More information on the Computational Toxicology Framework can be found at http://www.epa.gov/comptox/.

Minimum qualifications required: (Biologist): Bachelor's degree in biological sciences, agriculture, natural resource management, chemistry, or related disciplines appropriate to the position OR a combination of education and experience. (Chemist): Bachelor's degree in physical sciences, life sciences, or engineering that included 30 semester hours in chemistry, supplemented by course work in mathematics, and at least six semester hours of physics OR a combination of education and experience. All applicants must have one year of specialized experience in planning and coordinating environmental research activities including research milestones and budget needs; participating in an environmental research implementation team; communicating on the progress of research programs both orally and in writing; coordinating extramural activities in support of research programs; and developing quality assurance/quality control documents for an environmental research program and ensuring quality assurance/quality control objectives are met.

Minimum application materials required: Submit an online application, resume, and copy of college transcripts through Ezhire@EPA. Include narrative answers to more than 30 KSAs, including the following : 1) ability to program in JAVA, ORACLE, C++, or FORTRAN; 2) familiarity with new molecular approaches; 3) ability to organize data collected from other sources and integrate them with the data from personal research; 4) ability to communicate with other researchers; 5) ability to serve as a team leader to a research group and to work effectively and productively with a multidisciplinary science or research team; 6) ability to read, interpret, evaluate and synthesize, findings from a body of research on a pollutant or an environmental issue, and develop reports integrating the research findings; 7) ability to present findings to audiences outside the organization; 8) experience with harvest and storage of animal tissues in order to maintain RNA integrity; 9) experience with extraction and purification of high quality, nondegraded RNA; 10) experience with collecting and managing gene expression microassay results in a database; 11) knowledge of DNA sequencing and DNA sequence analysis software; 12) experience with digital imaging of DNA, image analysis of DNA microassays, PCR amplification of DNA, in situ DNA hybridization, in situ PCR amplification of DNA, DNA hybridization, and DNA sequencing; 13) skill in collecting, analyzing, and interpreting toxicity data.

Special requirements: Must pass a background investigation. Must be a U.S. citizen. Male applicants who turned age 18 after December 1959 must have registered with the Selective Service System.

Mathematical Statistician

Agency: Office of Water
Salary: $55,904 to $78,826
Location: Washington, D.C.

Job description summary: Provides statistical support services for data collection activities Communicates results of analysis to staff and management. Assesses statistical properties of state water-quality assessment methodologies. Reviews methodologies to evaluate the validity of statistical analysis and provides feedback on their adequacy. Applies current Geographic Information System tools to evaluate spatial patterns and relationships in monitoring data, to evaluate distributional and other assumptions, to present data clearly and concisely, and to identify outliers. Writes reports summarizing the statistical analysis, data reviews, results and recommendations. Provides briefings to project team on the results of the statistical analyses and evaluation of data.

Minimum qualifications required: Bachelor's degree: that included 24 semester hours of mathematics and statistics; OR a combination of education and experience. Must have at least one year of specialized experience, such as performing recurring or continuing complex mathematical statistical studies, evaluating the validity of smaller, less-complex scientific studies, or assisting in the development reports-based statistical analyses.

Minimum application materials required: Submit an online resume, college transcripts, and application through Ezhire@EPA. Respond in narrative form to the following KSAs: 1) ability to manage studies evaluating the environmental impacts of environmental regulations, policies, or issues related to the Clean Water Act and the Safe Drinking Water Act; 2) skill in a variety of statistical methods; 3) experience using statistical software and programming languages; 4) ability to develop statistical designs for experimental investigations in biological and environmental research; 5) ability to analyze ecological or environmental data using statistical methods; 6) ability to use statistical software applications to design and analyze environmental assessments and monitoring studies; 7) ability to use software to manipulate experimental data and to integrate scientific databases; 8) ability to develop numerical simulation studies; 9) ability to use statistical methods for the analysis of effects and data; 10) ability to develop mathematical and statistical models for biological and physical phenomena.

Special requirements: The person selected for this position is subject to a favorable pre-appointment background investigation and must successfully pass a background investigation.

Physical Scientist

Agency: Office of Air Quality Planning and Standards
Salary: $40,454 to $90,692
Location: Research Triangle Park, North Carolina

Job description summary: Serves as a project scientist with responsibility for coordinating and developing the design and application of complex air-quality models to assess the effectiveness of multipollutant emission control strategies. Applies, evaluates, and modifies atmospheric models; conducts model applications to address source/emissions/control data and projections, aerometric/meteorological data, and principles of atmospheric transport, dispersion, and transformation; supports studies and participates in multidisciplinary workgroups to conduct analyses of the "one-atmosphere" control concept; analyzes a wide variety of complex problems involving the air quality impact of pollution sources on single- and multipollutant control strategy alternatives; prepares and implements technical guidance and procedures and provides consultation related to the use of air quality models and the design/assessment of single- and multipollutant strategies to be used in federal, state, and local air pollution control programs for air toxics and criteria pollutants; presents findings to EPA managers, government officials, and industry; prepares technical papers, reviews, correspondence, and written reports on various aspects of air-quality modeling and control strategy analyses.

Minimum qualifications required: Bachelor's degree in physical science, engineering, or mathematics that included 24 semester hours in physical science; OR a combination of education and experience. Must have at least one year of specialized experience in or related to the line of work of the position as described in job summary.

Minimum application materials required: Submit an online resume, college transcript, and application through Ezhire@EPA. Include narrative responses to the following KSAs: 1) develop air-quality model applications to assess the pollutant control strategies as part of an assessment of air quality impacts; 2) experience in "one-atmosphere" integrated modeling sciences; 3) skill in technical and statistical analysis related to fine particles, ozone, visibility, or air toxics; 4) ability to determine the environmental impacts of criteria and toxic pollutants by applying dispersion models, photochemical grid models, and meteorological models; 5) ability to analyze air-quality impacts associated with multipollutant control strategies; 6) experience in developing and maintaining working relationships with a variety of personnel from various backgrounds and with various levels of professional credentials; 7) ability to apply statistical and graphical analysis to evaluate and interpret air-quality impacts of alternative control strategies; ability to conduct model performance evaluations; 8) experience in using and adapting the latest in computer hardware and software for air-quality modeling applications and technical data analysis; 9) skill in presenting technical briefings to program managers and stakeholder groups related to air-quality modeling for criteria and toxic pollutants.

Special requirements: As a condition of employment, male applicants born after December 31, 1959, must certify that they have registered with the Selective Service System, or are exempt from having to do so under Selective Service law.

Equal Employment Opportunity Commission

1801 L Street NW
Washington, D.C. 20507
202-663-4900

★ Web site: http://www.eeoc.gov/

★ Job vacancies:

★ USAJOBS By Phone: 912-757-3000

★ How to apply: http://www.eeoc.gov/soars/apply.html

★ Links to EEOC field offices: http://www.eeoc.gov/offices.html

The Equal Employment Opportunity Commission (EEOC) enforces laws which prohibit discrimination based on race, color, religion, sex, national origin, disability, or age in hiring, promoting, firing, setting wages, testing, training, apprenticeship, and all other terms and conditions of employment. The EEOC conducts investigations of alleged discrimination; makes determinations based on gathered evidence; attempts conciliation when discrimination has taken place; files lawsuits; and conducts voluntary assistance programs for employers, unions, and community organizations. The EEOC also has adjudicatory and oversight responsibility for all compliance and enforcement activities relating to equal employment opportunity among federal employees and applicants.

EEOC uses a Web-based employee recruitment system called Secure Online Automated Recruiting System (SOARS). SOARS allows job seekers to review vacancy announcements; answer position-specific questions; create, edit, and archive an electronic resume; and apply for EEOC's jobs online.

Sample Job Vacancy

Director, Communications Staff

Agency: Equal Employment Opportunity Commission
Salary: $100,231 to $130,305
Location: Washington, D.C.

Job description summary: Serves as a key communicator of EEOC policies and programs. Directs responses to information requests from the news media and the general public on the EEOC's programs. Recommends areas where EEOC should generate media interest. Represents the EEOC to the news media, nongovernment organizations, and the public, and is responsible for coordinating internal EEOC communications. Maintains an awareness of current issues and events, public attitudes, sensitivities and activities, and identifying impact upon and relationships to EEOC policies and programs. Speaks for the Director on EEOC policies, programs, and events. Reviews communications programs throughout EEOC to ensure continuing effectiveness. Continuously evaluates communications programs and recommends and implements changes based upon an analysis of findings.

Minimum qualifications required: At least one year of specialized experience where you served on panels, committees or task forces as a representative of the organization on technical or professional issues; served as an official spokesperson; lead briefings, meetings, or conferences; defended an organization's policies and activities to supportive or hostile audiences; or worked with key officials, managers, and technical personnel of an organization to achieve outreach and other strategic communications goals.

Minimum application materials required: Apply online via SOARS. Include narrative responses to the following KSAs: 1) ability to communicate organizational strategies, goals, objectives, or priorities; 2) ability to explain complex information orally and in writing; 3) ability to have good working relationships with key individuals and stakeholders and to deal with individuals who are difficult, hostile or distressed; 4) ability to manage time and resources; 5) ability to work under pressure; 6) ability to complete complex assignments requiring accurate, timely, and technically sound data; 7) skill in disseminating information through visual media; 8) ability to make presentations and briefings; 9) ability to write and edit speeches or testimony for high ranking officials; 10) ability to manage employees and projects.

Special requirements: Must be a U.S. citizen.

Export-Import Bank of the United States

811 Vermont Avenue NW
Washington, D.C. 20571
800-565-EXIM

★ Web site: http://www.exim.gov/

★ Job vacancies: http://www.exim.gov/about/jobs/current.html

★ USAJOBS By Phone: 912-757-3000

★ How to apply: http://www.exim.gov/about/jobs/howtoapply.html

★ Headquarters and regional offices contacts: http://www.exim.gov/contactus.html

★ Benefits: http://www.exim.gov/about/jobs/benefits.html

The Export-Import Bank of the United States (Ex-Im Bank) is the official export credit agency of the United States. Ex-Im Bank's mission is to assist in financing the export of U.S. goods and services to international markets. Ex-Im Bank enables U.S. companies–large and small–to turn export opportunities into real sales that help to maintain and create U.S. jobs and contribute to a stronger national economy. Ex-Im Bank does not compete with private sector lenders but provides export financing products that fill gaps in trade financing. It assumes credit and country risks that the private sector is unable or unwilling to accept. It also helps to level the playing field for U.S. exporters by matching the financing that other governments provide to their exporters. Ex-Im Bank provides working capital guarantees (preexport financing); export credit insurance (postexport financing); and loan guarantees and direct loans (buyer financing). No transaction is too large or too small. On average, 85 percent of its transactions directly benefit U.S. small businesses.

In addition to its headquarters in Washington, the Export-Import Bank operates six regional offices and employs about 400 people in positions such as business development specialist, loan specialist, engineer (electronics, civil, mechanical, electrical, industrial, environmental, mining), economist, attorney-advisor, resource manager (finance, accounting, human resources, information technology).

Sample Job Vacancy

Loan Specialist
Agency: Multibuyer Insurance Branch, Small and Medium Enterprises Division
Salary: $41,815 to $65,769
Location: Washington, D.C.

Job description summary: Analyzes export credit transactions and recommends actions regarding Ex-Im Bank support. Provides ongoing administration and monitoring of his own portfolio of insurance transactions.

Minimum qualifications required: One year of specialized experience performing financial analysis of business information for risk evaluation purposes; reviewing and evaluating applications for credit either bank or insurance; or other similar work to successfully perform the duties of the position. A master's degree in finance, business administration, international business, international relations, economics, or accounting may be substituted.

Minimum application materials required: Submit a resume, Optional Application for Federal Employment (OF 612), or Application for Federal Employment (SF 171). Include narrative responses to the following KSAs: 1) ability to analyze financial statements and other sources of business information such as credit reports and trade and bank references; 2) ability to prepare analytical/evaluative reports and other written material on a variety of credit, financial,

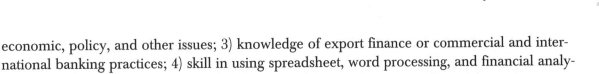

economic, policy, and other issues; 3) knowledge of export finance or commercial and international banking practices; 4) skill in using spreadsheet, word processing, and financial analysis software programs.

Special requirements: Must be a U.S. citizen.

Farm Credit Administration

1501 Farm Credit Drive
McLean, Virginia 22102-5090
703-883-4000

* Web site: http://www.fca.gov/
* Job vacancies: http://www.fca.gov/apps/jobs.nsf
* USAJOBS By Phone: 912-757-3000
* How to apply: http://www.fca.gov/howtoapply.htm
* Benefits: http://www.fca.gov/employeebenefits.htm
* Career development: http://www.fca.gov/careersdevelopment.htm
* FCA contacts: http://www.fca.gov/FCA-Contacts.htm
* Links to Farm Credit System institutions:
  http://www.fca.gov/apps/instit.nsf/Active%20Institutions%20Page?OpenPage

The Farm Credit Administration is responsible for ensuring the safe and sound operation of the banks, associations, affiliated service organizations, and other entities that collectively comprise what is known as the Farm Credit System, and for protecting the interests of the public and those who borrow from Farm Credit institutions or invest in Farm Credit securities. The major agency functions include conducting examinations of all System institutions; enforcing safe and sound banking practices, federal statutes, and FCA regulations; issuing and amending charters for System institutions; developing regulations; reviewing legal issues and resolving litigation; handling borrower-related issues and complaints; and administering the fiscal, personnel, and human resources of the agency. The agency's headquarters are in McLean, Virginia. It has field examination offices in Bloomington, Minnesota; Dallas, Texas; Denver, Colorado; and Sacramento, California.

Federal Communications Commission

445 Twelfth Street SW
Washington, D.C. 20554
888-225-5322

* Web site: http://www.fcc.gov/
* Job vacancies: http://www.fcc.gov/jobs/

★ USAJOBS By Phone: 912-757-3000

★ Headquarters contacts: http://www.fcc.gov/contacts.html

★ FCC regional and field offices: http://www.fcc.gov/eb/rfo/

★ Phone directory: http://www.fcc.gov/fcc-bin/findpeople.pl

The Federal Communications Commission (FCC) regulates interstate and foreign communications by radio, television, wire, satellite, and cable. It is responsible for the orderly development and operation of broadcast services and the provision of rapid, efficient nationwide and worldwide telephone and telegraph services at reasonable rates. Its responsibilities also include the use of communications for promoting safety of life and property and for strengthening the national defense.

The Commission staff is organized by function. There are six operating bureaus and 10 staff offices. The bureaus' responsibilities include processing applications for licenses and other filings; analyzing complaints; conducting investigations; developing and implementing regulatory programs; and taking part in hearings.

The FCC has three regional offices, 16 district offices, and nine resident agent offices located across the United States.

Selected Agencies Within FCC

The **Media Bureau** develops, recommends, and administers the policy and licensing programs relating to electronic media, including cable television, broadcast television, and radio, in the United States and its territories. The Media Bureau also handles postlicensing matters regarding direct broadcast satellite service.

★ Web site: http://www.fcc.gov/mb/

★ Headquarters contacts: http://www.fcc.gov/mb/mbstaff.html

The **Wireless Telecommunications Bureau** handles nearly all FCC domestic wireless telecommunications programs, policies, and outreach initiatives. Wireless communications services include amateur, cellular, paging, broadband PCS, public safety, and more.

★ Web site: http://wireless.fcc.gov/

★ Headquarters contacts: http://wireless.fcc.gov/organization/#structure

Other FCC Agencies

Consumer & Government Affairs Bureau
http://www.fcc.gov/cgb/

Enforcement Bureau
http://www.fcc.gov/eb/

International Bureau
http://www.fcc.gov/ib/

Wireline Competition Bureau
http://www.fcc.gov/wcb/

Sample Job Vacancies

Auditor

Agency: Office of the Inspector General
Salary: $72,108 to $110,775
Location: Washington, D.C.

Job description summary: Exercises technical direction over audits; performs systematic examination and appraisal of financial records, reports, management controls, policies and practices, etc., to ensure that legal economic and efficient expenditures are made; surveys organizational units to be audited to determine the purpose, scope, and objective of the unit or function; surveys accounting system; examines financial and other records to determine adherence to law, and prescribed policies; evaluates audit findings and drafts reports and substantiating papers, preparing recommendations; conducts conferences with program officials; conducts audits of FCC contractors; conducts audits of other funds under the control of the FCC, performs special audits involving suspected fraud, misapplications of funds, etc.; conducts inspections and examinations of nonfinancial accounting systems; prepares and maintains accurate working papers; and acts as Audit Lead in directing and/or reviewing the work of staff and contracted personnel assigned to a project.

Minimum qualifications required: Bachelor's degree in accounting or a related field that included 24 semester hours in accounting; OR a combination of education and experience equivalent to four years in accounting. Must have one year of specialized experience conducting examination and appraisals of financial records and reports, management controls, and policies and practices; acting as Audit Lead in directing or reviewing the work of staff or contracted personnel assigned to a project; and performing all facets of an audit report from initial audit survey through the drafting and issuance of a final audit report and oral presentation to management officials.

Minimum application materials required: Submit an Optional Application for Federal Employment (OF-612) or a resume. Include narrative responses to the following KSAs: 1) ability to plan, direct, and perform financial, program, and contract audits; 2) ability to formulate recommendations for corrective actions to address audit findings; 3) ability to produce written audit products; 4) ability to communicate orally with diverse individuals at all levels of authority within and outside of the agency.

Special requirements: Males over age 18 born after December 31, 1959, are required to have registered with the Selective Service System (or have an exemption).

Information Technology Specialist
Agency: Information Technology Center
Salary: $100,231 to $130,305
Location: Washington, D.C.

Job description summary: Provides leadership, management, and direction of major IT projects for knowledge capture and distribution in support of the FCC's and ITC's strategic goals and initiatives. Researches, analyzes, and evaluates new information technologies and knowledge management tools. Serves as a Contracting Officers Technical Representative (COTR) for assigned contracts in support of IT projects. Provides senior-level liaison, consultation, advice, coordination, and leadership on Commission-wide and Bureau/Office specific IT initiatives, training, systems, and processes. Serves as a senior member on various FCC councils and committees formed to review, recommend, and update IT strategies and related budgets.

Minimum qualifications required: One year of specialized experience applying IT theories, principles, concepts, standards and practices; providing leadership, management, and direction of major IT projects; identifying and recommending state-of-the art information technologies and knowledge management tools; and providing technical advice to managers on information technology. Demonstrated experience implementing and managing a document-management and collaboration project, incorporating taxonomy and classification methodologies.

Minimum application materials required: Submit an Optional Application for Federal Employment (OF-612) or a resume. Include narrative responses to the following KSAs: 1) ability to manage complex projects requiring change, technology, and contract management skills; 2) ability to lead successful knowledge management, research and behavioral-changing IT initiatives; 3) ability to manage and direct multidisciplinary teams; 4) ability to establish and maintain effective working relationships with individuals at all levels; 5) ability to communicate orally and in writing.

Special requirements: Males over age 18 born after December 31, 1959, are required to have registered with the Selective Service System (or have an exemption).

Federal Deposit Insurance Corporation

550 Seventeenth Street NW
Washington, D.C. 20429
202-393-8400

★ Web site: http://www.fdic.gov/

★ Job vacancies: http://www2.quickhire.com/fdic/fdicjobfamily.jsp

★ USAJOBS By Phone: 912-757-3000

★ How to apply for an FDIC job: http://www.fdic.gov/about/jobs/apply.html

★ Links to FDIC agencies and offices: http://www.fdic.gov/about/jobs/work.html

★ Student employment information: http://www.fdic.gov/about/jobs/stuemp.html

★ Employee benefits: http://www.fdic.gov/about/jobs/benefits.html

★ Recruiting locations: http://www.fdic.gov/about/jobs/recruit.html

★ Organizational directory:
http://www.fdic.gov/about/contact/FDICOrganizationalDirectory.html#HQDOA

The Federal Deposit Insurance Corporation (FDIC) insures bank and thrift deposits up to $100,000; periodically examines state-chartered banks that are not members of the Federal Reserve system for safety and for compliance with consumer protection laws; and liquidates the assets of failed banks or savings associations to reimburse insurance funds for the loss. As banking has transformed into e-banking, the FDIC also analyzes Internet-related risk, explores the ramifications of wireless banking, and looks into the issues of technology inter-operability.

The FDIC employs about 5,200 people. It is headquartered in Washington, D.C., but con-ducts much of its business in six regional offices and in field offices around the country. It has 14 divisions or offices at its headquarters. Types of careers available at FDIC include bank examiners, compliance examiners, economists, financial analysts, information technology pro-fessionals, administrative personnel, and attorneys. The FDIC employs students as summer interns, assisting economists as research assistants. Ideal candidates for interns are students who are in the process of obtaining a degree in finance, economics, or statistics.

To apply for a job at the FDIC, the agency requires one of the following: an Optional Application for Federal Employment (OF-612), a resume, or the old Application for Federal Employment (SF-171). Whichever document you submit must include all of the following information: the position title and announcement number on the first page of your applica-tion, as well as your name, address, Social Security Number, telephone numbers where you can be reached during the day, and citizenship. All application materials must be included with your original submission. FDIC recommends that you include with your application descriptions or examples of experience which demonstrate your possession of the knowledge, skills, and abilities identified in the qualification requirements and ranking factor sections of the vacancy announcement. Facsimiles and electronic transmittals (e-mail, disk) cannot be accepted unless specified on the vacancy announcement. Applications submitted in government-franked envelopes will not receive consideration.

Federal Election Commission

999 E Street NW
Washington, D.C. 20463
202-694-1100

★ Web site: http://www.fec.gov/

★ Job vacancies: http://www.fec.gov/jobs.htm

★ USAJOBS By Phone: 912-757-3000

★ FEC offices: http://www.fec.gov/pages/offices.htm

In 1975, Congress created the Federal Election Commission (FEC) to administer and enforce the Federal Election Campaign Act (FECA), the statute that governs the financing of federal elections. The duties of the FEC are to disclose campaign finance information, to enforce the provisions of the law such as the limits and prohibitions on contributions, and to oversee the public funding of presidential elections.

The Commission is made up of six members, who are appointed by the President and confirmed by the Senate. Each member serves a six-year term, and two seats are subject to appointment every two years.

Sample Job Vacancies

Attorney, Litigation Specialist
Agency: Litigation Division, Office of the General Counsel
Salary: $60,638 to $110,775
Location: Washington, D.C.

Job description summary: Researches and drafts papers; presents oral arguments when the Commission appears in court, at the trial and appellate levels. Drafts a variety of legal documents, including complaints, answers, briefs, motions, and other documents incident to trying the case as assigned. Participates in negotiating settlements and prepares the settlement agreement and other necessary papers. Advises the Commission on actions relating to his or her cases and represents the Commission in court as assigned.

Minimum qualifications required: A law degree, bar membership and one year of professional attorney experience. Excellent oral communication skills as well as strong analytical skills and the ability to research complex legal issues and to write clearly, concisely and persuasively about difficult issues of statutory and constitutional law. Deposition, discovery and other litigation skills and experience are desirable. Knowledge of election law, administrative law, and investigative experience are helpful

Minimum application materials required: Submit an Optional Application for Federal Employment (OF-612), an Application for Federal Employment (SF-171), or a resume, along with a copy of your law school transcript. Include one writing sample that reflects your ability to analyze sophisticated legal issues.

Special requirements: Must pass a background investigation. A one-year probationary period is also required.

Docket Technician
Agency: Office of Complaints Examination and Legal Administration (CELA),
Office of the General Counsel
Salary: $34,184 to $49,216
Location: Washington, D.C.

Job description summary: Provides administrative and clerical support for CELA activities and establishes and maintains all permanent enforcement files. Maintains, extracts, and tracks case-related statistical information in various electronic spreadsheets, and tracks and prepares regular reports for all civil penalty agreements and payments. Implements new and revised reporting methods; prepares and maintains files; circulates documents to the Commission; tracks civil penalty payments; prepares monthly reports; archives closed cases; maintains paper manuals; and assists in maintaining, extracting, and tracking case-related statistical information in various electronic spreadsheets. Works closely with other CELA staff especially the Paralegal Specialists and the CELA Supervisory Attorney and must be knowledgeable of the various data systems utilized by those positions to assist them and handle routine matters in their absence.

Minimum qualifications required: Must possess one year of specialized experience; OR one year of graduate-level education; OR an undergraduate degree with superior academic achievement at the undergraduate level. Specialized experience includes skill in operating personal computers and word processing software to prepare documents and reports; skill in using Excel (or similar spreadsheet programs) to maintain, modify, merge, enter, extract, and present statistical data; and skill as a qualified typist. Must be able to type at least 40 words per minute with three or less errors.

Minimum application materials required: Submit an Optional Application for Federal Employment (OF-612), and Application for Federal Employment (SF-171), or a resume. Indicate typing speed, and include narrative answers to the following KSAs: 1) knowledge of office practices and procedures required to perform functions of the office; 2) ability to plan, organize, and prioritize work to meet office objectives, workload demands and deadlines; 3) ability to manage and maintain records and files; 4) skill in verifying data and making appropriate corrections and revisions in automated systems; 5) skill in utilizing software programs to extract information from automated systems or databases; 6) ability to review data from automated systems or databases to support record-keeping activities; 7) ability to perform analysis and to review materials and data for suitability and relevance; 8) ability to work effectively under pressure of tight time frames and rigid deadlines; 9) ability to express oneself in a clear, concise, and cordial manner with skill in written communications to prepare documents and reports and skill in oral communications to obtain and provide information; and 10) ability to work with staff in a team environment.

Special requirements: Must pass a background investigation. A one-year probationary period is also required.

Federal Housing Finance Board

1777 F Street NW
Washington, D.C. 20006
202-408-2500

★ Web site: http://www.fhfb.gov/index.htm

★ Job vacancies: http://www.fhfb.gov/CareerOps/Jobs.htm

★ USAJOBS By Phone: 912-757-3000

* Employee handbook:
  http://www.fhfb.gov/CareerOps/empGuides/EEOHandbook04203-B.doc

* Mailing addresses for FHL Banks: http://www.fhfb.gov/FHLB/fhlbs_banks.htm

* Employee benefits: http://www.fhfb.gov/CareerOps/Jobs.htm

* Employee directory: http://www.fhfb.gov/AboutUs/phonelist.asp

The Federal Housing Finance Board regulates the 12 Federal Home Loan (FHL) Banks that were created in 1932 to improve the supply of funds to local lenders that, in turn, finance loans for home mortgages. The FHL Banks and their 8,104 member-owners, which constitute the FHL Bank System, form a cooperative partnership that supports community-based financial institutions and facilitates their access to credit. The Finance Board ensures that the FHL Banks, which are privately capitalized, government-sponsored enterprises, operate in a safe and sound manner, carry out their housing and community development finance mission, and remain adequately capitalized and able to raise funds in the capital markets.

Selected Agencies Within FHLB

The **Office of Finance** (OF) issues and services all debt securities for the FHL Banks, while obtaining the most cost-effective terms possible, given the needs of investors and dealers. It also analyzes and develops new funding opportunities. The OF also provides the FHL Banks with credit and general capital market information/data, and manages their relationship with the credit rating agencies.

* Web site: http://www.fhlb-of.com/mission/of_frame.html

* Job vacancies: http://www.fhlb-of.com/mission/of_frame.html

Sample Job Vacancy

Bank Examiner
Agency: Federal Housing Finance Board
Salary: $94,913 to $155,386
Location: Washington, D.C.

Job description summary: Responsible for the development of examination and supervisory guidance, briefing and position paper and memoranda for specific matters, which includes the various risks that may be encountered by the FHL Banks and Office of Finance. Participates in the development and execution of a quality assurance program for ensuring the transparency and integrity of the supervisory program. May participate at the on-site examinations as a member of the examinations team.

Minimum qualifications required: Bachelor's degree in a related field. Must have one year of specialized experience in a related position. Must have experience assessing credit, market, and operational risks as well as accounting and corporate governance issues.

Minimum application materials: Submit an Optional Application for Federal Employment (OF-612), an Application for Federal Employment (SF-171), or a resume. Respond in narrative form to the following KSAs: 1) knowledge of current bank examination or audit practices; 2) experience in assessing a financial institution's credit, market, and operational risks; 3) skill in written program development for addressing supervisory issues emerging from economic, legislative, policy, and business changes and trends that affect the integrity and performance of the FHL Banks; 4) ability to analyze and resolve complex or controversial issues and provide technical advice and assistance on difficult matters; 5) skill in oral presentations for technical and nontechnical audiences.

Special requirements: Must be a U.S. citizen.

Federal Labor Relations Authority

1400 K Street NW
Washington, D.C. 20005
202-218-7000

- ★ Web site: http://www.flra.gov/

- ★ Job vacancies: http://www.flra.gov/29-jobs.html

- ★ USAJOBS By Phone: 912-757-3000

- ★ Links regional offices: http://www.flra.gov/gc/regions/map.html

- ★ How to apply: http://www.flra.gov/hrd/hrd_how.html

- ★ Employee benefits: http://www.flra.gov/hrd/hrd_bnf.html

- ★ Career information: http://www.flra.gov/hrd/hrd_job.html

The Federal Labor Relations Authority (FLRA) oversees the Federal service labor-management relations program. It administers the law that protects the right of the 1.9 million worldwide employees of the federal government to organize, bargain collectively, and participate through labor organizations of their own choosing in decisions affecting them. FLRA also ensures compliance with the statutory rights and obligations of federal employees and the labor organizations that represent them in their dealings with federal agencies.

FLRA employs approximately 215 people, about half of whom are in the Washington, D.C., headquarters offices, and the remainder divided among seven regional offices. The majority of FLRA employees are attorneys or labor relations specialists. FLRA consists of three major components: the Authority, the Office of the General Counsel, and the Federal Service Impasses Panel.

Sample Job Vacancy

Labor Relations Specialist
Agency: Office of the General Council
Salary: $81,602 to $106,086
Location: Washington, D.C.

Job description summary: Handles the most complex and significant representation cases and complex unfair labor practice and compliance cases and issues in the regional office; represents the Office of the General Counsel in novel or complex cases or issues which have national implications; opens and investigates cases involving petitions that involve nationwide reorganizations or complex accretion and successorship issues; investigates challenged ballots or objections to an election which are filed following a highly contested election having sensitive, national or political impact; schedules and conducts complex mail, manual, or combination elections; drafts Decisions and Orders on complex representation issues for the regional director.

Minimum qualifications required: Must possess one year of experience performing work related to labor economics; labor relations; collective bargaining in commerce, industry, or government; or labor law.

Minimum application materials required: Submit resume, application, and narrative answers to the following KSAs: 1) expert understanding of public or private sector labor law, regulations, policies and practices; 2) expert knowledge of public or private-sector case law and procedures in representation case handling; 3) knowledge of public or private-sector case law and procedures in unfair labor practice case handling; 4) ability to facilitate resolution of representations and unfair labor practice cases; 5) knowledge and ability to gather and analyze complex factual and legal issues and to arrive at practical solutions to problems which are unusual or highly complicated; 6) ability to establish and maintain effective working relationships; 7) skill in effective written and oral communications.

Special requirements: Must be a U.S. citizen.

Federal Maritime Commission

800 North Capitol Street NW
Washington, D.C. 20573-0001
202-523-5707

★ Web site: http://www.fmc.gov/

★ Job vacancies: http://www.fmc.gov/jobs/jobs.htm

★ USAJOBS By Phone: 912-757-3000

★ Contact information for FMC area representatives:
http://www.fmc.gov/About%20the%20Commission_Copy.htm#Area%20Representatives

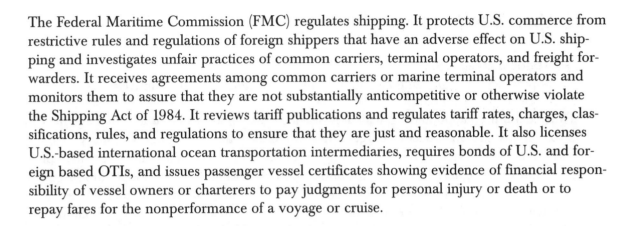

The Federal Maritime Commission (FMC) regulates shipping. It protects U.S. commerce from restrictive rules and regulations of foreign shippers that have an adverse effect on U.S. shipping and investigates unfair practices of common carriers, terminal operators, and freight forwarders. It receives agreements among common carriers or marine terminal operators and monitors them to assure that they are not substantially anticompetitive or otherwise violate the Shipping Act of 1984. It reviews tariff publications and regulates tariff rates, charges, classifications, rules, and regulations to ensure that they are just and reasonable. It also licenses U.S.-based international ocean transportation intermediaries, requires bonds of U.S. and foreign based OTIs, and issues passenger vessel certificates showing evidence of financial responsibility of vessel owners or charterers to pay judgments for personal injury or death or to repay fares for the nonperformance of a voyage or cruise.

Selected Agencies Within FMC

The **Bureau of Trade Analysis** (BTA) reviews agreements and monitors the activities of common carriers. It also reviews and analyzes service contracts, monitors rates of government controlled carriers, reviews carrier published tariff systems, and responds to inquiries or issues that arise concerning service contracts or tariffs. The BTA also is responsible for competition oversight and market analysis, focusing on activity that is substantially anti-competitive and market distorting. It is an expert organization on the economics of international liner shipping and maritime agreements, especially with respect to issues of competition and unfair trade practices as they may affect the interests of the shipping public and U.S. international trade.

★ Web site: http://www.fmc.gov/jobs/jobs.htm

Other FMC Agencies

Bureau of Enforcement
http://fmc.gov/. Then click on About the Commission. Then click on Bureau of Enforcement.

Bureau of Consumer Complaints & Licensing
http://fmc.gov/. Then click on About the Commission. Then click on Bureau of Consumer Complaints & Licensing.

Federal Mediation and Conciliation Service

2100 K Street NW
Washington, D.C. 20427
202-606-8100

★ Web site: http://www.fmcs.gov/internet/

★ Job vacancies:
http://www.fmcs.gov/internet/itemDetail.asp?categoryID=41&itemID=17625

★ USAJOBS By Phone: 912-757-3000

★ Mediator recruitment bulletin (PDF format):
   http://www.fmcs.gov/assets/files/HumanResources/MED04.pdf

★ Regional offices:
   http://www.fmcs.gov/internet/itemDetail.asp?categoryID=107&itemID=16282

The Federal Mediation and Conciliation Service (FMCS) assists labor and management in resolving disputes in collective bargaining contract negotiation through voluntary mediation and arbitration services; provides training to unions and management in cooperative processes to improve long-term relationships under the Labor Management Cooperation Act of 1978; provides alternative dispute resolution services and training to government agencies, including the facilitation of regulatory negotiations under the Administrative Dispute Resolution Act and the Negotiated Rulemaking Act of 1996; and awards competitive grants to joint labor-management committees to encourage innovative approaches to cooperative efforts.

In addition to administrative personnel, the FMCS primarily employs mediators. Stationed throughout the country, mediators perform duties in three major areas: collective bargaining mediation, relationship development training (preventive mediation), and outreach. Recruitment for mediators is continuous, with application materials available online. (*See* FMCS's Mediator Recruitment Bulletin.)

Sample Job Vacancy

Mediator
Agency: Federal Mediation and Conciliation Service
Salary: $62,905
Location: locations nationwide

Job description summary: Mediators serve as neutral and completely impartial parties in the collective bargaining process and other alternative dispute resolution processes. The mediator's knowledge of collective bargaining, understanding of labor-management problems, and possession of the ability to influence bargainers in the adjustment of their differences, contributes toward the settlement of labor-management conflicts as well as other disputes. In addition to entering into the specific labor-management dispute situations, the mediator has a continuing responsibility to prevent labor disputes from developing through active participation in relationship building activities and public information programs with labor and management organizations.

Minimum qualifications required: Applicants must have the demonstrated capacity to become full service mediators, that is, those who can enter a tension-filled labor dispute over terms of a collective bargaining agreement, while at the same time be able to deliver preventive mediation services. Must have substantial full-time experience (acquired over the last 10 years) in the negotiation of collective bargaining agreements in a leadership role or a similar role in agreement administration, including utilization of varied bargaining processes, substantial knowledge of contract language, familiarity with a broad scope of subjects, experience in numerous and diverse bargaining circumstances, and knowledge of joint processes to improve labor-management relationships. Must have the capacity to perform successfully collective bargaining mediation, relationship development training, and outreach. Candidates who fall short in meeting the qualification requirements may be considered for developmental positions. Availability of these positions is limited as they are located at our larger field offices where mentoring with an experienced mediator is possible.

Minimum application materials required: Submit an Optional Application for Federal Employment (OF-612) or a resume. Your application must include completed copies of FMC's Office Location Form, Supplemental References Form, and Background Survey Questionnaire, as well as written responses to the following KSAs: 1) knowledge of economic, management and labor trends, and of current developments and problems in the field of labor-management relations and with changes and trends in union agreements; 2) advanced knowledge of collective bargaining practices gained through progressively responsible and successful experience in the negotiation or administration of collective bargaining agreements and the resolution of labor-management conflict; 3) ability or potential to assess, design, deliver, and evaluate processes aimed at improving relationships or organizational effectiveness; 4) knowledge of conflict resolution; 5) knowledge of the general structure, functions, policies, and practices of employer and labor organizations; 6) familiarity with the applicable laws governing collective bargaining, wages, hours, benefits, etc.; 7) faculty for sound presentation and facilitation skills that includes effective communication skills (both verbal and written); 8) ability to chair meetings and lead discussions; 9) ability to use personal computers and various software packages.

Special requirements: Must pass a complete physical examination, undergo a suitability/ background investigation, possess a valid driver's license, indicate a willingness to accept assignment to any location in the United States based on the needs of the Service, and must present proof of U.S. citizenship.

Federal Reserve System

Twentieth Street and Constitution Avenue NW
Washington, D.C. 20551
202-452-3000

★ Web site: http://www.federalreserve.gov/

★ Job vacancies: http://www.federalreserve.gov/careers/default.cfm

★ USAJOBS By Phone: 912-757-3000

★ Job line: 800-448-4894

★ Internships: http://www.federalreserve.gov/careers/info.cfm?WhichCategory=8

★ Benefits: http://www.federalreserve.gov/careers/info.cfm?WhichCategory=57

The Federal Reserve System (Fed), the central bank of the United States, is charged with administering and formulating the Nation's credit and monetary policy. Through its supervisory and regulatory banking functions, the Federal Reserve maintains the safety and soundness of the nation's economy, responding to the nation's domestic and international financial needs and objectives. Its major responsibility is in the execution of monetary policy. It also performs other functions, such as the transfer of funds, handling government deposits and debt issues, supervising and regulating banks, and acting as lender of last resort.

The System consists of the Board of Governors in Washington, D.C.; the 12 Federal Reserve Banks and their 25 branches and other facilities situated throughout the country; the Federal Open Market Committee; the Federal Advisory Council; the Consumer Advisory Council; the Thrift Institutions Advisory Council; and the nation's financial institutions, including commercial banks, savings and loan associations, mutual savings banks, and credit unions.

Selected Agencies Within the Fed

The 12 **Federal Reserve Banks** operate under the general supervision of the Board of Governors in Washington. Each Bank has a nine-member board of directors that oversees its operations. Federal Reserve Banks generate their own income, primarily from interest earned on government securities that are acquired in the course of Federal Reserve monetary policy actions. A secondary source of income is derived from the provision of priced services to depository institutions, as required by the Monetary Control Act of 1980. Federal Reserve Banks are not, however, operated for a profit, and each year they return to the U.S. Treasury all earnings in excess of Federal Reserve operating and other expenses.

★ District 1 (Boston) Web site: http://www.bos.frb.org/

★ District 1 job vacancies:
   https://careers.peopleclick.com/Client40_FRBBoston/bu1/External_Pages/jobsearch.asp?

★ District 2 (New York) Web site: http://www.newyorkfed.org/

★ District 2 job vacancies: http://www.newyorkfed.org/careers/current_openings.html

★ District 3 (Philadelphia) Web site: http://www.phil.frb.org/

★ District 3 job vacancies:
   http://careers.peopleclick.com/client40_frbphilly/bu1/external_pages/jobsearch.asp

★ District 4 (Cleveland) Web site: http://www.clevelandfed.org/

★ District 4 job vacancies: http://www.clevelandfed.org/HR/Index.cfm

★ District 5 (Richmond) Web site: http://www.rich.frb.org/

★ District 5 job vacancies:
   http://careers.peopleclick.com/Client40_FRBRichmond/bu1/External_Pages/JobSearch.asp

★ District 6 (Atlanta) Web site: http://www.frbatlanta.org/

★ District 6 job vacancies:
   http://careers.peopleclick.com/client40_frbatlanta/bu1/external_pages/jobsearch.asp

★ District 7 (Chicago) Web site: http://www.chicagofed.org/

★ District 7 job vacancies:
   http://careers.peopleclick.com/Client40_FRBChicago/BU1/External_Pages/JobSearch.asp

★ District 8 (St. Louis) Web site: http://www.stlouisfed.org/

★ District 8 job vacancies: http://www.stlouisfed.org/about/jobsearch.html

★ District 9 (Minneapolis) Web site: http://www.minneapolisfed.org/

★ District 9 job vacancies: http://www.minneapolisfed.org/info/career/peopleclick/

★ District 10 (Kansas City) Web site: http://www.kansascityfed.org/

★ District 10 job vacancies: http://www.kansascityfed.org/humanres/currentopenings.htm

★ District 11 (Dallas) Web site: http://www.dallasfed.org/

★ District 11 job vacancies: http://careers3.peopleclick.com/client40_frbdallas/bu1/external_pages/jobsearch.asp

★ District 12 (San Francisco) Web site: http://www.frbsf.org/

★ District 12 job vacancies: http://www.frbsf.org/federalreserve/careers/jobs.html

Other Fed Agencies

Federal Reserve Board
http://www.federalreserve.gov?

Federal Open Market Committee
http://www.federalreserve.gov/pubs/frseries/frseri2.htm

Federal Advisory Council
http://www.federalreserve.gov/generalinfo/adviscoun/fac.htm

Consumer Advisory Council
http://www.federalreserve.gov/generalinfo/adviscoun/cac/default.htm

Thrift Institutions Advisory Council
http://www.federalreserve.gov/generalinfo/adviscoun/tiac.htm

Sample Job Vacancies

Administrative Assistant
Agency: Federal Reserve Bank of San Francisco
Salary: $36,200 to $51,200
Location: San Francisco, California

Job description summary: Provides word processing, typing and editorial support; answers and screens a high volume of incoming calls, taking and directing accurate messages; assists in assuring office efficiency by opening and routing mail, providing copier support, maintaining accurate department records by daily filing and updating; maintains attendance and vacation records; orders supplies; makes travel arrangements and arranges and coordinates meetings, conferences, and other projects; acts as back-up to other departmental staff assistant; acts as the department receptionist, greeting internal and external visitors when they arrive on the floor.

Minimum qualifications required: High school diploma or general education degree (GED) with three years of office administrative experience or combination of equivalent training and experience; the ability to write routine reports and correspondence; effective communication skills; and a demonstrated proficiency in computer skills and software products for word processing, spreadsheet, database, and presentation.

Minimum application materials required: Complete and submit an online application and resume.

Economist

Agency: Supervision, Regulation & Credit Department, Federal Reserve Bank of Boston
Salary: $69,832 to $125,698
Location: Boston, Massachusetts

Job description summary: Produces high-quality research for publication in referred journals; advises senior management on policy issues related to the regulation of banks and financial markets; and participates in credit and operational risk assessments of large complex banks.

Minimum qualifications required: Ph.D. in economics, finance, or a related field; demonstrated research capability; and strong written and oral communication skills. Relevant industry experience would also be a positive consideration.

Minimum application materials required: Complete and submit an online application and resume.

Junior Budget Analyst

Agency: Federal Reserve Bank of St. Louis
Salary: $40,454 to $52,591
Location: St. Louis, Missouri

Job description summary: Supports preparation of annual project, operating, and business line budgets, and all associated duties. Assists with monitoring actual expenses incurred by department, district, and other districts. Assists in researching budget variances to report or respond to department and bank management, and to Treasury customers. Assists with estimating usage of automated applications and environments, and monitoring charge-backs. Assists with various analytical projects.

Minimum qualifications required: Bachelor's degree in accounting or finance. Proven ability to communicate effectively orally and in writing with various levels of Bank management. Demonstrated high degree of skill for analyzing both financial data, and associated business needs. Demonstrated ability to research project and operating budget variances and draft appropriate explanations. Strong experience with accessing and downloading data from automated expense data collection systems. Demonstrated ability to prepare complex Excel spreadsheets. Strong working knowledge of MS Word and PowerPoint.

Minimum application materials required: Complete and submit an online application and resume.

Federal Retirement Thrift Investment Board

1250 H Street NW
Washington, D.C. 20005
202-942-1600

★ Web site: http://www.frtib.gov/

★ Job vacancies: http://www.frtib.gov/personnel/index.html

★ USAJOBS By Phone: 912-757-3000

★ Job Information Line: 202-942-1687

The Federal Retirement Thrift Investment Board administers the Thrift Savings Plan, which provides Federal employees the opportunity to save for additional retirement security. It is one of the smaller federal departments, with just over 100 employees.

Federal Trade Commission

600 Pennsylvania Avenue NW
Washington, D.C. 20580
202-326-2222

★ Web site: http://www.ftc.gov/index.html

★ USAJOBS By Phone: 912-757-3000

★ Regional offices: http://www.ftc.gov/ro/romap2.htm

★ Job opportunities, internships, student employment:
  http://www.ftc.gov/ftc/oed/hrmo/jobops.htm

★ Guide to the FTC: http://www.ftc.gov/bcp/conline/pubs/general/guidetoftc.htm

★ Employee benefits: http://www.ftc.gov/ftc/oed/hrmo/benefits.htm

The Federal Trade Commission (FTC) works to ensure the smooth operation of the American free market system. It enforces federal consumer protection laws that prevent fraud, deception, and unfair business practices as well as federal antitrust laws that prohibit anticompetitive mergers and other business practices that restrict competition and harm consumers. In addition, the Commission conducts economic research and analysis to support its law enforcement efforts and to contribute to the policy deliberations of the Congress, the executive branch, other independent agencies, and state and local governments.

The FTC hires attorneys, economists, paralegals, and administrative support personnel, among others. It recruits annually for entry-level attorney positions. The Bureau of Competition generally employs the largest number of new law school graduates.

Selected Agencies Within FTC

The **Bureau of Consumer Protection** protects consumers against unfair, deceptive, or fraudulent practices by enforcing a variety of consumer protection laws enacted by Congress, as well as trade regulation rules issued by the Commission. It investigates companies and industries, engages in litigation, makes rules, and educates consumers and businesses. The Bureau of Consumer Protection is divided into seven divisions: The Division of Advertising Practices, the Division of Enforcement, the Division of Financial Practices, the Division of Marketing Practices, the Division of Planning & Information, the International Division of Consumer Protection, and the Office of Consumer and Business Education.

★ Web site: http://www.ftc.gov/bcp/bcp.htm

Other FTC Agencies

Bureau of Competition

http://www.ftc.gov/bc/mission.htm

Bureau of Economics

http://www.ftc.gov/be/index.htm

General Services Administration

1800 F Street NW
Washington, D.C. 20405
202-708-5082

★ Web site: http://www.gsa.gov/

★ Job vacancies: https://jobs.quickhire.com/scripts/gsa.exe/runuserinfo?Haveusedbefore=5

★ USAJOBS By Phone: 912-757-3000

★ GSAJobs: http://www.gsa.gov. Then click on GSAjobs.

★ Application FAQs: http://www.gsa.gov. Then click on GSAjobs. Then click on FAQ.

★ Links to GSA regional offices: http://www.gsa.gov. Then click on About GSA. Then click on Regions.

★ Key staff: http://www.gsa.gov. Then click on Key Staff.

The General Services Administration (GSA) establishes policy for and provides economical and efficient management of government property and records, including construction and operation of buildings; procurement and distribution of supplies; utilization and disposal of real and personal property; transportation, traffic, and communications management; and management of the government-wide automatic data processing resources program.

The GSA organization consists of the Federal Supply Service, the Federal Technology Service, the Public Buildings Service, the Office of Governmentwide Policy, and various Staff Offices, including the Office of Small Business Utilization, the Office of Citizen Services and Communications, and the Office of Civil Rights. Eleven regional offices extend GSA's outreach to federal customers nationwide.

GSA has just over 13,000 employees who provide valuable services to support other federal agencies and, in some cases, the general public. GSA support can include office space, equipment, supplies, telecommunications, and information technology. GSA also plays a key role in developing and implementing policies that affect many government agencies.

Selected Agencies Within GSA

The **Federal Supply Service** (FSS) serves the federal community offering business, administrative, and mission solutions, and provides a source for virtually every commercial product or service an agency might need. With a business volume topping $25 billion, FSS offers more services than any commercial enterprise in the world. FSS also brings hundreds of thousands of federal customers together with more than 9,000 contractors.

★ Web site: http://www.gsa.gov. Then choose Federal Supply Service from drop-down menu.

★ Job vacancies: https://jobs.quickhire.com/scripts/gsa.exe/runuserinfo?Haveusedbefore=5

Other GSA Agencies

Citizen Services and Communications
http://www.gsa.gov. Then choose Citizen Services and Communications from drop-down menu.

Federal Technology Service
http://www.gsa.gov. Then choose Federal Technology Service from drop-down menu.

Office of Governmentwide Policy
http://www.gsa.gov. Then choose Office of Governmentwide Policy from drop-down menu.

Office of Small Business Utilization
http://www.gsa.gov. Then choose Office of Small Business Utilization from drop-down menu.

Public Buildings Service
http://www.gsa.gov. Then choose Public Buildings Service from drop-down menu.

Sample Job Vacancies

Appraiser
Agency: Portfolio Management Division, Public Buildings Service
Salary: $72,108 to $93,742
Location: Washington, D.C.

Job description summary: Performs a variety of complex appraisals and related services for valuing commercial, industrial, and residential properties, unimproved land, and special purpose properties which GSA and other federal agencies propose to lease, purchase, sell, transfer, outlease, condemn, grant partial interests, or value for prospectus and asset management purposes.

Minimum qualifications required: Must demonstrate at least one year of specialized experience equivalent in a real estate program with responsibility for performing the following types of duties: acquiring assets, investing in assets, managing tenant relationships, managing operations and maintenance of facilities, and disposing of assets.

Minimum application materials required: Register with General Services Administration's (GSAjobs) online application system and respond in narrative form to the following KSAs: 1) experience performing real property appraisals; 2) ability to communicate orally and in writing.

Special requirements: Must pass a background security investigation. Male applicants born after December 31, 1959, must have registered with the Selective Service System, or prove they are exempt.

Architect
Agency: Public Buildings Service
Salary: $59,570 to $92,090
Location: Atlanta, Georgia

Job description summary: Serves as a senior architect with overall responsibility for the design management of designated major design, construction, renovation, or alteration projects. Projects assigned typically encompass the largest, most complex, highly visible activities of the region or those with the highest dollar value.

Minimum qualifications required: Bachelor's degree in architecture or related field which included 60 semester hours of course work in architecture or related discipline; OR a combination of education and experience that furnished a thorough knowledge of the arts and sciences underlying professional architecture and a good understanding of architectural principles, methods and techniques and their applications to the design and construction or improvement of buildings. Must have at least one year of specialized experience in professional architectural work which typically requires the application of architectural principles, theories, concepts, methods, and techniques and an understanding and skill to use pertinent aspects of the construction industry, engineering, and the physical sciences related to the design and construction of new or the improvement of existing buildings.

Minimum application materials required: Register with General Services Administration's (GSAjobs) online application system. Application includes more than 20 KSAs, including the following: 1) ability to apply principles, practices, and procedures of engineering, landscape architecture, or architecture to manage, plan, design or oversee construction projects; 2) ability to serve as contracting officer's representative (COR) on construction projects; 3) ability to participate in environmental and cultural compliance activities involved in facility construction; 4) ability to work with unusual natural, or cultural resources planning issues related to construction projects; 5) ability to deal with others on sensitive issues in a tactful and diplomatic manner; 6) ability to study, investigate, and resolve problems occurring in planning and design modifications; 7) ability to prepare a variety of written products using good grammar, spelling, and punctuation; 8) ability to maintain contacts with a variety of individuals in connection with engineering, landscape architecture, or architecture work; 9) ability to direct multidiscipline teams in accomplishment of environmentally and culturally sensitive planning, design, or construction projects; 10) ability to use effective leadership skills to guide project formulation and development through to completion.

Customer Relations Specialist
Agency: Public Buildings Service
Salary: $85,210 to $110,775
Location: Washington, D.C.

Job description summary: Develops and maintains strategic and operational relationships with a wide range of customers. Develops consistent and effective customer coverage strategies across the Public Buildings Service (PBS) and the General Services Administration (GSA). Serves as an advocate for customers at GSA. Implements the PBS customer-coverage strategies and collaborates with appropriate customer services offices across GSA. Supports national accounts by listening, setting expectations, providing feedback, explaining processes, coaching, and delivering on commitments. Builds customer focus into all processes to deliver overall customer satisfaction across GSA with the customer. Utilizes a national Customer Relations Management program to support/execute the customer coverage strategies. Communicates customer coverage strategies, plans, projects, and results to nationwide network of regional account managers and to appropriate PBS organizations.

Minimum qualifications required: At least one year of specialized experience that reflects the building and maintaining of customer relationships and the maintenance of customer satisfaction in the management of commercial or federal real estate projects or programs (leasing, design, and construction or facilities/property/asset management). Such experience must include a working knowledge of the functions, policies, programs, procedures, regulations, and laws associated with a national commercial/federal real estate organization.

Minimum application materials required: Register with General Services Administration's (GSAjobs) online application system and respond in narrative form to the following KSAs: 1) skill in evaluating and analyzing financial and operational data to formulate recommendations for improvements in quality and level of services; 2) ability to work with customers to identify real estate problems or opportunities and develop strategies to resolve or promote with procedures, products, or services; 3) experience analyzing customer needs and providing recommendations to the agency (customer); 4) experience researching, analyzing, and responding to customer inquiries and complaints regarding products or services.

Materials Handler

Agency: Federal Supply Service
Salary: $16.86 to $19.73/hour
Location: Camden and Burlington Counties, New Jersey

Job description summary: Performs the full range of warehouse duties to accomplish export or domestic functions, including receiving, locating, storing, and rewarehousing materials, commodities, or equipment in accordance with established procedures and operating requirements; determines sequence of loading and unloading, develops space utilization plans, and implements the movement of materials from dock to bin or from storage to shipping; processes documents and verifies the quantity and condition of materials and equipment handled. Places, marks, and seals items in containers, cartons, and boxes using appropriate cushioning materials, protective wrapping materials, and sealing devices.

Minimum qualifications required: Must be able to do the work of a materials handler without more than normal supervision. Must be able to interpret instructions. Must have knowledge of the operation of materials handling equipment and of safe work practices.

Minimum application materials required: Register with General Services Administration's (GSAjobs) online application system and respond in narrative form to more than 50 KSAs.

Purchasing Agent

Agency: Public Buildings Service
Salary: $33,333 to $43,338
Location: San Francisco, California

Job description summary: Receives requisitions or other purchase requests and effects the procurement (below $25,000) of building services: Makes sure funds are available; prepares Requests for Purchase (RFP) under established guidelines; maintains bidders mailing lists and other sources; compares prices; follows through on the transactions including preparation and mailing of solicitations, opening, and review of bids; codes and processes invoices; prepares all documents for certification by the contracting officer before processing; records contract and purchase order transactions on the field office log books; collects data and prepares reports on procurement; monitors need for contract renewal; receives and responds to contract correspondence.

Minimum qualifications required: Must have at least one year of specialized experience that demonstrates a knowledge of the following: purchasing and requisitioning methods; federal procurement regulations; accounting codes and NEAR system requirements. Must be able to type 40 words per minute (with less than three errors).

Minimum application materials required: Register with General Services Administration's (GSAjobs) online application system. Application includes more than 20 KSAs, including the following: 1) maintains files and records; 2) codes documents for filing; 3) maintains requisitions for purchase of different goods or services; 4) sets up files; 5) maintains all directives, manuals, supply schedules, catalogs and orders received; 6) processes work authorization requests for services; 7) researches reports to insure correct procurement obligations and payments are entered; 8) maintains list of prospective bidders and solicits quotations or offers in writing and by telephone.

Structural Engineer

Agency: Design and Construction Division, Public Buildings Service
Salary: $59,570 to $92,090
Location: Atlanta, Georgia

Job description summary: Acts as the regional technical expert on structural engineering. Manages the development, coordination, and implementation of a region-wide seismic upgrade/repair program. Prepares and evaluates designs with particular attention to seismic safety. Prepares statements of scope and detailed instructions for consulting engineers; checks consulting engineers' reports and recommendations; evaluates engineering assumptions and calculations. Prepares or checks detailed estimates for the structural and civil engineering portions of projects for new construction, building rehabilitation, and seismic strengthening. Interprets technical data pertaining to contracts. Checks submittals for technical feasibility, adequacy, and compliance with specifications. Serves as structural and civil engineering representative of GSA at preconstruction conferences. Provides expert consultation for the development and implementation of facilities projects from project conceptualization to final design and construction. Ensures that structural engineering aspects of all projects meet code as well as other requirements. Assists in translating requirements into structural engineering concepts by accomplishing feasibility studies and designs, which are then discussed with the customer.

Minimum qualifications required: Must have a combination of college-level education, training, or technical experience that furnished (1) a thorough knowledge of the arts and sciences underlying professional engineering and (2) a good understanding, both theoretical and practical, of structural design principles, methods, and techniques and their applications to the design and construction or improvement of buildings. Must have one year of specialized experience in the design and construction of projects totaling $30 million or more at any one time, where you have had responsibility for coordinating structural design with the activities of architects, engineers, tenant agencies, construction managers, and contractors. The level of project experience should include at least one project of 100,000 gross square feet or more, involving multiple tenants, or more than one phase of construction. Experience should also include directing the structural design aspects of a project, including planning, predesign, A/E selection, site selection, all design efforts, monitoring construction operations to evaluate progress, and ensuring compliance with design requirements.

Minimum application materials required: Register with General Services Administration's (GSAjobs) on-line application system and respond in narrative form to the following KSAs: 1) experience in the design of complex structural systems and knowledge of structural principles and problem solving; 2) involvement in the design of new high-rise structures and seismic strengthening of existing buildings; 3) experience in performing structural investigation and coordination with other design disciplines; 4) ability to apply a variety of structural computer software programs to real property management projects concerned with design contracting, buildings management, or project management; 5) knowledge of foundation design, structural analysis, security design and seismology; 6) experience in seismic design in regions of high seismicity, innovative technology such as base isolators or dampers, load path, and system analysis; 7) knowledge of wind load design and blast design.

Merit Systems Protection Board

Fifth Floor
1615 M Street NW
Washington, D.C. 20419
202-653-7200

- ★ Web site: http://www.mspb.gov/

- ★ Job vacancies: http://www.mspb.gov/business/humanresource.html

- ★ USAJOBS By Phone: 912-757-3000

- ★ Links to MSPB headquarters and regional offices: http://www.mspb.gov/contactinguspage.html

The Merit Systems Protection Board protects the integrity of federal merit systems and the rights of Federal employees working in the systems. In overseeing the personnel practices of the federal government, the Board conducts special studies of the merit systems, hears and decides charges of wrongdoing and employee appeals of adverse agency actions, and orders corrective and disciplinary actions when appropriate. The Merit Systems Protection Board is a successor agency to the United States Civil Service Commission. In addition to its headquarters in Washington, D.C., MSPB has five regional and three field offices.

National Aeronautics and Space Administration

300 E Street SW
Washington, D.C. 20546
202-358-0000

- ★ Web site: http://www.nasa.gov/

- ★ Job vacancies: http://nasajobs/nasa.gov/

- ★ USAJOBS By Phone: 912-757-3000

★ How to apply: http://www.nasajobs.nasa.gov/how/index.htm

★ Benefits: http://www.nasajobs.nasa.gov/benefits/index.htm

★ Career development: http://nasapeople.nasa.gov/training/

★ Recruitment calendar: http://nasajobs.nasa.gov/recruit/calendar/index.cfm

★ Astronaut selection and training: http://astronauts.nasa.gov/

★ Student employment: http://www.nasajobs.nasa.gov/stud_opps/index.htm

The National Aeronautics and Space Administration conducts research for the solution of flight problems within and outside the Earth's atmosphere and develops, constructs, tests, and operates aeronautical and space vehicles. It conducts activities required for the exploration of space with manned and unmanned vehicles and arranges for the most effective utilization of the scientific and engineering resources of the United States with other nations engaged in aeronautical and space activities for peaceful purposes.

NASA employs more than 18,000 people in more than 15 facilities around the country. Sixty percent of NASA employees are in the professional, scientific, or engineering fields (accounting, aerospace engineering, biology, computer engineering, computer science, general engineering, meteorology); 24 percent are in administrative or managerial fields (administrative specialist, budget analyst, contract specialist, information technology specialist, public affairs specialist,); seven percent are in clerical and administrative support (accounting technician, clerk-typist, management assistant, office automation clerk, procurement clerk, secretary); nine percent are in technical and medical support (electronics technician, engineering technician, meteorological technician); less than one percent are in the trades and labor (high voltage electrician, instrument maker, model maker, utility systems repair).

Selected Agencies Within NASA

The **Office of Earth Science** works to improve life on planet Earth. Its research yields information about Earth's land, atmosphere, ice, oceans, and life that is obtainable in no other way. Global changes require global-scale observations and models, and many regional and local changes are only truly understood when seen in their global context. Research conducted by the Earth Science Enterprise advances the interdisciplinary field of Earth system science and contributes to NASA's mission to understand and protect our home planet. Earth Science Enterprise plays a vital role in three key challenges facing America and the world today: climate change, homeland security, and educating the next generation of explorers.

★ Web site: http://www.earth.nasa.gov/flash_top.html

★ Job vacancies: http://nasajobs.nasa.gov/

The **Office of Space Flight** provides many critical enabling capabilities that make possible much of the science, research, and exploration achievements of the rest of NASA. It is responsible for three major programs: the International Space Station, the Space Shuttle program, and Flight Support.

★ Web site: http://www.hq.nasa.gov/osf/

★ Job vacancies: http://nasajobs.nasa.gov

The **Glenn Research Center** is responsible for developing and transferring critical technologies that address national priorities in aeropropulsion and space applications. Its work is focused on research for new aeropropulsion technologies, aerospace power, microgravity science, electric propulsion, and communications technologies for aeronautics, space, and aerospace applications.

★ Web site: http://www.grc.nasa.gov/

★ Job vacancies: http://www.grc.nasa.gov/WWW/OHR/next3.htm

★ Volunteer information: http://www.grc.nasa.gov/WWW/PAO/html/volunteer.htm

★ Internships: http://www.grc.nasa.gov/WWW/OEP/student1.htm

★ Benefits: http://www.grc.nasa.gov/WWW/OHR/next4.htm

The **Jet Propulsion Laboratory** is managed for NASA by the California Institute of Technology and is NASA's lead center for robotic exploration of the Solar System. It is responsible for the Spirit and Opportunity rovers that landed on Mars, the comet-chasing Stardust spacecraft, and Cassini spacecraft set to explore Saturn. JPL also manages NASA's Deep Space Network, an international network of antennas that supports communications between distant spacecraft and the Earth-based teams who manage them, and the Spitzer Space Telescope and Galaxy Evolution Explorer, which are capturing images of distant galaxies.

★ Web site: http://www.jpl.nasa.gov/

★ Job vacancies: http://hq.jpl.aspdeploy.com/Hirequest/seeker.html

★ Student employment: http://careerlaunch.jpl.nasa.gov/college.htm

★ Employee services: http://www.jpl.nasa.gov/about_JPL/employee_services.cfm

Other NASA Agencies

Ames Research Center
http://www.arc.nasa.gov/index.cfm?flash5=true

Dryden Flight Research Center
http://www.dfrc.nasa.gov/

Goddard Space Flight Center
http://www.gfsc.nasa.gov/

Goddard Institute for Space Studies
http://www.giss.nasa.gov/

Johnson Space Center
http://www.jsc.nasa.gov/

Kennedy Space Center
http://www.ksc.nasa.gov/

Langley Research Center
http://www.larc.nasa.gov/

Marshall Space Flight Center
http://www.msfc.nasa.gov/

Office of Aerospace Technology
http://www.aerospace.nasa.gov/aboutus/index.htm

Office of Biological and Physical Research
http://spaceresearch.nasa.gov/

Office of Space Science
http://spacescience.nasa.gov/index.htm

Stennis Space Center
http://www.ssc.nasa.gov/

Sample Job Vacancies

Assistant, Aerospace Flight Systems
Agency: Marshall Space Flight Center
Salary: $50,020 to $63,967
Location: Huntsville, Alabama

Job description summary: Oversees the planning and implementation of mission and payload integration for multiuse racks, including analytical integration; verification; definition and development of integration hardware and software; and support to physical integration. Interfaces with payload users and crew representatives and provides technical expertise for the integration of payloads into the multiuse racks. Coordinates the maintenance and update of payload integration documentation and requirement definition. Ensures safety requirements are met by the integrated hardware in the development of integrated safety documentation activities. Oversees Certificate of Flight Readiness submittals for the integrated rack. Monitors contractor activities in the day-to-day performance in the area of integration.

Minimum qualifications required: Bachelor of science degree that included 30 semester hours of course work in a combination of mathematics, statistics, and computer science. Must have one year of specialized experience in the development of systems engineering analyses and performance assessments of existing integration processes.

Minimum application materials required: Submit an online resume through NASA STARS (STaffing and Recruitment System). Applicants will no longer submit KSAs or verification information at the time of application; however, if selected you must provide any relevant verification information, such as transcripts or veterans' preference validation.

Change and Integration Specialist

Agency: Glenn Research Center
Salary: $71,171 to $92,524
Location: Brook Park, Ohio

Job description summary: Provides authoritative change management guidance, oversight, representation, and delivery of programs and services for the Center in support of complex, agency-wide initiatives, including the NASA Transformation, the NASA Shared Services Center, E-government, and Full Cost. Manages the impact of these changes on the Center's training and development function. Builds organizational supports and process through consulting, facilitating, developing, managing, coordinating, and evaluating various administrative and change management practices and resources. Identifies and resolves resource and interface issues; redesigns policies, processes, roles and procedures; and develops and implements appropriate organizational interventions.

Minimum qualifications required: Must have one year of specialized experience in a wide range of qualitative and quantitative methods for the assessment and improvement of program effectiveness or the improvement of complex management process and systems.

Minimum application materials required: Submit an online resume through NASA STARS (STaffing and Recruitment System). Applicants will no longer submit KSAs or verification information at the time of application; however, if selected you must provide any relevant verification information, such as transcripts or veterans' preference validation.

Electronics Engineer

Agency: NASA Headquarters
Salary: $100,231 to $130,305
Location: Washington, D.C.

Job description summary: Serves as the agency authority on technical committees and advisory groups concerned with establishing and administering standards for engineering programs of national or international scope. Applies spectrum engineering and regulatory initiatives in such areas as International Telecommunications Union R-Sector, SG-7, and Interdepartmental Radio Advisory Committee (IRAC) forums. Consults on extremely complex or controversial legal or technical problems related to spectrum/regulatory matters of national and international import. Manages overall development of projects of highly complex electro-political issues associated with NASA's Level One Spectrum Management Program. Interacts with senior management to formulate agreements and plans for institutional support of activities in areas of space flight highly dependent on spectrum access and use. Serves as a technical authority in the development and interpretation of guidelines in spectrum engineering, interacting with the formal spectrum regulatory community at a senior level. Serves as expert authority and leader in electronics engineering, specifically national and international spectrum management. Represents NASA before all branches of the federal government and other high level audiences regarding all aspects of spectrum management and related regulatory policies and programs.

Minimum qualifications required: Bachelor of Science degree with a major in engineering, physical science, mathematics, life sciences, computer science, or other field of science. Must

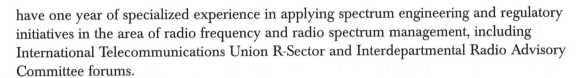

have one year of specialized experience in applying spectrum engineering and regulatory initiatives in the area of radio frequency and radio spectrum management, including International Telecommunications Union R-Sector and Interdepartmental Radio Advisory Committee forums.

Minimum application materials required: Submit an online resume through NASA STARS (STaffing and Recruitment System). Applicants will no longer submit KSAs or verification information at the time of application; however, if selected you must provide any relevant verification information, such as transcripts or veterans' preference validation.

Special requirements: Applicant must hold, or be able to attain a Top Secret clearance for this position.

Management Support Assistant

Agency: Marshall Space Flight Center
Salary: $33,247 to $43,221
Location: Huntsville, Alabama

Job description summary: Performs and assists with a broad range of management, administrative, and clerical functions in support of the mission of the office. Assists with special studies and reviews. Reviews, maintains, and disseminates highly scientific, financial, administrative, or other reports, or documentation. Uses office automation tools to create, edit, or reformat a wide range of documents. Serves as the focal point for information on the processing and status of reports and work in progress

Minimum qualifications required: Must have one year of specialized experience that includes knowledge of capabilities, operating characteristics, and advanced functions of office automation tools (i.e., Word, Excel, PowerPoint, spreadsheets, graphics, and database systems), procurement of supplies, and budget planning and tracking.

Minimum application materials required: Submit an online resume through NASA STARS (STaffing and Recruitment System). Applicants will no longer submit KSAs or verification information at the time of application; however, if selected you must provide any relevant verification information, such as transcripts or veterans' preference validation.

Resources Analyst

Agency: Goddard Space Flight Center
Salary: $60,638 to $78,826
Location: Greenbelt, Maryland

Job description summary: Performs budget work for Agency programs, identifies relationships between projected major program changes and the projected budget, forecasts shortfalls and actions necessary to accommodate the changes, prepares special analyses of fund expenditures as necessary, and evaluates the effect of cost and program changes on the budget execution process. Reviews and coordinates accounting records and prepares apportionments, allocations, and operating budgets. Monitors, tracks, and reports on program obligations. Conducts year-end closing activities and reconciles with accounting records. Performs cost accounting functions conducting a wide range of cost accounting processes. Prepares and processes monthly cost accruals. Analyzes significant costs variances and assists managers in making recommendations. Conducts cost reporting and serves as the point of contact on matters related to cost presentation. Reviews historical data and current trends to validate and consolidate requests and estimates. Prepares annual budget formulation documents in final form, and ensures that all reconciliations are made as to workload data, accuracy, and distribution of programs.

Minimum qualifications required: Must have one year of specialized experience in contract cost accruals and contractor financial data analysis, including both budget formulation and execution experience.

Minimum application materials required: Submit an online resume through NASA STARS (STaffing and Recruitment System). Applicants will no longer submit KSAs or verification information at the time of application; however, if selected you must provide any relevant verification information, such as transcripts or veterans' preference validation.

Secretary

Agency: NASA Headquarters
Salary: $37,858 to $49,216
Location: Washington, D.C.

Job description summary: Manages office operations and activities. Coordinates with key staff members to provide background on the subject matter of meetings and conferences. Performs administrative and clerical support functions to identify workflow problems or situations and recommends changes as appropriate. Screens all telephone calls and visitor requests, handling procedural matters and determining appropriate staff members for technical inquiries. Manages correspondence services, reviewing incoming and outgoing, establishing and maintaining a tracking system. Performs proofreading and editing of finished documents for grammar, punctuation, spelling, and clarity of expression. Composes nontechnical correspondence and reports. Makes all necessary arrangements for travel and prepares travel orders and vouchers.

Minimum qualifications required: Must possess one year of specialized experience in performing a broad range of secretarial and administrative activities, such as maintaining supervisor's calendar, scheduling meetings, completing travel arrangements, reviewing and managing office correspondence, and using standard office automation equipment. Must be able to type at least 40 words per minute.

Minimum application materials required: Submit an online resume through NASA STARS (STaffing and Recruitment System). Applicants will no longer submit KSAs or verification information at the time of application; however, if selected you must provide any relevant verification information, such as transcripts or veterans' preference validation.

Space Planner Specialist

Agency: NASA Headquarters
Salary: $60,638 to $78,826
Location: Washington, D.C.

Job description summary: Plans, manages, oversees, and coordinates all phases of projects for interior space design, construction, and renovation; produces scenarios for design and layout of office space using Computer Assisted Design (CAD) drawings including furnishings, lighting, heating, ventilation, telephone, and electrical; maintains liaison with contractors; provides space planning and architectural design services to insure effective space utilization; facilitates and negotiates with contractors, vendors, and senior management for project design, schedule, and costs; serves as task monitor or Contracting Officer Technical Representative for Headquarters design and furniture contracts; determines standard and project management controls for inclusion in statement of work products for contracts.

Minimum qualifications required: Must have one year of specialized experience in space utilization assessments using space planning and architectural design services to ensure productive and efficient work environments.

Minimum application materials required: Submit an online resume through NASA STARS (STaffing and Recruitment System). Applicants will no longer submit KSAs or verification information at the time of application; however, if selected you must provide any relevant verification information, such as transcripts or veterans' preference validation.

National Archives and Records Administration

8601 Adelphi Road
Park, Maryland 20740-6001
866-272-6272

★ Web site: http://www.archives.gov/

★ Job vacancies: http://www.archives.gov/careers/employment/all_candidates/all_candidates.html

★ USAJOBS By Phone: 912-757-3000

★ How to apply: http://www.archives.gov/careers/employment/how_to_apply.html

★ Benefits: http://www.archives.gov/careers/employment/benefits.html

★ Career Development Resource Center: http://www.archives.gov/careers/career_development_in_govt.html

★ Internship information:
http://www.archives.gov/careers/internships/about_internships.html

★ Volunteer information: http://www.archives.gov/careers/volunteering/volunteering.html

★ Links to NARA facilities nationwide: http://www.archives.gov/facilities/index.html

★ Staff contacts: http://www.archives.gov/facilities/staff_contacts.html

The National Archives and Records Administration (NARA) ensures, for citizens and federal officials, ready access to essential evidence that documents the rights of American citizens, the actions of federal officials, and the national experience. It establishes policies and procedures for managing U.S. government records and assists federal agencies in documenting their activities, administering records management programs, scheduling records, and retiring noncurrent records; accessions, arranges, describes, preserves, and provides access to the essential documentation of the three branches of government; manages the presidential libraries system; and publishes the laws, regulations, and presidential and other public documents. It also assists the Information Security Oversight Office, which manages federal classification and declassification policies, and the National Historical Publications and Records Commission, which makes grants to help nonprofit organizations identify, preserve, and provide access to materials that document American history. NARA has more than 30 sites across the country—regional archives and records services facilities, presidential libraries, and three major buildings in the Washington, D.C., area.

Selected Agencies Within NARA

The **Presidential Library** system is made up of 10 Presidential Libraries. This nationwide network of libraries is administered by the Office of Presidential Libraries located in College Park, Maryland. These are not traditional libraries, but rather repositories for preserving and making available the papers, records, and other historical materials of U.S. presidents since Herbert Hoover.

Each Presidential Library contains a museum and provides an active series of public programs. When a president leaves office, NARA establishes a presidential project until a new presidential library is built and transferred to the government.

★ Web site: http://www.archives.gov/presidential_libraries/index.html

★ Job vacancies: http://www.archives.gov/careers/employment/all_candidates/all_candidates.html

★ Headquarters contacts: http://www.archives.gov/presidential_libraries/contact_information.html

★ George Bush Presidential Library and Museum: http://bushlibrary.tamu.edu/

★ Jimmy Carter Library and Museum: http://www.jimmycarterlibrary.gov/

★ William J. Clinton Presidential Library: http://www.clintonlibrary.gov/

★ Dwight D. Eisenhower Library and Museum: http://www.eisenhower.utexas.edu/

★ Gerald R. Ford Library and Museum: http://www.fordlibrarymuseum.gov/

★ Herbert Hoover Presidential Library-Museum: http://hoover.archives.gov/

★ Lyndon Baines Johnson Library and Museum: http://www.lbjlib.utexas.edu/

★ John F. Kennedy Library and Museum: http://www.jfklibrary.org/

★ Nixon Presidential Materials Staff: http://www.archives.gov/nixon/

★ Ronald Reagan Presidential Library: http://www.reagan.utexas.edu/

★ Franklin D. Roosevelt Presidential Library and Museum:
  http://www.fdrlibrary.marist.edu/

★ Truman Presidential Museum and Library: http://www.trumanlibrary.org/

NARA has nine **regional records services** centers, plus the national personnel Records
Center, that manage historically valuable records that are primarily of regional or local
interest.

★ Web site: http://www.archives.gov/facilities/records_centers.html

★ Job vacancies: http://www.archives.gov/careers/employment/all_candidates/
  all_candidates.html

★ Northeast Region (Boston): http://www.archives.gov/facilities/ma/boston.html

★ Northeast Region (Pittsfield): http://www.archives.gov/facilities/ma/pittsfield.html

★ Mid-Atlantic Region:
  http://www.archives.gov/midatlantic/fed_agency_services/fed_agency_services.html

★ Southeast Region: http://www.archives.gov/facilities/ga/atlanta.html

★ Great Lakes Region (Chicago): http://www.archives.gov/facilities/il/chicago.html

★ Great Lakes Region (Dayton): http://www.archives.gov/facilities/oh/dayton.html

★ Central Plains Region (Kansas City):
  http://www.archives.gov/facilities/mo/kansas_city.html

★ Central Plains Region (Lee's Summit): http://www.archives.gov/facilities/mo/
  lees_summit.html

★ Southwest Region: http://www.archives.gov/facilities/tx/fort_worth.html

★ Rocky Mountain Region: http://www.archives.gov/facilities/co/denver.html

★ Pacific Region (Laguna Niguel): http://www.archives.gov/facilities/ca/laguna_niguel.html

★ Pacific Region (Seattle): http://www.archives.gov/facilities/ca/san_francisco.html

★ Pacific Alaska Region: http://www.archives.gov/facilities/ak/anchorage.html

★ National Personnel Records Center: http://www.archives.gov/facilities/mo/st_louis.html

Other NARA Agencies

Federal Register
http://www.archives.gov/federal_register/index.html

Information Security Oversight Office
http://www.archives.gov/isoo/index.html

National Archives Trust Fund Board
http://www.archives.gov/about_us/basic_laws_and_authorities/nara_trust_fund_board.html

National Historical Publications and Records Commission
http://www.archives.gov/grants/index.html

Records Management
http://www.archives.gov/records_management/index.html

Sample Job Vacancies

Archives Technician
Agency: Office of Presidential Libraries, Ronald Reagan Presidential Library
Salary: $28,902 to $37,578
Location: Simi Valley, California

Job description summary: Performs archival duties involving customer service, reference, arrangement, description, evaluation, and preservation/rehabilitation of classified and unclassified historical materials. Assists researchers in filling forms for reproductions as well as for Freedom of Information Act requests, and mandatory review requests. Conducts in-depth research and responds to written and oral inquiries. Prepares internal finding aids, such as document, folder, and shelf lists; registers; indexes; card files; and lists of security classified documents withdrawn from collections. Performs detailed arrangement work. Searches for missing information and documents. Assists in the accessioning and disposal of records, books, serials, and pamphlets.

Minimum qualifications required: Bachelor's degree. Must have one year of specialized experience conducting research in historical materials and responding to reference inquiries; preparing detailed finding aids for historical materials; and accessioning and disposing of records.

Minimum application materials required: Submit a resume, Optional Application for Federal Employment (OF-612), or Application for Federal Employment (SF-171). Include narrative responses to the following KSAs: 1) knowledge of the life of the president and related historical and political aspects of his presidency in order to provide reference services; 2) knowledge of archival and library science principles and techniques, finding aids, and research tools; 3) ability in written and oral expression; 4) knowledge of computer software and programs (Windows, MS Office, Word, Access) and Web page editing.

Special requirements: Must be a U.S. citizen.

Audiovisual Technician
Agency: Office of Records Administration, Archives I Theater
Salary: $34,184 to $44,439
Location: Washington, D.C.

Job description summary: Works theater events in the absence of the theater manager; coordinates and supervises audiovisual support and crowd control for film screenings, lectures, conferences, symposia, videoconferences and theatrical performances; assists with videotaping, audio recording sound system setups, and projectionist activities for meetings, seminars and special events; assists with the acquisition and transportation of film prints; conducts basic video and audiotape dubbing and editing; assists with telephone reservations and inquiries; writes material for the Calendar of Events and other appropriate material for publication and publicity purposes.

Minimum qualifications required: One year of specialized experience using motion picture projection systems in a theater environment; operating and maintaining film projectors, videotape recorders and speakers; and communicating information to the public regarding schedules and programming.

Minimum application materials required: Submit a resume, Optional Application for Federal Employment (OF-612), or Application for Federal Employment (SF-171). Include narrative responses to the following KSAs: 1) use 35mm slide projectors and videodisc and videotape recorders; 2) videotape meetings, seminars, or special events; 3) set up audio recording sound systems and set up and run projectors for meetings, seminars, or special events; 4) dub and edit videotape and audiotape; 5) adjust, maintain, and trouble-shoot lenses, aspect ratio, and major screen types; 6) apply knowledge of noise reduction techniques in a theater environment; 7) operate and maintain speakers and amplifiers; 8) coordinate audiovisual support for a theater; 9) locate audiovisual programs available from commercial distributors, film archives, museums, or other educational institutions; 10) conduct research about recently published works.

Special requirements: Must be a U.S. citizen. Must pass a background investigation.

Secretary

Agency: National Personnel Records Center
Salary: $30,762 to $39,996
Location: College Park, Maryland

Job description summary: Receives visitors, incoming telephone calls, and incoming correspondence and reports and refers matters to the appropriate people. Maintains office files and records. Maintains desk appointment calendar for supervisor. Uses a variety of office equipment and software to prepare documents. Reviews materials to ensure correct punctuation, capitalization, spelling, grammar, and format. Makes travel arrangements and prepares required travel documents. Maintains time and attendance records. Orders office supplies and equipment. Coordinates meetings and conferences. Monitors the workflow and coordinates work assignments.

Minimum qualifications required: Must be able to type at least 40 words per minute. Must have one year of specialized experience in receiving and screening visitors and incoming telephone calls, arranging travel, preparing time and attendance records; ordering supplies and maintenance services; composing correspondence; using typewriter, word processor, and personal computer and establishing and maintaining office files.

Minimum application materials required: Submit a resume, Optional Application for Federal Employment (OF-612), or Application for Federal Employment (SF-171). Include narrative responses to more than 20 KSAs.

Special requirements: Must be a U.S. citizen. Male applicants born after December 31, 1959, must certify that they have registered with the Selective Service System or are exempt from having to do so.

Supervisory Museum Curator

Agency: Office of Presidential Libraries, William J. Clinton Presidential Library
Salary: $58,665 to $76,261
Location: Little Rock, Arkansas

Job description summary: Plans, formulates, designs, constructs, and installs exhibits. Selects material for exhibit. Prepares exhibit catalogs, news releases, or public announcements of new exhibit openings, and general information leaflets on exhibits and museum programs. Evaluates museum objects offered as gifts to the Library. Monitors the registration and cataloging of museum objects. Oversees rehabilitation, repair, and preservation of the museum collections. Provides information about museum objects and programs to many sources. Assists in planning and supervising special activities. Maintains close liaison with the Library's Foundation members. Supervises managerial and administrative activities, including budget, personnel, space management, procurement, and security. Responsible for the physical care, maintenance, preservation, and security of the museum areas and collections.

Minimum qualifications required: Bachelor's degree in museum work or history; OR a combination of education and experience. Must have one year of specialized experience, such as planning, supervising, and executing programs and activities of a museum.

Minimum application materials required: Submit a resume, Optional Application for Federal Employment (OF-612), or Application for Federal Employment (SF-171). Include narrative responses to the following KSAs: 1) knowledge of professional museum collections management; 2) ability to conduct historical research and prepare exhibits; 3) knowledge of presidential history and related historical and political issues and events; 4) ability to supervise; 5) ability to communicate orally and in writing.

Special requirements: Must be a U.S. citizen.

National Credit Union Administration

1775 Duke Street
Alexandria, Virginia 22314-3428
703-518-6300

★ Web site: http://www.ncua.gov/

★ Job vacancies: http://www.ncua.gov/AboutNCUA/vacancies/vacancies.html

★ USAJOBS By Phone: 912-757-3000

★ Organization chart and links to regional offices:
   http://www.ncua.gov/AboutNCUA/org/OrgChart.htm

The National Credit Union Administration (NCUA) is the federal agency that charters and supervises federal credit unions and insures savings in federal and most state-chartered credit unions across the country through the National Credit Union Share Insurance Fund (NCUSIF), a federal fund backed by the full faith and credit of the United States government. In addition to its headquarters in Alexandria, Virginia, NCUA has five regional offices and an Asset Management and Assistance Center in Austin, Texas.

Sample Job Vacancy

Credit Union Examiner

Agency: National Credit Union Administration
Salary: $28,847 to $59,345
Location: Phoenix, Arizona

Job description summary: Conducts credit union examinations, analyzes operations, and prepares reports and gives oral presentations of examination findings, conclusions, and recommendations to credit union leadership. Works from home and selects own schedule. Works independently and in small groups and serves a variety of large and small credit unions.

Minimum qualifications required: Bachelor of science degree in economics or a bachelor's degree in accounting, business, business administration, finance, marketing, or another directly related business field with a grade point average of 3.5 or higher in the major field or graduation in the top third of the graduating class or major subdivision or election to a National Scholastic Honor Society; OR one year of graduate education in the above fields. Must have one year of specialized experience that included duties such as preparing or analyzing financial statements; posting and/or balancing general ledger accounts in accordance with Generally Accepted Accounting Principles (GAAP); and auditing, examining, and appraising financial records or statements for completeness and internal accuracy in accordance with Generally Accepted Auditing Standards (GAAS).

Minimum application materials required: Complete and submit an occupational questionnaire along with a resume and any supporting documentation (college transcripts). Respond in narrative form to the following KSAs: 1) knowledge of business theory; 2) skill in the development of written reports; 3) skill in verbal communication; 4) ability to plan, organize, and manage work processes by initiating work and operating independently; 5) ability to evaluate financial statements and use mathematics to determine relevant qualitative facts; 6) ability to use a personal computer to create documents, spreadsheets, etc., and analyze information in an Internet or Intranet environment.

Special requirements: Must complete six months of intensive classroom and on-the-job training. Because of the nature of the work, you must have an acceptable credit history. Male applicants born after December 31, 1959, must certify that they have registered with the Selective Service System, or are exempt from having to do so.

National Foundation on the Arts and the Humanities

1100 Pennsylvania Avenue NW
Washington, D.C. 20506-0001
202-682-5400 (NEA); 202-606-8400 (NEH); 202-606-8536 (IMLS)

The National Foundation on the Arts and the Humanities (NFAH) consists of the National Endowment for the Arts, the National Endowment for the Humanities, the Federal Council on the Arts and the Humanities, and the Institute of Museum and Library Services. A fourth entity, the Federal Council on the Arts and the Humanities, assists the Endowments and the Council in coordinating their programs and other activities with those of Federal agencies. Each Endowment is advised on its respective grantmaking and related policies, programs, and procedures by its own national council, composed of the endowment chairman and other members appointed by the president and confirmed by the Senate. Members of Congress, appointed by the leadership of the House and the Senate, serve in an ex officio, nonvoting capacity on the National Council on the Arts.

Agencies Within NFAH

National Endowment for the Arts (NEA) makes grants that support projects of artistic excellence in an effort to preserve and enhance the nation's cultural heritage. Grants are made to nonprofit arts organizations, units of state or local government (such as school districts and local arts agencies), and federally recognized tribal communities or tribes, for dance, design, folk and traditional arts, literature, media arts, multidisciplinary, museum, music, musical theater, opera, presenting, theater, and visual arts projects. Competitive fellowships are awarded to published creative writers and literary translators of exceptional talent; honorific fellowships are given to jazz masters and significant, influential master folk and traditional artists. NEA also works in partnership with the 56 state and special jurisdictional arts agencies and their regional arts organizations to support projects that foster creativity, preservation, arts learning, and outreach to underserved communities. NEA dedicates 40 percent of its program appropriation to this purpose.

The NEA accepts interns throughout the year in many of the Arts Endowment's offices. Internships offer a national overview of arts activities across the country. Interns work in assisting the staff with a variety of tasks related to the process of awarding federal grants. A variety of resources are available for participants of the NEA Internship Program: an extensive arts library and meetings of advisory panels and the National Council on the Arts.

★ Web site: http://www.arts.gov/

★ Job vacancies: http://www.arts.gov/about/Jobs/JobsMenu.html

★ Headquarters contacts: http://www.arts.gov:591/staff/staff.html

★ Internship information: http://www.arts.gov/about/Jobs/Internships.html

★ NEA Arts newsletter: http://www.arts.gov/about/NEARTS/index.html

The **National Endowment for the Humanities** (NEH) makes grants that support research, education, preservation, and public programs in the humanities. The term "humanities" includes the study of the following: language, both modern and classical; linguistics; literature; history; jurisprudence; philosophy; archeology; comparative religion; ethics; the history, criticism, and theory of the arts; and those aspects of the social sciences that employ historical or philosophical approaches. NEH makes grants to individuals, groups, or institutions (schools, colleges, universities, museums, public television stations, libraries, public agencies, and non-profit private groups) to increase understanding and appreciation of the humanities.

★ Web site: http://www.neh.gov/

★ Job vacancies: http://www.neh.gov/whoweare/jobs.html

★ Headquarters contacts: http://www.neh.gov/whoweare/officedirectory.html

★ Legal internship program: http://www.neh.gov/whoweare/legalinternship.html

★ Humanities magazine: http://www.neh.gov/news/humanities.html

★ State humanities councils: http://www.neh.gov/whoweare/statecouncils.html

★ Employee directory: http://www.neh.gov/whoweare/staffdirectory.html

The **Institute of Museum and Library Services** (IMLS) makes grants to museums and libraries. IMLS combines administration of federal museum programs formerly carried out by the Institute of Museum Services and Federal library programs formerly carried out by the Department of Education. In addition to providing distinct programs of support for museums and libraries, IMLS encourages collaboration between these community resources. The Institute's library programs help libraries use new technologies to identify, preserve, and share library and information resources across institutional, local, and state boundaries and to reach those for whom library use requires extra effort or special materials. Museum programs strengthen museum operations, improve care of collections, increase professional development opportunities, and enhance the community service role of museums. All IMLS competitive awards are reviewed by volunteer library and museum professionals.

★ Web site: http://www.imls.gov/

★ Job vacancies: http://www.imls.gov/about/abt_empl.htm

★ Headquarters contacts: http://www.imls.gov/utility/contact.htm

★ Legal internship program: http://www.imls.gov/about/lawstud.htm

★ Primary Source newsletter: http://www.imls.gov/whatsnew/new_imls.htm#ps

★ Volunteer reviewer information: http://www.imls.gov/grants/review/rev_how.htm

Sample Job Vacancy

Division Specialist (Opera)
Agency: National Endowment for the Arts
Salary: $41,815 to $78,826
Location: Washington, D.C.

Job description summary: Receives, reviews, and processes all applications from opera field (including organizing them for grant review and determining on-site visit requirements) and follows applications through the complete review process. Processes rejections, revised budget, and grant awards. Answers questions concerning the applications and prepares written materials/reports for presentation to, or review by the National Council on the Arts. Reviews budgetary and descriptive information on all applications from the opera field. Monitors grantee performance through review of progress, interim, and final reports; amendment requests; and conversations with the grantee to ensure that the grantee is functioning in accordance with the terms and conditions of the grant.

Minimum qualifications required: At least one year of specialized experience in or directly related to opera field and grantmaking that has equipped the applicant with the knowledge, skills, and abilities to successfully perform the duties of the position.

Minimum application materials required: Optional Application for Federal Employment (OF-612), or a resume, or any other written application format of your choice. Respond to the following KSAs 1) knowledge of the opera discipline and its artistic values (such as repertoire, vocal artistry, staging, etc.); 2) knowledge of the opera field's current needs and directions; 3) knowledge of Arts Endowment programs and grant-making policies; 4) skill in oral and written communication; 5) skill in working in an automated environment.

National Labor Relations Board

1099 Fourteenth Street NW
Washington, D.C. 20570
202-273-1000

- ★ Web site: http://www.nlrb.gov/

- ★ Job vacancies: http://www.nlrb.gov/nlrb/about/careers/default.asp

- ★ USAJOBS By Phone: 912-757-3000

- ★ Student employment programs: http://www.nlrb.gov/nlrb/about/careers/student.asp

- ★ Regional offices: http://www.nlrb.gov/nlrb/offices/
  default.asp?theZip=showall&theorder=region

- ★ Application forms: http://www.nlrb.gov/nlrb/about/careers/appforms.asp

The National Labor Relations Board is vested with the power to prevent and remedy unfair labor practices committed by private sector employers and unions and to safeguard employees' rights to organize and determine whether to have unions as their bargaining representative. The agency has two major, separate components. The Board itself has five members and primarily acts as a quasi-judicial body in deciding cases on the basis of formal records in administrative proceedings. The General Counsel is independent from the Board and is responsible for the investigation and prosecution of unfair labor practice cases and for the general supervision of the 34 NLRB field offices in the processing of cases.

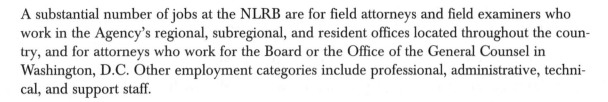

A substantial number of jobs at the NLRB are for field attorneys and field examiners who work in the Agency's regional, subregional, and resident offices located throughout the country, and for attorneys who work for the Board or the Office of the General Counsel in Washington, D.C. Other employment categories include professional, administrative, technical, and support staff.

National Railroad Passenger Corporation (Amtrak)

60 Massachusetts Avenue NE
Washington, D.C. 20002
202-906-3000

★ Web site: http://www.amtrak.com/

★ Job vacancies: http://www.teamrewards.net/home/public_index.jsp

★ Job line: 877-268-7251 (877-AMTRAK1)

The National Railroad Passenger Corporation (Amtrak) operates intercity passenger trains, at an average of 212 trains per day, serving over 540 station locations in 46 states, over a system of approximately 22,000 route miles. Of this route system, Amtrak owns less than 1,000 track miles in the Northeast Corridor (Washington-New York-Boston; New Haven-Springfield; Philadelphia-Harrisburg), and several other small track segments throughout the country. Amtrak owns or leases its stations and owns its own repair and maintenance facilities. Amtrak employs a total work force of approximately 22,205 and provides all reservation, station, and on-board service staffs, as well as train and engine operating crews.

To find out about current job openings at Amtrak, call the Job Line. To apply for a job from the Job Line, write the specific job title and posting number on your resume and mail it to the appropriate address listed on the Job Line. Amtrak does not accept faxed resumes, and resumes without a job title or posting number will be returned. New jobs are added regularly, so make sure to check back often for the latest job opportunities. Applicants can also apply for Amtrak jobs online at the Teamrewards Web site.

National Science Foundation

4201 Wilson Boulevard
Arlington, Virginia 22230
703-292-5111

★ Web site: http://www.nsf.gov/

★ Job vacancies: http://www.nsf.gov. Then click on Career Opportunities.

★ USAJOBS By Phone: 912-757-3000

★ Student employment information: http://www.nsf.gov/oirm/hrm/jobs/student.htm

★ New graduate employment information:
http://www.nsf.gov/oirm/hrm/jobs/special.htm#scholar

★ Salary and benefits: http://www.nsf.gov/oirm/hrm/jobs/salary.htm

★ Work environment: http://www.nsf.gov/oirm/hrm/jobs/worklife.htm

★ New employee orientation information: http://www.nsf.gov/oirm/hrm/orientation/

The National Science Foundation (NSF) promotes the progress of science and engineering by awarding grants, contracts, and fellowships that support research and education programs. Its major emphasis is on high-quality, merit-selected research–the search for improved understanding of the fundamental laws of nature upon which our future well-being as a nation depends. Its educational programs are aimed at ensuring increased understanding of science and engineering at all educational levels and maintaining an adequate supply of scientists, engineers, and science educators to meet our country's needs.

NSF employs scientists, engineers, and educators in seven directorates on rotational assignment from academia, industry, or other eligible organizations to further the Agency's mission of supporting the entire spectrum of science and engineering research and education. The most frequently used programs are the Visiting Scientist, Engineer, and Educator (VSEE) Program and the Intergovernmental Personnel Act (IPA) Program.

Selected Agencies Within NSF

The **Directorate for Biological Sciences** promotes scientific progress in biology largely through grants to colleges, universities, and other institutions, especially in those areas where NSF has major responsibility. The Foundation is the nation's principal supporter of fundamental academic research on plant biology, environmental biology, and biodiversity. Other divisions include integrative organismal biology, molecular and cellular biology, and the plant genome research project.

★ Web site: http://www.nsf.gov/bio/

★ Job vacancies: http://www.nsf.gov/bio/jobs.htm

★ Staff directory: http://www.nsf.gov/staff/orgpage.cfm?key=48

The **Directorate for Engineering** promotes the progress of engineering in order to enable the country's capacity to perform. The Directorate sponsors programs in nanotechnology, biocomplexity, cyberinfrastructure, human and social dynamics, sensors and networks, and earthquake simulation. It administers the NSF's Small Business Innovation Research (SBIR) program.

★ Web site: http://www.geo.nsf.gov/geo/about/overview.htm

★ Job vacancies: http://www.eng.nsf.gov/jobopportunities/

★ Staff directory: http://www.nsf.gov/staff/orgpage.cfm?key=50

Other NSF Agencies

Directorate for Computer and Information Science and Engineering
http://www.cise.nsf.gov/

Directorate for Education and Human Resources
http://www.ehr.nsf.gov/

Directorate for Geosciences
http://www.geo.nsf.gov/

Directorate for Mathematical and Physical Sciences
http://www.nsf.gov/home/mps/start.htm

Directorate for Social, Behavioral, and Economic Sciences
http://www.nsf.gov/sbe/start.htm

Sample Job Vacancies

Chemical Oceanographer
Agency: Directorate for Geosciences
Salary: $66,229 to $104,336
Location: Arlington, Virginia

Job description summary: Assists in the implementation, review, funding, postaward management, and evaluation of the program and in the integration with other programs supported by the Division. Designs and implements the proposal review and evaluation process. Selects individuals to provide reviews on proposals. Conducts final review of proposals and evaluations, and recommends acceptance or declination. Monitors on-going grants, contracts, interagency, and cooperative agreements to ensure fulfillment of commitments to NSF. Evaluates progress of awards through review and evaluation of reports and publications submitted by awardees or meetings at NSF and during site visits. Assists in establishing goals and objectives, initiating new program thrusts and phasing out old projects. Recommends new policies to improve the activities and management of the program.

Minimum qualifications required: Must have a Ph.D. or equivalent experience in chemical oceanography, marine chemistry, marine geochemistry, or related disciplinary fields, plus four or more years of research experience beyond the Ph.D. Familiarity with a broad spectrum of the ocean science research community and demonstrated administrative ability are desired. Applicants who are multifaceted and have multidisciplinary experience and capabilities are also desired.

Minimum application materials required: Submit an Optional Application for Federal Employment (OF-612), an Application for Federal Employment (SF-171), or a resume.

Computer Scientist
Agency: Directorate for Computer and Information Science and Engineering
Salary: $85,210 to $132,791
Location: Arlington, Virginia

Job description summary: Maintains balance of support for all the needs of the research and education enterprise either through program, division, directorate, Foundation, or interagency activities. Manages program resources. Incorporates cross-directorate responsibilities into program administration. Manages an effective, timely merit review process, with attention to increasing the size and quality of the reviewer pools and insuring participation by women, minorities, and disabled scientists. Provides scientific expertise, evaluation, and advice for other programs in NSF, including international programs, other research programs, and cross-directorate programs. Advises and assists in the development of short- and long-range plans, establishing goals for research programs. Plans the budget for the programs. Allocates resources within that budget, distributing scarce resources among major competitive programs, and manages postaward evaluation.

Minimum qualifications required: Must have a Ph.D. or equivalent experience in computer science, computer engineering, communication, information/computational science, or allied disciplines, plus six or more years of successful research, research administration, or managerial experience beyond the Ph.D. in an area supported by the program. Also desirable is knowledge of general scientific community, skill in written communication and preparation of technical reports, and ability to communicate orally, and several years of successful independent research of the kind normally expected of the academic rank of associate professor or higher.

Minimum application materials required: Submit an Optional Application for Federal Employment (OF-612), an Application for Federal Employment (SF-171), or a resume.

Special requirements: Must pass a background investigation. Satisfactory completion of a one-year trial period is required.

Science and Engineering Assistant
Agency: National Science Board Office
Salary: $27,597 to $65,769
Location: Washington, D.C.

Job description summary: Assists in producing NSB reports and working papers. Develops relevant data that can be used in preparing analytical and interpretive reports and guides. Writes thank you notes and reminders, takes minutes and provides feedback to executive staff.

Minimum qualifications required: Must have a bachelor's degree in science or engineering.

Minimum application materials required: Submit an Optional Application for Federal Employment (OF-612), an Application for Federal Employment (SF-171), or a resume.

Special requirements: Must pass a background investigation.

Social Scientist
Agency: Division of Behavioral and Cognitive Sciences (BCS), Directorate for Social, Behavioral, and Economic Sciences
Salary: $27,597 to $65,796
Location: Arlington, Virginia

Job description summary: Provides ad hoc support for special requests and inquiries that require a scientific background to properly respond. Provides scientific assistance to BCS in all phases of the proposal review process and coordinates proposal review activities with SBE Divisions and other directorates. Assists with the screening of proposals and develops factual information about grants to ascertain whether the research is normally supported by BCS programs. Participates in ad hoc reviewer identification by reading professional journals and conducting library research.

Minimum qualifications required: Must have a bachelor's degree in any of the following social and behavioral sciences: archaeology; archaeometry; cognitive neuroscience; cultural anthropology; developmental and learning sciences; geography and regional sciences; linguistics; physical anthropology and social psychology. Some administrative, managerial, or professional experience related to the position is desirable.

Minimum application materials required: Submit an Optional Application for Federal Employment (OF-612), an Application for Federal Employment (SF-171), or a resume along with letters of recommendation from professionals who can comment on your capabilities. Application must include narrative answers to the following KSAs: 1) knowledge of the principles, theories and methods of social and/or behavioral science; 2) ability to use computer software, database systems, and Web-based systems; 3) ability to organize and gather scientific and administrative data for use in the preparation of analytical and interpretative reports and guides; 4) ability to communicate orally and in writing to the scientific community and individuals at all levels; 5) ability to organize review panels.

Special requirements: Must pass a background investigation.

National Transportation Safety Board

490 L'Enfant Plaza SW
Washington, D.C. 20594
202-314-6000

★ Web site: http://www.ntsb.gov/

★ Job vacancies: http://www.ntsb.gov/vacancies/listing.htm

★ USAJOBS By Phone: 912-757-3000

★ Regional offices, aviation: http://www.ntsb.gov/Abt_NTSB/regions/aviation.htm

★ Field offices, railroad: http://www.ntsb.gov/Abt_NTSB/regions/railroad.htm

★ Field offices, highway: http://www.ntsb.gov/Abt_NTSB/regions/highway.htm

★ Student internship positions: http://www.ntsb.gov/vacancies/student_internships_AS.htm

★ Headquarters contacts: http://www.ntsb.gov/Info/sources.htm

The National Transportation Safety Board (NTSB) investigates more than 2,000 accidents each year, including every civil aviation accident in the United States and significant accidents in the other modes of transportation. It also conducts special investigations and safety studies, and issues safety recommendations to prevent future accidents. Over the past three decades, investigators have developed their own expertise in specialized areas, and are often consulted by other safety professionals. The NTSB has prepared its investigators by developing and conducting its own accident investigation training at the NTSB Academy, located on the campus of George Washington University in Ashburn, Virginia.

The NTSB employs about 400 people across the country. To view vacancies and apply for a job, visit the NTSB SafetyJobs Web site. Except in extreme hardship cases, NTSB only accepts applications online through SafetyJobs. Before using the system to apply for jobs, you must first register by providing basic background and employment information. During the registration process you may cut and paste your resume into the SafetyJobs system, and choose to receive e-mail notification for vacancy announcements of interest to you. When applying for a job you will be asked to answer job-related questions specific to each announcement. SafetyJobs uses the answers provided in the application to automatically qualify and rate applications in a fair and objective manner.

Nuclear Regulatory Commission

Washington, D.C. 20555
301-415-7000

★ Web site: http://www.nrc.gov/

★ Job vacancies: http://www.nrc.gov/who-we-are/employment/nrcareers.html

★ USAJOBS By Phone: 912-757-3000

★ Student employment: http://www.nrc.gov/who-we-are/employment/student-prog.html

★ Career paths: http://www.nrc.gov/who-we-are/employment/careers.html

★ Salaries and career advancement: http://www.nrc.gov/who-we-are/employment/salaries.html

★ Employee benefits: http://www.nrc.gov/who-we-are/employment/benefits.html

★ Graduate fellowships: http://www.nrc.gov/who-we-are/employment/grad-fel-prog.html

★ Office locations: http://www.nrc.gov/who-we-are/locations.html

The Nuclear Regulatory Commission (NRC) licenses and regulates civilian use of nuclear energy to protect public health and safety and the environment. This is achieved by licensing people and companies to build and operate nuclear reactors and other facilities and to own and use nuclear materials. The Commission makes rules and sets standards for these types of licenses. It also carefully inspects the activities of the people and companies licensed to ensure compliance with the safety rules of the Commission.

The NRC uses an online job application system called NRCareers, designed to make it easier and more efficient to apply for positions with NRC. NRCareers lets you browse current job vacancies; create, edit, and store your resume electronically; and apply for specific NRC jobs online.

The NRC hires budget analysts, auditors, accountants, management analysts, program analysts, human resources specialists, contract specialists, and secretaries and office automation assistants; attorneys; general, nuclear, mechanical, chemical, structural, electrical, environmental, materials, software, and human factors engineers; communications specialists, computer specialists, IT project managers, systems administrators, computer systems analysts, Web masters, and information management specialists; investigators, analysts, and law enforcement specialists; chemists, nuclear physicists, radiation biologists, physical scientists, materials scientists, health physicists, geologists, hydrologists, and seismologists; security and safeguards analysts with physical, personnel, information, and operational security knowledge as well as individuals with experience in the physical protection, surveillance, control, and accounting of nuclear material.

Selected Agencies Within NRC

The **Office of Investigations** develops policy, procedures, and quality control standards for investigations of licensees, applicants, their contractors or vendors, including the investigations of all allegations of wrongdoing by other than NRC employees and contractors.

★ Web site: http://www.nrc.gov/who-we-are/organization/oifuncdesc.html

★ Job vacancies: http://www.nrc.gov/who-we-are/employment/nrcareers.html

★ Field offices: http://www.nrc.gov/who-we-are/organization/oifuncdesc.html#fo

The **Office of Nuclear Reactor Regulation** is responsible for ensuring the public health and safety through licensing and inspection activities at all nuclear power reactor facilities in the United States.

★ Web site: http://www.nrc.gov/who-we-are/organization/nrrfuncdesc.html

★ Job vacancies: http://www.nrc.gov/who-we-are/employment/nrcareers.html

The **Office of State and Tribal Programs** is responsible for establishing and maintaining effective communications and working relationship between the NRC and states, local government, other federal agencies and Native American Tribal Governments.

★ Web site: http://www.nrc.gov/who-we-are/organization/ospfuncdesc.html

★ Job vacancies: http://www.nrc.gov/who-we-are/employment/nrcareers.html

Other NRC Agencies

Advisory Committee on Nuclear Waste
http://www.nrc.gov/who-we-are/organization/acrsfuncdesc.html#acnw

Advisory Committee on Reactor Safeguards
http://www.nrc.gov/who-we-are/organization/acrsfuncdesc.html#acrs

Atomic Safety and Licensing Board Panel
http://www.nrc.gov/who-we-are/organization/aslbpfuncdesc.html

Office of Enforcement
http://www.nrc.gov/who-we-are/organization/oefuncdesc.html

Office of Nuclear Material Safety and Safeguards
http://www.nrc.gov/who-we-are/organization/nmssfuncdesc.html

Office of Nuclear Regulatory Research
http://www.nrc.gov/who-we-are/organization/resfuncdesc.html

Office of Nuclear Security and Incident Response
http://www.nrc.gov/who-we-are/organization/nsirfuncdesc.html

Region I
http://www.nrc.gov/who-we-are/organization/rifuncdesc.html

Region II
http://www.nrc.gov/who-we-are/organization/riifuncdesc.html

Region III
http://www.nrc.gov/who-we-are/organization/riiifuncdesc.html

Region IV
http://www.nrc.gov/who-we-are/organization/rivfuncdesc.html

Sample Job Vacancies

Emergency Response Coordinator
Agency: Office of Nuclear Security and Incident Response
Salary: $72,108 to $93,742
Location: Montgomery County, Maryland

Job description summary: Provides advice, technical evaluation, and coordination of a program to address topics and problems associated with the NRC assessment of protective measures taken in response to a nuclear emergency. Assists in the coordination of the training and other support provided to the NRC Headquarters emergency response teams. Provides assistance in the development of analytical tools required to perform analyses during an emergency.

Minimum qualifications required: Bachelor's degree in a related field, OR at least one year's experience performing like or similar duties. Must be able to evaluate and assess engineering and scientific issues in response to an incident or emergency event and recommend courses of action.

Minimum application materials required: Submit an online resume via NRCareers. Respond in narrative form to the following KSAs: 1) knowledge of the principles and practices of radiological incident or emergency preparedness, and incident or emergency plan development; 2) knowledge of Federal and State legislation, Executive Orders, and government regulations related to incident or emergency preparedness and planning programs; 3) ability to assess engineering or scientific issues under stressful situations that occur during an emergency or event; 4) ability to present technical information both orally and in writing.

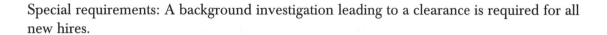

Special requirements: A background investigation leading to a clearance is required for all new hires.

International Relations Specialist

Agency: Office of International Programs
Salary: $27,597 to $54,360
Location: Montgomery County, Maryland

Job description summary: Coordinates, implements, and plans administrative activities in support of NRC's international nuclear safety cooperation and assistance activities. Recommends policies and procedures regarding specific program activities.

Minimum qualifications required: Bachelor's degree with a major in international law and international relations, political science, economics, history, sociology, geography, social or cultural anthropology, law, statistics, or in the humanities. Must have one year of specialized experience that clearly demonstrates knowledge of the principles and policies of the U.S. government regarding nuclear policies and programs related to principles of international relations.

Minimum application materials required: Submit an online resume via NRCareers. Respond in narrative form to the following KSAs: 1) ability to learn international affairs and U. S. political issues sufficient to identify countries with which the U. S. has significant differences in regard to international terrorism, nuclear proliferation or safeguards and nuclear arms control matters; 2) ability to establish effective working relationships; 3) skill in communicating information, ideas and advice in a clear, concise and logical manner, both orally and in writing; 4) ability to use information technology in support of responsibilities and activities of this position.

Special requirements: A background investigation leading to a clearance is required for all new hires.

IT Specialist

Agency: Quality Assurance and Technology Direction Branch
Salary: $85,210 to $110,775
Location: Montgomery County, Maryland

Job description summary: Assesses new and emerging technologies and develops policies, standards, and guidelines relating to NRC's Architecture and Technology programs. This includes assisting in the development of the technology plan; coordinating the planning, assessment, and implementation of information technology; and assisting customers with their projects to ensure that the proposed technologies in their screening forms and business cases are compatible with the Agency's infrastructure.

Minimum qualifications required: Bachelor's degree in a related field. Must have at least one year of specialized experience that demonstrates knowledge of new and emerging technologies, government policies, industry's best practices, and regulations and rules relating to architecture and technology.

Minimum application materials required: Submit an online resume via NRCareers. Respond in narrative form to the following KSAs: 1) ability to assess and evaluate new and emerging and technology standards for incorporation into NRC`s infrastructure; 2) knowledge of information technology issues unique to federal agencies and other large scientific, technical, or legal organizations, and actions required to mitigate or resolve these problems; 3) ability to evaluate complex programmatic problems and to communicate complex IT technical issues to executive level management in an effective manner; 4) knowledge of federal or private sector project management and contracting practices and ability to ensure that project objectives are accomplished as planned on schedule, within established funding levels, and are consistent with standard business practices, agency policy and guidelines, and federal regulations; 5) ability to communicate effectively, both orally and in writing.

Special requirements: A background investigation leading to a clearance is required for all new hires.

Physical Security Inspector

Agency: Division of Reactor Safety
Salary: $71,617 to $93,104
Location: Dallas-Fort Worth Metro Area

Job description summary: Conducts inspections of performance at licensee nuclear power reactors to assure the existing security, safeguards, and fitness-for-duty programs provide the intended level of protection. Follows up on identified problems to ensure that NRC licensees have taken appropriate corrective action.

Minimum qualifications required: One year of specialized experience which demonstrates a thorough knowledge of the theories, principles, and practices in physical security systems, process equipment, and procedures at nuclear power plants with particular emphasis in the areas of vulnerability assessment and knowledge of response force capabilities; detection and assessment hardware; defensive strategies; and, response tactics.

Minimum application materials required: Submit an online resume via NRCareers. Respond in narrative form to the following KSAs: 1) knowledge of physical protection systems, processes, techniques, equipment, handheld weapons, explosive devices, and procedures at an NRC-licensed facility; 2) ability to perform field and program assessments of plant security systems/processes; 3) experience in evaluating facility physical security plans, contingency response plans, security force training plans, fitness-for-duty programs and processes, and access authorization programs at an NRC-licensed facility; 4) experience evaluating potential threat information and implementing or recommending appropriate response actions at an NRC-licensed facility; 5) knowledge of and coordination with other federal, state, and local response organizations, and members of the public; 6) ability to communicate effectively both orally and in writing.

Special requirements: Must pass a drug test and a background investigation.

Office of Personnel Management

1900 E Street NW
Washington, D.C. 20415-0001
202-606-1800

★ Web site: http://www.opm.gov/

★ Job vacancies: http://jobsearch.usajobs.opm.gov/a9opm.asp

★ USAJOBS By Phone: 912-757-3000

★ Contact information: http://apps.opm.gov/opmorgchart/

★ Salaries and wages: http://www.opm.gov/oca/04tables/index.asp

★ Student jobs: http://www.studentjobs.gov/

★ Federal career intern information: http://www.opm.gov/careerintern/

★ Basic employment and benefit information:
http://www.opm.gov/Employment_and_Benefits/

The Office of Personnel Management administers a merit system to ensure compliance with personnel laws and regulations and assists agencies in recruiting, examining, and promoting people on the basis of their knowledge and skills, regardless of their race, religion, sex, political influence, or other nonmerit factors. Its role is to provide guidance to agencies in operating human resources programs which effectively support their missions and to provide an array of personnel services to applicants and employees. The Office supports government program managers in their human resources management responsibilities and provides benefits to employees, retired employees, and their survivors.

Sample Job Vacancies

Human Resource Specialist
Agency: Talent Management Group, Center for Human Capital Management,
Office of Personnel Management
Salary: $50,593 to $93,742
Location: Washington, D.C., Metro Area

Job description summary: Advises management officials on the application of provisions of federal employee and labor relations statutes, regulations, and case law. Serves as a technical advisor in the field of employee and labor relations agency-wide.

Minimum qualifications required: Ph.D., OR one year of specialized experience related to the work of the position, OR a combination of experience and education.

Minimum application materials required: Submit an online resume, supporting documentation, and application questionnaire. Questionnaire requires narrative responses to the following KSAs: 1) application of laws, executive orders, regulations, decisions, principles, practices, and techniques of employee and labor relations; 2) conducts research on sensitive employee relations issues; 3) analyzes regulations, policies and actions having impact on employee and labor relations; 4) provides policy advice in the areas of leave, attendance, hours of duty, grievances, adverse actions and other labor and employee relations matters; 5) advises top officials on the application of provisions of employee and labor relations statues, regulations, and case law; 6) recommends strategies for developing, implementing, and evaluating employee relations programs; 7) consults with union and management on grievances, arbitration and labor relations law.

Investigations Technician

Agency: Center for Federal Investigative Services
Salary: $24,083 to $43,388
Location: Boyers, Pennsylvania

Job description summary: Provides technical assistance to investigators who are reviewing personnel background investigations or adjudicating suitability for employment. Reviews investigative cases for suitability and personnel security purposes; performs postaudit of work done by contractors to ensure accuracy and completeness; and prepares and gives feedback to the contractor, gathering and compiling data to prepare periodic oversight reports. Performs data entry duties associated with the scheduling, review, and closing of investigations.

Minimum qualifications required: Associate's degree, OR at least one year of progressively responsible clerical, office, or other work that indicates the ability to acquire the particular competencies needed to perform the duties of this position.

Minimum application materials required: Submit an online resume, supporting documentation, and application questionnaire. Questionnaire requires narrative responses to the following KSAs: 1) customer service ability; 2) decision making ability; 3) interpersonal relations skills; 4) office automation skills; 5) written and oral communications skills; 6) reasoning ability; 7) self management ability; 8) team work; 9) ability to apply laws and regulations.

Test Administrator

Agency: Office of Personnel Management
Salary: $10.31/hour
Location: Guam

Job description summary: Administers written tests for federal employment, and Armed Services Vocational Aptitude Battery Enlistment tests, and DoD Student tests. Responsible for security of test materials.

Minimum qualifications required: Associate's degree, OR at least one year of progressively responsible clerical, office or other work (i.e., teaching) which indicates the ability to orally present information to individuals or groups, ability to handle administrative and clerical processes, and ability to establish effective relationships with customers.

Minimum application materials required: Submit an online resume, supporting documentation, and application questionnaire. Questionnaire has more than 20 KSAs, including the following: 1) administer written tests; 2) ensure test conditions in a test room are conducive to the best possible test performance by applicants; 3) maintain control in the test room to ensure against cheating and test material losses; 4) give oral instructions to others, such as how to complete; 5) verify shipments of controlled materials; 6) report invoice or material discrepancies; 7) audit and account for all material.

Special requirements: Must have a valid driver's license. Must be a U.S. citizen. Males born after December 31, 1959, must have registered with the Selective Service.

Overseas Private Investment Corporation

1100 New York Avenue NW
Washington, D.C. 20527
202-336-8400

★ Web site: http://www.opic.gov/

★ Job vacancies: http://www.usajobs.opm.gov/

★ USAJOBS By Phone: 912-757-3000

★ Internship information: http://www.opic.gov/HRM/internships/interns_aboutopic.asp

★ Basic employment information: http://www.opic.gov/hrm/hrm.asp

The Overseas Private Investment Corporation (OPIC) helps U.S. businesses invest overseas, fosters economic development in new and emerging markets, complements the private sector in managing the risks associated with foreign direct investment, and supports U.S. foreign policy. By expanding economic development in host countries, OPIC-supported projects can encourage political stability, free market reforms, and U.S. best practices. OPIC projects also support American jobs and exports. Because OPIC charges market-based fees for its products, it operates on a self-sustaining basis at no net cost to taxpayers. The OPIC staff consists of approximately 200 employees, all based in Washington, D.C.

Peace Corps

1111 Twentieth Street NW
Washington, D.C. 20526
202-692-2000

★ Web site: http://www.peacecorps.gov/

★ Job vacancies (domestic): http://www.peacecorps.gov/index.cfm?shell=pchq.jobs.domvac

★ Job vacancies (overseas):
   http://www.peacecorps.gov/index.cfm?shell=pchq.jobs.overseasvac

★ Job vacancies (headquarters): http://www.peacecorps.gov/index.cfm?shell=pchq.jobs.hqop

★ USAJOBS By Phone: 912-757-3000

★ Regional recruitment offices:
   http://www.peacecorps.gov/index.cfm?shell=pchq.jobs.regrecop

★ Professional medical opportunities:
   http://www.peacecorps.gov/index.cfm?shell=pchq.jobs.overseasop.medical

★ How to apply: http://www.peacecorps.gov/index.cfm?shell=pchq.jobs.howtoapply

★ Salary and benefits:
   http://www.peacecorps.gov/index.cfm?shell=pchq.jobs.workingpc.salary

★ Basic employment information: http://www.peacecorps.gov/index.cfm?shell=pchq.jobs

The mission of the Peace Corps is to help the people of interested countries in meeting their need for trained men and women, and to help promote better mutual understanding between Americans and people of other countries. The Peace Corps consists of a Washington, D.C., headquarters; 11 area offices; and overseas operations in 70 countries, utilizing more than 7,000 volunteers.

To fulfill the Peace Corps mandate, men and women are trained for a 9- to 14-week period in the appropriate local language, the technical skills necessary for their particular job, and the cross-cultural skills needed to adjust to a society with traditions and attitudes different from their own. Volunteers serve for a period of two years, living among the people with whom they work, and serving in six program areas: education, health and HIV/AIDS, environment, information technology, agriculture, and business development.

The most common international employment opportunities within the Peace Corps are Country Director (CD) and Associate Director (APCD). Occasionally, Peace Corps recruits MDs or DOs for Area Peace Corps Medical Officers for the Africa Region. There are 11 Peace Corps recruiting offices throughout the United States where staff identify and select the volunteers. One of the key positions in these offices is the regional recruiter. Peace Corps also seeks physicians, nurse practitioners, and physician assistants with independent practice experience for two-year contract positions overseas as Peace Corps Medical Officers (PCMOs). PCMOs provide health care, education, counseling, and manage the Volunteer health care delivery system in the country of assignment.

Selected Agencies Within Peace Corps

Since its inception in 1989 by Paul D. Coverdell, **World Wise Schools** has helped more than one million U.S. students communicate directly with Peace Corps Volunteers all over the world. Initially set up as a correspondence "match" program between Volunteers and U.S. classes, World Wise Schools has expanded its scope over the past 10 years by providing a broad range of resources for educators—including award-winning videos, teacher guides, classroom speakers, a newsletter and online resources.

★ Web site: http://www.peacecorps.gov/wws/index.html

★ Contact information: http://www.peacecorps.gov/wws/contacts/index.html

Other Peace Corps Agencies

Crisis Corps

http://www.peacecorps.gov/index.cfm?shell=resources.former.crisiscorps

Fellows/USA

http://www.peacecorps.gov/index.cfm?shell=learn.whyvol.eduben.fellows

Sample Job Vacancies

Assessment and Placement Assistant

Agency: Volunteer Recruitment and Selection
Salary: $34,531 to $41,232
Location: Washington, D.C.

Job description summary: Performs initial screening of applications using Peace Corps criteria and guidelines and gathers missing documents and information; identifies applicants with skill suitability or legal qualification issues that need follow-up by specialist; communicates information to applicants regarding their status and placement; and provides general administrative support to two placement specialists including data entry, record keeping, running computer reports, maintaining filing systems, and caseload management.

Minimum qualifications required: Bachelor's degree. Must have one year of specialized experience in or related to the work of this position.

Minimum application materials required: E-mailed and faxed applications are preferred. Include narrative answers to the following KSAs: 1) ability to work effectively and accurately under pressure of deadlines or heavy workloads; 2) ability to work with the public in providing customer service and assistance in resolving problems through clear explanation of interrelated systems; 3) ability to assume responsibility and work independently setting work priorities and coordinating workloads; 4) experience which provides an understanding of the demands and constraints of working in a cross-cultural international environment and the ability to communicate those factors to others.

Special requirements: Must pass a background security investigation. The selectee must be able to obtain and keep a Top Secret security clearance.

Associate Peace Corps Director, Administrative Officer

Agency: Europe, Mediterranean, and Asia Division
Salary: $37,694 to $68,315
Location: Rabat, Morocco

Job description summary: Responsible for overseas post administrative operations, including budget formulation and execution, human resource management, procurement, contracts, property management, computer systems maintenance, and general services support.

Minimum qualifications required: Bachelor's degree. Must have one year of specialized experience in or related to the work of this position.

Minimum application materials required: E-mailed and faxed applications are preferred. Include narrative answers to the following KSAs: 1) overseas experience in a multicultural setting in a developing country; 2) skill in developing annual and multi-year budget projections; 3) knowledge of accounting, including monitoring the status of funds, and preparing financial reports; 4) knowledge of overseas procurement; 5) skill in supervising administrative operations.

Special requirements: Must pass a background security investigation. The selectee must be able to obtain and keep a Top Secret security clearance.

Human Resources Specialist

Agency: Office of Human Resources Management, Peace Corps Headquarters
Salary: $53,325 to $96,643
Location: Washington, D.C.

Job description summary: Provides advice, counsel, and guidance on all operational personnel matters including: staffing and recruitment, position management and classification, pay administration, federal benefits, personnel procedures, policies, and regulations. Leads and participates in special projects and programs and coordinates recruitment and selection of U.S. direct-hire staff for overseas positions.

Minimum qualifications required: Bachelor's degree in a related field. Must have one year of specialized experience in or related to the work of this position.

Minimum application materials required: E-mailed and faxed applications are preferred. Include narrative answers to the following KSAs: 1) ability to display tact and diplomacy and maintain effective working relationships with management, staff, subordinates, and people at all levels; 2) ability to serve as an advisor in an excepted service workforce environment; 3) ability to provide customer service through oral and written communications.

Special requirements: Must pass a background security investigation.

Program Specialist

Agency: Office of Administrative Services, Reference Research, and Distribution Division (RRD)
Salary: $43,209 to $63,453
Location: Washington, D.C.

Job description summary: Implements and coordinates property management systems, providing procedural management for the control and accountability of all agency personal property; assists with the review of contract obligations, ensuring contract company fulfills their contractual obligations; conducts analytical studies of support-related functions and procedures within the RRD; and formulates and presents oral and written reports and correspondence.

Minimum qualifications required: Bachelor's degree. Must have one year of specialized experience in or related to the work of this position.

Minimum application materials required: E-mailed and faxed applications are preferred. Include narrative answers to the following KSAs: 1) ability to prepare and present reports, studies, critiques, and solutions in writing; 2) ability to monitor contractor performance; 3) knowledge of supply regulations, policies and procedures.

Special requirements: Must pass a background security investigation.

Regional Safety and Security Officer

Agency: Office of Safety and Security, Volunteer Safety and Overseas Security Division
Salary: $46,519 to $84,309
Location: Worldwide

Job description summary: Provides support to country directors in a specified subregion in collaboration with their senior staff and State Department regional security officers posted in the assigned subregion. Assists the country directors in developing safety and security strategies, procedures, and training consistent with the Volunteer Safety Support System and the policies and standards set forth by the Agency. Collects and disseminates resources throughout the subregion; assesses existing safety and security training for staff and Volunteers; assists in developing training guidelines and modules; designs and delivers regional safety and security training workshops; conducts post and subregional safety and security assessments of Peace Corps residences and offices and Volunteer housing and sites to ensure they are consistent with Agency standards; and assists the country director and headquarters staff in managing safety and security crisis situations.

Minimum qualifications required: Bachelor's degree. Must have one year of specialized experience in or related to the work of this position.

Minimum application materials required: E-mailed and faxed applications are preferred. Include narrative answers to the following KSAs: 1) strong interpersonal and communications skills (oral and written); 2) ability in facilitating group processes and building consensus; 3) ability to work collaboratively with other agencies on issues related to personal safety and security; 4) ability to coordinate and supervise the work of others to accomplish established goals, setting priorities, and meeting deadlines; 5) proficiency in the official language of one of the three regions; 6) knowledge of the culture, history, politics, etc. of one of the three regions.

Special requirements: Must pass a background security investigation.

Telecommunications Specialist

Agency: Office of the Chief Information Officer
Salary: $34,531 to $63,453
Location: Washington, D.C.

Job description summary: Responsible for the day-to-day operation of the Peace Corps' Cable Room, which includes receiving, sorting, assigning action and distributing all incoming/outgoing classified and unclassified telegram traffic to and from overseas posts; maintains a secure log and filing system for all classified telegrams. Hand-delivers all classified telegrams to the proper office and obtains a valid receipt signature. Maintains close contact with the Department of State Communications Branch to keep abreast of changes in work methods and functions affecting international communications needs. Performs duties and functions associated with Call Center operations. Monitors and maintains existing inventory and provides end-user training and analysis and recommendations on the selection of new devices. Administers agency federal calling card inventory. Orders staff calling cards, provides training, and resolves carrier actions. Acts as a backup for video conferencing.

Minimum qualifications required: Bachelor's degree. Must have one year of specialized experience in or related to the work of this position.

Minimum application materials required: Submit a resume or Optional Application for Federal Employment (OF-612). E-mailed and faxed applications are preferred. Include narrative answers to the following KSAs: 1) ability to follow instructions, organize, and prioritize tasks in a systematic procedure; 2) ability to communicate orally and in writing; and 3) experience preparing and formatting telegrams

Special requirements: Must pass a background security investigation.

Pension Benefit Guaranty Corporation

1200 K Street NW
Washington, D.C. 20005
202-326-4000

★ Web site: http://www.pbgc.gov/

★ Job vacancies: http://jobsearch.usajobs.opm.gov/

★ USAJOBS By Phone: 912-757-3000

★ PBGC Job Information Line: 202-326-4111

★ Contact information: http://www.pbgc.gov/contacts/default.htm

★ Employee benefits: http://www.pbgc.gov/about/pbgc-benefits.htm

★ Employee directory: http://www.pbgc.gov/contacts/employee/default.htm

The Pension Benefit Guaranty Corporation (PBGC) guarantees payment of nonforfeitable pension benefits in covered private-sector defined benefit pension plans. PBGC is not funded by general tax revenues. PBGC collects insurance premiums from employers that sponsor insured pension plans, earns money from investments, and receives funds from pension plans it takes over. PBGC protects the pensions of nearly 44.3 million working people in more than 31,000 private-sector defined benefit pension plans, including over 1,600 multiemployer plans. These pension plans provide a specified monthly benefit at retirement, usually based on salary or a stated dollar amount and years of service.

PBGC has approximately 750 employees with many different skills. PBGC staff includes accountants; actuaries; attorneys; auditors; budget, financial, and management analysts; computer, pension law, and public affairs specialists; administrative personnel; and many more.

Selected Agencies Within PBGC

The Corporate Finance and Negotiations Department (CFND) is responsible for analyzing the financial conditions of companies with over $50 million in aggregate unfunded benefit liabilities or more than 5,000 plan participants. CFND monitors the risk these companies present to the pension plan and PBGC by tracking company and industry developments, analyzing transactions, and intervening to formulate, recommend, and pursue recoveries that obtain maximum protection for plan participants and the PBGC. When plans terminate and PBGC becomes the trustee of the plan, CFND facilitates the smooth transition of plans from company to PBGC trusteeship.

★ Web site: http://www.pbgc.gov/about/departments.htm

Other PBGC Agencies

Contracts and Controls Review Department
http://www.pbgc.gov/about/departments.htm

Insurance Operations Department
http://www.pbgc.gov/about/departments.htm

Participant and Employer Appeals Department
http://www.pbgc.gov/about/departments.htm

Sample Job Vacancies

Actuary
Agency: Insurance Operations Department
Salary: $29,696 to $55,934
Location: Washington, D.C.

Job description summary: Reviews termination cases to determine that all required plan information is included. Identifies additional information required or items needing clarification. Analyzes plan documents of terminated pension plans to determine benefit entitlement and calculates benefit amounts for plan participants. Determines present value of benefits and allocates pension plan assets by priority categories. Produces benefit statements for plan participants and automated benefit redetermination programs to be used by Pension Law Specialists for participants entering pay status.

Minimum qualifications required: Bachelor's degree in actuarial science or mathematics. Must have one year of experience actuarial analyses and knowledge of the laws, regulations and policies governing pension plans.

Minimum application materials required: Submit a resume, Optional Application for Federal Employment (OF-612), Application for Federal Employment (SF-171), or any other written format that includes the necessary information specified in the announcement. In addition submit separate narrative statements addressing the following KSAs: 1) knowledge of the general principles and practices of actuarial science; 2) knowledge of the theory, funding and operation of defined benefit pension plans under ERISA which include experience with interpretation of plan documents, funding determinations (valuations), pension law, plan determinations, and liability calculations; 2) ability to communicate clearly, both orally and in writing; 3) skill in using computers with standard PC software packages such as Lotus 1-2-3, Excel, WordPerfect or Paradox.

Special requirements: Males born after December 31, 1959, must have registered for Selective Service.

Collections Analyst

Agency: Financial Operations Department
Salary: $60,638 to $93,742
Location: Washington, D.C.

Job description summary: Manages an extensive caseload of money owed to PBGC. Reviews and updates debtor databases and letter generation system. Reviews investigation reports and legal determinations to assess the financial impact on the collections program. Supports OGC in litigation and formal proceedings to collect unpaid accounts. Manages efforts with DMS to collect recalcitrant debtor accounts and other monies owed to PBGC. Assists the Policies, Procedures and Controls Division (PPCD), OGC, and CPRD in collection matters and on studies of debt enforcement.

Minimum qualifications required: Bachelor's degree in a related field. One year of specialized experience in debt collection and assessment, judicial decisions concerning debt collections, and collection practices and procedures, in order to apply new concepts and standards to complex, unprecedented cases, provide guidance to contractor and other staff, and function as a technical authority in litigation support and staff studies.

Minimum application materials required: Submit a resume, Optional Application for Federal Employment (OF-612), Application for Federal Employment (SF-171), or any other written format that includes the necessary information specified in the announcement. In addition submit separate narrative statements addressing the following KSAs: 1) skill in debt collection and assessment, judicial decisions concerning debt collections, and collection practices and procedures; 2) skill in communicating both orally and in writing; 3) skill in the use of data processing applications for management and reporting of financial data; 4) skill in researching financial information and analyzing data to make sound proposals and determinations.

Special requirements: Everyone must serve a one-year probationary period.

Railroad Retirement Board

844 North Rush Street
Chicago, Illinois 60611-2092
312-751-4777

★ Web site: http://www.rrb.gov/

★ Job vacancies: http://www.usajobs.opm.gov/

★ USAJOBS By Phone: 912-757-3000

★ Field offices: http://www.rrb.gov/field.html

The Railroad Retirement Board (RRB) determines and pays comprehensive retirement-survivor and unemployment-sickness benefits for the nation's railroad workers and their families. To this end, the RRB employs field representatives to assist railroad personnel and their families in filing claims for benefits, examiners to adjudicate the claims, and information technology staff to maintain earnings records, calculate benefits, and process payments. The RRB also employs actuaries to predict the future income and outlays of the railroad retirement system, statisticians and economists to provide vital data, and attorneys to interpret legislation and represent the RRB in litigation. Internal administration requires a procurement staff, a budget and accounting staff, and personnel specialists. The Inspector General employs auditors and investigators to detect any waste, fraud, or abuse in the benefit programs.

Securities and Exchange Commission

450 Fifth Street NW
Washington, D.C. 20549
202-942-4150

★ Web site: http://www.sec.gov/

★ Job vacancies: http://www.sec.gov/jobs.shtml

★ USAJOBS By Phone: 912-757-3000

★ How to apply: http://www.sec.gov/jobs/jobs_apply.shtml

★ Regional and district offices: http://www.sec.gov/contact/addresses.htm

★ Internships: http://www.sec.gov/jobs/jobs_students.shtml

The primary mission of the U.S. Securities and Exchange Commission (SEC) is to protect investors and maintain the integrity of the securities markets. SEC requires public companies to disclose meaningful financial and other information to the public, which provides a common pool of knowledge for all investors to use to judge for themselves if a company's securities are a good investment. The SEC also oversees other key participants in the securities world, including stock exchanges, broker-dealers, investment advisors, mutual funds, and public utility holding companies. Here again, the SEC is concerned primarily with promoting disclosure of important information, enforcing the securities laws, and protecting investors who interact with these various organizations and individuals. Crucial to the SEC's effectiveness is its enforcement authority. Each year the SEC brings 400 to 500 civil enforcement actions against individuals and companies that break the securities laws. Typical infractions include insider trading, accounting fraud, and providing false or misleading information about securities and the companies that issue them.

The SEC consists of five presidentially appointed Commissioners, four Divisions and 18 Offices. With approximately 3,100 staff, the SEC is small by federal agency standards. Headquartered in Washington, D.C., the SEC has 11 regional and district Offices throughout the country. It hires attorneys, accountants, securities compliance examiners, IT specialists, and economists, along with administrative and office support specialists.

SEC uses the AVUE online system to manage its vacancy announcements. After registering on the AVUE site, you can build and maintain a personal profile and apply for SEC vacancies online. You may also elect to have the system notify you by e-mail of the status of your application throughout the entire recruitment process.

Selected Agencies Within SEC

The **Division of Corporation Finance** oversees corporate disclosure of important information to the investing public. Corporations are required to comply with regulations pertaining to disclosure that must be made when stock is initially sold and then on a continuing and periodic basis. The Division's staff routinely reviews the disclosure documents filed by companies. The staff also provides companies with assistance interpreting the Commission's rules and recommends to the Commission new rules for adoption.

★ Web site: http://www.sec.gov/divisions/corpfin.shtml

Other SEC Agencies

Office of Economic Analysis
http://www.sec.gov/about/economic.shtml

Division of Enforcement
http://www.sec.gov/divisions/enforce.shtml

Division of Investment Management
http://www.sec.gov/divisions/investment.shtml

Division of Market Regulation
http://www.sec.gov/divisions/marketreg.shtml

Office of Administrative Law Judges
http://www.sec.gov/about/offices/oalj.htm

Office of Compliance Inspections and Examinations
http://www.sec.gov/about/offices/ocie.htm

Office of Filings and Information Services
http://www.sec.gov/info/edgar/ofis.shtml

Office of International Affairs
http://www.sec.gov/about/offices/oia.htm

Office of Investor Education and Assistance
http://www.sec.gov/investor.shtml

Sample Job Vacancies

Trial Attorney
Agency: Division of Enforcement
Salary: $123,982 to $158,844
Location: Washington, D.C.

Job description summary: Represents the SEC in complex civil federal district court actions and administrative proceedings brought to enforce the federal securities laws. Is responsible for all aspects of the litigation, including the preparation and filing of pleadings, motions, briefs, and other court papers; discovery; trial; and settlement negotiations. Effectively and aggressively prosecutes civil actions that frequently raise complex and factual issues and in which the defendants are often represented by highly skilled defense counsel. Oversees SEC investigative attorneys, accountants, and support staff who assist in the conduct of the litigations. Advises senior enforcement division staff and the SEC's chairman and commissioners concerning litigation-related issues that arise in proposed and pending enforcement actions.

Minimum qualifications required: Must be an active member of the Bar and must have either a minimum of four years of specialized experience as a practicing attorney or one year of specialized professional legal experience that demonstrates knowledge of trial techniques, the Federal Rules of Civil Procedure, and the Federal Rules of Evidence.

Minimum application materials required: Submit a resume or the Optional Application for Federal Employment (OF-612). Include narrative responses to the following KSAs: 1) experience litigating and trying complex cases in federal or state courts or before Administrative Law Judges; 2) experience taking depositions and/or investigative testimony; 3) experience preparing pleadings, briefs, and other court papers involving complex legal issues; 4) knowledge of the federal securities statutes, rules, and regulations administered by the Commission, the Federal Rules of Civil Procedure, and the Federal Rules of Evidence; 5) ability to work effectively with others on a litigation team and to deal and negotiate effectively with opposing counsel.

Disclosure Assistant
Agency: Division of Investment Management
Salary: $29,939 to $46,662
Location: Washington, D.C.

Job description summary: Establishes and maintains databases, files, records, and indexes. Works with Division and Commission databases and record keeping systems. Performs program-related research; keeps abreast of work currently pending or in progress; and types highly technical, financial, and accounting memoranda. Receives and screens telephone calls and visitors; reviews and disseminates mail; monitors, records, and maintains necessary records of time and attendance and STATS for staff; makes arrangements for conferences and travel; schedules appointments for the assistant director and other staff members. Maintains manual and computerized log of correspondence, filings, and periodic reports.

Minimum qualifications required: Bachelor's degree, OR one year of specialized experience related to the duties of the position. Must be able to type 40 words per minute. Must also have experience working effectively in a team-oriented environment and possess the ability to interact well with others in work situations where there are frequent time constraints, variable deadlines, and other job-related demands.

Minimum application materials required: Submit a resume or Optional Application for Federal Employment (OF-612). Respond in narrative form to the following KSAs: 1) good computer skills and demonstrated ability in using a variety of software and databases; 2) ability to set-up and maintain office files; 3) knowledge of administrative procedures regarding travel and time and attendance; 4) ability to work well with others with professionalism and to work cooperatively as part of a group.

Securities Compliance Examiner

Agency: Central Regional Office
Salary: $54,975 to $121,465
Location: Denver, Colorado

Job description summary: Performs compliance examinations and investigations of investment companies and investment advisers, broker-dealers, and/or transfer agents. Examines the operations and financial conditions of companies, the adequacy of books and records, procedures for safeguarding funds and securities, and methods of doing business. Prepares required schedules, worksheets, and narrative materials; evaluates findings and formulates conclusions concerning the degree of compliance with statutory and/or regulatory requirements. Conducts conferences and interviews with a variety of company personnel in order to determine possible regulatory violations, and with officers and partners of registrants, private investors, attorneys, CPA's, industry and banking officials, and law enforcement officials on matters relevant to the examination. Prepares report of findings as well as correspondence to entity outlining deficiencies and corrective actions to be taken.

Minimum qualifications required: Master's degree or Ph.D. in accounting, business administration, finance, or related field of study. Must have at least one year of progressively responsible specialized experience in the application of accounting and auditing work related to the position.

Minimum application materials required: Apply by submitting a resume or Optional Application for Federal Employment (OF-612).

Staff Accountant

Agency: Central Regional Office
Salary: $44,943 to $52,760
Location: Denver, Colorado

Job description summary: Assists with completion of compliance examinations and inspections. Reviews and analyzes the books, records, and activities of underwriters, brokers, dealers, investment companies, investment advisers, transfer agents, or other persons registered with the SEC, as well as records of banks and other entities to determine whether transactions and conduct are in compliance with the SEC's rules, regulations and procedures; prepares charts, schedules, and reports of findings. Recommends courses of action. Interviews accounting professionals and securities industry participants regarding financial statements, audits, and securities transactions.

Minimum qualifications required: Bachelor's degree in accounting or in a related field of study; OR at least four years of accounting/auditing experience: OR an equivalent combination of accounting experience and college-level education.

Minimum application materials required: Apply by submitting a resume or Optional Application for Federal Employment (OF-612).

Selective Service System

National Headquarters
Arlington, Virginia 22209-2425
703-605-4000

- ★ Web site: http://www.sss.gov/Default.htm
- ★ Job vacancies: http://www.sss.gov/Job%20Opportunities.htm
- ★ USAJOBS By Phone: 912-757-3000
- ★ Reserve forces officer information: http://www.sss.gov/rfo.htm
- ★ Regional offices: http://www.sss.gov/struct.htm
- ★ Volunteer as a local board member: http://www.sss.gov/fslocal.htm

The Selective Service System provides untrained manpower to the armed forces in an emergency and operates an Alternative Service Program during a draft for men classified as conscientious objectors. The Selective Service System's structure consists of the national headquarters, data management center, and three region headquarters. About 200 full-time employees, including 16 military officers, work in these locations. Also part of Selective Service is a field structure of military reservists and civilian volunteer board members. Each state, the District of Columbia, and U.S. territories also has a state director. Selective Service's reservists, board members, and state directors are the Agency's standby components. They serve part-time for the Agency, remaining trained and ready to be called into service in the event of a draft.

Small Business Administration

409 Third Street SW
Washington, D.C. 20416
202-205-6600

- ★ Web site: http://www.sba.gov/
- ★ Job vacancies: http://www.sba.gov/jobs/

★ USAJOBS By Phone: 912-757-3000

★ SBA regional offices: http://www.sba.gov/aboutsba/regoffices.html

★ SBA local offices: http://www.sba.gov/aboutsba/dis_offices.html

★ Business Information Centers contact information:
http://www.sba.gov/aboutsba/bics_full.html#al

★ Benefits: http://www.sba.gov/gopher/Ops/SBA/empl8.txt

★ Employee directory: http://www.sba.gov/aboutsba/find.html

The fundamental purposes of the Small Business Administration (SBA) are to aid, counsel, assist, and protect the interests of small business; ensure that small business concerns receive a fair portion of government purchases, contracts, and subcontracts, as well as of the sales of government property; make loans to small business concerns, state and local development companies, and the victims of floods or other catastrophes, or of certain types of economic injury; and license, regulate, and make loans to small business investment companies.

SBA has 70 district and 10 regional offices. The SBA offers a wide range of careers, including economic development specialist, business opportunity specialist, personnel specialist, criminal investigator, loan specialist, industrial specialist, contract specialist, procurement analyst, clerical and administrative support positions, accountant, auditor, economist, and attorney.

Selected Agencies Within SBA

The **Office of Entrepreneurial Development** helps small businesses start, grow, and compete in global markets by providing training, counseling, and access to resources. It offers the following programs and resources: the Small Business Development Centers, SCORE, the Small Business Training Network, Native American Assistance, Business & Community Initiatives, and Women's Business Ownerships.

★ Web site: http://www.sba.gov/ed/index.html

★ Job vacancies: http://www.sba.gov/jobs/

★ Small Business Development Centers: http://www.sba.gov/sbdc/

★ SCORE: http://www.score.org/

★ The Small Business Training Network: http://www.sba.gov/training/

★ The Office of Native American Affairs: http://www.sba.gov/naa/

★ Business and Community Initiatives: http://www.sba.gov/bi/

★ The Office of Women's Business Ownership: http://www.sba.gov/ed/wbo/index.html

The **Office of Government Contracting and Business Development** helps small, disadvantaged, and women-owned businesses build their potential to compete more successfully in a global economy. It administers the Office of Government Contracting; the Office of Federal Contract Assistance for Women Business Owners; the Office of Business Development; the

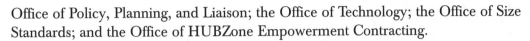

Office of Policy, Planning, and Liaison; the Office of Technology; the Office of Size Standards; and the Office of HUBZone Empowerment Contracting.

★ Web site: http://www.sba.gov/gcbd/

★ Job vacancies: http://www.sba.gov/jobs/

★ Office of Government Contracting: http://www.sba.gov/GC/

★ Office of Technology: http://www.sba.gov/sbir/

★ Office of Size Standards: http://www.sba.gov/size/

★ Office of HUBZone Empowerment Contracting: https://eweb1.sba.gov/hubzone/internet/

Other SBA Programs and Offices

8(a) Business Development
http://www.sba.gov/8abd/

Financial Assistance
http://www.sba.gov/financing/

Investment Division
http://www.sba.gov/INV/

Office of Advocacy
http://www.sba.gov/ADVO/

Office of Disaster Assistance
http://www.sba.gov/disaster_recov/index.html

Office of Hearings and Appeals
http://www.sba.gov/oha/

Office of International Trade
http://www.sba.gov/oit/

Office of Lender Oversight
http://www.sba.gov/olo/

Office of the National Ombudsman
http://www.sba.gov/ombudsman/

Office of Surety Guarantees
http://www.sba.gov/osg/

Office of Veterans Business Development
http://www.sba.gov/VETS/

Small Disadvantaged Business
http://www.sba.gov/sdb/

Sample Job Vacancy

Deputy District Director

Agency: St. Louis District Office

Salary: $82,713 to $107,528

Location: St. Louis, Missouri

Job description summary: Formulates and finalizes the District's operating plans and budget. Assists the district director in administering the operations of small business advisory councils and the Service Corps of Retired Executives (SCORE). Works with community leaders and state officials on agency programs, and serves as the key liaison person with local, city, state, and federal government entities. Assists in internal administrative functions of the District Office that include personnel, budget, program management, and staff utilization. Advises on problems that impact on operating programs; hears group grievances and reviews serious disciplinary cases and disciplinary programs. Participates in implementing the Equal Employment Opportunity Program.

Minimum qualifications required: Bachelor's degree. Must have one year of specialized experience which is in or directly related to the line of work of the position.

Minimum application materials required: Submit an Optional Application for Federal Employment (OF-612) or a resume. Include narrative responses to the following KSAs: 1) ability to direct, coordinate and manage a program or divisional operation engaged in the delivery of services; 2) knowledge of business management methods, practices and techniques; 3) skill in meeting, dealing, negotiating or maintaining effective working relationships with diverse individuals or groups; 4) ability to supervise.

Special requirements: Must be a U.S. citizen. Musts pass a background security investigation.

Social Security Administration

6401 Security Boulevard

Baltimore, Maryland 21235

410-965-1234

★ Web site: http://www.ssa.gov/

★ Job vacancies: http://jobsearch.usajobs.opm.gov/a9ssajob.asp

★ USAJOBS By Phone: 912-757-3000

★ How to apply: http://www.ssa.gov/careers/application.htm

★ Student employment: http://www.ssa.gov/careers/students&grads.htm

★ Field offices' personnel offices: http://www.ssa.gov/careers/nearestyou.htm

★ Hearings and appeals offices: http://www.ssa.gov/careers/OHAoffices.htm

★ Teleservice program service, regional, and headquarters' personnel offices: http://www.ssa.gov/careers/nearestyou.htm

★ Recruiting events: http://www.ssa.gov/careers/recruiting.htm

★ Training and development: http://www.ssa.gov/careers/training&dev.htm

★ Benefits: http://www.ssa.gov/careers/pay&benefits.htm

The Social Security Administration manages the country's social insurance program, consisting of retirement, survivors, and disability insurance programs, commonly known as Social Security. It also administers the Supplemental Security Income program for the aged, blind, and disabled. The Administration is responsible for studying the problems of poverty and economic insecurity among Americans and making recommendations on effective methods for solving these problems through social insurance. The Administration also assigns Social Security numbers to U.S. citizens and maintains earnings records for workers under their Social Security numbers.

In addition to its headquarters in Baltimore, Maryland, SSA has over 1,300 field offices, 140 hearing offices, 37 teleservice centers, six program service centers, and 10 regional offices all over the country. It employs more than 65,000 people in several areas: public contact positions (claims representative, claims authorizer, benefit authorizer, service representative, and teleservice representatives), information technology (software development, network services, systems analysis, Web development, and data management), law (staff attorneys, attorney-advisors, administrative law judges, and attorney-examiners), law enforcement (criminal investigators), and management/administrative and support (management analysts, budget analysts, human resource specialists, program analysts, staff assistants).

Selected Agencies Within SSA

The **Office of Hearings and Appeals** (OHA) administers the hearings and appeals program for the Social Security Administration (SSA). Administrative Law Judges (ALJs) conduct hearings and issue decisions. The Appeals Council considers appeals from hearing decisions, and acts as the final level of administrative review for the Social Security Administration.

★ Web site: http://www.ssa.gov/oha/

★ Hearings offices: http://www.ssa.gov/oha/ho_locator.html

★ Job opportunities: http://www.ssa.gov/careers/

★ Legal career opportunities: http://www.ssa.gov/careers/legalcareers.htm

The **Social Security Advisory Board** (SSAB) is an independent, bipartisan board that advises the president, the Congress, and the Commissioner of Social Security on matters related to the Social Security and Supplemental Security Income programs.

★ Web site: http://www.ssab.gov/NEW/default.htm

★ Headquarters contacts: http://www.ssab.gov/NEW/contact.htm

Other SSA Agencies

Office of International Programs
http://www.ssa.gov/international/inter_intro.html

Office of the Chief Actuary
http://www.ssa.gov/OACT/index.html

Office of the Inspector General
http://www.ssa.gov/oig/

Sample Job Vacancies

Claims Assistant

Agency: Social Security Administration
Salary: $26,699 to $34,714
Location: Bloomington, Indiana

Job description summary: Reviews files and documents for completeness and accuracy. Requests supporting evidence. Abstracts data from documents. Prepares certification and refers complex issues and discrepancies to claims representatives and service representatives or to supervisory personnel. Receives incoming mail and telephone calls, answers routine inquiries and provides status reports on pending cases, refers technical inquiries to the responsible staff member. Establishes and maintains files, controls pending cases, records workload, and prepares periodic and special workload reports.

Minimum qualifications required: Must be able to type 40 words per minute. Must have one year of specialized experience in or related to the position being filled.

Minimum application materials required: Complete and submit an Occupational Questionnaire and either a resume or Optional Application for Federal Employment (OF-612). Application must include narrative answers to the following KSAs: 1) use a computer to access data, records or other information and to process and analyze data; 2) use word processing software to produce documents; 3) use a computer to confirm information; 4) answer general or routine inquiries; 5) assist customers with processes, procedures or issues; 6) prepare routine written correspondence; 7) receive telephone calls and route to the appropriate personnel; 8) request information from various sources; 9) sort, control, and route work or information; 10) search for records, files or missing inventory.

Special requirements: Must be a U.S. citizen. Males born after December 31, 1959, must have registered with the Selective Service System. Must pass a background investigation check. All selectees are required to complete an 11-week technical training class. All selectees are required to serve a one-year probationary period.

Contact Representative

Agency: Social Security Administration
Salary: $24,075 to $33,026
Location: Martinsburg, West Virginia

Job description summary: Interviews beneficiaries and the general public to determine the nature of their problem; explain technical information, gather facts, and resolve problems relating to Social Security programs.

Minimum qualifications required: One year of specialized experience performing the following tasks: 1) applying laws, rules, or regulations and written guidelines; 2) communicate orally in order to provide information, assistance, or instructions to members of the general public or their representatives; 3) performs administrative and clerical processes using a computer to reconcile discrepancies, associate documents with related files/records; 4) write correspondence in response to inquires and drafts a variety of other written products. Applicants will be required to participate in a panel interview to demonstrate an aptitude for meeting and dealing with the public.

Minimum application materials required: Complete and submit an Occupational Questionnaire and either a resume or Optional Application for Federal Employment (OF-612). Application must include narrative answers to the following KSAs: 1) ability to communicate orally with individuals from various socio-economic backgrounds and intellectual levels; 2) ability to interpret and apply laws, regulations, and operating procedures; 3) ability to process work in a computer environment; 4) ability to use reasoning to analyze issues to make decisions and resolve problems; 5) ability to organize, prioritize, and process a large volume of work within established deadlines.

Special requirements: Must be a U.S. citizen. Males born after December 31, 1959, must have registered with the Selective Service System. Must pass a background investigation check. All selectees are required to complete an 11-week technical training class. All selectees are required to serve a one-year probationary period.

Human Resources Assistant
Agency: Center for Human Resources, Social Security Administration
Salary: $29,904 to $38,880
Location: Richmond, California

Job description summary: Provides administrative and clerical support to the benefits team and assists in planning, organizing, and implementing employee benefits. Maintains automated databases and control logs. Will gradually receive more advanced assignments through the training period until the selectee reaches the full performance level of the position.

Minimum qualifications required: Bachelor's degree, OR one year of specialized experience performing clerical duties without supervision, and ability to type 40 words per minute.

Minimum application materials required: Complete and submit an Occupational Questionnaire and either a resume or Optional Application for Federal Employment (OF-612). Application must include narrative answers to the following KSAs: 1) experience extracting information and obtaining background material for reports and meetings; 2) experience in developing and maintaining files; 3) skill in researching, developing, and assembling background information; 4) experience in answering basic inquiries; 5) skill in developing and maintaining effective working relationships at all levels; 6) ability to deal effectively with employees and visitors when providing customer service or assistance; 7) experience coordinating with upper level staff in resolving complex issues; 8) experience explaining regulatory and procedural requirements pertaining to employment.

Special requirements: Must be a U.S. citizen. Males born after December 31, 1959, must have registered with the Selective Service System. Must pass a background investigation check. All selectees are required to complete an 11-week technical training class. All selectees are required to serve a one-year probationary period.

Math Statistician

Agency: Office of Research, Evaluation, and Statistics, Office of the Deputy Commissioner for Policy
Salary: $100,231 to $130,305
Location: Woodlawn, Maryland

Job description summary: Serves as the senior advisor on statistical matters. Recommends and implements statistical policies, assures that appropriate methodologies and practices are used, and serves as the spokesperson in statistical matters for the Office of Research, Evaluation, and Statistics. Provides technical consultation and support to staff and management in other offices within the Social Security Administration.

Minimum qualifications required: Bachelor's degree in mathematics and statistics. Must have one year of experience directly related to the major duties of the position.

Minimum application materials required: Complete and submit an Occupational Questionnaire and either a resume or Optional Application for Federal Employment (OF-612). Application must include narrative answers to the following KSAs: 1) knowledge of mathematical/statistical techniques and theories; 2) skill in adapting or developing new methodology for application to research highly complex projects; 3) skill in expressing and presenting ideas and recommendations; 4) ability to maintain effective working relationships with all levels of management.

Special requirements: Must be a U.S. citizen. Males born after December 31, 1959, must have registered with the Selective Service System. Must pass a background investigation. Must complete an 11-week technical training class. All selectees are required to serve a one-year probationary period.

Social Insurance Specialist

Agency: Social Security Administration
Salary: $26,699 to $29,761
Location: Fergus Falls, North Dakota

Job description summary: Conducts interviews to obtain, clarify, and verify information about initial and continuing eligibility for retirement, survivors, disability, and health insurance benefits, and eligibility for supplemental security income including state supplements. Resolves discrepancies, clarifies issues and makes final decisions for initial and continuing claims for benefits and payments.

Minimum qualifications required: Three years of general experience as a claims clerk, law clerk, contact representative, claims agent, claims adjuster, claims examiner, or voucher examiner. Applicants will be required to participate in a panel interview to demonstrate an aptitude for meeting and dealing with the public. This interview will cover typical situations, which might be encountered on the job, in person or over the telephone. Must demonstrate qualities such as clarity of speech, ability to listen, ability to establish confidence and put others at ease and the ability to organize and express thoughts clearly.

Minimum application materials required: Complete and submit an Occupational Questionnaire (156 questions, see vacancy announcement) and either a resume or Optional Application for Federal Employment (OF-612).

Special requirements: Must be a U.S. citizen. Males born after December 31, 1959, must have registered with the Selective Service System. Must pass a background investigation. All selectees are required to complete an 11-week technical training class. All selectees are required to serve a one-year probationary period.

Tennessee Valley Authority

400 West Summit Hill Drive
Knoxville, Tennessee 37902
202-898-2999

★ Web site: http://www.tva.gov/

★ Job vacancies: http://www.tva.gov/employment/currentjobs.htm

★ USAJOBS By Phone: 912-757-3000

★ Internship information: http://www.tva.gov/employment/internships.htm

★ Co-op jobs: http://www.tva.gov/employment/coop.htm

★ Jobs for college recruits: http://www.tva.gov/employment/positions.htm

★ Jobs requiring 2- or 4-year technical degree:
  http://www.tva.gov/employment/om_jobs.htm

★ Professional, technical, and administrative jobs:
  http://www.tva.gov/employment/expro_jobs.htm

★ How to apply for a TVA job: http://www.tva.gov/employment/applynow.htm

The Tennessee Valley Authority (TVA) is a wholly owned government corporation responsible for managing the nation's fifth-largest river system and the area's resources, working to protect the environment through clean-air and water initiatives, and fostering a healthy economy in the Tennessee Valley. It is America's largest public power company, with 31,658 megawatts of dependable generating capacity spread over 80,000 square miles in seven southeastern states, with 13,000 employees. TVA's power facilities include 11 fossil plants, 29 hydroelectric dams, three nuclear plants, six combustion turbine plants, a pumped-storage facility, and 17,000 miles of transmission lines. Through 158 locally owned distributors, TVA provides power to nearly 8.5 million residents in the Tennessee Valley. It operates a national laboratory for environmental research that focuses on the cleanup and protection of land, air, and water resources. It also participates in economic and community development programs by providing technical assistance in industrial development, waste management, tourism promotion, and community preparedness.

Sample Job Vacancies

Atmospheric Analyst
Agency: Tennessee Valley Authority
Salary: Varies
Location: Muscle Shoals, Alabama

Job description summary: Develops and tests computer model code to support modeling and data analysis activities, scientific computations, data management, and the graphical presentation of data; recommends new methods for data archiving, database management, data visualization, model code development, and debugging; evaluates performance of computer models to identify and correct computational problems and code errors; prepares and delivers scientific presentations on computer modeling technology to groups within and outside TVA and writes conference papers to promote new techniques and model approaches developed at TVA; keeps abreast of atmospheric modeling research; serves in national scientific and engineering organizations to help transfer technology to and from TVA, maintain state-of-the-art technical expertise, and recommend directions for future model development programs.

Minimum qualifications required: Bachelor of science degree in computer science, atmospheric science, physics, meteorology, chemistry, environmental engineering, or a closely related discipline, and a minimum of two years' experience in work with similar duties and responsibilities. Experience with the application of complex computer code to solve physical problems or complex mathematical equations. Experience with writing, debugging, compiling, linking, and running computer code (especially FORTRAN 90) on UNIX and/or LINUX operating systems.

Minimum application materials required: Submit a scannable resume and TVA's Applicant Information Sheet (follow instructions on TVA's How to Apply page of their Web site).

Industrial Hygienist
Agency: Tennessee Valley Authority
Salary: Varies
Location: Newport, Indiana, and Pine Bluff, Arkansas

Job description summary: Serves as industrial hygiene expert with responsibility for supporting major projects involving comprehensive IH and safety support. Defines scope and nature of IH and safety portions of projects, estimates, and budget requirements, and develops and certifies appropriate IH and safety work plans and schedules. Serves as onsite health and safety officer for large, complex projects such as hazardous waste cleanups, chemical weapons demilitarization, and process plant demolition. Provides IH and occupational health and safety consultation to project management, including developing project safety and health plans, conducting workers' health and safety training, monitoring worker exposure to hazardous agents, and investigating worker injuries and illnesses. Prepares project completion reports or technical IH and safety reports. Conducts nonroutine IH and OH&S studies covering emerging technologies, newly identified health hazards, and exposure profiles for epidemiology investigations. Periodically evaluates, certifies, and audits the status of IH safety practices, procedures, and controls utilized by operating organizations.

Minimum qualifications required: Bachelor of science degree in physical sciences, engineering, biological sciences, or related discipline. Master's degree in industrial hygiene preferred. At least five years' experience in IH or other interdisciplinary health or safety fields.

Minimum application materials required: Submit a scannable resume and TVA's Applicant Information Sheet (follow instructions on TVA's How to Apply page of their Web site).

Special requirements: Must be certified by American Board of Industrial Hygiene or Board of Certified Safety Professionals.

Mechanical Technician Trainee
Agency: Tennessee Valley Authority
Salary: $38,275 to $54,675
Location: Allen Fossil Plant, Memphis, Tennessee

Job description summary: This is a two-and-a-half-year paid training program that consists of a combination of on-the-job and classroom instruction. Upon the successful completion of training, the position of Mechanical Technician trainee leads to the position of Mechanical Technician. This position includes shift work, overtime, callouts, outage work and schedules, and working weekends and holidays. Mechanical technicians maintain power station mechanical and electrical equipment. They perform preventive maintenance routines, failure analysis, and corrective maintenance tasks on equipment like valves, pumps, boilers, motor bearings, drive mechanisms, and steam turbines. They also dismantle and reassemble equipment.

Minimum qualifications required: Associate of applied science degree in mechanical engineering technology or industrial maintenance. Must be able to frequently lift up to 50 pounds and occasionally lift up to 100 pounds. In addition, trainees are expected to be prepared for class, including homework assignments, out of class readings, pop quizzes, written exams, and oral exams. Students will be required to exhibit skills required to perform certain tasks through the use of qualification cards.

Minimum application materials required: Submit a scannable resume and TVA's Applicant Information Sheet (follow instructions on TVA's How to Apply page of their Web site).

Special requirements: Position requires S03-respirator exam and respirator fit testing and ability to distinguish colors.

Nuclear Environmental Technician
Agency: Tennessee Valley Authority
Salary: Varies
Location: Browns Ferry Nuclear Plant, Athens, Alabama

Job description summary: Performs environmental surveillance duties required to monitor the operation of the nuclear plant reactor and support systems or to support the operation of the nuclear sites through the conduct of radiological environmental monitoring. Operates sampling equipment such as air sampling systems used in the radiological environmental monitoring program. Performs operational QA/QC checks on equipment, and maintains records required to document correct operation of instrumentation. Performs data entry to support the performance of environmental surveillance activities, performs calculations to produce the final results, and maintains records of surveillance or inspection activities. Performs sample collection routines. May provide technical supervision for entry-level environmental technicians.

Minimum qualifications required: Associate's degree in environmental science, chemistry, health physics, or related science or comparable training program with field experience. Must have competence as an environmental technician (radiological) as demonstrated by progressive experience. Must have knowledge of the basics of environmental science, radiation measurement, quality control for environmental sampling, environmental monitoring equipment, chemistry lab techniques, personal computer use, mathematics, lab safety.

Minimum application materials required: Submit a scannable resume and TVA's Applicant Information Sheet (follow instructions on TVA's How to Apply page of their Web site).

Procurement Agent
Agency: Tennessee Valley Authority
Salary: Varies
Location: Browns Ferry Nuclear Plant, Athens, Alabama

Job description summary: Performs both standard and nonstandard transactions associated with the supply chain job family. Typical duties include selecting, applying, and explaining procedures and practices to identify and resolve discrepancies, research information sources, and document and coordinate results. Interviews suppliers and conducts local sourcing activities for nominal products and services not covered by presourced contracts, and executes contracts, agreements, and releases. Prepares supplier documentation and procedures to ensure compliance with requirements. Prepares material release documents and purchase requisitions based on requests from end-users. Expedites materials for all assigned activities. Sells surplus material, schedules transportation, and resolves transportation claims. Responds to diverse businesses on standard and nonstandard matters and plans supplier events. Creates requisitions and enters procurement transactions into supply chain management software. Keys data into various business reporting systems and runs reports. Creates presentation documents and flowcharts. Maintains tracking of performance indicators using spreadsheets.

Minimum qualifications required: Bachelor of science degree in business administration or related field, or equivalent experience. Participation in CM/CA training modules desirable.

Minimum application materials required: Submit a scannable resume and TVA's Applicant Information Sheet (follow instructions on TVA's How to Apply page of their Web site).

United States Agency for International Development

1300 Pennsylvania Avenue NW
Washington, D.C. 20523-0001
202-712-0000

★ Web site: http://www.usaid.gov/

★ Job vacancies: http://www.usaid.gov/careers/

★ USAJOBS By Phone: 912-757-3000

★ Internship and new graduate information: http://www.usaid.gov/careers/nepanno2.html

★ USAID mission directory: http://www.usaid.gov/locations/missiondirectory.html

★ USAID mission Web sites: http://www.usaid.gov/missions/

★ Fellows program: http://www.usaid.gov/about/employment/fellows/

★ Technical advisor program: http://www.usaid.gov/about/employment/taacs/taacs.html

★ Working for USAID: http://www.usaid.gov/careers/

★ Organization chart: http://www.usaid.gov/about_usaid/orgchart.html

★ Employment FAQs: http://www.usaid.gov/careers/cpfaqn.html

The U.S. Agency for International Development (USAID) administers U.S. foreign economic and humanitarian assistance programs worldwide. It is the principal U.S. agency to extend assistance to countries recovering from disaster, trying to escape poverty, and engaging in democratic reforms. Under the foreign policy guidance of the secretary of state, USAID supports long-term and equitable economic growth and advances U.S. foreign policy objectives by supporting: economic growth, agriculture, and trade; global health; and, democracy, conflict prevention, and humanitarian assistance. It provides assistance in four regions of the world: Sub-Saharan Africa; Asia and the Near East; Latin America and the Caribbean; and Europe and Eurasia. USAID has field offices around the world. It works in close partnership with private voluntary organizations, indigenous organizations, universities, American businesses, international agencies, other governments, and other U.S. government agencies. USAID has working relationships with more than 3,500 American companies and over 300 U.S.-based private voluntary organizations.

All vacancies in USAID are filled through Avue Digital Services (AVUE), an automated application system. Each announcement is listed on the HR Web site with a direct link to USAJOBS. Applicants can simply click on the vacancy number identified and go immediately to USAJOBs. Once at USAJOBs, you can either review the individual announcement OR go directly to the AVUE online employment site, register, and then apply for the job. A paper applications are also accepted.

Selected Agencies Within USAID

The **Bureau for Africa** oversees assistance programs in 22 field missions and three regions. Central to USAID's assistance programs in Africa are four new initiatives to improve education, increase agricultural productivity, promote trade with Africa, and protect the Congo Basin Forest. The Initiative to End Hunger in Africa focuses on programs to improve the use of modern technology and increase agricultural productivity and income for small-scale farmers. Through the Trade for African Development and Enterprise (TRADE) initiative USAID will work to improve the trade and investment environment and promote the fuller integration of Africa into the global economy. The Congo Basin Forest Partnership supports efforts to conserve the outstanding forest and wildlife resources of the Congo Basin Forest, the second largest remaining tropical forest in the world.

★ Web site: http://www.usaid.gov/locations/sub-saharan_africa/

★ Country and regional programs: http://www.usaid.gov/locations/sub-saharan_africa/countries/

The **Bureau for Democracy, Conflict and Humanitarian Assistance** works to promote democracy, resolve conflicts, and provide humanitarian assistance to those in need. In the area of democracy it seeks to strengthen the rule of law, promote competitive elections, develop a politically active civil society, and encourage more transparent and accountable governments. In the area of humanitarian assistance, it runs a variety of programs that provide assistance to victims of foreign disasters, displaced children and orphans, those disabled by conflict in need of prosthetics, and victims of torture. In the area of conflict it is examining how its longer-term assistance in the areas of democracy and governance, economic growth, agriculture, and the environment, and health can help reduce tensions before conflict occurs or build a more sustainable peace once conflict ends.

★ Web site for democracy and governance:
http://www.usaid.gov/our_work/democracy_and_governance/

★ Web site for Humanitarian Assistance:
http://www.usaid.gov/our_work/humanitarian_assistance/

★ Web site for Conflict management: http://www.usaid.gov/our_work/cross-cutting_programs/conflict/

★ Office of Democracy and Governance:
http://www.usaid.gov/our_work/democracy_and_governance/technical_areas/dg_office/index.html

The **Bureau for Economic Growth, Agriculture, and Trade** works to support the efforts of low-income countries to improve the levels of income their citizens enjoy as well as with farmers, scientists, businesses, and local communities in an effort to increase agricultural production and profit.

★ Web site for economic growth and trade:
http://www.usaid.gov/our_work/economic_growth_and_trade/

★ Web site for agriculture: http://www.usaid.gov/our_work/agriculture/

Other USAID Agencies

Bureau for Asia and the Near East
http://www.usaid.gov/locations/asia_near_east/

Bureau for Europe and Eurasia
http://www.usaid.gov/locations/europe_eurasia/

Bureau for Global Health
http://www.usaid.gov/our_work/global_health/

Bureau for Latin America and the Caribbean
http://www.usaid.gov/locations/latin_america_caribbean/

Bureau for Policy and Program Coordination
http://www.usaid.gov/policy/

Sample Job Vacancies

Auditor
Agency: Office of Inspector General
Salary: $65,809 to $96,643
Location: Budapest, Cairo, Dakar, Manila, Pretoria, and San Salvador

Job description summary: Foreign Service Auditors are required to perform audits of Agency programs in accordance with generally accepted government auditing standards. The purpose of these audits is to determine whether the programs are being carried out in compliance with laws, regulations, and agreements; are being administered efficiently and economically; and are achieving the desired results or benefits. This work requires the development of audit programs and procedures necessary to conduct audits; the ability to write clear, concise audit reports; and the coordination of audit matters with USAID and with other U.S. and foreign government agencies.

Minimum qualifications required: Twenty-four semester hours in accounting or auditing courses of appropriate type and quality; OR a certificate as a Certified Public Accountant or a Certified Internal Auditor, obtained through written examination; OR completion of the requirements for a degree that included substantial course work in accounting or auditing. Additional related finance/accounting experience, a CPA, working knowledge of consumer software (Microsoft, Word Perfect, Quattro Pro, etc.) and foreign language proficiency (particularly French or Spanish) is highly desirable. The ability to communicate both orally and in writing is essential for all candidates under consideration.

Minimum application materials required: Submit a resume, Optional Application for Federal Employment (OF-612), or Application for Federal Employment (SF-171). In addition, applicants must include a two- or three-page typed autobiography which discusses your personal background, interests, hobbies and travel, professional experience that was not included in the employment application, and motivation for applying for a Foreign Service Auditor career.

Special requirements: Position requires a top secret security clearance. Upon selection, applicants must provide sufficient information to support the investigation.

Food for Peace Officer

Agency: The U.S. Agency for International Development
Salary: $65,809 to $96,643
Location: Worldwide

Job description summary: Assists in the planning, analysis, negotiation, implementation, and evaluation of USAID emergency and nonemergency food programs. Responsible for food security programming and monitoring all uses of USAID P.L. 480 supplied food. Provides assistance to host government authorities and to Private Voluntary Organizations (PVOs) and Non-Governmental Organizations (NGOs) on food security needs assessments and on technical and financial aspects of project/program design, accountability, monitoring, and reporting. Ensures that proposed projects/programs meet USAID criteria and are properly documented.

Minimum qualifications required: Bachelor's degree plus seven years of relevant experience of which three years is relevant overseas experience; OR a Master's degree in a relevant major plus five years of relevant experience of which three years is relevant overseas experience; OR a Ph.D. in a relevant major with three years of relevant experience of which two years is relevant overseas experience. Relevant majors are public administration, business administration, agriculture, agri-business, agricultural economics, and public health/nutrition. Relevant experience is defined as developing, evaluating, and monitoring programs concerned with providing food to alleviate hunger and malnutrition, to assist economic and social development or the management of food supplies under emergency conditions.

Minimum application materials required: Applications for this position are only accepted online through Avue and must include written responses to the following KSAs: 1) ability to communicate effectively orally and in writing; 2) ability to manage and build teams; 3) knowledge of emergency and nonemergency food aid programs and activities.

Special requirements: Foreign Service members must be able to serve at any overseas post. Many facilities are remote, unhealthy, or have limited medical support. Therefore, each applicant must meet medical fitness standards which are, of necessity, often more rigorous than those of other professions. Prior to being appointed to the Foreign Service, applicants must have a thorough medical examination and receive an unlimited medical clearance for assignment worldwide.

Public Health Advisor

Agency: Bureau for Global Health
Salary: $74,335 to $110,775
Location: Washington, D.C.

Job description summary: Serves as a senior technical expert and advisor on development assistance activities in the area of public health. Supports geographic or region activities by reviewing and analyzing data; developing strategies, analytical models, and methodologies; and providing assistance and advice on issues related to Latin America and the Caribbean.

Mentors and works with new foreign service officers and mission staff to ensure the mission is able to carry out its mandates. Supports agency-wide activities within the public health area by reviewing and analyzing data; developing strategies, and methodologies; and providing assistance and advice on regional issues.

Minimum qualifications required: Must have one year of specialized experience that provided: 1) knowledge of organizational, operational, and programmatic practices applied by agencies engaged in health-related activities; 2) knowledge of the methods used to develop and deliver public health programs in state and local settings; 3) knowledge of a specialized public health program; 4) skill in the application of administrative methods necessary for working within a health organization and carrying out specific program functions; 5) skill in oral and written communications, gathering and conveying information, making oral presentations, and preparing reports, correspondence, and other written materials.

Minimum application materials required: Applicants must complete an applicant questionnaire form and respond to the following KSAs: 1) ability to communicate in writing; 2) ability to work effectively with a diverse group of professionals; 3) ability to plan and execute work within a team environment; 4) ability to lead and manage a team of professionals.

Special requirements: Candidates for this position must have experience living and working overseas and working, directly, or indirectly with an international organization.

United States International Trade Commission

500 E Street SW
Washington, D.C. 20436
202-205-2000

★ Web site: http://www.usitc.gov/

★ Job vacancies: http://jobsearch.usajobs.opm.gov/tc00.asp

★ USAJOBS By Phone: 912-757-3000

★ Employee directory: ftp://ftp.usitc.gov/pub/telephone/itcphone.pdf

The U.S. International Trade Commission (ITC) is an independent, nonpartisan, quasi-judicial federal agency that provides trade expertise to both the legislative and executive branches of government, determines the impact of imports on U.S. industries, and directs actions against certain unfair trade practices, such as patent, trademark, and copyright infringement. The ITC staff of about 365 individuals includes international trade analysts (investigators and experts in particular industries), international economists, attorneys, and technical support personnel.

The ITC performs a number of functions. In countervailing duty and antidumping investigations, for example, the ITC works in concert with the U.S. Department of Commerce. The Commerce Department determines whether the alleged subsidies or dumping are actually occurring, while the ITC determines whether the U.S. industry is materially injured by reason of the dumped or subsidized imports. The ITC also assesses whether U.S. industries are being seriously injured by fairly traded imports and can recommend to the president that relief be provided to facilitate positive adjustment to import competition.

Through its research program, the ITC conducts objective studies on many international trade matters and has an extensive library of international trade resources called the National Library of International Trade, which is open to the public. The ITC frequently holds public hearings as part of its investigations and studies. It makes determinations in investigations involving unfair practices in import trade, mainly involving allegations of infringement of U.S. patents and trademarks by imported goods. If it finds a violation of the law, the ITC may order the exclusion of the imported product from the United States. Finally, the ITC is responsible for continually reviewing the Harmonized Tariff Schedule of the United States (HTS), a list of all the specific items that are imported into and exported from the United States, and for recommending modifications to the HTS that it considers necessary or appropriate.

Sample Job Vacancy

Staff Assistant

Agency: Office of Administration, Office of Human Resources, U.S. International Trade Commission
Salary: $37,858 to $49,216
Location: Washington, D.C.

Job description summary: Performs a wide range of support activities which may include: maintaining a formal system of procedures and administrative controls; producing a wide variety of reports and other documents; receiving visitors and calls for offices; maintaining calendars, making appointments, and arranging conferences; making travel arrangements; controlling correspondence; and drafting letters, memoranda, and other documents.

Minimum qualifications requirements: Must have one year of specialized experience in or related to the work of the position described. Must be able to type 40 words per minute.

Minimum application materials required: Complete an online application and resume or submit an Optional Application for Federal Employment (OF-612). Include narrative answers to the following KSAs: 1) ability to provide administrative support to an organization; 2) ability to facilitate, plan, schedule, coordinate, and control the work of an organization; 3) skill in the use of personal computers and word processing software.

Special requirements: Must be a U.S. citizen. Must obtain a Secret security clearance.

United States Postal Service

475 L'Enfant Plaza SW
Washington, D.C. 20260-0010
202-268-2000

★ Web site: http://www.usps.gov/

★ Job vacancies, mail processing: http://www.usps.com/employment/maildeliveryjobs.htm

★ Job vacancies, corporate: http://www.usps.com/employment/corporatejobs.htm

★ USAJOBS By Phone: 912-757-3000

★ Internship information:

★ Management internship information: http://www.usps.com/employment/internprograms/managementinternprogram.htm

★ Career development information: http://www.usps.com/employment/careerdev.htm

★ Employment requirements: http://www.usps.com/employment/employrequirements.htm

★ Employee benefits: http://www.usps.com/employment/compbenefits.htm

★ Exam information for entry-level jobs:
http://www.usps.com/cpim/ftp/pubs/pub60a/pub60a.html#508hdr7

The United States Postal Service (USPS) provides mail processing and delivery services to individuals and businesses within the United States. USPS is committed to serving customers through the development of efficient mail-handling systems and operates its own planning and engineering programs. It also protects the mails from loss or theft and apprehends those who violate postal laws.

USPS has approximately 776,000 career employees and handles about 207 billion pieces of mail annually. In addition to the national headquarters, there are area and district offices supervising approximately 38,000 post offices, branches, stations, and community post offices throughout the United States. USPS is the only Federal agency whose employment policies are governed by a process of collective bargaining under the National Labor Relations Act.

Selected Agencies Within USPS

The **U.S. Postal Inspection Service** is the Federal law enforcement agency which has jurisdiction in criminal matters affecting the integrity and security of the mail. Postal Inspectors enforce more than 200 federal statutes involving mail fraud, mail bombs, child pornography, illegal drugs, and mail theft, as well as being responsible for the protection of postal employees.

★ Web site: http://www.usps.com/postalinspectors/

★ Headquarters contacts: http://www.usps.com/postalinspectors/fraud/ContactUs.htm

The **Office of the Inspector General** (OIG) is independent of postal management and reports directly to the nine presidential appointed governors of the USPS. The primary purpose of the OIG is to prevent, detect, and report fraud, waste, and program abuse, and promote efficiency in the operations of the Postal Service. The OIG has "oversight" responsibility for all activities of the Postal Inspection Service, a major federal law enforcement agency.

★ Web site: http://www.uspsoig.gov/

★ Job vacancies: http://www.uspsoig.gov/employment.aspx

Sample Job Vacancies

City Carrier
Agency: U.S. Postal Service
Salary: Hourly
Location: Nationwide

Job description summary: Travels planned routes to deliver and collect mail, typically on foot or by vehicle, outdoors in all weather.

Minimum qualifications required: Must have a current valid state driver's license and safe driving record. Must pass test 470.

Minimum application materials required: During the opening period indicated on the test announcements for test 470, apply by phone or online. You will be prompted through the application process. At least one week before the test date, you will be mailed a scheduling package indicating when and where to report for the test. Applicant instructions and sample questions will also be included. A passing score on test 470 qualifies you to continue in the hiring process but does not guarantee employment with the Postal Service. If you qualify, your name is listed on an entrance register to be considered with other applicants for vacant positions.

Special requirements: Must be a U.S. citizen at least 18 years of age or 16 with a high school diploma. Must possess basic competency in English. Males born after December 31, 1959, must be registered with the Selective Service System. Must pass an extensive criminal history check, a urinalysis drug screen, and undergo a medical assessment.

Maintenance Mechanic
Agency: U.S. Postal Service
Salary: Hourly
Location: Nationwide

Job description summary: Performs semiskilled preventive, corrective, and predictive maintenance tasks associated with the upkeep and operation of various types of mail processing, buildings, building equipment, and customer service and delivery equipment.

Minimum qualifications required: Must pass exam 933.

Minimum application materials required: During the opening period indicated on the test announcements for test 933, apply by phone or online. You will be prompted through the application process. At least one week before the test date, you will be mailed a scheduling package indicating when and where to report for the test. Applicant instructions and sample questions will also be included. A passing score on test 933 qualifies you to continue in the hiring process but does not guarantee employment with the Postal Service. If you qualify, your name is listed on an entrance register to be considered with other applicants for vacant positions.

Special requirements: Must be a U.S. citizen at least 18 years of age or 16 with a high school diploma. Must possess basic competency in English. Males born after December 31, 1959,

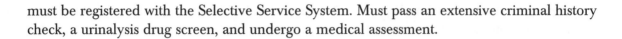

must be registered with the Selective Service System. Must pass an extensive criminal history check, a urinalysis drug screen, and undergo a medical assessment.

Mail Handler

Agency: U.S. Postal Service
Salary: Hourly
Location: Nationwide

Job description summary: Loads and unloads containers of mail; transports mail and empty equipment throughout a building; opens and empties sacks of mail.

Minimum qualifications required: Must be able to lift heavy objects. Must pass test 470.

Minimum application materials required: During the opening period indicated on the test announcements for test 470, apply by phone or online. You will be prompted through the application process. At least one week before the test date, you will be mailed a scheduling package indicating when and where to report for the test. Applicant instructions and sample questions will also be included. A passing score on test 470 qualifies you to continue in the hiring process but does not guarantee employment with the Postal Service. If you qualify, your name is listed on an entrance register to be considered with other applicants for vacant positions.

Special requirements: Must be a U.S. citizen at least 18 years of age or 16 with a high school diploma. Must possess basic competency in English. Males born after December 31, 1959, must be registered with the Selective Service System. Must pass an extensive criminal history check, a urinalysis drug screen, and undergo a medical assessment.

Tractor Trailer Operator

Agency: U.S. Postal Service
Salary: Hourly
Location: Nationwide

Job description summary: Operates heavy-duty tractor trailers either in over-the-road service, city shuttle service, or trailer spotting operations.

Minimum qualifications required: Must have at least two years of driving experience, with at least one year of full-time experience (or equivalent) driving at least a seven-ton capacity truck or 16-passenger bus. At least six months of the truck driving experience must be with tractor-trailers. The driving must have taken place in the United States or its possessions or territories, or in U.S. military installations worldwide. Safe driving record required. At the time of appointment, you must have a valid Commercial Driver's License from the state in which you live, with air brakes certification, for the type(s) of vehicle(s) used on the job.

Minimum application materials required: Must complete an assessment questionnaire online or by phone. Questionnaire asks for specific information concerning an applicant's driving history and safety record. Prior to completing this questionnaire, applicants are given the opportunity to request (or if online, print), an assessment worksheet to help them prepare for the questionnaire. You must receive a passing score of 70 on the assessment to receive further employment consideration. If you are determined to be eligible, you will continue the process for employment consideration.

Special requirements: Must be a U.S. citizen at least 18 years of age or 16 with a high school diploma. Must possess basic competency in English. Males born after December 31, 1959, must be registered with the Selective Service System. Must pass an extensive criminal history check, a urinalysis drug screen, and undergo a medical assessment.

Boards, Commissions, and Committees

American Battle Monument Commission

2300 Clarendon Boulevard
Arlington, Virginia 22201
703-696-6897

★ Web site: http://www.abmc.gov/
★ USAJOBS By Phone: 912-757-3000

The American Battle Monuments Commission is a small independent agency of the Executive Branch of the federal government. It is responsible for commemorating the services of the American Armed Forces where they have served since the U.S. entry into World War I through the establishment of suitable memorial shrines; designing, constructing, operating, and maintaining permanent American military burial grounds in foreign countries; controlling the design and construction of U.S. military monuments and markers in foreign countries by other U.S. citizens and organizations; and encouraging the maintenance of such monuments and markers by their sponsors.

The American Battle Monuments Commission has two major subordinate regions: The European Region in Paris, France, and the Mediterranean Region in Rome, Italy. The Washington Office directs the operations of three separate cemeteries: The Mexico City National Cemetery, the Corozal American Cemetery in Panama, and the Manila American Cemetery in the Republic of the Philippines.

Broadcasting Board of Governors

330 Independence Avenue SW
Washington, D.C. 20237
703-756-6012

★ Web site: http://www.bbg.gov/

★ Job vacancies: http://jobsearch.usajobs.opm.gov/

★ USAJOBS By Phone: 912-757-3000

The Broadcasting Board of Governors (BBG) is an independent, autonomous entity responsible for all U.S. government and government-sponsored, nonmilitary, international broadcasting. The mission of U.S. international broadcasting is to promote the open communication of information and ideas, in support of democracy, and the freedom to seek, receive, and impart information, worldwide. The mission of the BBG is to ensure and safeguard the integrity, quality, and effectiveness of the nation's international broadcasters.

Every week, more than 100 million listeners, viewers, and Internet users around the world turn on, tune in, and log on to U.S. international broadcasting programs. The day-to-day broadcasting activities are carried out by the individual BBG international broadcasters: the Voice of America (VOA), Alhurra, Radio Sawa, Radio Farda, Radio Free Europe/Radio Liberty (RFE/RL), Radio Free Asia (RFA), and Radio and TV Martí, with the assistance of the International Broadcasting Bureau (IBB).

Selected Agencies Within BBG

Radio Free Europe/Radio Liberty is a private, nonprofit, U.S. government-funded radio broadcaster to Central, Southeastern, and Eastern Europe; the Caucasus; and Central and Southwestern Asia. RFE/RL broadcasts more than 1,000 hours of programming in 29 languages every week. All RFE/RL broadcasts are also streamed live and on-demand over the Internet; audio, video, and text in English and the broadcast languages is available from its Web site.

★ Web site: http://www.rferl.org/

★ Job vacancies: http://www.rferl.org/about/jobs/

★ Contact information: http://www.rferl.org/about/default.asp#contact

The **Voice of America** broadcasts on radio and television in 44 languages to an estimated 96 million people each week. VOA radio provides around-the-clock news and features. It focuses on countries that lack a strong, independent media. VOA-TV produces programs in more than 20 languages, including news reports, feature magazines, and live call-in shows.

TV broadcasts include original and acquired programs that reflect American life along with discussions on United States foreign and domestic policies. VOA's Internet provides continually updated news and information with photos, audio, and video.

★ Web site: http://www.voanews.com/

★ Job vacancies: http://www.voa.gov/vacancies/personnel.html

★ 24-hour job line: 202-619-0909

★ Internship information: http://www.voa.gov/interns/

Other BBG Agencies

Alhurra
http://199.239.255.9/

The Office of Cuba Broadcasting (Radio and TV Martí)
http://www.martinoticias.com/default.asp

Radio Farda
http://www.radiofarda.com/

Radio Free Asia
http://www.rfa.org/front/

Radio Sawa
http://www.radiosawa.com/

Sample Job Vacancies

Electronics Engineer
Agency: Broadcasting Board of Governors
Salary: $72,108 to $110,775
Location: Washington, D.C.

Job description summary: Responsible for designing, developing, and modifying high power short-wave, medium wave, FM, and television transmission facilities at the International Broadcasting Bureau (IBB), Affiliate, and leased sites worldwide. Leads multidisciplined technical teams of engineers from project inception through project completion; develops project reports, schedules, and budgets. Serves as an authoritative technical source within the Division in the application of engineering theories and concepts relating to the design and development of communications and broadcasting systems and subsystems. Conducts or directs studies and analyses to determine the feasibility of various engineering-related approaches for future RF systems and to solve current problems. Serves as the Authorized Representative of the Contracting Officer (AR/CO) on assigned projects. Serves as an expert in RF systems engineering, and as such provides high level technical representation for the IBB in contracts with engineers, architects, and planners in both government and industry in the field of broadcast systems and facility design.

Minimum qualifications required: Bachelor of Science degree or higher in engineering OR at least four years of college-level education, training, or technical experience that furnished understanding of the engineering sciences and techniques. Must have current registration as a professional engineer OR evidence of having passed the Engineering-in-Training (EIT) examination OR evidence of successful completion of at least 60 semester hours of courses in the physical, mathematical, and engineering sciences and in engineering PLUS one year of professional engineering experience. Graduate education related to the requirements of this position may be substituted for experience.

Must have theoretical knowledge of medium and shortwave transmitters, FM transmitters, and TV transmitters and of high-power medium and shortwave antennas, FM and TV antennas, matching and phasing networks, and RF transmission lines and RF switches.

Minimum application materials required: Optional Application for Federal Employment (OF-612), a resume, OR any other written format. Must include narrative responses to the following KSAs: 1) technical expertise in the field of radio and television transmission equipment and experience managing complex projects and leading multi-disciplined teams; 2) experience administering contracts, with demonstrated ability to write concise statements of work, technical specifications, tasking documents, project plans, project schedules, and administrative correspondence; 3) knowledge of federal government procurement practices and policies.

TV Production Specialist
Agency: Indonesian Service
Salary: $50,593 to $65,769
Location: Washington, D.C.

Job description summary: Responsible for assisting and producing news and information segments for Indonesian television broadcasts. Performs subject and story research; calls and develops sources; researches and logs raw video material and news feeds; writes basic stories for on camera, voice over, or narrated reporter package. Conducts interviews with officials and personalities and assists or performs electronic news gathering in the field. Responsible for the Service's video and audio equipment and its operational readiness. Serves as liaison with stringers and correspondents on tape and equipment issues.

Minimum qualifications required: Must have one year of specialized experience within this field or a field that is closely related at a level close to the work of this job that has given you the particular knowledge, skills, and abilities required to perform successfully. Must be able to conceptualize, identify, develop, and write news and feature stories for on camera, making sure stories are geared to the needs of an Indonesian audience. Must be able to organize, manage and coordinate the various resources, both human and material, to produce a high quality television segment or program. Must be able to perform subject and story research to insure the accuracy, comprehensiveness, and balance of news and information stories.

Minimum application materials required: Submit resume and written responses to the following KSAs: 1) knowledge of a wide range of principles, practices methods and techniques for communicating information through TV, including knowledge of all phases of TV production; 2) ability to edit and assemble the video material into a finished piece ready for air; 3) knowledge of the social, cultural, historical, political and economic situations in Indonesia, the United States, and the world in general.

Special requirements: Candidates must provide show tapes of their TV production skills in PAL OR NTSC format.

Presidio Trust

P.O. Box 29052
34 Graham Street
San Francisco, California 94129
415-561-5300

★ Web site: http://www.presidiotrust.gov/

★ Job vacancies: http://www.presidio.gov/TrustManagement/TrustEmployment/

★ USAJOBS By Phone: 912-757-3000

★ Volunteer information: http://www.presidio.gov/About_the_Presidio/volunteeropportunities/

★ Contracting opportunities: http://www.presidio.gov/TrustManagement/TrustContracts/

★ General employment information:
http://www.presidio.gov/TrustManagement/TrustEmployment/EmploymentInformation.htm

The Presidio, a 1,491-acre sight overlooking San Francisco Bay, had been a military post since 1776, when the Spanish established a post there. From 1846 until 1994, when it became part of the National Park Service, the Presidio served as a United States military base. It is now part of the 75,500-acre Golden Gate National Recreation Area (GGNRA), the world's largest national park in an urban area. The Presidio Trust was created in 1996 to manage the interior lands of the park.

Its mission is to preserve and enhance the natural, cultural, scenic, and recreational resources of the Presidio for public use in perpetuity, and to achieve long-term financial sustainability. These efforts encompass the natural areas, wildlife, and native habitats of the park, as well as the historic structures and designed landscapes that make the park a National Historic Landmark District.

Sample Job Vacancies

Environmental Protection Specialist
Agency: Presidio Trust
Salary: Varies
Location: The Presidio

Job description summary: Assists the NEPA Compliance Manager and other Trust staff (project managers) in completing necessary paperwork for review. Responsible for preparing agendas, assisting in coordinating, and recording minutes of interdisciplinary team meetings, and distributing correspondence within the Trust or to other agencies or entities outside the Trust for review and comment. Tracks projects for compliance review and keeps compliance records for the file. Serves as "caretaker" of the Trust's NEPA files to ensure that the environmental and project tracking databases are organized and complete for public inspection. Ensures that Presidio projects under review keep moving in an expeditious a manner.

Collects, analyzes, and interprets reconnaissance-level information in support of environmental documentation for Presidio projects. Conducts training sessions on the NEPA for Trust staff.

Minimum qualifications required: Must perform professional work with a minimum of supervision; analyze and compile information and prepare reports; and understand and carry out oral and written directions. Basic administrative skills including information management, project tracking, standard computer use, and word processing.

Requires education/training/experience equivalent to bachelor's degree in city planning, architecture, or closely related planning/environmental field. Working knowledge of NEPA and other planning and environmental laws. Recent experience in performing environmental planning duties under direction and ability to independently accomplish planning tasks for a government agency or environmental consulting firm preferred.

Minimum application materials required: Download and submit an application from the Web site.

Heavy Mobile Equipment Operator
Agency: Presidio Trust
Salary: Varies
Location: The Presidio

Job description summary: Operates a variety of wheeled and tracked construction equipment and vehicles, including backhoes, loaders, landscaping tractors, skid steer tractor, roller/compactor, dump truck, and street sweeper. Repairs potholes and constructs new paved areas. Acts as flagger/spotter on roadway work; sets barricades, cones, and signage for worksite safety; cleans culverts, curbs, and gutters. Paints curbs and roadway markings; assists masons in mixing and pouring concrete; sets concrete forms and removes rubble and debris. Demolishes concrete sidewalks, curbs, and walls. Performs trail work such as brush clearing, trail grading, cleaning drainage channels, etc.; builds fences, steps, and wooden retaining walls. Moves various construction materials. Assists machine shop mechanic in servicing, fueling, and maintaining vehicles and equipment.

Minimum qualifications required: Requires extensive and prolonged physical activity (digging, jack hammering, bending, lifting, walking, and standing for prolonged periods). Must be able to lift items weighing up to 100 pounds. Requires class B driver license and extensive equipment operating experience.

Minimum application materials required: Download and submit an application from the Web site.

United States Holocaust Memorial Museum

100 Raoul Wallenberg Place SW
Washington, D.C. 20024
202-488-0400

★ Web site: http://www.ushmm.org/

★ Job vacancies: https://secure.ushmm.org/museum/. Click on Employment Opportunities.

★ USAJOBS By Phone: 912-757-3000

★ Internship and volunteer information: http://www.ushmm.org/museum/volunteer_intern/

The United States Holocaust Memorial Museum is America's national institution for the documentation, study, and interpretation of Holocaust history. The Museum's primary mission is to advance and disseminate knowledge about the Holocaust; to preserve the memory of those who suffered; and to encourage visitors to reflect upon the moral and spiritual questions raised by the events of the Holocaust as well as their own responsibilities as citizens of a democracy.

Chartered by a unanimous Act of Congress in 1980 and located adjacent to the National Mall in Washington, D.C., the Museum strives to broaden public understanding of the history of the Holocaust through multifaceted programs, such as exhibitions; research and publication; collecting and preserving material evidence, art and artifacts relating to the Holocaust; annual Holocaust commemorations known as Days of Remembrance; distribution of educational materials and teacher resources; and public programming designed to enhance understanding of the Holocaust and related issues, including those of contemporary significance.

Sample Job Vacancy

Director, Western Regional Office

Agency: United States Holocaust Memorial Museum
Salary: Varies
Location: Los Angeles, California

Job description summary: Serves as the Museum's professional development presence in the western United States. Manages all regional development initiatives and creates and implements fundraising strategies, donor cultivation, and major gift solicitation.

Minimum qualifications required: Must have a minimum of seven years of successful experience raising funds from high-level donors.

Minimum application materials required: Apply online or by mail. KSAs: 1) demonstrated proficiency with the fundamentals of philanthropic support; 2) knowledge of generally accepted fundraising techniques, principles and ethics, gift processing, data management, donor recognition, acknowledgements, and gift substantiation; 3) knowledge of and experience with nonprofit and community groups to cultivate new and diverse prospects; 4) knowledge of the Museum's history, purpose and mission, of the varied functions and programs of the Development Office; 5) strong communication and interpersonal skills to communicate effectively and diplomatically.

Special requirements: A background security investigation will be required for all new hires.

Quasi-Official Agencies

Legal Services Corporation

3333 K Street NW
Washington, D.C. 20007-3522
202-295-1500

★ Web site: http://www.lsc.gov/

★ Job vacancies: http://www.lsc.gov/employ.htm

★ USAJOBS By Phone: 912-757-3000

★ Staff directory: http://www.lsc.gov/welcome/wel_staf.htm

★ Links to LSC funded programs: http://www.lsc.gov/links.htm

★ LSC programs by state: http://www.lsc.gov/fundprog.htm

The Legal Services Corporation is a private, nonprofit organization that provides legal assistance for noncriminal proceedings to those who would otherwise be unable to afford such assistance. It is governed by an 11-member board of directors, appointed by the president with the advice and consent of the senate.

LSC does not provide legal assistance directly; it funds more than 140 legal aid programs across the country and makes grants to and contracts with individuals, firms, corporations, and organizations for the purpose of providing legal assistance to these clients.

Job vacancies posted on LSC's Web site are for its headquarters only. Legal Services Corporation grantee programs are private entities and conduct their own independent application and hiring process. As such, any individual with an interest in employment opportunities at one of the grantee programs should contact that program directly.

Sample Job Vacancy

Vice President of Government Relations and Public Affairs
Agency: Legal Services Corporation
Salary: Dependent upon qualifications and experience
Location: Washington, D.C.

Job description summary: Participates as part of LSC's Senior Management Team in developing and implementing LSC policy; develops and implements a plan with the president for the LSC authorization and appropriations process, including assisting in the development of the narrative section of the budget, written testimony, preparation of witnesses, legislative drafting, and preparation of other materials requested by Congress and the administration. Maintains liaison with authorization and appropriation committees of Congress and other congressional committees or members as appropriate; acts as liaison with federal agencies that support legal services and related activities or whose policies affect legal services programs and clients; monitors selected legislative activities that affect LSC; coordinates responses to inquiries from members of Congress, public officials, and others regarding LSC and its grantees; oversees all communications in consultation with the president between the administration, Congress, federal agencies, state and local governments, the media, and the general public; oversees preparation and publication of LSC materials including, Equal Justice Magazine, the LSC Annual Report; and content of the LSC Web site Home Page; supervises staff of the Office of Governmental Relations and Public Affairs.

Minimum qualifications required: J.D. and 10 years of relevant experience (legal, legislative, managerial or communications) including significant experience on the Hill or as a lobbyist; or any equivalent combination of education and related experience with a demonstrated track record. Excellent working knowledge and understanding of the legislative process.

Ability to understand complex legal, factual, and financial concepts relating to LSC and the delivery of legal services to the poor and to express them succinctly for congressional staff, the media and the public. Ability to oversee publication and distribution of a special interest magazine as well as raise funds for same.

Minimum application materials required: Submit a detailed chronological resume with cover letter, including salary history.

Smithsonian Institution

1000 Jefferson Drive SW
Washington, D.C. 20560
202-357-2700.

- ★ Web site: http://www.smithsonian.org
- ★ Job vacancies: http://www.si.edu/ohr/job.htm
- ★ USAJOBS By Phone: 912-757-3000
- ★ Internship and fellowship information: http://www.si.edu/ohr/job.htm
- ★ How to apply: http://www.si.edu/ohr/apply.htm
- ★ Application tips: http://www.si.edu/ohr/tips.htm
- ★ Contact information: http://www.si.edu/contacts/
- ★ Volunteer information: http://www.si.edu/resource/faq/volunteer/start.htm
- ★ Benefits: http://www.si.edu/ohr/benefits.htm
- ★ Human resources contact information: http://www.si.edu/ohr/contact.htm

The Smithsonian Institution is an independent trust instrumentality of the United States which comprises the world's largest museum and research complex. The Smithsonian includes 16 museums and galleries, the National Zoo, and research facilities in several states and the

Republic of Panama. It holds more than 143 million artifacts and specimens in its trust for the American people.

The Smithsonian is dedicated to public education, national service, and scholarship in the arts, sciences, history, and culture. It was created by an act of August 10, 1846, to carry out the terms of the will of British scientist James Smithson (1765-1829), who in 1826 had bequeathed his entire estate to the United States "to found at Washington, under the name of the Smithsonian Institution, an establishment for the increase and diffusion of knowledge among men."

The Smithsonian, with over 6,000 people at facilities in six states, the District of Columbia and the Republic of Panama requires a variety of skills to support its operations. It employs crafts people in virtually every trade to maintain and restore the historic buildings; horticulturalists and gardeners to design and maintain the grounds and display gardens; administrative and support staff to manage human resources, contracts, accounting, and finance; engineers and architects to oversee the design of new facilities and manage construction and renovation projects; scientists to do basic and applied research in a wealth of scientific disciplines as varied as astronomy, anthropology, botany, ecology, mineral sciences, earth sciences, and veterinary medicine; historians, art historians, and archivists to collect and interpret the nation's history.

There are also a variety of positions that are unique to the museum world, such as museum director, curator, conservator, and exhibit designer.

Selected Agencies Within the Smithsonian

The **Archives of American Art** contains the nation's largest collection of documentary materials reflecting the history of visual arts in the United States. On the subject of art in America, it is the largest archives in the world, holding more than 13 million documents. The Archives gathers, preserves, and microfilms the papers of artists, craftsmen, collectors, dealers, critics, and art societies.

These papers include manuscripts, letters, diaries, notebooks, sketchbooks, business records, clippings, exhibition catalogs, transcripts of tape-recorded interviews, and photographs of artists and their work.

★ Web site: http://archivesofamericanart.si.edu/

★ Job vacancies: http://www.usajobs.opm.gov/

★ Internships, fellowships, volunteers: http://archivesofamericanart.si.edu/volintfe.htm

★ Contact information: http://archivesofamericanart.si.edu/contact.htm

★ Hours and locations: http://archivesofamericanart.si.edu/contact.htm#rescntr

The **National Air and Space Museum** was created to memorialize the development and achievements of aviation and space flight. It collects, displays, and preserves aeronautical and space flight artifacts of historical significance as well as documentary and artistic materials related to air and space. Among its artifacts are full-size planes, models, and instruments.

Highlights of the collection include the Wright brothers' Flyer, Charles Lindbergh's *Spirit of St. Louis,* a Moon rock, and Apollo spacecraft. The exhibitions and study collections record human conquest of the air from its beginnings to recent achievements. The principal areas in which work is concentrated include flight craft of all types, space flight vehicles, and propulsion systems

★ Web site: http://www.nasm.si.edu

★ Job vacancies: http://www.nasm.si.edu/getinvolved/employment/

★ Explainers program: http://www.nasm.si.edu/getinvolved/explainers/

★ Internships and fellowships: http://www.nasm.si.edu/getinvolved/internfellow.cfm

★ Department and staff contacts: http://www.nasm.si.edu/museum/departments.cfm

★ Contact information: http://www.nasm.si.edu/help/contact.cfm

The **National Museum of American History**'s mission is to inspire a broader understanding of the United States and its people. In that capacity, the Museum provides learning opportunities, stimulates the imagination of visitors, and presents challenging ideas about the nation's past. The Museum's exhibits provide a unique view of the American experience. Emphasis is placed upon innovative individuals representing a wide range of cultures, who have shaped our heritage, and upon science and the remaking of our world through technology.

Exhibits draw upon strong collections in the sciences and engineering, agriculture, manufacturing, transportation, political memorabilia, costumes, musical instruments, coins, armed forces history, photography, computers, ceramics, and glass. Classic cars, icons of the American Presidency, First Ladies' gowns, the Star-Spangled Banner flag, Whitney's cotton gin, Morse's telegraph, the John Bull locomotive, Dorothy's ruby slippers from *The Wizard of Oz,* and other American icons are highlights of the collection.

★ Web site: http://www.americanhistory.si.edu/

★ Job vacancies: http://www.americanhistory.si.edu/careers/index.htm

★ Internship and fellowship information:
   http://www.americanhistory.si.edu/interns/index.htm

★ Volunteer information: http://www.americanhistory.si.edu/youmus/volunter.htm

The **National Zoological Park** encompasses 163 acres along Rock Creek Park in Northwest Washington, D.C. Established in 1889, the Zoo is developing into a biopark with live animals, botanic gardens, and aquaria, and artworks with animal themes.

The collection today has animals ranging in size and diversity from leaf-cutter ants to giraffes. Research on genetics, animal behavior, and reproductive studies has given the National Zoo a leadership role among the Nation's conservation institutions.

★ Web site: http://www.si.edu/natzoo/

★ Job vacancies: http://www.sihr.si.edu/job.htm

★ General employment and internship information:
   http://nationalzoo.si.edu/Audiences/JobSeekers.cfm

★ Volunteer information: http://nationalzoo.si.edu/Support/Volunteer/

The **National Museum of Natural History** is dedicated to understanding the natural world and the place of humans in it. The Museum's permanent exhibits focus on human cultures, Earth sciences, biology, and anthropology, with the most popular displays featuring gemstones such as the Hope diamond, dinosaurs, insects, marine ecosystems, birds, and mammals.

The Museum's encyclopedic collections comprise more than 125 million specimens, making the Museum one of the world's foremost facilities for natural history research. The museum's four departments are anthropology, mineral sciences, paleobiology, and systematic biology. Doctorate-level staff researchers ensure the continued growth and value of the collection by conducting studies in the field and laboratory.

★ Web site: http://www.mnh.si.edu/

★ Job vacancies: http://www.sihr.si.edu/job.htm

★ General employment, internship, and volunteer information:
   http://www.mnh.si.edu/info_desk.html#vie

Smithsonian Institution Libraries include more than one million volumes (among them 40,000 rare books) with strengths in natural history, art, science, humanities, and museology. Many volumes are available through interlibrary loan.

★ Web site: http://www.sil.si.edu/

★ Job vacancies: http://www.sil.si.edu/About/job.htm

★ Internships: http://www.sil.si.edu/researchintern/internship.htm

★ Contact information: http://www.sil.si.edu/About/contact.htm

The **John F. Kennedy Center for the Performing Arts** is the only official memorial in Washington, D.C., to President Kennedy. Since its opening in 1971, the Center has presented a year-round program of the finest in music, dance, and drama from the United States and abroad.

Visitor services are provided by the Friends of the Kennedy Center volunteers. Free performances are given every day on the Millennium Stage in the Grand Foyer.

★ Web site: http://www.kennedy-center.org/

★ Job vacancies: http://www.kennedy-center.org/jobs/

★ Volunteer information: http://www.kennedy-center.org/support/volunteers/

★ General employment benefits: http://www.kennedy-center.org/jobs/benefits.html

★ Applicant FAQ: http://www.kennedy-center.org/jobs/applicant-faq.html

The **National Gallery of Art** houses one of the finest collections in the world, illustrating Western man's achievements in painting, sculpture, and the graphic arts. The collections, beginning with the thirteenth century, are rich in European old master paintings and French, Spanish, Italian, American, and British eighteenth- and nineteenth-century paintings; sculpture from the late Middle Ages to the present; Renaissance medals and bronzes; Chinese porcelains; and about 90,000 works of graphic art from the twelfth to the twentieth centuries.

The Micro Gallery is the most comprehensive interactive multimedia computer system in any American art museum. Thirteen computers enable visitors to see in magnified detail nearly every work of art on display in the permanent collection and provide access to information about artists, geographic areas, time periods, pronunciations (with sound), and more.

★ Web site: http://www.nga.gov/

★ Job vacancies: http://jobsearch.usajobs.opm.gov/

★ Volunteer information: http://www.nga.gov/ginfo/involved.htm#volunteer

★ Internships and fellowships: http://www.nga.gov/education/interned.htm

★ General employment information: http://www.nga.gov/resources/employ.htm

★ Contact information: http://www.nga.gov/xio/phone.htm

Other Smithsonian Agencies

Anacostia Museum and Center for African American History and Culture
http://www.si.edu/anacostia

Arthur M. Sackler Gallery
http://www.asia.si.edu

Center for Folk Life and Cultural Heritage
http://www.folklife.si.edu

Cooper-Hewitt National Design Museum
http://www.si.edu/ndm

Freer Gallery of Art
http://www.asia.si.edu

Hirshhorn Museum and Sculpture Garden
http://www.hirshhorn.si.edu

International Center
http://www.si.edu/intrel/

National Museum of African Art
http://www.nmafa.si.edu

National Museum of the American Indian
http://www.nmai.si.edu

National Portrait Gallery
http://www.npg.si.edu

National Postal Museum
http://www.si.edu/postal

Renwick Gallery
http://www.saam.si.edu/collections/exhibits/renwick25

Smithsonian American Art Museum
http://www.saam.si.edu

Smithsonian Astrophysical Observatory
http://www.harvard.edu/sao-home.html

Smithsonian Center for Materials Research and Education
http://www.si.edu/scmre/

Smithsonian Environmental Research Center
http://www.serc.si.edu

Smithsonian Institution Archives
http://www.si.edu/archives/

Smithsonian Institution Traveling Exhibition Service
http://www.si.edu/organiza/offices/sites

Smithsonian Marine Station
http://www.sms.si.edu

Smithsonian Tropical Research Institute
http://www.stri.org

Woodrow Wilson International Center for Scholars
http://www.wilsoncenter.org

Sample Job Vacancies

Docent Coordinator
Agency: Smithsonian American Art Museum, Education Office
Salary: $41,815 to $65,769
Location: Washington, D.C.

Job description summary: Administers the docent program ensuring quality performance by up to 100 volunteers. Develops tours for the museum with other staff. Recruits and selects new docents. Plans and monitors basic training for new docents, ongoing training for all, and special training for new exhibitions and initiatives. Ensures that accessibility concerns are addressed for visitors to the museum. Promotes tour offerings and other activities by preparing brochures and flyers, writing notices for the museum members' calendars, and maintaining current information on the museum's Web site. Researches and proposes partnership and funding opportunities. Coordinates fundraising activities with the museum's development office.

Minimum qualifications required: Must have one year of specialized experience in or related to the work of the position as described above; OR a master's degree; OR a combination of education and experience.

Minimum application materials required: Submit an Optional Application for Federal Employment (OF-612), an Application for Federal Employment (SF-171), or a resume.

Respond in narrative form to the following KSAs: 1) ability to develop and manage a volunteer program, including tour and resource development; 2) knowledge of museum education programs; 3) knowledge of art history, American history, or social/cultural studies; 4) ability to work within a team as well as in a leadership role; 5) skill in written and oral communication; 6) skill in the use of computer programs including word processing, desktop publishing, and financial or project management software.

Sales Store Clerk

Agency: Freer Gallery of Art and Arthur M. Sackler Gallery
Salary: $20,138 to $28,565
Location: Washington, D.C.

Job description summary: Greets and offers assistance to customers; provides knowledgeable information to customers selecting merchandise. Operates cash register, gives change, and maintains and counts stock. Performs appropriate housekeeping in assigned areas. Observes all visitors to maintain security precautions.

Minimum qualifications required: Must have three months' general experience in clerical, office, or other work, or have a high school diploma or equivalent.

Minimum application materials required: Submit an Optional Application for Federal Employment (OF-612), an Application for Federal Employment (SF-171), or a resume. Respond in narrative form to the following KSA: Knowledge of technical practices and materials used in sales and cashier work.

Public Affairs Specialist

Agency: National Portrait Gallery
Salary: $41,815 to $65,769
Location: Washington, D.C.

Job description summary: Serves as principle publicist for all aspects of the National Portrait Gallery (NPG), its assigned exhibitions, and public programs. Devises media plan which includes researching and writing press releases, fact sheets, and public service announcements; planning press packets and overseeing design/printing of special materials; planning and working with office staff to hold press preview events; scheduling and coordinating interviews with staff; collecting relevant media clips, etc. Maintains relationships with local and national media and seeks new press contacts, introducing them to NPG and asking them to incorporate material about NPG in their reporting and features. Supplies media contacts with regular written updates on the Gallery's activities. Fields requests for images requested by media and for film crews requesting shootings in the museum. Works with other External Affairs staff on the coordination of special events. Oversees production of NPG newsletter. Represents NPG at meetings of various tourism industry organizations.

Minimum qualifications required: Must have one year of experience in or related to the work of the position as described above; OR a master's degree in a related field; OR a combination of education and experience.

Minimum application materials required: Submit an Optional Application for Federal Employment (OF-612), an Application for Federal Employment (SF-171), or a resume. Respond in narrative form to the following KSAs: 1) knowledge of and experience with a variety of print, broadcast, internet, and mass media outlets; 2) ability to establish and maintain relationships with media contacts, special interest groups, individuals and the public; 3) knowledge of public events management such as catering, audiovisual management, security, etc; 4) knowledge of computer applications such as WordPerfect, Word, Excel, PowerPoint, desktop publishing software and Adobe Acrobat; 5) ability to plan and coordinate special events and conferences.

Veterinary Medical Officer
Agency: National Zoological Park
Salary: $72,108 to $93,742
Location: Washington, D.C.

Job description summary: Provides the clinical and surgical care of the animals and supervises the preventative medical procedures. Supervises the maintenance of the hospital, keeping it in a state of readiness to meet the clinical and surgical demands of the NZP; supervises the clinical intern, preceptor, hospital animal keepers, and hospital biological technicians and assists in their training in various aspects of zoological medicine. Advises on problems in the general care and maintenance of the animals; responsible for the maintenance of the medical records program of all related medical information; supervises appropriate procedures to check accuracy of data entered; participates in the preparation of reports. Examines animals to be shipped and conducts the appropriate tests enforcing regulations concerning quarantine requirements of imported animals entering the collections. Summarizes the data collected from independent clinical studies into a scientific format for publication in appropriate peer-reviewed journals; maintains up-to-date familiarity with veterinary medical information and new drug developments; maintains a close liaison with the Department of Pathology, coordinating the necropsy findings and the results of clinical laboratory tests.

Minimum qualifications required: Must have Doctor of Veterinary Medicine degree. Must have one year of progressively responsible professional veterinary experience with demonstrated ability to perform total health in the practice of zoological medicine for the care to a variety of animal species.

Minimum application materials required: Submit an Optional Application for Federal Employment (OF-612), an Application for Federal Employment (SF-171), or a resume. Respond in narrative form to the following KSAs: 1) ability to supervise a work force of different levels of expertise; 2) knowledge of biology, husbandry, and medicine of exotic animals in captivity; 3) ability to conduct applied clinical research in zoological medicine by appropriate publications in the scientific literature; 4) ability to teach the concepts and practice of zoological medicine to veterinary medical students, zoologists, and graduate veterinarians.

United States Institute of Peace

Suite 200, 1200 Seventeenth Street NW
Washington, D.C. 20036-3011
202-457-1700

★ Web site: http://www.usip.org

★ Job vacancies: http://www.usip.org/jobs/index.html

★ USAJOBS By Phone: 912-757-3000

★ Fellowship program: http://www.usip.org/fellows/index.html

★ Contact information: http://www.usip.org/aboutus/contact.html

★ Programs and projects: http://www.usip.org/aboutus/programs.html

The United States Institute of Peace is an independent, nonpartisan federal institution created by Congress to promote the prevention, management, and peaceful resolution of international conflicts. Established in 1984, the Institute meets its congressional mandate through an array of programs, including research grants, fellowships, professional training, education programs from high school through graduate school, conferences and workshops, library services, and publications.

Sample Job Vacancies

Program Officer (Northeast Asia)
Program: Research & Studies Program
Salary: Commensurate with experience
Location: Washington, D.C.

Job description summary: Conceives, designs, and implements study projects relating to the prevention, management, and resolution of conflict in Northeast Asia (China, Japan, Koreas, Taiwan). The work will entail research and writing for publication, organizing workshops and conferences, and representing the Institute at pertinent meetings. Study subjects may range from specific conflicts to broader issues such as regional capacity building for conflict prevention and peacekeeping, lessons learned in mediation, the role of nonstate actors in peace processes, economic factors in civil conflict, and the challenge of postconflict reconstruction including demobilization, disarmament, and reintegration.

Minimum qualifications required: Ph.D. in international relations or a related field, or equivalent professional experience in government or the nongovernmental sector; demonstrated expertise relating to conflict prevention, management, and resolution in East Asia; excellent writing and oral communications skills; ability to work independently and yet collegially with staff and external organizations and individuals.

Additional qualifications include: specific experience and study of the issues in northeast Asia and skill in a foreign language germane to the area, especially Chinese. Candidates should also demonstrate good computer skills (Macintosh preferred) especially in word processing and Internet navigation.

Minimum application materials required: Submit a resume or Curriculum Vitae along with a cover letter that specifically addresses the desired qualifications for the positions and a salary history.

Program Officer (Post-Conflict Reconstruction)

Program: Peace and Stability Operations Program
Salary: Commensurate with experience
Location: Washington, D.C.

Job description summary: Conceives, coordinates, and moderates a series of working group sessions and drafts brief analytical reports to examine past failures and future policy options related to U.S. and international intervention in postconflict reconstruction. The project will focus specifically on the following topics: civilian/military planning, assessment of postconflict requirements, mass media, telecommunications, the role of women, disarmament, demobilization and reintegration, transitional justice and reconciliation, and the successor generation.

Minimum qualifications required: Master's degree in international relations; two or more years of international practitioner field experience in a government, military, NGO, or international organization capacity in a post-conflict environment; excellent writing and oral presentational skills.

Minimum application materials required: Submit a resume or Curriculum Vitae along with a cover letter that specifically addresses the desired qualifications for the positions and a salary history.

Special requirements: Must be a U.S. citizen.

Selected Multilateral Organizations

International Monetary Fund

700 Nineteenth Street NW
Washington, D.C. 20431
202-623-7000

★ Web site: http://www.imf.org/

★ Job vacancies: http://www.imf.org/external/np/adm/rec/vacancy.htm

★ USAJOBS By Phone: 912-757-3000

★ Internship information: http://www.imf.org/external/np/adm/rec/job/summint.htm

★ Research assistants program: http://www.imf.org/external/np/adm/rec/job/rap.htm

★ IMF contacts: http://www.imf.org/external/np/exr/contacts.htm

The International Monetary Fund IMF is an international organization of 184 member countries. It was established to promote international monetary cooperation, exchange stability, and orderly exchange arrangements; to foster economic growth and high levels of employment; and to provide temporary financial assistance to countries to help ease balance of payments adjustment.

It employs three main functions: surveillance, technical assistance, and lending to meet these objectives. Surveillance is the regular dialogue and policy advice that the IMF offers to each of its members. Once a year, the IMF conducts in-depth appraisals of each member country's economic situation, then discusses with the country's authorities the policies that are most conducive to stable exchange rates and a growing a prosperous economy. The IMF provides technical assistance to help member countries strengthen their capacity to design and implement effective policies.

Technical assistance is offered in fiscal policy, monetary policy, and macroeconomic and financial statistics. Finally, when a member country has balance of payment problems, the IMF provides financial assistance in the form of loans. The IMF employs about 2,690 people from 141 countries.

Selected Agencies Within IMF

The **Joint Vienna Institute** is an international training institute located in Vienna, Austria. It offers a comprehensive program of seminars in specialized topics aimed at mid- and senior-level officials and private sector managers in transition economies.

★ Web site: http://vi.null2.net

Other IMF Agencies

The IMF Institute
http://www.imf.org/external/np/ins/english/index.htm

Singapore Regional Training Institute
http://www.imf-sti.org/

Sample Job Vacancies

Assistant Editor
Agency: IMF Institute
Salary: Varies
Location: Washington, D.C.

Job description summary: Coordinates and administers Distance Learning (DL) Program; plans, develops, edits, proofreads, and produces the Institute's main publications, select working papers, books, and case studies, as well as course revision material for the DL; writes speeches, briefs, and overviews as requested by senior management; contributes to the department's Web development strategy

Minimum qualifications required: Advanced degree in a field related to the editor's work (such as English), plus a minimum of four years of relevant professional experience. Must have a thorough knowledge of English structure and syntax and proven editorial experience. Strong knowledge of and experience in information technology, including electronic documentation, presentation software, and Web site design and communications are desirable. Strong communications skills, in particular the ability to think strategically; knowledge of languages other than English would be an advantage.

Minimum application materials required: Complete and submit an online application.

Economist

Agency: IMF Institute
Salary: Varies
Location: Washington, D.C.

Job description summary: Desk economists are responsible for keeping abreast of economic developments in the country (countries) for which they are responsible, alerting management to significant economic changes and issues as they arise, and coordinating the report written after visits (missions) to the country. Economists in a functional department (such as Fiscal Affairs or Monetary and Exchange Affairs Department) are responsible for handling aspects of the IMF's work, such as public expenditure, debt management, exchange rate management, banking supervision, etc. to ensure that the IMF applies "best practices" in the advice it gives and treats countries in an even-handed manner.

Minimum qualifications required: Master's degree in macroeconomics or a related subject. Further postgraduate studies, including a Ph.D., are desirable. Five to fifteen years of experience as a professional handling economic policy issues at the national level. Such experience is usually gained in a Central Bank, Ministry of Finance, other international financial institution, or in a research institute or academia provided that you have been exposed to policy making.

Minimum application materials required: Complete and submit an online application.

Staff Assistant

Agency: IMF Institute
Salary: Varies
Location: Washington, D.C.

Job description summary: The role of Assistants has been changing. The IMF no longer needs assistants with just secretarial skills but is looking for those with writing, office management, computer, and database management skills. The IMF is particularly interested in finding bilingual assistants who are native speakers of Arabic, Chinese, French, Portuguese, or Spanish. Staff Assistant positions are filled with candidates resident in the local Washington, D.C. area.

Minimum qualifications required: Proficiency in Excel and Word; ability to pass a test of office skills, given in English; excellent interpersonal skills and ability to work in a team environment; minimum of two years of relevant work experience in a similar capacity.

Minimum application materials required: Complete and submit an online application.

Organization of American States

1889 F Street NW
Washington, D.C. 20006
202-458-3000

★ Web site: http://www.oas.org/

★ Job vacancies:
http://www.oas.org/main/main.asp?sLang=E&sLink=http://www.oas.org/consejo

★ USAJOBS By Phone: 912-757-3000

★ Internship information: http://www.oas.org/main/english/ then click on Opportunities & Jobs and then Internships

★ Fellowship information: http://www.oas.org/main/english/ then click on Opportunities & Jobs and then Fellowships

★ Links to OAS member states:
http://www.oas.org/main/main.asp?sLang=E&sLink=../../documents/eng/oasinbrief.asp

The Organization of American States (OAS) brings together the countries of the Western Hemisphere to strengthen cooperation and advance common interests. It is the region's premier forum for multilateral dialogue and concerted action. The OAS works to promote good governance and democracy, strengthen human rights, foster peace and security, expand trade, and address the complex problems caused by poverty, drugs, and corruption.

Through decisions made by its political bodies and programs carried out by its General Secretariat, the OAS seeks to promote greater inter-American cooperation and understanding. All 35 independent countries of the Americas have ratified the OAS Charter and belong to the Organization. Cuba remains a member, but its government has been excluded from participation in the OAS since 1962.

The principal organs of the OAS are as follows: the General Assembly, which is normally composed of the foreign ministers of the member states and meets at least once a year to decide the general action and policy of the Organization; the Meeting of Consultation of Ministers of Foreign Affairs, which meets on call to consider urgent matters of common interest or threats to the peace and security of the hemisphere; the Permanent Council, composed of Ambassadors/Permanent Representatives at headquarters, which meets twice a month; the

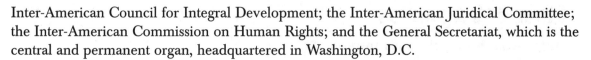

Inter-American Council for Integral Development; the Inter-American Juridical Committee; the Inter-American Commission on Human Rights; and the General Secretariat, which is the central and permanent organ, headquartered in Washington, D.C.

The OAS has six specialized organizations that handle technical matters of common interest. They are the Pan American Health Organization (PAHO), Inter-American Children's Institute (IIN), Inter-American Commission of Women (CIM), Inter-American Indian Institute (III), Pan American Institute of Geography and History (PAIGH), and the Inter-American Institute for Cooperation on Agriculture (IICA).

Selected Agencies Within OAS

The **Pan American Health Organization** (PAHO) is an international public health agency with 100 years of experience in working to improve health and living standards of the countries of the Americas.

It serves as the specialized organization for health of the Inter-American System. It also serves as the Regional Office for the Americas of the World Health Organization and enjoys international recognition as part of the United Nations system.

★ Web site: http://www.paho.org/

★ Job vacancies: http://www.paho.org/English/AM/HRM/RE/HRM-vacancies.htm

★ Headquarters and country offices: http://www.paho.org/english/paho/fieldoffices.htm

★ Regional centers, institutes, and programs: http://www.paho.org/english/paho/centers.htm

★ General employment information: http://www.paho.org/english/AM/HRM/RE/HRM-geninfo.htm

★ Internship information: http://www.paho.org/English/AM/HRM/RE/HRM-internship.htm

★ How to apply for PAHO vacancies: http://www.paho.org/English/AM/HRM/RE/HRM-apply.htm

The **Inter-American Institute for Cooperation on Agriculture** was founded as an institution for agricultural research and graduate training in tropical agriculture. In response to changing needs in the Americas, the Institute gradually evolved into an agency for technical cooperation in the field of agriculture.

These changes were officially recognized through the ratification of a new Convention on December 8, 1980. The Institute's purposes under the new Convention are to encourage, facilitate, and support cooperation among its member states so as to promote agricultural development and rural well-being.

★ Web site: http://www.iicanet.org/

★ Job vacancies: http://www.iicanet.org/oportunidades/

★ Headquarters contacts: http://www.iicanet.org/contactos/

Other OAS Agencies

Inter-American Children's Institute
http://www.iin.oea.org

Inter-American Commission of Women
http://www.oas.org/cim/default.htm

Inter-American Indian Institute
http://www.ini.gob.mx/iii/index.html

Panamerican Institute of Geography and History
http://www.ipgh.org.mx/

Sample Job Vacancies

Advisor in Family and Community Health
Agency: Pan America Health Organization
Salary: $58,041
Location: Quito, Ecuador

Job description summary: Contributes to the development of family and community health by identifying and analyzing local experiences in the country and by identifying and documenting key elements for success, lessons learned, and good practices. Promotes and implements essential action plans starting from the development of community family health policies within the laws and judicial legal mechanisms. Coordinates and supports the implementation of activities promoted by the main Centers and strengthens training in the area of reproductive health. Cooperates to develop the Action Plan for the elimination of congenital Rubella in Ecuador and maintains the plan for the eradication of Measles, Polio, and Neonatal Tetanus.

Minimum qualifications required: Master's degree in public health, family health, epidemiology, community, or social health, with experience in sexual reproductive health. Must have seven years of experience in management, negotiation of project plans, inter sectors health and social programs, with special emphasis on health of children, adolescents, women, family, and community. Must have two years of experience in international cooperation, together with essential programs or projects that promote the vital cycle of the quality of health and life.

Minimum application materials required: Online applications are strongly encouraged.

Special requirements: Must have a very good knowledge of Spanish and a working knowledge of English.

Country Representative
Agency: Inter-American Institute for Cooperation on Agriculture
Salary: Varies
Location: San Jose, Costa Rica

Job description summary: Provides leadership in agricultural technical cooperation and policy activities with national, provincial, and municipal authorities, and with public, private,

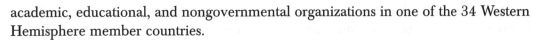

academic, educational, and nongovernmental organizations in one of the 34 Western Hemisphere member countries.

Minimum qualifications required: Master's degree or Ph.D. in agricultural sciences, natural resources, economics, agricultural economics, business or public administration. Minimum of seven years' professional experience in agricultural or rural development, in increasingly broader positions. Proven leadership abilities and skills in management, diplomacy, technical cooperation, and administration; experience in negotiating and working with national and local government officials to develop integrated approaches on agricultural issues and rural development.

Relevant experience in at least one of the Institute's strategic areas: Trade Policy and Agribusiness Development, Agricultural Research and Technical Innovation, Agricultural Health and Food Safety, Sustainable Rural Development, and Agricultural Education and Training. Must be a citizen of one of the Institute's member states, but by the Institute's statutes may not serve in one's own country. Excellent oral and written communication skills in English or Spanish, and basic fluency in the other; knowledge of Portuguese or French is a plus.

Minimum application materials required: Submit curriculum vitae by mail.

United Nations

New York, New York 10017
212-963-1234

* Web site: http://www.un.org
* Job vacancies: https://jobs.un.org/release1/vacancy/vacancy.asp
* USAJOBS By Phone: 912-757-3000
* How to apply for a UN job: https://jobs.un.org/release1/info/guide.asp?lang=1200
* Application FAQs: http://www.unvolunteers.org/
* Internship information: http://www.un.org/Depts/OHRM/examin/internsh/intern.htm
* Volunteer information: http://www.unvolunteers.org/
* Links to member states: http://www.un.org/members/index.html
* General Assembly: http://www.un.org/ga/58/
* Security Council: http://www.un.org/Docs/sc/
* Economic and Social Council: http://www.un.org/esa/coordination/ecosoc/
* Trusteeship Council: http://www.un.org/documents/tc.htm
* International Court of Justice: http://www.icj-cij.org/
* UN Offices, Programs, Funds, and Regional Commissions: http://www.un.org/Depts/otherprgs.htm
* Departments of the UN Secretariat: http://www.un.org/Depts/index.html

The United Nations (UN) is an international organization that was set up in accordance with the Charter drafted by governments represented at the Conference on International Organization meeting at San Francisco and signed on June 26, 1945.

The UN consists of 191 member states, of which 51 are founding members. The purposes of the UN are to maintain international peace and security; to develop friendly relations among nations; to achieve international cooperation in solving international problems of an economic, social, cultural, or humanitarian character and in promoting respect for human rights; and to be a center for harmonizing the actions of nations in the attainment of these common ends.

The principal organs of the UN are the General Assembly, the Security Council, the Economic and Social Council, the Trusteeship Council, the International Court of Justice, and the Secretariat.

All UN Member States are represented in the General Assembly—"parliament of nations"—which meets to consider the world's most pressing problems. Each member state has one vote. The Assembly cannot force action by any state, but its recommendations are an important indication of world opinion and represent the moral authority of the community of nations.

The Security Council has primary responsibility for maintaining international peace and security. The Council may convene at any time, whenever peace is threatened. Under the Charter, all Member States are obligated to carry out the Council's decisions. There are 15 Council members. Five of these—China, France, the Russian Federation, the United Kingdom, and the United States—are permanent members. The other 10 are elected by the General Assembly for two-year terms.

Decisions of the Council require nine yes votes. The Council can take measures to enforce its decisions, such as imposing economic sanctions or an arms embargo. On rare occasions, the Council has authorized member states to use "all necessary means," including collective military action, to see that its decisions are carried out.

The Economic and Social Council, under the overall authority of the General Assembly, coordinates the economic and social work of the United Nations and the UN family of organizations. The Council has 54 members, elected by the General Assembly for three-year terms. The Council's subsidiary bodies meet regularly and report back to it. The Commission on Human Rights, for example, monitors the observance of human rights throughout the world.

Other bodies focus on such issues as social development, the status of women, crime prevention, narcotic drugs and environmental protection. Five regional commissions promote economic development and cooperation in their respective regions.

The Trusteeship Council was established to provide international supervision for 11 Trust Territories administered by seven Member States and ensure that adequate steps were taken to prepare the Territories for self-government or independence. By 1994, all Trust Territories had attained self-government or independence. Its work completed, the Trusteeship Council now consists of the five permanent members of the Security Council. It has amended its rules of procedure to allow it to meet as and when the occasion may require.

The International Court of Justice, also known as the World Court, is the main judicial organ of the UN. Consisting of 15 judges elected jointly by the General Assembly and the Security

Council, the Court decides disputes between countries. Participation by states in a proceeding is voluntary, but if a state agrees to participate, it is obligated to comply with the Court's decision. The Court also provides advisory opinions to the General Assembly and the Security Council upon request. The Court is located in The Hague in The Netherlands.

The Secretariat carries out the substantive and administrative work of the UN as directed by the General Assembly, the Security Council, and the other organs. At its head is the Secretary-General, who provides overall administrative guidance.

The Secretariat consists of departments and offices with a total staff of some 7,500 under the regular budget, and a nearly equal number under special funding. They are drawn from some 170 countries. Duty stations include UN Headquarters in New York, as well as UN offices in Geneva, Vienna, Nairobi, and other locations.

The International Monetary Fund, the World Bank and 12 other independent organizations known as "specialized agencies" are linked to the UN through cooperative agreements. These agencies, among them the World Health Organization and the International Civil Aviation Organization, are autonomous bodies created by intergovernmental agreement.

They have wide-ranging international responsibilities in the economic, social, cultural, educational, health, and related fields. Some of them, like the International Labour Organization and the Universal Postal Union, are older than the UN itself.

In addition, a number of UN offices, programmes and funds—such as the Office of the UN High Commissioner for Refugees (UNHCR), the UN Development Programme (UNDP), and the UN Children's Fund (UNICEF)—work to improve the economic and social condition of people around the world. They report to the General Assembly or the Economic and Social Council.

All these organizations have their own governing bodies, budgets and secretariats. Together with the United Nations, they are known as the UN family, or the UN system. Together, they provide technical assistance and other forms of practical help in virtually all economic and social areas.

Selected UN Programs and Funds

The **United Nations Children's Fund** (UNICEF) advocates for the protection of children's rights to help meet their basic needs and help them reach their full potential. It is committed to ensuring special protection for the most disadvantaged children—victims of war, disasters, extreme poverty, all forms of violence, and exploitation and those with disabilities—and aims, through its country programs, to promote the equal rights of women and girls and to support their full participation in the political, social and economic development of their communities.

UNICEF works for the benefit of the world's children in five broad areas: child protection, girls' education, HIV/AIDS prevention and care, immunization, and early childhood health and education.

★ Web site: http://www.unchs.org/vacancy/internship.asp

★ Job vacancies: http://www.unicef.org/about/employ/index_currentvacancies.html

★ Careers at UNICEF: http://www.unicef.org/about/employ/index.html

★ Benefits: http://www.unicef.org/about/employ/index_benefits.html

★ How to apply: http://www.unicef.org/about/employ/index_apply.html

★ Employment qualifications:
http://www.unicef.org/about/employ/index_qualifications.html

★ Young professional program: http://www.unicef.org/about/employ/index_ypp.html

★ Junior professional program: http://www.unicef.org/about/employ/index_jpp.html

★ Internships: http://www.unicef.org/about/employ/index_internship.html

★ Volunteers: http://www.unicef.org/about/employ/index_volunteers.html

The **United Nations Conference on Trade and Development** aims at the development-friendly integration of developing countries into the world economy. It performs research, policy analysis, and data collection; provides technical assistance to developing countries; and serves as a forum for intergovernmental discussions related to trade and development.

★ Web site: http://www.unctad.org/

★ Job vacancies: http://www.unctad.org/Templates/Page.asp?intItemID=2105&lang=1

★ Internship information:
http://www.unctad.org/Templates/Page.asp?intItemID=2106&lang=1

★ Recruitment information:
http://www.unctad.org/Templates/Page.asp?intItemID=2104&lang=1

★ Member countries: http://www.unctad.org/Templates/Page.asp?intItemID=1929&lang=1

The **Office of the United Nations High Commissioner for Human Rights** works to keep the vision of a world in which the human rights of all are fully respected and enjoyed in conditions of global peace to the forefront through constant encouragement of the international community and its member states to uphold universally agreed human rights standards. OHCHR alerts governments and the world community to the daily reality that these standards are too often ignored or unfulfilled, and seeks to be a voice for the victims of human rights violations everywhere.

It presses the international community to take the steps that can prevent violations, including support for the right to development.

★ Web site: http://www.ohchr.org/english/

★ Job vacancies: http://www.ohchr.org/english/about/vacancies/index.htm

★ Internship program: http://www.ohchr.org/english/about/internship.htm

★ Fellowship program: http://www.ohchr.org/english/issues/indigenous/fellowship.htm

The **United Nations High Commissioner for Refugees** leads and coordinates international action to protect refugees and resolve refugee problems worldwide. Its primary purpose is to safeguard the rights and well-being of refugees. It strives to ensure that everyone can exercise the right to seek asylum and find safe refuge in another state, with the option to return home voluntarily, integrate locally, or to resettle in a third country.

In more than five decades, the agency has helped an estimated 50 million people restart their lives. Today, a staff of around 5,000 people in more than 120 countries continues to help some 17 million persons.

★ Web site: http://www.unhcr.ch/cgi-bin/texis/vtx/home

★ Job vacancies: http://www.unhcr.ch/cgi-bin/texis/vtx/home/ and click on Careers in the Quick Find drop-down box. Then click on Vacancy Announcements.

★ How to apply: http://www.unhcr.ch/cgi-bin/texis/vtx/home/. Click on Careers in the Quick Find drop-down box and then click on Background Information and How to Apply.

★ Careers and recruitment: http://www.unhcr.ch/cgi-bin/texis/vtx/admin?id=3ba1bdcb7

★ Junior professional officer program: http://www.unhcr.ch/cgi-bin/texis/vtx/home/ and click on Careers in the Quick Find drop-down box. Then click on The Junior Professional Officer Programme.

★ Standard post profiles (job descriptions): http://www.unhcr.ch/cgi-bin/texis/vtx/home/ and click on Careers in the Quick Find drop-down box. Then click on Standard Post Profiles.

UN-HABITAT, The **United Nations Human Settlements Program** promotes socially and environmentally sustainable towns and cities with the goal of providing adequate shelter for all.

★ Web site: http://www.unchs.org/

★ Job vacancies: http://www.unchs.org/vacancy/index.asp

★ Headquarters contacts: http://www.unchs.org/contacts/overview.asp

★ Internship information: http://www.unchs.org/vacancy/internship.asp

★ Regional offices: http://www.unchs.org/offices/offices.asp

The **United Nations Research Institute for Social Development** is an autonomous UN agency engaging in multidisciplinary research on the social dimensions of contemporary problems affecting development. Through its research, UNRISD stimulates dialogue and contributes to policy debates on key issues of social development within and outside the UN system.

The Institute has sought to promote a holistic and multidisciplinary approach to social development by focusing on decision-making processes, often conflicting social forces, and the question of who wins and who loses as economies grow or contract and societies change.

★ Web site: http://www.unrisd.org/

★ Job vacancies: http://www.unrisd.org/ and then click on About UNRISD. Click on About the Institute and then on Working at UNRISD.

★ Headquarters contacts: http://www.unrisd.org/ and then click on About UNRISD. Click on Contact Details.

Other UN Entities

Commission on Human Rights
http://www.unhchr.ch/html/menu2/2/chr.htm

Commission on Narcotic Drugs
http://www.unodc.org/unodc/cnd.html

Commissions on Crime Prevention and Criminal Justice
http://www.uncjin.org/Documents/documents.html#Commission

Commission on Sustainable Development
http://www.un.org/esa/sustdev/csd/csd13/csd13.htm

Commission on Status of Women
http://www.un.org/womenwatch/daw/csw/

Commission on Population and Development
http://www.un.org/esa/population/cpd/aboutcom.htm

Commission for Social Development
http://www.un.org/esa/socdev/csd/

Department for Disarmament Affairs
http://disarmament.un.org:8080/

Department of Peacekeeping Operations
http://www.un.org/Depts/dpko/dpko/index.asp

Department of Political Affairs
http://www.un.org/Depts/dpa/

Economic Commission for Africa
http://unstats.un.org/unsd/statcom/commission.htm

Economic Commission for Europe
http://www.unece.org/

Economic Commission for Latin America and the Caribbean
http://www.eclac.cl/default.asp?idioma=IN

Economic and Social Commission for Asia and the Pacific
http://www.unescap.org/

Economic and Social Commission for Western Asia
http://www.escwa.org.lb/

Joint United Nations Program on HIV/AIDS
http://www.unssc.org/web1/

International Research and Training Institute for the Advancement of Women
http://www.un-instraw.org/en/index.html

International Trade Centre
http://www.intracen.org/index.htm

Office for the Coordination of Humanitarian Affairs
http://ochaonline.un.org/

Office of the High Representative for the Least Developed Countries, Landlocked Developing Countries, and Small Island Developing States
http://www.un.org/special-rep/ohrlls/ohrlls/default.htm

Permanent Forum on Indigenous Issues
http://www.un.org/esa/socdev/unpfii/index.html

Statistical Commission
http://unstats.un.org/unsd/statcom/commission.htm

United Nations Capital Development Fund
http://www.uncdf.org/

United Nations Development Fund for Women
http://www.unifem.org/

United Nations Drug Control Program
http://www.intracen.org/index.htm

United Nations Environment Program
http://www.unep.org/

United Nations Forum on Forests
http://www.un.org/esa/forests/

United Nations Interregional Crime and Justice Research Institute
http://www.unicri.it/

United Nations Institute for Disarmament Research
http://www.unidir.org/

United Nations Office on Drugs and Crime
http://www.unodc.org/unodc/index.html

United Nations Office for Project Services
http://www.unops.org/web_forms/welcome.htm

United Nations Population Fund
http://www.uncdf.org/

United Nations Relief and Works Agency for Palestine Refugees in the Near East
http://www.un.org/unrwa/

United Nations System Staff College
http://www.unssc.org/web1/

United Nations University
http://www.unu.edu/

United Nations Volunteers
http://www.unv.org/

World Food Program
http://www.wfp.org/

Sample Job Vacancies

Associate Air Operations/Aviation Officer
Agency: United Nations Organization Mission in the Democratic Republic of Congo
Salary: $55,346
Location: Kinshasa

Job description summary: Manages the Aviation Policy Sub-Unit and administers all policy activities related to quality assurance and standardization, including risk management. Coordinates aviation operations policy compliance activities within the DPKO Mission's Aviation Safety program and current UN Air Operations Manual, Military/Civil Aviation Local Area Procedures (LAPs). Establishes relationships and builds trust with the personnel of ground handling companies and Civil Aviation Authorities. Coordinates with Section Aviation MovCon Officers and Air Liaison Officers to ensure standards are maintained in the sectors according to standardized policy and ensures compliance with the host country's airports authority and CAA on issues and matters concerning airfields/helipads operation. Produces a range of policy documentation including aircraft performance and carrier assessment reports.

Minimum qualifications required: Bachelor's degree in a communications-related field or aviation management OR an equivalent combination of relevant education and professional development in an aviation-related occupation. At least five years' professional experience, with a minimum of two years at the international level.

Must possess the following competencies: 1) demonstrated conceptual, analytical, and evaluative skills and the ability to conduct research and analysis, identify issues, formulate opinions and make recommendations; 2) exposure to the full range of air operations and air safety issues; 3) ability to comprehend and reconcile the diverse features of air operations; 4) ability to establish priorities, plan, coordinate, and monitor the work plan of those under supervision; 5) strong communication and analytical skills, including the ability to articulate ideas in clear, concise style; 6) ability to identify key issues in complex situations, to assess information and the potential impact of recommendations and proposed courses of action, to treat sensitive and confidential information appropriately and to make difficult decisions when necessary; 7) excellent interpersonal skills, including ability to operate effectively across Organization boundaries; 8) ability to establish and maintain effective partnerships and working relations in a multicultural, multiethnic environment with sensitivity and respect for diversity; 9) computer literacy; 10) ability to manage the development and adoption of new applications for air operations.

Minimum application materials required: Apply online by opening a "My UN" account online. After opening the account, applicants may apply for vacancies using the Personal History Profile (PHP) provided.

Chinese Interpreter
Agency: Department for General Assembly and Conference Management
Salary: $68,306
Location: New York, New York

Job description summary: Provides interpretation into Chinese of speeches and statements given in English and into English of statements and speeches given in Chinese. May occasionally be assigned to sensitive meetings and function as team leader of all interpreters assigned to the same meeting.

Minimum qualifications required: Bachelor's degree and at least two years of internationally recognized professional interpreting experience. Must have passed the United Nations Chinese Interpreters' examination. Perfect command of Chinese and English is required. Knowledge of an additional official UN language is an asset.

Must possess the following competencies 1) punctuality, ability to work under stress, willingness to travel and keep flexible working hours; 2) good interpersonal and communication skills; 3) ability to establish and maintain effective working relations as a team member in a multicultural, multiethnic environment with sensitivity and respect for diversity; 4) desire to constantly improve linguistic skills, monitor own work, and be prepared for meetings.

Minimum application materials required: Apply online by opening a "My UN" account online. After opening the account, applicants may apply for vacancies using the Personal History Profile (PHP) provided.

Drug Control Officer

Agency: United Nations Office on Drugs and Crime
Salary: $68,306
Location: Vienna, Austria

Job description summary: Advises government officials and international and regional bodies on control measures related to chemicals scheduled under the 1988 Convention. Answers queries on potential use of chemicals in illicit drugs manufacture. Carries out analytical research, detects trends, and compiles analytical parts of surveys and background information on illicit trafficking in precursors and chemicals. Identifies and investigates deficiencies and cases of noncompliance with the 1988 Convention and recommends corrective action. Advises on technical questions related to chemical control systems, data evaluation systems, assessment methods, methods of data recording, etc. Attends policy-making and technical meetings and represents INCB at those meetings. Prepares correspondence with governments, letters, mission reports, analyses, briefings, presentations, enforcement strategies, policy proposals and documents, etc. Liaises with counterparts in UN and ODC, other organizations, and specialized agencies, particularly with the World Customs Organization (WCO) and ICPO/Interpol. Maintains and supervises precursor database systems. Trains national drug control administrators.

Minimum qualifications required: Bachelor's degree in social sciences or other relevant disciplines OR the equivalent combination of education and experience in any of those areas. Minimum of five years of professional experience at the international level in areas related to drug control, international relations, or public administration. Excellent knowledge of English and Spanish, including drafting ability. Experience in international drug control; knowledge of additional UN official languages. Ability to expeditiously deal with operational information.

Must possess the following competencies: 1) reliability and discretion in dealing with confidential and sensitive operational information; 2) knowledge and understanding of drug and precursor control; 3) research, analytical and problem-solving skills; 4) ability to establish and maintain productive partnerships with clients and to gain their trust and respect; 5) ability to identify clients' needs and priorities and to match them with the Office's operational priorities; 6) Very good oral and written communication skills; 7) fully proficient with computer technology; 8) good interpersonal skills and ability to establish and maintain effective partnerships and working relations in a multicultural, multiethnic environment with sensitivity and respect for diversity.

Minimum application materials required: Apply online by opening a "My UN" account online. After opening the account, applicants may apply for vacancies using the Personal History Profile (PHP) provided.

Economic Affairs Officer

Agency: Trade and Regional Integration Division (TRID), Economic Commission for Africa
Salary: $68,306
Location: Addis Ababa

Job description summary: Coordinates and conducts research and studies on African development; assists with macroeconomic studies on African development; collects, collates and analyzes economic research data; identifies and analyzes policy proposals; provides input for advocating for ECA policies and programs to a range of stakeholders. Participates in team projects; prepares documents and other communications such as results of studies, reports, letters, proposals, Web site texts and speeches; provides inputs and makes timely contributions to the Division's work plan; assists with the implementation of policy and programme initiatives; assists with identifying and recruiting consultants; and participates in missions as a resource person.

Minimum qualifications required: Master's or doctorate degree in economics or development economics with an emphasis on macroeconomics or regional integration. At least five years of progressively responsible experience in applying the principles of economic and social development, preferably in the context of Africa. Practical experience in trade or regional integration gained through involvement in program development or implementation, research, teaching, or related work and specific experience with Computable General Equilibrium modeling on international economics is also required. Record of relevant publications would be an asset. Strong computer skills are required, including the use of software relating to macroeconomic research and analysis, proficiency with spreadsheet and database applications, word processing, presentation programs, and the Internet.

Must possess the following competencies: 1) demonstrated in-depth technical knowledge and proven analytical skills in aspects of economic and social development in the African context; 2) good problem-solving ability; 3) ability to plan, coordinate, and monitor own work plan and that of the others; 4) ability to manage conflicting priorities; 5) sound drafting ability, particularly in preparing reports that are clear and concise, and well developed oral presentation skills; 6) ability to apply good interpersonal skills.

Minimum application materials required: Apply online by opening a "My UN" account online. After opening the account, applicants may apply for vacancies using the Personal History Profile (PHP) provided.

Special requirements: Fluency in spoken and written English or French is required; working knowledge of the other is highly desirable.

Human Rights Officer

Agency: Office of the High Commissioner for Human Rights
Salary: $84,400
Location: Geneva, Switzerland

Job description summary: Acts as Secretary of the Committee against Torture and the Secretary of the United Nations Voluntary Fund for Victims of Torture. Prepares documentation for the Committee sessions and draft-guidelines for following-up Committee recommendations. Oversees preparation and conduct of inquiries and implementation of the recommendations resulting from such inquiries. Facilitates and assists in the adoption of measures to rationalize the functioning of the treaty body system. Prepares legal analyses and drafts legal background papers for the Committee and other human rights treaty bodies, related to State reporting procedures. Undertakes research into the travaux préparatoires of relevant human rights treaties and monitors relevant developments in regional human rights institutions. Prepares and participates in missions relating to State reporting procedures. Prepares the documentation for the Meetings of the States Parties to the Convention and participates in their organization.

Minimum qualifications required: Masters degree, preferably in law, political science, international relations or other disciplines related to human rights. A combination of relevant academic qualifications and extensive experience may be accepted in lieu of the advanced degree. At least seven years of progressively responsible experience in human rights field, including three years at the international level, preferably within the UN. Very good knowledge of international human rights machinery and treaties. Experience with project management, finance, and fundraising.

Must possess the following competencies: 1) comprehensive knowledge of a range of human rights issues; 2) very good knowledge of institutional mandates, policies and guidelines related to human rights, in particular treaty body monitoring mechanisms; 3) good analytical and research skills, including ability to evaluate and integrate information from a variety of sources; 4) excellent communication skills, including the ability to convey complex concepts and recommendations at senior levels, both orally and in writing, in a clear, concise style; 5) ability to interact and to establish and maintain effective working relations both as a team member and team leader, with people of different national and cultural backgrounds; 6) ability to oversee work of more junior staff and to plan and organize own work and that of others.

Minimum application materials required: Apply online by opening a "My UN" account online. After opening the account, applicants may apply for vacancies using the Personal History Profile (PHP) provided.

Special requirements: Fluency in oral and written English or French; working knowledge of the other.

Prepress Technician (Platemaker)
Agency: Department for General Assembly and Conference Management
Salary: $58,123
Location: New York, New York

Job description summary: Receives work submitted in digital and conventional form for processing and provides plates for the printing presses; receives and processes hard copy for digital output to plate or film for offset printing, scans from hard copy and is responsible for the output of digitally prepared plates and film for offset printing. In the absence of the Working Leader, Prepress, responsible for the output of offset plates.

Minimum qualifications required: High school education or equivalent. Four-year apprenticeship, followed by course work in a formal printing trade school, highly desirable. Several years of experience including four years of practical prepress experience including digital and conventional prepress plus on-the-job experience within the Organization. Advanced skills with graphic arts software applications required.

Must possess the following competencies: 1) keeps abreast of microcomputer applications, especially graphic arts/layout applications and prepress software; 2) willingness to learn new skills; 3) works collaboratively with colleagues; 4) ability to work in a multicultural, multiethnic environment with sensitivity and respect for diversity; 5) good interpersonal skills.

Minimum application materials required: Apply online by opening a "My UN" account online. After opening the account, applicants may apply for vacancies using the Personal History Profile (PHP) provided.

Radio Producer (Arabic)
Agency: Department of Public Information
Salary: $68,306
Location: New York, New York

Job description summary: Researches, writes, narrates, produces and broadcasts radio news, feature/documentary programs in Arabic on the global activities of the UN; monitors the activities of organizations, funds, and programs within the UN System. Liaises with departments of the UN System and other relevant sources on topical issues for radio programming; conducts interviews, gathers audio material, performs audio desktop editing and management of sound files; undertakes digital editing and recording; generates original materials and other actuality for programming; liaises with broadcasting and nongovernmental organizations regarding usage of radio programs; contributes ideas to program planning and promotional efforts.

Minimum qualifications required: Masters degree in broadcast journalism/communications, with knowledge of international affairs or political science. Five to seven years experience in national or international broadcasting as a writer/producer or editor. Training in digital desktop sound editing, Internet research, and electronic posting is required.

Must possess the following competencies: 1) in-depth background and practical experience in radio broadcast journalism with proven written and on-air presentation skills; 2) ability to work under pressure and meet tight deadlines; 3) good knowledge of the UN System and its work; 4) political awareness and judgment as well as ability to keep abreast of international current affairs developments; 5) good communications research and analytical skills; 6) ability to plan and organize efficiently to ease pressure of working under strict deadlines; 7) hands-on practical experience in digital desktop sound editing, Internet research, and electronic posting; 8) ability to write crisply and concisely making use of sound and words and to make clear on-air presentations; 9) good interpersonal skills and ability to establish and maintain harmonious working relationships with colleagues in a multicultural environment.

Minimum application materials required: Apply online by opening a "My UN" account online. After opening the account, applicants may apply for vacancies using the Personal History Profile (PHP) provided.

Special requirements: Fluency in written and oral Arabic is required.

Selected Bilateral Organization

International Boundary and Water Commission, United States and Mexico

Suite C-310, 4171 North Mesa Street
El Paso, Texas 79902
800-262-8857

★ Web site: http://www.ibwc.state.gov/

★ Job vacancies: http://www.ibwc.state.gov/html/job_announcements.html

★ USAJOBS By Phone: 912-757-3000

★ Headquarters contacts: http://www.ibwc.state.gov/html/staff_by_divisionx.html

Established in 1889, the International Boundary and Water Commission (IBWC) has responsibility for applying the boundary and water treaties between the United States and Mexico and settling differences that may arise out of these treaties. The IBWC is an international body composed of the United States Section and the Mexican Section, each headed by an Engineer-Commissioner appointed by his or her respective president.

Sample Job Vacancy

Office Clerk
Agency: International Boundary and Water Commission, United States and Mexico
Salary: $8.30 to $10.38/hour
Location: El Paso, Texas

Job description summary: Performs simple and routine clerical duties such as the following: receives inquiries, including telephone calls and visitors; takes and relays messages; files and retrieves a variety of records, manuals, and other information; distributes mail; makes photocopies; and operates a computer terminal to prepare routine documents.

Minimum qualifications required: Must be able to type 40 words per minute. Must be currently enrolled as a degree/certificate seeking student taking at least a half-time course load.

Minimum application materials required: Submit an Application for Federal Employment (SF-171), an Optional Application for Federal Employment (OF-612), or a resume. The following documents are also required: Declaration for Federal Employment (OF-306), Ability to Drive Safely (IBWC Form 336), proof of current enrollment. In addition, include narrative responses to the following KSAs: 1) knowledge of simple clerical procedures such as taking and relaying messages, typing simple documents such as forms, address labels, etc, and filing; 2) basic skill in operating a personal computer.

Part III

Special Federal Job Opportunities

CHAPTER 7

Special Federal Job Opportunities for Veterans

If you're a military veteran, Uncle Sam wants you. This time, though, you can leave the uniforms in your closet because Uncle Sam wants you dressed in civvies for your new career as a civilian government employee.

If you meet certain criteria, you'll receive hiring preference for many federal job openings, eligibility for special hiring programs open only to veterans, and preference if your agency has layoffs (in government jargon they're called "reductions in force").

Note: No Guarantees for Veterans

Being a veteran does not guarantee you a federal job—it just improves your chances of getting one. You still must meet the job's basic qualification requirements to be considered.

As a bonus, if you get a government job you may run into military buddies who served with you because veterans fill about 25 percent of all executive branch jobs. That's nearly half a million jobs.

Veterans' preference has existed for nearly 150 years, back to the days of the Civil War. Recognizing that people who serve in the nation's armed forces make sacrifices, Congress has tried to ensure that veterans who seek federal jobs are not penalized for their time in military service. Veterans' preference recognizes the economic loss suffered by citizens who have served in the military, restores veterans to a favorable competitive position for federal employment, and acknowledges the larger obligation owed to veterans who suffered disabling wounds.

Qualifying veterans who meet the requirements for a federal job are awarded extra "points." Every federal applicant is scored on a scale that ranges from zero to 100. These scores are based either on answers to a written examination or an evaluation of the applicant's education and experience. To be considered for a job opening, an applicant must achieve a score of at least 70.

Veterans get 5 or 10 points added to their score depending on their circumstances, pushing them above candidates who have similar backgrounds but haven't served in the military. Since in most cases federal agencies are limited to considering the three candidates who score the highest, the extra points veterans receive can tip the selection process in their favor.

Veterans' preference applies to permanent and temporary jobs in the competitive and excepted services of the executive branch. It does not apply to positions in the Senior Executive Service or in the legislative and judicial branches *unless* the positions are in the competitive service, such as jobs at the Government Printing Office.

The rules regarding veterans' preference, like most government rules, are extremely complex. We'll explore the highlights–the information you really need to know if you're a veteran. To avoid crossing your eyes, however, we won't describe every possible nuance or contingency in excruciating detail.

Who Qualifies for Veterans' Preference?

It's probably easiest to start by listing who is *not* eligible for veterans' preference:

★ Veterans who did not receive an honorable or general discharge when they left military service.

★ Military retirees at the rank of major, lieutenant commander, or higher *unless* they are disabled veterans.

★ Members of the National Guard and Reserves who went on active duty only for training purposes.

Qualifications for a 5-Point Preference

Five points are added to the score of a veteran who served in one of the following situations:

★ For more than 180 days, any part of which occurred after January 31, 1955, and before October 15, 1976.

★ During the Gulf War from August 2, 1990, through January 2, 1992.

★ In a campaign or expedition for which a campaign medal was authorized. This includes El Salvador, Grenada, Haiti, Lebanon, Panama, Somalia, southwest Asia, Bosnia, and the global war on terrorism.

Qualifications for a 10-Point Preference

Ten points are added to the score of

★ A veteran who served any time and who (1) has a present service-connected disability or (2) is receiving compensation, disability retirement benefits, or a pension from the military or the Department of Veterans Affairs. Individuals who received a Purple Heart qualify as disabled veterans.

★ A spouse of certain deceased veterans who has not remarried.

★ A spouse of a veteran who is unable to work because of a service-connected disability.

★ The mother of a veteran who died in service or who is permanently and totally disabled.

How Veterans' Preference Is Applied

Veterans' preference is applied in a variety of ways depending on the type of job, the number of points the applicant receives, and other circumstances:

★ For scientific and professional positions in grades GS-9 and higher, all candidates—both veterans and non-veterans—are ranked by their overall score. The scores of applicants who qualified for veterans' preference have been boosted by 5 or 10 points, depending on the nature of their preference, but these applicants do not receive any other special consideration in hiring.

★ For all other positions, the names of veterans who qualified for a 10-point preference *and* who have a compensable, service-connected disability of 10 percent or more are placed ahead of the names of all other eligible candidates.

The names of other veterans who qualified for a 10-point preference, veterans who received a 5-point preference, and non-veterans are then ranked by their overall score.

★ Examinations for certain jobs are only open to applicants who qualify for veterans' preference as long as such applicants are available. The jobs include custodian, guard, elevator operator, and messenger.

★ People who qualify for a 10-point preference may apply for any federal jobs subject to competition where a non-temporary appointment has been made within the previous three years.

★ A person who is unable to apply for an open competitive job because of military service may apply after the position's closing date.

In the last two situations, interested veterans should contact the agency that announced the position for further information.

Consulting the "Veterans' Preference Advisor"

The Department of Labor has created a handy online "Veterans' Preference Advisor" that helps veterans determine the preference to which they're entitled, the benefits associated with the preference, and the steps necessary to file a complaint if a federal agency fails to provide the required benefits.

Using the system simply requires clicking on the applicable answers to some questions. The Veterans' Preference Advisor is available at http://www.dol.gov/elaws/vetspref.htm.

Veterans Usually Get Required Preferences

Veterans usually receive proper consideration in federal hiring, according to a study released by the Office of Personnel Management. OPM launched the study after veterans groups raised concerns about whether veterans who applied for federal jobs received the required preferences.

But the OPM study did find some problems:

★ Over the previous two years, the government had hired 8,000 lawyers and 95,000 student trainees without a clear understanding of how to apply veterans' preferences.

★ Officials in many offices that were part of the excepted service, rather than the competitive service, incorrectly believed they did not have to comply with veterans' preferences laws and rules.

★ The hiring of disabled veterans was "very uneven" among government agencies and "most managers were unaware of specific initiatives by their agency to hire disabled veterans," the report said.

Special Hiring Programs for Veterans

The OPM report said 41 percent of veterans entered the federal workforce through special hiring programs that seek to recruit veterans. In government-speak, these programs are called "special appointing authorities for veterans."

Several different programs exist. All are optional for federal agencies, so a specific agency may or may not use particular programs.

Veterans' Recruitment Appointment

The largest program is the Veterans' Recruitment Appointment (VRA), under which agencies can hire an eligible veteran without competition. The veteran must meet the basic qualification requirements for the job and must have served on *active duty,* not active duty for training.

Agencies can use the VRA to fill jobs at any grade through General Schedule 11 (GS-11) or the equivalent. VRA applicants are hired under excepted appointments to positions that are otherwise in the competitive service. After two years of satisfactory performance, the agency must convert the veteran to a normal competitive service appointment.

Once VRAs are hired, they're treated like any other competitive service employee and may be promoted, reassigned, or transferred. VRA hires who have less than 15 years of education must complete a training program established by the agency.

To apply for VRA, veterans should directly contact the personnel office at the federal agency where they are interested in working to find out more about VRA opportunities.

Program for Veterans with Disabilities

Another program provides special benefits to veterans who have disabilities of 30 percent or more. These veterans can be hired under temporary or term appointments for any job where they meet the requirements. Unlike the VRA program, there is no grade limitation. After demonstrating satisfactory performance, the veteran may be converted at any time to a normal competitive service appointment.

To apply for this program, veterans should contact the personnel office at the federal agency where they want to work to inquire about opportunities. As part of the hiring process, veterans must submit a copy of a letter dated within the previous 12 months from the Department of Veterans Affairs or the Department of Defense certifying that they receive compensation for a service-connected disability of 30 percent or more.

Two Online Guides to Special Hiring Programs

Two publications by the Office of Personnel Management describe other special hiring programs for veterans. The "VetsInfo Guide" (http://www.opm.gov/veterans/html/vetsinfo.asp) is aimed at veterans, while the longer and more detailed "VetGuide" (http://www.opm.gov/veterans/html/vetguide.asp) is aimed at federal personnel specialists and managers. Be careful using these publications, however, since both were seriously outdated when this book was being written.

How to Find a Federal Job If You're a Veteran

Veterans who want to work for the federal government have two primary methods for finding a job.

The first and most effective is to contact the personnel office at the agency where you're interested in working to ask about opportunities. If you qualify for one of the special hiring programs for veterans, be sure to mention this.

The second method is to look for job openings at USAJOBS, the official job site for the federal government. On an average day, USAJOBS provides complete information about 16,000 to 18,000 federal job openings. You can access USAJOBS online at http://usajobs.opm.gov or by telephone at 703-724-1850 (TDD 978-461-8404). We discuss how to use USAJOBS in detail in Chapter 2.

Which Agencies Hire the Most Veterans?

Not surprisingly, the majority of veterans in the federal government work in civilian jobs at agencies that are part of the Department of Defense. The Department of the Army employs 17.4 percent of all veterans in the federal government, the Department of the Navy 15 percent, the Department of the Air Force 13.2 percent, and other Defense Department agencies 6.3 percent, according to the latest statistics available.

The Department of Veterans Affairs also is a big employer of veterans. It accounts for 13.8 percent of all veterans in the federal government. All other agencies combined account for 34.2 percent of veterans in federal jobs.

Outside the Defense Department and the Veterans Administration, some of the federal agencies that have the highest percentages of veterans on their staffs include the Department of Energy, the Department of Justice, and the Department of Transportation.

CHAPTER 8

Special Federal Job Opportunities for People with Disabilities

Some people with disabilities, whether physical or mental, qualify for special federal hiring programs where they do not have to compete with other applicants. These programs are not widely advertised, however, so people with disabilities must be aggressive in pursuing them.

Of course, people with disabilities also can compete for federal jobs by applying through vacancy announcements. Federal law bars agencies from discriminating against people with disabilities. Law also requires agencies to provide reasonable accommodations to applicants and employees when needed.

If you've looked at some federal job announcements, you've probably seen statements similar to the following: "This agency provides reasonable accommodation to applicants with disabilities where appropriate.

"If you need reasonable accommodation for any part of the application and hiring process, notify the agency. Determinations on requests for reasonable accommodation will be made on a case-by-case basis."

Federal Government Aggressively Hires People with Disabilities

For years, the federal government has aggressively hired people with disabilities. Over the last decade, people with various types of disabilities have consistently constituted about 7 percent of the federal workforce.

This has translated into the government employing between 120,000 and 145,000 people with disabilities annually.

What Constitutes a Disability?

The Rehabilitation Act of 1973, which protects executive branch applicants and employees against employment discrimination based on disability, defines a person with a disability as someone who

★ Has a physical or mental impairment that substantially limits one or more of the person's major life activities. A "physical or mental impairment" means one of the following:

  • Any physiological disorder, condition, cosmetic disfigurement, or anatomical loss affecting one or more systems such as neurological, musculoskeletal, special sense organs, cardiovascular, reproductive, digestive, respiratory, genito-urinary, hemic and lymphatic, skin, and endocrine.

  • Any mental or psychological disorder, such as mental retardation, organic brain syndrome, emotional or mental illness, and specific learning disabilities.

★ Has a history of such an impairment or is perceived by others as having such an impairment.

Examples of "major life activities" include caring for yourself, performing manual tasks, walking, seeing, hearing, speaking, breathing, learning, concentrating, and working.

The Rehabilitation Act also requires federal agencies to provide reasonable accommodation for known physical or mental limitations of applicants and employees, unless doing so would cause "undue hardship." In addition, Executive Order 13164, which was issued on July 26, 2000, requires federal agencies to develop written procedures for providing reasonable accommodation.

Reasonable accommodation "is any change to a job, the work environment, or the way things are usually done that allows an individual with a disability to apply for a job, perform job functions, or enjoy equal access to benefits available to other individuals in the workplace," according to a publication from the Office of Personnel Management.

Accommodations can range from providing application forms in alternative formats such as large print or Braille to providing a sign language interpreter for someone who is deaf. The government must pay for the accommodations.

Tip: Make Your Needs Known

Applicants or employees with disabilities are responsible for making their needs known.

For example, if you're applying for a federal job but have a disability that makes it impossible for you to type, you must alert the agency as soon as possible if you cannot fill out the online resume builder that it requires.

Special Hiring Authorities

The majority of people with disabilities who work for the federal government were hired in open competitions. However, special hiring authorities exist where competition is not required for people with disabilities.

These rules cover people with mental retardation; people with severe physical disabilities; people with psychiatric disabilities; disabled veterans who are enrolled in a Department of Veterans Affairs training program; and veterans who are 30 percent or more disabled. Agencies are not required to use these special hiring authorities.

If you wish to be considered under the special hiring authorities, you must contact a counselor at either your state vocational rehabilitation agency or, if you're a veteran, at the Vocational Rehabilitation and Employment Service at the Department of Veterans Affairs. They will prepare and review the necessary documents.

You should ask them to give you a "certification" statement that

★ Verifies that you have a severe disability and are therefore eligible under the Schedule A special hiring authority.

★ States that you are able to perform the duties of the job for which you're applying.

★ Lists any needed reasonable accommodation.

Once you have the certification statement, you have two options:

1. You can send an application and the certification to the Selective Placement Coordinator at the agency where you'd like to work.

2. You can contact the person at the agency who handles the Selective Placement program (it's sometimes called the Disability Employment program). These agency representatives can help match your core skills, along with any needed reasonable accommodations, with available jobs. You'll find them in either the human resources department or the Equal Employment Opportunity office of each agency.

A directory of Selective Placement program coordinators at federal agencies is available online at http://apps.opm.gov/sppc_directory.

Sometimes the certification is done in two steps. The first step is a letter from the counselor certifying that you are disabled and eligible for employment under the special hiring authorities. This type of certification is sufficient for an applicant to be considered for any job.

The second step occurs after you have been tentatively selected for the position. It requires a second letter that must state the counselor has evaluated the job tasks and determined you are able to perform the essential duties of the position. The letter also must state what reasonable accommodations, if any, are sought.

To be hired, you must meet all basic qualification requirements for the job. You also must be able to perform the job's essential functions, either with or without reasonable accommodation. In determining whether you can perform the job's functions, the hiring agency must conduct an individualized assessment. The agency cannot exclude from consideration an entire group of people with a particular disability.

If you're hired under a special hiring authority, you'll probably spend your first two years in the excepted service. After two years of satisfactory performance, you may be converted to an appointment in the competitive service.

More Federal Resources on Disabilities

More information about federal employment of people with disabilities is available from the Office of Personnel Management at http://www.opm.gov/disability/index.asp. Another useful site is DisabilityInfo.gov (http://www.disabilityinfo.gov), which is a gateway to federal information and resources about disabilities.

CHAPTER 9

Special Federal Job Opportunities for Students

The federal government offers more internship and employment opportunities for students and recent college graduates today than ever before. Some of the internships lead directly into good federal jobs, and acceptance of some job offers results in the government paying up to $60,000 toward your college loans.

That's right: Up to *$60,000* in debt vanishes.

Unfortunately, the government does not maintain a centralized list of all the internship and employment opportunities that it offers to students and recent graduates. The purpose of this chapter is to highlight some of the largest programs and point you in the right direction so you can get information about the rest.

Internships

Just like with the private sector, an internship with the federal government is a great way to obtain some work experience, check out a place where you may later want to work, and get your foot in the door for future job openings. Internships are invaluable, especially in today's tight job market.

When many people think about federal internships, the place that comes immediately to mind is Washington, D.C. Each year thousands of young people descend on Washington to participate in government internships.

You shouldn't forget, however, that internship opportunities also exist at many local and regional offices of federal agencies throughout the country.

Wherever you intern with the federal government, you'll end up with an impressive experience to list on your resume—even if you don't end up working for the government.

Any federal office where you apply for an internship will ask you questions, and you need to ask some questions of your own to try to ensure, as much as possible, that you'll have a worthwhile experience.

Most offices try hard to make sure you learn as much as possible during your internship, but a few simply chain interns to fax and photocopy machines for their entire stays.

Before accepting an internship, you should consider asking questions such as:

★ What will my primary duties be as an intern?

★ What will a typical day be like?

★ How many other interns do you expect will work at your office during my stay?

Many young people gravitate toward Capitol Hill and Congress for their internships. It's useful to keep in mind, however, that agencies throughout the federal government—the Smithsonian Institution, the Library of Congress, the Environmental Protection Agency, and the State Department, to name just a few—also offer internships.

Some of the best-known intern programs include

★ The elite Presidential Management Fellows Program, which is designed to attract to government service outstanding graduate students who are committed to leading and managing public policies and programs. Fellows receive an initial two-year appointment that starts at GS-9 and can move to GS-11 in the second year. Upon completion of the program, fellows are eligible for appointment to permanent federal jobs and promotion to GS-12. Applicants must be nominated by their schools. More info: http://www.usajobs.opm.gov/EI18.asp.

★ The Career Intern Program, which is designed to help federal agencies recruit top undergraduate and graduate students for a variety of occupations. The internship lasts for two years, and interns are usually initially employed at the GS-5, GS-7, or GS-9 levels. Upon successful completion of the internship, interns may be eligible for permanent placement within an agency. Each agency develops its own program, and individuals interested in the program must contact specific agencies. Interns can be hired at any time during the year. More info: http://www.opm.gov/careerintern/index.asp.

★ The White House Internship Program, which provides interns with a unique opportunity to observe government officials and gain practical knowledge about the daily operations of the White House. Interns work in a variety of White House offices, including communications, legislative affairs, presidential correspondence, public liaison, scheduling, and faith-based and community initiatives, among others. Internships are unpaid and cannot exceed ninety days in length. Applicants must be U.S. citizens, enrolled in a college or university, and willing to undergo a security clearance prior to working at the White House. More info: http://www.whitehouse.gov/government/wh-intern.html.

Many agencies run their own intern programs besides participating in government-wide efforts such as the Presidential Management Fellows Program. Here are two examples:

★ The State Department uses close to 1,000 interns annually, split evenly between positions in the United States and positions at U.S. embassies in foreign countries. The department seeks students with a broad range of majors, including business, public administration, social work, economics, information management, journalism, and biological and engineering sciences, as well as majors directly related to international affairs. Applicants must be U.S. citizens in good academic standing, and must qualify to receive a Secret or Top Secret clearance. More info: http://www.careers.state.gov/student/prog_intrn.html.

★ The Emerging Leaders Program at the Department of Health and Human Services provides two-year internships for recent college graduates that can lead to permanent employment. Over the last three years the department has taken on nearly 250 recent college graduates. "Managers and supervisors throughout the department are continually amazed that employees right out of school are able to come in and make such an immediate impact," said Ed Sontag, the department's chief human capital officer, at a congressional hearing. More info: http://www.hhs.gov/careers/elp.html.

Federal agencies and departments usually post information about internship programs on their Web sites. Internship information is sometimes included under a broad category such as "Employment" or "Jobs" at a Web site.

Note: URLs for Agency Internship Web Pages

In Part II of this book, listings for specific agencies include the URL for their internship page if one is available.

Although the government does not have a centralized source for information about all federal internship opportunities, the Office of Personnel Management provides links to student employment pages for a wide variety of agencies at http://www.studentjobs.gov/agencies.asp.

Two other lists from the Office of Personnel Management may be helpful as you search for the perfect internship:

★ The list at http://www.studentjobs.gov/d_internship.asp provides brief descriptions and links to more information for dozens of state and federal government internship programs.

★ The list at http://www.usajobs.opm.gov/EI-13.asp provides detailed information about a number of federal internship programs that are sponsored by private organizations.

College Loan Repayments

If you're like most college students and have tens of thousands of dollars in college loans to repay, Uncle Sam may be able to help. If you qualify and work at one of the participating federal agencies, the government will repay up to $60,000 of your loans. That's quite an incentive to work for the federal government—which is exactly why the program was created in fiscal year 2001.

Participating agencies can offer to repay federally insured student loans as an incentive to attract top candidates or to retain excellent employees. Agencies can agree to repay up to $10,000 for an employee in a calendar year, with total payments capped at $60,000 for each employee. In return, the employee must sign an agreement promising to work for the agency for a minimum of three years.

Penalty for Breaking Your Work Agreement

The penalty for breaking that promise to work for three years is stiff. If you leave the agency at any time during the three-year period, you must reimburse the agency for every penny that it paid toward your loans.

There's only one exception: If you transfer to another federal agency and your service agreement does not specifically require repayment upon a transfer. But your new agency is not obligated to honor your previous agreement.

The student loan repayment program is in its infancy, but it's growing as agencies realize the program's power as an incentive. According to the most recent data, the 24 participating agencies repaid more than $9.1 million in student loans for 2,077 employees.

That was a big jump from 2002, when the 16 participating agencies repaid more than $3.1 million in student loans for 690 employees. Since the program's inception, the State Department has been its biggest user. In fiscal year 2003, the department repaid more than $3.2 million in loans for 660 employees.

Note: Agencies Not Required to Do Student Loan Repayment

Agencies are not required to participate in the student loan repayment program, and those that do are largely free to make their own rules. For example, they may extend the required period of service beyond the three years established by law.

More information about the program, including a list of participating agencies, is available at http://www.opm.gov/oca/PAY/StudentLoan/index.asp.

Part IV

Appendixes

Federal Jobs by College Major

No matter what your college major might be, the federal government has a job for you. Look through this list until you find your major, and then look under it for the types of jobs that may be available. But keep three things in mind:

★ The jobs listed under each major are usually examples, not an all-inclusive list.

★ If you don't have a college degree, in many cases work experience in the field is just as good.

★ If you're looking for an administrative job, you often can qualify with a degree in any academic major.

Any Major

Administrative Officers

Air Traffic Controllers

Civil Rights Analysts

Claims Examiners

Contact Representatives

Contract Administrators

Environmental Protection

General Investigators

Internal Revenue Officers

Logistics Managers

Management Analysts

Paralegal Specialists

Personnel Occupations

Public Affairs

Supply Managers

Writers and Editors

Accounting

Accountants

Auditors

Contract Specialists

Financial Administrators

Financial Institution Examiners

Financial Managers

Government Accountability Office Evaluators

Intelligence Specialists

Internal Revenue Agents

Agriculture

Agricultural Commodity Graders

Agricultural Engineers

Agricultural Management Specialists

Agricultural Market Reporters

Agricultural Marketing Specialists

Agricultural Program Specialists

Foreign Agriculture Affairs Specialists

Soil Conservationists

Soil Scientists

Agronomy

Agricultural Management Specialists

Agronomists

Soil Conservationists

Soil Scientists

Anthropology

Anthropologists

Management Analysts

Museum Curators

Museum Specialists

Program Analysts

Archeology

Archeologists

Museum Curators

Museum Specialists

Architecture

Architects

Construction Analysts

Construction Control Inspectors

Landscape Architects

Naval Architects

Program Analysts

Arts, Fine and Applied

Arts Specialists

Audio-Visual Production Specialists

Exhibits Specialists

General Arts and Information Specialists

Illustrators

Photographers

Recreation and Creative Arts Therapists

Visual Information Specialists

Astronomy

Astronomers and Space Scientists

Geodesists

Aviation

Air Navigators

Air Safety Investigators

Air Traffic Controllers

Aircraft Operators

Aircrew Technicians

Aviation Safety Inspectors

Biology

Entomologists

Fishery Biologists

General Biological Scientists

Government Accountability Office Evaluators

Microbiologists

Range Conservationists

Wildlife Biologists

Zoologists

Botany

Agronomists

Botanists

Forestry Technicians

Geneticists

Horticulturists

Plant Pathologists

Plant Physiologists

Plant Protection and Quarantine Specialists

Range Conservationists

Business

Budget Analysts

Business and Industry Specialists

Commissary Store Managers

Contract Specialists

Government Accountability Office Evaluators

Import Specialists

Internal Revenue Officers

Miscellaneous Administrative and Programs Specialists

Quality Assurance Specialists

Trade Specialists

Cartography

Cartographers

Cartographic Technicians

Geodetic Technicians

Chemistry

Chemical Engineers

Chemists

Consumer Safety Officers

Environmental Engineers

Food Technologists

Government Accountability Office Evaluators

Health Physicists

Intelligence Specialists

Toxicologists

Communications

Communications Specialists

Public Affairs Specialists

Technical Writers and Editors

Telecommunications Managers

Writers and Editors

Computer Science

Computer Programmers

Computer Science Specialists

Computer Specialists

Management Analysts

Program Managers

Corrections

Correctional Institution Administrators

Correctional Officers

Program Analysts

Counseling

Chaplains

Education and Vocational Training Specialists

Educational Services Specialists

Equal Opportunity Compliance Specialists

Personnel Specialists

Psychologists

Psychology Aides and Technicians

Social Service Aides and Assistants

Social Service Representatives

Vocational Rehabilitation Specialists

Criminal Justice/Law Enforcement

Border Patrol Agents

Criminal Investigators

Game Law Enforcement Agents

Government Accountability Office Evaluators

Internal Revenue Officers

Police Officers

United States Marshals

Dietetics and Nutrition

Dietitians

Food Technologists

Nutritionists

Economics

Actuaries

Budget Analysts

Contract Specialists

Economists

Financial Analysts

Financial Institution Examiners

Government Accountability Office Evaluators

Loan Specialists

Trade Specialists

Transportation Industrial Analysts

Education

Education and Training Specialists

Education and Vocational Training Specialists

Educational Program Specialists

Educational Services Specialists

Employee Development Specialists

Instructional Systems Specialists

Public Health Educators

Training Instructors

Vocational Rehabilitation Specialists

Electronics Technology

Communications Specialists

Electronics Mechanics

Electronics Technicians

Patent Examiners

Employee/Labor Relations

Contractor Industrial Relations Specialists

Employee Relations Specialists

Hearing and Appeals Specialists

Labor Management Relations Examiners

Labor Relations Specialists

Mediators

Salary and Wage Administrators

Workers Compensation Claims Examiners

Engineering (Any Specialty)

Aerospace Engineers

Biomedical Engineers

Civil Engineers

Computer Engineers

Electrical Engineers

Electronics Engineers

General Engineers

Industrial Engineers

Mechanical Engineers

Nuclear Engineers

English and Literature

Editorial Assistants

Management Analysts

Miscellaneous Administrative and Programs Specialists

Printing Specialists

Program Analysts

Program Managers

Public Affairs Specialists

Technical Writers and Editors

Writers and Editors

Environmental Studies

Ecologists

Environmental Health Technicians

Environmental Protection Assistants

Environmental Protection Specialists

Fish and Wildlife Refuge Management

General Fish and Wildlife Administrators

Government Accountability Office
Evaluators

Miscellaneous Administrative and
Programs Specialists

Toxicologists

Epidemiology

Environmental Health Technicians

General Health Scientists

Industrial Hygienists

Microbiologists

Finance

Appraisers and Assessors

Budget Analysts

Financial Administrators

Financial Analysts

Financial Institution Examiners

Securities Compliance Examiners

Tax Examiners

Trade Specialists

Fish, Game, and Wildlife Management

Fish and Wildlife Refuge Management

Fishery Biologists

Game Law Enforcement Agents

General Biological Scientists

General Fish and Wildlife Administrators

Soil Conservationists

Wildlife Biologists

Wildlife Rescue Managers

Food Technology and Safety

Consumer Safety Inspectors

Consumer Safety Officers

Dietitians and Nutritionists

Food Assistance Program Specialists

Food Technologists

Toxicologists

Foreign Language

Air Safety Investigators

Border Patrol Agents

Customs Inspectors

Equal Employment Opportunity
Specialists

Foreign Affairs Specialists

Foreign Agricultural Affairs Specialists

Intelligence Specialists

Language Specialists

Forestry

Fish and Wildlife Refuge Management

Foresters

General Fish and Wildlife Administrators

Management Analysts

Program Analysts

Soil Conservationists

Geography

Cartographers

Geographers

Geology

General Physical Scientists

Geodesists

Geologists

Hydrologists

Oceanographers

Geophysics

General Physical Scientists

Geophysicists

Health

Environmental Health Technicians

General Health Scientists

Health Physicists

Health System Administrators

Health System Specialists

Industrial Hygienists

Public Health Programs Specialists

Safety and Occupational Health
Management Specialists

History

Archives Technicians

Archivists

Exhibits Specialists

Historians

Intelligence Specialists

Management Analysts

Miscellaneous Administrative and
Programs Specialists

Museum Curators

Program Analysts

Home Economics

Consumer Safety Officers

Food Technologists

Horticulture

Agricultural Marketing Specialists

General Biological Scientists

Horticulturists

Plant Physiologists

Plant Protection and Quarantine Specialists

Hospital Administration

Administrative Officers

General Health Scientists

Health System Administrators

Health System Specialists

Hospital Housekeepers

Miscellaneous Administrative and
Programs Specialists

Public Health Programs Specialists

Human Resource Management

Apprenticeship and Training
Representatives

Employee Development Specialists

Equal Employment Opportunity
Specialists

Military Personnel Management Specialists

Personnel Management Specialists

Personnel Staffing Specialists

Position Classification Specialists

Hydrology

Environmental Engineers

Environmental Protection Specialists

Fish and Wildlife Refuge Management

General Fish and Wildlife Administrators

Hydrologists

Program Analysts

Industrial Management

Business and Industry Specialists

Equipment Specialists

Industrial Hygienists

Industrial Property Managers

Industrial Specialists

Management Analysts

Production Controllers

Program Analysts

Property Disposal Specialists

Quality Assurance Specialists

Insurance

Crop Insurance Administrators

Miscellaneous Administrative and
Programs Specialists

Program Analysts

Social Insurance Administrators

Social Insurance Claims Examiners

Unemployment Insurance Specialists

International Relations

Foreign Affairs Specialists

Foreign Agricultural Affairs Specialists

Intelligence Specialists

International Relations Workers

Language Specialists

Public Affairs Specialists

Trade Specialists

Journalism

Agricultural Market Reporters

Printing Specialists

Program Analysts

Public Affairs Specialists

Technical Writers and Editors

Writers and Editors

Law

Administrative Law Judges

Attorneys

Government Accountability Office
Evaluators

Hearing and Appeals Specialists

Legal Instruments Examiners

Paralegal Specialists

Patent Attorneys

Tax Law Specialists

Law Enforcement

Alcohol, Tobacco, and Firearms Inspectors

Border Patrol Agents

Criminal Investigators

Customs Inspectors

Game Law Enforcement Agents

Immigration Inspectors

Inspections, Investigations, and
Compliance Specialists

Police Officers

United States Marshals

Liberal Arts/Humanities

Contact Representatives

Customs Inspectors

Education Services Specialists

Equal Opportunity Compliance Specialists

Management Analysts

Personnel Management Specialists

Program Analysts

Social Insurance Claims Examiners

Veterans Claims Examiners

Library Science

Librarians

Library Technicians

Medical Record Librarians

Technical Information Services

Management

Administrative Officers

Administrators

Logistics Management Specialists

Management Analysts

Manpower Development Specialists

Miscellaneous Administrative and Program Specialists

Program Analysts

Support Services

Management, Facilities

Commissary Store Managers

Correctional Institution Administrators

Distribution Facility and Storage Managers

Equipment Specialists

Facility Managers

General Facilities and Equipment Managers

Housing Managers

Industrial Property Managers

Production Controllers

Management Information Systems

Computer Science Specialists

Computer Specialists

Financial Managers

Logistics Management Specialists

Management Analysts

Miscellaneous Administrative and Programs Specialists

Operations Research Analysts

Program Analysts

Program Managers

Marketing

Agricultural Marketing Specialists

Bond Sales Promotion Representatives

Business and Industry Specialists

Contract Specialists

Inventory Management Specialists

Packaging Specialists

Property Disposal Specialists

Supply Specialists

Trade Specialists

Mathematics

Actuaries

Cartographers

Computer Science Specialists

Mathematical Statisticians

Mathematicians

Operations Research Analysts

Statisticians

Medical Support

Diagnostic Radiological Technicians

Medical Instrument Technicians

Medical Record Technicians

Medical Technicians

Nuclear Medicine Technicians

Pathology Technicians

Therapeutic Radiological Technicians

Meteorology

General Physical Scientists

Meteorologists

Natural Resource Management

Fish and Wildlife Administrators

General Biological Scientists

Program Analysts

Wildlife Biologists

Wildlife Refuge Management

Nursing

Nurses

Physicians' Assistants

Park and Recreation Management

Foresters

Management Analysts

Outdoor Recreation Planners

Park Rangers

Recreation and Creative Arts Therapists

Recreation Specialists

Pharmacy

Consumer Safety Inspectors

Consumer Safety Officers

Pharmacists

Pharmacologists

Physical Education

Corrective Therapists

Outdoor Recreation Planners

Program Analysts

Recreation Aides and Assistants

Recreation and Creative Arts Therapists

Recreation Specialists

Sports Specialists

Physical Science

General Physical Scientists

Metallurgists

Physicists

Physics

Astronomers and Space Scientists

General Physical Scientists

Geodesists

Geophysicists

Health Physicists

Hydrologists

Oceanographers

Patent Examiners

Physicists

Planning, Community or City

Community Planners

Realtors

Political Science/Government

Archivists

Budget Analysts

Foreign Affairs Specialists

Government Accountability Office Evaluators

Historians

Miscellaneous Administrative and Program Specialists

Program Analysts

Public Affairs Specialists

Social Scientists

Psychology

Educational Services Specialists

Employee Development Specialists

Government Accountability Office Evaluators

Personnel Management Specialists

Personnel Staffing Specialists

Position Classification Specialists

Psychologists

Recreation and Creative Arts Therapists

Public Administration

Budget Analysts

Employee Development Specialists

Employee Relations Specialists

Government Accountability Office Evaluators

Housing Managers

Management Analysts

Manpower Development Specialists

Miscellaneous Administrative and Program Specialists

Program Analysts

Public Utilities Specialists

Public Health

Environmental Health Technicians

Food Assistance Program Specialists

Food Inspectors

Health System Administrators

Health System Specialists

Industrial Hygienists

Public Health Educators

Public Health Programs Specialists

Social Insurance Administrators

Veterans Claims Examiners

Public Relations

Contact Representatives

Foreign Affairs Specialists

Foreign Agricultural Affairs Specialists

Public Affairs Specialists

Purchasing

Business and Industry Specialists

Commissary Store Managers

Contract Specialists

Purchasing Specialists

Real Estate

Building Managers

Business and Industry Specialists

Contract Specialists

Housing Managers

Realtors

Rehabilitation Therapy

Corrective Therapists

Manual Arts Therapists

Occupational Therapists

Physical Therapists

Prosthetic Representatives

Rehabilitation Therapy Assistants

Social Work

Food Assistance Program Specialists

Psychology Aides and Technicians

Recreation Specialists

Social Science Aides and Technicians

Social Scientists

Social Service Aides and Assistants

Social Service Representatives

Social Workers

Sociology

Government Accountability Office Evaluators

Program Analysts

Social Science Aides and Technicians

Social Scientists

Social Service Aides and Assistants

Social Service Representatives

Sociologists

Statistics

Actuaries

Computer Science Specialists

Mathematical Statisticians

Operations Research Analysts

Program Analysts

Statisticians

Transportation Industry Analysts

Surveying

Geodesists

Land Surveyors

Systems Analysis

Computer Science Specialists

Computer Specialists

Management Analysts

Miscellaneous Administrative and Programs Specialists

Program Analysts

Theology

Chaplains

Program Analysts

Social Workers

Transportation

Cargo Schedulers

Highway Safety Specialists

Marine Cargo Specialists

Traffic Management Specialists

Transportation Industry Analysts

Transportation Loss/Damage Claims Examiners

Transportation Operators

Transportation Specialists

Travel Assistants

Zoology

Animal Scientists

Physiologists

Zoologists

Sample Federal Job Vacancy Announcement

As explained in Chapter 2, don't be intimidated by federal vacancy announcements. Although usually quite long, an announcement explains the job opening, its location, salary, qualifications required, and more. Announcements also tell you exactly how to apply and the deadline for your application materials.

To prepare you for your first encounter with a federal vacancy announcement, we've reproduced the complete text for one that appeared on the USAJOBS Web site. (We modified the dates and the agency contact information because the announcement will have expired by the time you read this information.)

So take a deep breath, take your time, and refer to Chapter 2 for a clear explanation of the main parts of an announcement.

Note: Some Sections on Announcements May Not Apply to You

Most announcements include sections on veterans' preference, or preferential hiring for qualified veterans; the Career Transition Assistance Program (CTAP), or preferential hiring for federal employees whose jobs have been eliminated; and merit promotion procedures, or application instructions for current federal employees. Skip these sections if they do not apply to you.

Announcements also include equal opportunity statements, information for applicants with disabilities who need assistance, and sometimes, admonitions to tell the truth on applications.

Department: Department of Agriculture

Agency: Agriculture, Natural Resources Conservation Service

Job Announcement Number: NRCS-KY-05-02B (NON-STATUS)

NON-STATUS (DEU) VACANCY ANNOUNCEMENT

ANNOUNCEMENT NUMBER: NRCS-KY-05-02B (Non-Status)

TYPE OF APPOINTMENT & WORK SCHEDULE: Permanent Full-Time

POSITION TITLE, SERIES AND GRADE: DISTRICT CONSERVATIONIST (SUPERVISORY), GS-457-11

SALARY RANGE: GS-11 = $48,947

OPENING DATE: October 26, 20xx

CLOSING DATE: December 1, 20xx

APPLICATIONS MUST BE RECEIVED IN THE HUMAN RESOURCES OFFICE BY THE CLOSE OF BUSINESS (5 p.m.) ON: December 1, 20xx.

THIS POSITION HAS NO PROMOTION POTENTIAL

THE DUTY LOCATION AND ORGANIZATION: 3–Vacancies

USDA-NRCS–Versailles, Kentucky (Responsible for two (2) Counties Woodford and Jessamine)

USDA-NRCS–Hodgenville, Kentucky

USDA-NRCS–Harrodsburg, Kentucky

"The Natural Resources Conservation Service provides leadership in a partnership effort to help people conserve, maintain, and improve our natural resources and environment." (http://www.nrcs.usda.gov/).

WHO MAY APPLY: Applications will be accepted from all qualified U. S. citizens. You need not be a current or former Federal employee to apply; however, you must be a U.S. citizen. Status Applicants (Current or former Federal employees) must apply under vacancy announcement number NRCS-KY-05-02A (STATUS).

Relocation expenses are not authorized for this position.

Please read the entire vacancy announcement and follow all application instructions. Failure to submit all required documents will result in your application not being considered.

NOTE: To receive preference, eligible veterans claiming 5-Point Preference must submit a copy of their DD-214, all 10-Point Preference Eligibles must submit a completed Standard Form 15 (SF-15, Application for 10-Point Veteran Preference), and a letter from the Veteran's Administration (VA) dated within the last 12 months outlining the percentage of their service connected disability.

MAJOR DUTIES:

Directs the field level operation and provides technical assistance to individuals and groups on soil and water conservation systems.

Acts as a technical advisor in a leadership role and provides guidance to the conservation district board of supervisors on long-range programs coordinated for which the agency is responsible.

Receives and services referrals for the Environmental Quality Incentives Programs (EQIP) and other agency state programs.

Provides advice and counsel on all aspects of programs for which the agency is responsible.

Works with the Engineering Job Approval Classification Chart or with engineers in the planning and application of conservation systems.

Identifies areas in the county with special soil and/or water resource management problems.

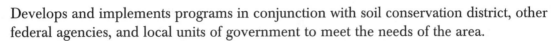

Develops and implements programs in conjunction with soil conservation district, other federal agencies, and local units of government to meet the needs of the area.

QUALIFICATIONS REQUIRED:

The qualifications for this position are described below and are published in the "Qualification Standards Operating Manual". See http://www.opm.gov/qualifications/index/htm.

QUALIFICATIONS REQUIRED:

http://www.opm.gov/qualifications
http://www.opm.gov/qualifications/SEC-IV/A/GS-PROF.HTM
http://www.opm.gov/qualifications/SEC-IV/B/GS0400/0457.HTM

To be basically qualified for this job, you must have:

A. Degree: soil conservation or related agricultural or natural resource discipline such as agronomy, soil science, forestry, agricultural education, or agricultural engineering. The study must have included 30 semester hours in a natural resource or agricultural field, including at least 12 semester hours in a combination of soils and crops or plant science. Of the 12 semester hours, a minimum of 3 semester hours must have been in soils and 3 semester hours in crops or plant science.

OR

B. Combination of education and experience—at least 30 semester hours in one or more of the disciplines as shown in A above, including at least 12 semester hours in a combination of soils and crops or plant science, plus appropriate experience or additional education. Of the 12 semester hours, a minimum of 3 semester hours must have been in soils and 3 semester hours in crops or plant science.

In addition to meeting the basic entry qualification requirements, applicants must have specialized experience and/or directly related education. Applicant must have one year of specialized experience equivalent to the next lower grade, which has equipped the applicant with the particular knowledge, skills, and abilities to successfully perform the duties of the position. Experience is typically in or related to the work of the position described.

Specialized experience is experience that equipped the applicant with the particular knowledge, skills, and abilities to perform successfully the duties of the position, and that is typically in or related to the work of the position to be filled. To be creditable, specialized experience must have been equivalent to at least the next lower grade level in the normal line of progression for the occupation in the organization. Some examples of specialized experience are – Providing technical assistance to contractors and others regarding the construction and maintenance of engineering structures, Acting as a technical advisor in a leadership role, providing guidance to the conservation district board of supervisors in the development and implementation of a long-range program coordinated with the agency programs and field level activities, etc. – this is not all inclusive.

For the GS-11 position, applicants must have 1 year specialized experience equivalent to at least the GS-09 level or 3 years of progressively higher level graduate education leading to a Ph.D. degree or Ph.D. or equivalent doctoral degree.

Note: Education and experience may be combined for all grade levels for which both education and experience are acceptable.

Credit will be given for appropriate qualifying unpaid experience or volunteer work such as community, cultural, social service, and professional association activities on the same basis as for unpaid experience. To receive proper credit for unpaid experience or volunteer work, fully describe your responsibilities and show the actual time (years, months, and hours per week) spent in such activities.

Transcripts are mandatory for all positions advertised in the GS-457 job series.

NOTE: YOU MUST SUBMIT A TRANSCRIPT(S) TO VERIFY CLASSES, HOURS AND TO DETERMINE BASIC ELIGIBLITY FOR THE POSITION.

KNOWLEDGES, SKILLS AND ABILITIES REQUIRED (KSA's):

KSA Responses are limited to one (2) pages per KSA (anything beyond two pages will not be considered).

The following knowledges, skills and abilities (KSAs) are required for this job. For each KSA, you must prepare a two page or less written statement that explains how you meet the specific KSA. Failure to submit a response for each KSA will negatively affect your eligibility and/or rating for this position.

a. KNOWLEDGE OF LAND AND WATER RESOSURCE ACTIVITIES in order to accomplish conservation planning and application of soil and water conservation practices.

b. ABILITY TO RESEARCH, ANALYZE, AND INTERPRET INFORMATION in order to develop and analyze the use of land and water resource data in the district which includes collection of information on soil resources, existing land use, and conservation treatment needs and interpreting and explaining summarized data to other local agencies and groups.

c. ABILITY TO PROVIDE TECHNICAL ASSISTANCE TO DISTRICTS in order to develop and implement the district work plan.

d. ABILITY TO SUPERVISE AND MANAGE A STAFF in order to direct field office operation and provide technical guidance and leadership to nonprofessional employees in development, analysis, and use of land and water resource data in the district.

e. ABILITY TO COMMUNICATE WITH OTHERS (ORALLY, TDY, LIP READING, SIGN LANGUAGE, ETC.) in order to provide information, advice, and guidance to technical program officials; persuade; and provide/obtain information from agency employees, state, and local planning commissions, and other organizations on a variety of controversial issues.

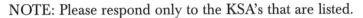

NOTE: Please respond only to the KSA's that are listed.

Credit will be given for appropriate qualifying unpaid experience or volunteer work such as community, cultural, social service, and professional association activities on the same basis as for unpaid experience. To receive proper credit for unpaid experience or volunteer work, fully describe your responsibilities and show the actual time (years, months, and hours per week) spent in such activities.

NOTE: Please respond to only the KSA's that are listed.

BASIS OF RATING:

Your rating will be based on an evaluation of your experience as it relates to the qualification requirements and on the knowledge, skills, and abilities (KSA's) listed. You should provide detailed evidence of your possession of the KSA's in your application as well as in your KSA responses with clear concise examples that include level of accomplishment, and degree of responsibility.

For CTAP and ICTAP, well-qualified means that the applicant meets the qualification standard and eligibility requirements for the position, meets minimum educational and experience requirements, meets all selective factors where applicable, and is able to satisfactorily perform the duties of the position upon entry.

PAY, BENEFITS, AND WORK SCHEDULE:

This is a permanent, career-conditional appointment. Selectee will be eligible for health and life insurance, annual leave (vacation), sick leave and will be covered under the Federal Employees Retirement System, Thrift Savings Plan or Civil Service Retirement System (CSRS).

The work schedule is full time (40 hours per week).

All Federal employees are required by Public Law 104-134 to have federal payments made by Direct Deposit.

Your pay grade and step will be set in accordance with Federal pay regulations.

Management has the prerogative to select at any grade level for which this position has been advertised. If you are placed in this position at a grade lower than the target grade (i.e. the promotion potential grade), you may be promoted to the target grade without further competition. However, there is no commitment or obligation on the part of management to promote you. Your promotion will depend upon the continuing need for that level of work to be performed and your ability to perform the higher level duties.

CONDITIONS OF EMPLOYMENT:

If you are selected for this position you will be required to:

★ complete a one year probationary period, and

★ complete a Declaration for Federal Employment (OF-306) to determine your suitability for Federal employment, authorize a background investigation, and certify the accuracy of all the information in your application (or resume).

A background security investigation will be required for all new appointments. Your continued employment will be subject to your successful completion of a background security investigation and favorable adjudication. Failure to successfully meet these requirements will be grounds for termination.

If you are a male over age 18 who was born after December 31, 1959, you must have registered with the Selective Service System (or have an exemption) to be eligible for a Federal job.

You must be a United States Citizen or National (resident of American Samoa and Swains Island) to be considered for this job.

Your Social Security Number is requested to uniquely identify your records from those of other applicants who may have the same name. Failure to provide your SSN in your application package will result in your application not being processed.

OTHER INFORMATION:

If you make a false statement in any part of your application (or resume), you may not be hired, or you may be removed after being hired.

You will be contacted regarding the status of your application. Selections normally take approximately eight weeks after the closing date of the announcement.

Information on Special Hiring Authorities

Are you:

★ a 30% compensably disabled Veteran (http://www.opm.gov/veterans/html/vetguide.htm),

★ a VRA eligible (http://www.opm.gov/veterans/html/vetguide.htm),

★ a person with a severe physical handicap (http://www.opm.gov/disability/), or

★ a former Peace Corps or VISTA Volunteer?

If so, we may be able to consider you under a special hiring authority. You must tell us in your application under which of these special hiring authorities you wish to be considered. If you want to be considered under a special hiring authority as well as the regular competitive process, you must submit two complete applications and request the dual consideration. When only one application is received from a special hiring authority eligible, it will be considered under the appropriate special hiring authority only. You must submit proof of your eligibility with your application or you will not be considered under a special hiring authority. The VRA hiring authority is limited to positions at the GS-11 level and below.

Information on Veterans' Preference (http://www.opm.gov/veterans/html/vetguide.htm)

If you served on active duty in the United States Military and were separated under honorable conditions, you may be eligible for Veterans' Preference. What types of preference are there?

★ 5-point preference is granted if you entered the military service prior to October 14, 1976, or if your service began after October 15, 1976, and you received a campaign badge or expeditionary medal. You must submit a copy of your DD-214 with your application package, by the closing date of the announcement, or you will not receive 5-point preference.

★ 10-point preference is granted if you are a disabled Veteran; you received a Purple Heart; you are the spouse or mother of a 100% disabled Veteran; or you are the unremarried widow (or widower) or the mother of a deceased Veteran. You must submit, with your application package by the closing date of the announcement, a copy of your DD-214, SF-15 Application for 10-point Veterans' Preference, plus the required proof of eligibility as indicated on the back of that form or you will not receive 10-point preference.

Information on ICTAP/CTAP-

Individuals who have special priority selection eligibility under the Agency Career Transition Assistance Program (CTAP) or the Interagency Career Transition Assistance Program (ICTAP) must be well qualified for the position to receive consideration for special priority selection. See Basis for Rating for definition of "well qualified". Federal employees seeking CTAP/ICTAP eligibility must submit proof that they meet the requirements of 5 CFR 30.605 (a) for CTAP and 5 CFR 330.704 for ICTAP. This includes proof of eligibility, a copy of their most recent Performance Rating and a copy of their most recent SF-50 noting current position, grade level, and duty location. Please annotate your application to reflect that you are applying as a CTAP or ICTAP eligible.

NRCS provides reasonable accommodations to applicants with disabilities. If you need a reasonable accommodation for any part of the application and hiring process, please notify us. The decision on granting reasonable accommodation will be on a case-by-case basis.

HOW TO APPLY:

Applications submitted by facsimile or other electronic means will not be accepted.

Applications submitted by email will not be accepted.

Submit your application package directly to the Human Resources Office by close of business (5 p.m.) on the closing date. Late applications will result in your application not being considered. There will be no exceptions.

SUBMIT YOUR APPLICATION PACKAGE TO:

USDA-NRCS
Human Resources Office
7891 Mason Drive
Smithville, Kentucky 40522

Attn: Mary P. Jones

CONTACT PERSON FOR ADDITIONAL INFORMATION:

Name: Mary P. Jones

Phone: (866) 234-XXXX

Items 1 through 3 are required documents that must be submitted by every applicant:

1. An OF-612 Application for Federal Employment, resume, or any other form of application. You do not need to send both an OF-612 and a resume. If you use a resume, it must include all of the information listed below under "Required Information on Resume". If your application or resume does not include the required information, you may lose consideration for the job. OF-612 forms may be obtained on the Internet at www.opm.gov/forms/html/of.htm, or by calling the number listed under 'Contact'.

2. A separate, written response to each of the knowledges, skills, and abilities listed in this vacancy announcement. Do not submit more than 2 pages per KSA response. Responses to generic KSAs are not acceptable. See "Basis of Rating" for more details. Failure to submit KSA responses as specifically instructed may negatively impact your rating.

3. A legible copy of all college transcripts. If the qualification standard for this position has specific educational requirements or permits the substitution of education for experience (see the section entitled "Qualifications Required") and you wish to qualify based on this substitution, you must submit a legible copy of your transcript(s) for your undergraduate and graduate education. It is your responsibility to demonstrate that you possess the required education. See "Qualifications Required".

In addition, the following documentation must be submitted if applicable:

4. Documentation verifying Veterans status or Special Hiring Authority eligibility. See "Other Information" for details.

5. Documentation verifying ICTAP/CTAP eligibility. See "Other Information" for details.

What other important things do you need to know about submitting a successful application package?

1. Do not send position descriptions, manuscripts, personal endorsements, training certificates, publications, work samples, or any other unsolicited material. They will be discarded. References to these items may be made in your application, resume, or KSA responses.

2. Do not submit your application materials in a notebook, binder, or other cumbersome covering. It will be discarded. Cover letters are acceptable.

3. You cannot use postage-paid government envelopes, messenger envelopes, federal stamps, and federal postage meters to file your applications. It is a violation of USDA regulations. Applications received directly or indirectly through these means will not be considered.

4. Application packages will not be returned to you.

5. If you wish to have education acquired outside the United States credited for the educational requirements of this position, you must prove that it has been evaluated as equivalent to the education gained in accredited United States colleges and universities. Submit documentation of your education to a private organization that specializes in interpretation of foreign educational credentials for a determination. The Council on Postsecondary

Accreditation may be of assistance in providing information on these organizations (www.ed.gov/offices/OPE/accreditation/accredus.html). The processing of this vacancy announcement will not be delayed pending receipt of your evaluation materials.

6. A professional application gives a positive impression to hiring managers. It is recommended that you make the effort to assure your application is neat, legible, error free, easy to read, and concise.

INFORMATION THAT IS REQUIRED IN A FEDERAL RESUME:

If you prepare a resume, be sure you provide all of the information listed below. This is the same information that is identified on the OF-612 application form, which can be found at www.opm.gov/forms/html/of.htm. You don't need to send both an OF-612 application form and a resume.

Tell us what job you are applying for, i.e.

★ The announcement number, title and grade.

Provide all of the following.

★ Full name, mailing address and day/evening telephone numbers

★ Social Security Number.

★ Country of Citizenship.

★ Highest Federal civilian grade held, job series, and dates of employment in grade.

Education:

★ High School name, city, state and zip code, date of diploma or GED.

★ Colleges and/or Universities attended, city, state and zip code

★ Major field(s) of study.

★ Type and year of degree(s) received.

Work experience related to the job for which you are applying:

★ Job title.

★ Duties and accomplishments.

★ Number of hours per week.

★ Employers name and address.

★ Supervisor's name and phone number.

★ Starting and ending dates of employment (month and year).

★ Salary.

★ Indicate if your current supervisor may be contacted.

Other Qualifications:

★ Job-related training courses (title and year).

★ Job-related skills (e.g., other languages, computer software/hardware, tools, machinery, typing speed, etc.)

★ Job-related certificates and licenses.

★ Job-related honors, awards, and special accomplishments (e.g. publications, memberships in professional or honor societies, leadership activities, public speaking, performance awards, etc.) Do not send copies of documents unless specifically requested.

Veterans Preference:

★ Indicate if you are claiming 5 points (attach DD 214) or 10 points (attach an Application for 10 Point Veterans' Preference (SF-15) and proof required as indicated on the SF-15.)

USDA prohibits discrimination in all its programs and activities on the basis of race, color, national origin, gender, religion, age, disability, political beliefs, sexual orientation, and marital or family status. Not all prohibited basis apply to all programs. Persons with disabilities who require alternative means for communication of program information (Braille, large print, audiotape, etc.) should contact USDA's TARGET Center at (202) 720-2600 (voice and TDD). To file a complaint of discrimination, write USDA, Director, Office of Civil Rights, Room 326-W, Whitten Building, 14th and Independence Avenue, SW, Washington, D.C. 20250-9410 or call (202) 720-5964 (voice or TDD).

Federal agencies must provide reasonable accommodation to applicants with disabilities where appropriate. Applicants requiring reasonable accommodation for any part of the application and hiring process should contact the hiring agency directly. Determinations on requests for reasonable accommodation will be made on a case-by-case basis.

Social Security Number—Your Social Security Number is requested under the authority of Executive Order 9397 to uniquely identify your records from those of other applicants who may have the same name. As allowed by law or Presidential directive, your Social Security Number is used to seek information about you from employers, schools, banks, and others who may know you. Failure to provide your Social Security Number on your application materials, will result in your application not being processed

Privacy Act—Privacy Act Notice (PL 93-579): The information requested here is used to determine qualifications for employment and is authorized under Title 5 U.S.C. 3302 and 3361.

Signature—Before you are hired, you will be required to sign and certify the accuracy of the information in your application.

False Statements—If you make a false statement in any part of your application, you may not be hired; you may be fired after you begin work; or you may be subject to fine, imprisonment, or other disciplinary action.

Selective Service—If you are a male applicant born after December 31, 1959, you must certify that you have registered with the Selective Service System, or are exempt from having to do so under the Selective Service Law.

The United States Government does not discriminate in employment on the basis of race, color, religion, sex, national origin, political affiliation, sexual orientation, marital status, disability, age, membership in an employee organization, or other non-merit factor.

Send Mail to:

Department Of Agriculture
7891 Mason Drive
Smithville, Kentucky 40522
Fax: (866) 234-XXXX

For questions about this job:
Mary P. Jones
Phone: (866) 234-XXXX
Fax: (866) 234-XXXX
Internet: MJ@xx.usda.gov

USAJOBS Control Number: 322540

Sample Federal-Style Resumes

As we explain in Chapter 3, you can't use your regular resume when applying for a federal job. Your standard resume can serve as the base for your federal-style resume, but the government requires more information.

Federal-style resumes may run two to four pages because of the information that's required or that you have the option to include. You can format your federal-style resume any way you like.

Take advantage of a paper resume's flexibility by choosing a format that highlights your strengths. If you are a recent graduate, for example, you might place education before work experience. The only limitation when applying for a federal job is that you must list jobs in reverse chronological order, so start with your most recent job. Each page should include the vacancy announcement number and your name and Social Security number.

Following are examples of federal-style resumes; see Chapter 3 for details.

Sample Resume 1

John Smith
5837 Custis Parkway, Falls Church, VA 24001
Home: 202-123-4567; Work: 202-890-1234
E-mail: johnsmith@yahoo.com

Social Security Number:	123-45-6789
Country of Citizenship:	United States
Veterans' Preference:	N/A
Highest Grade:	GS-0201-14, 07/2001-Present
Contact Current Supervisor:	Yes

JOB INFORMATION

Announcement Number:	W80043
Job Title:	Personnel Management Administrator
Grade:	GS-15

WORK EXPERIENCE

U.S. Office of Personnel Management   **Dates Employed: 07/2001-Present**
1900 E Street   **Grade Level: GS-14/4**
Room 888   **Hours Per Week: 40**
Washington, DC 22745-8943

Personnel Management Manager
Supervise a staff of 11 GS-4 through GS-13 clerks and specialists. Responsible for implementing a new, highly visible Government-wide human resources initiative that markets Federal employment opportunities to college students through the Internet. Duties include overseeing and evaluating the design and content of the interactive Web site; developing and evaluating policies regarding site content; negotiating with contractors that are creating the site's architecture; coordinating implementation issues with another OPM department that will respond to queries generated by the site; reporting about the initiative's progress to senior OPM officials; and disseminating information about the initiative to Federal agencies, State and local governments, and colleges and universities. Previously played a key role in developing and implementing USAJOBS, a Web site that serves as a one-stop source for information about Federal job openings. Supervisor: Eric Jones. May be contacted; phone 202-231-3333.

EDUCATION

Masters in Public Administration, 06/2001
George Mason University
Fairfax, VA 12345
GPA: 3.9 out of 4.0

Bachelors in Political Science, 06/1999
George Mason University
Fairfax, VA 12345
Major: Political Science
GPA: 3.8 out of 4.0

High School Diploma, 05/1995
Mount Vernon High School
Mount Vernon, VA 12121
GPA: 3.5 out of 4.0

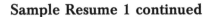

Sample Resume 1 continued

John Smith, page 2
Social Security Number: 123-45-6789
Announcement Number: W80043

JOB-RELATED TRAINING COURSES

Advanced Employee Relations, 2005
Grievance Handling, 2004
Adverse and Conduct-Based Actions, 2003
Position Classification, 2002
Basic Employee Relations, 2002
Seminar for New Managers, 2001

JOB-RELATED SKILLS

Strong project management, team building, and interpersonal communication skills. Proficient in Excel, PowerPoint, and numerous Web browsers for PCs and Macs. Fluent in Spanish.

JOB-RELATED HONORS, AWARDS, AND MEMBERSHIPS

American Society of Public Administrators
OPM Director's Award for Excellence, 07/2004
OPM Director's Award for Excellence, 03/2003
OPM Director's Award for Excellence, 08/2002

Sample Resume 2

Sarah Jones

Current Address:
134 Valley Drive, Apt. 29
Foster, NY 12345
Home: (585) 123-4567
Cell: (585) 987-6543
E-mail: sjones@esu.edu
Social Security Number: 123-45-6789
Citizenship: United States
Veterans' Preference: N/A
Vacancy Announcement Number: JP-04-131-DEU
Job Title, Series, Grade: Writer-Editor, GS-1082-11/12/13

Permanent Address:
1472 Seger Road
McKinley, NY 98765
(978) 437-6932

EDUCATION

Eastern State University
1478 Hotchkiss Drive
Foster, NY 98765
- Bachelor of Arts, expected June 2005
- Major: Journalism
- Minor: Political Science
- Current GPA: 3.4/4.0

McKinley High School
123 Rosemary Lane
McKinley, NY 37593
Diploma received June 2001

RELEVANT EXPERIENCE

General Assignment Reporter/Photographer   **Summer 2003, 2004**
The McKinley Enterprise
123 State Street, McKinley, NY 98765
- Filled in for vacationing staff members.
- Responsible for covering beats, generating ideas for feature stories, editing wire service copy, editing and laying out the Home section, and shooting photographs for own stories and as assigned.
- Supervisor: Managing Editor Walter Smith. Phone: (978) 879-4721. May be contacted.

Staff Member   **September 2001-Present**
The Eastern Echo
120 Jones Hall, Eastern State University, Foster, NY 12345
- Rose from student housing reporter for three-day-a-week college newspaper in freshman year to editor-in-chief in senior year.
- Responsibilities grew each year and involved supervising other student reporters or editors starting in sophomore year.
- As editor-in-chief in senior year, responsibilities include supervising and mentoring junior editors and reporters, planning news coverage with other editors, developing and overseeing the budget in conjunction with the faculty adviser, and representing the newspaper at meetings before the Student Publications Board.
- Salary rose from $5 per story in freshman year to $150 per week in senior year.
- Supervisor: Professor Larry Smith. Phone: (585) 483-2943. May be contacted.

Sample Resume 2 continued

Sarah Jones
Page 2

Social Security Number: 123-45-6789
Vacancy Announcement Number: JP-04-131-DEU
Job Title, Series, Grade: Writer-Editor, GS-1082-11/12/13

OTHER ACTIVITIES

Volunteer   **09/2002 – Present**
Foster Shelter for the Homeless
834 Ripley Blvd., Foster, NY 12345

- Initially responsible for checking residents in and out, washing bedding, and helping prepare meals.
- Responsibilities expanded to include coordinating and scheduling student volunteers.
- Supervisor: Shelter Director Karen Smith. Phone: (585) 451-2390.

HONORS

- Scholarship from the Scripps-Howard Foundation, 2003 – present
- Award from the New York Scholastic Press Association for writing the best editorial in a New York high school newspaper, 2000.

Sample Resume 3

Henrietta R. Jacobsen
12924 Reed Avenue   □   Town, MD 12435
Cell (343) 323-3434   □   Home (343) 323-3433
HJacobsen@email.net

Social Security Number: 323-1XXX
Citizenship: United States
Veterans' Preference and Federal Civilian Status: N/A

Job Title: Investigator, GS-1811-07
Announcement Number: DD-3223

EDUCATION

University of Chicago, Chicago, IL 60660
B.A., June 2003
Major: Psychology
GPA: 3.3 out of 4.0

Washington High School, Chicago, IL, 1999

WORK EXPERIENCE

Security Officer   July 2003 - Present
Merced Mall, Town, MD 12435 $26,000/year
                                                      38 hours/week

Patrol mall and parking areas on foot. Interview, detain, and apprehend
suspects and witnesses. Resolve conflicts. Prepare and process reports.
Maintain fitness and weapons qualifications. Supervisor: Joe Johnson, (323)
XXX-1234. May be contacted.

School Psychologist Assistant   January 2001 - May 2003
Jackson School, Chicago, IL 60665 $15/hour
                                                      20 hours/week

Worked in a correctional facility for juvenile females. Coordinated group
therapy, exercise programs, and arts programs. Supervisor: Mary Gibson,
(324) 567-0988.

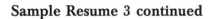

Sample Resume 3 continued

Henrietta R. Jacobsen
Social Security Number: 323-1XXX
Job Title: Investigator, GS-1811-07
Announcement Number: DD-3223
Page 2

JOB-RELATED SKILLS

Research, leadership, report writing, organizational skills, and communication skills. Fluent in Spanish.

COMPUTER SKILLS

Microsoft Excel, Microsoft Word, PageMaker

HONORS

Neighborhood Safety Council, Member of the Year Award, 2005

Honor Society, 2002-2003

AVAILABILITY

Can work emergency duty, after hours, and weekends. Willing to travel.

Helpful Web Sites for Federal Job Seekers

The Web is full of many sites that provide information on federal jobs. This appendix describes and helps you pinpoint the most useful sites.

USAJOBS

http://usajobs.opm.gov

USAJOBS is the official jobs site for the federal government. It has a searchable database of federal job openings that typically contains 16,000 to 18,000 jobs, search agents that send you e-mail messages when jobs meeting your criteria are listed, an online resume builder that you can use to quickly apply for many federal jobs, and publications about working for the federal government.

The jobs database primarily lists executive branch positions, but it also lists some jobs in other branches of government and at independent agencies.

USAJOBS: Careers

http://career.usajobs.opm.gov

This site helps users explore their career interests. Different sections help you find jobs for which you're best suited based on your interests, help you match your interests to specific jobs, provide descriptions and minimum qualification requirements for specific federal jobs, and match federal jobs to jobs in the private sector.

USAJOBS: Publications

http://www.usajobs.opm.gov/faqs.asp

This page at USAJOBS offers dozens of publications about working for the federal government. They cover topics such as employment of non-citizens, employment opportunities for attorneys, federal employment overseas, federal qualification requirements, the hiring of postal employees, pay and benefits, and summer employment opportunities for students, among others.

Air Force Civilian Employment

https://ww2.afpc.randolph.af.mil/resweb

Information about civilian job opportunities with the Air Force is available at this site, which also has job listings.

Army Civilian Employment

http://www.cpol.army.mil/employ

This site describes working for the Army as a civilian, and also has job listings.

Central Intelligence Agency: Careers

http://www.cia.gov/employment

This site provides information about various career paths at the Central Intelligence Agency, lists job openings, and describes numerous programs for students.

Because the CIA's work is classified and prospective hires are extensively screened, the application process can last more than a year.

Congressional Budget Office: Employment

http://www.cbo.gov/EmploymentIntro.cfm

The Congressional Budget Office is a nonpartisan agency that produces policy analyses, cost estimates, and budget and economic projections for Congress. The site has information about working at the CBO and announcements about job openings at the agency.

Defense Civilian Careers

http://www.go-defense.com

The Department of Defense operates this site, which describes civilian career opportunities.

Government Accountability Office: Employment Opportunities

http://www.gao.gov/jobopp.htm

The nonpartisan Government Accountability Office is often referred to as the investigative arm of Congress. Its Web site provides background about the agency and job listings.

Government Printing Office: Careers

http://www.gpo.gov/careers/index.html

The Government Printing Office is part of the legislative branch. Its Web site has career information and announcements about job openings.

Library of Congress: Jobs and Fellowships

http://www.loc.gov/hr/employment

This site provides information about working at the Library of Congress, which includes the Congressional Research Service. It also has listings for job vacancies.

National Security Agency: Careers

http://www.nsa.gov/careers/index.cfm

Collecting signals intelligence is the primary job of the super-secret National Security Agency. Its Web site offers information about working at the agency, details about student programs, and job listings.

Navy Civilian Employment

http://www.donhr.navy.mil/jobs

Civilian jobs in the Navy are the focus of this site, which also has job listings.

Nuclear Regulatory Commission: Employment Opportunities

http://www.nrc.gov/who-we-are/employment.html

Extensive information about working at the Nuclear Regulatory Commission, an independent agency that regulates the nation's nuclear power plants, is available at this site. It also features an online job application system.

OPM: Career Opportunities

http://www.opm.gov/Career_Opportunities

The Office of Personnel Management offers numerous publications about career opportunities with the federal government through this Web page.

The publications discuss topics such as benefits for new federal employees; career development programs; and special employment programs for people with disabilities, military veterans, and students.

OPM: Electronic Forms

http://www.opm.gov/Forms

Just about any form you'll ever need regarding federal employment is available through this page at the Office of Personnel Management's Web site.

OPM: Employment and Benefits

http://www.opm.gov/Employment_and_Benefits/index.asp

Publications available through this page at the Office of Personnel Management Web site cover topics such as fair hiring practices, leave programs, retirement benefits, the General Schedule salary system, and performance appraisal.

Peace Corps: Jobs

http://WWW.PEACECORPS.GOV/index.cfm?shell=pchq.jobs

This site provides information about working at the headquarters of the Peace Corps in Washington, D.C.

Studentjobs.gov

http://www.studentjobs.gov

Studentjobs.gov, which provides information about federal jobs for students, is an offshoot of USAJOBS. Its searchable database contains listings from USAJOBS of federal job openings that are available to students.

Today's Military: Careers

http://www.todaysmilitary.com/mc/t13_mc_milcar.php

The Department of Defense operates this site, which provides information about different types of careers available in the military.

U.S. Courts: Employment Opportunities

http://www.uscourts.gov/employment.html

This site is the best source for job listings in the judicial branch. It provides information about job vacancies at the U.S. Supreme Court and at various U.S. Courts of Appeals, U.S. District Courts, and U.S. Bankruptcy Courts around the country.

The job listings are incomplete because individual courts may post vacancy announcements only on their own Web sites.

U.S. House of Representatives: Employment Opportunities

http://www.house.gov/cao-hr

This site is the key source for information about vacancies in staff jobs at the U.S. House of Representatives. Unfortunately, the U.S. Senate does not operate a comparable site.

U.S. Postal Service Employment

http://www.usps.com/employment

The U.S. Postal Service is an independent agency that operates its own employment system. The Web site provides details about the USPS hiring process and lists job openings.

Index

D

© 2005 • JIST Works

© 2005 • JIST Works